101 Sample Write-Ups for Documenting Employee Performance Problems

101 Sample Write-Ups for Documenting Employee Performance Problems

A Guide to Progressive Discipline & Termination

3RD EDITION

PAUL FALCONE

AMACOM AMERICAN MANAGEMENT ASSOCIATION
New York ▪ Atlanta ▪ Boston ▪ Chicago ▪ Kansas City ▪ San Francisco
Washington, D.C. Brussels ▪ Mexico City ▪ Tokyo ▪ Toronto

SOCIETY FOR HUMAN
RESOURCE MANAGEMENT

Bulk discounts available. For details visit:
www.amacombooks.org/go/specialsales
Or contact special sales: Phone: 800-250-5308 E-mail: specialsls@amanet.org
View all the AMACOM titles at: www.amacombooks.org
American Management Association: www.amanet.org

Names: Falcone, Paul, author.
Title: 101 sample write-ups for documenting employee performance problems : a guide to progressive discipline
    & termination / Paul Falcone.
Description: Third Edition. | New York : AMACOM, [2017] | Revised edition of the author's 101 sample write-
    ups for documenting employee performance problems, c2010. | Includes bibliographical references and index.
Identifiers: LCCN 2017009481 (print) | LCCN 2017019053 (ebook) | ISBN 9780814438589 (E-book) | ISBN
    9780814438558 (pbk.)
Subjects: LCSH: Employees--Dismissal of. | Labor discipline. | Problem employees.
Classification: LCC HF5549.5.D55 (ebook) | LCC HF5549.5.D55 F35 2017 (print)
    | DDC 658.3/13--dc23
LC record available at https://lccn.loc.gov/2017009481

About AMA

American Management Association (www.amanet.org) is a world leader in talent development, advancing the skills of individuals to drive business success. Our mission is to support the goals of individuals and organizations through a complete range of products and services, including classroom and virtual seminars, webcasts, webinars, podcasts, conferences, corporate and government solutions, business books, and research. AMA's approach to improving performance combines experiential learning—learning through doing—with opportunities for ongoing professional growth at every step of one's career journey.

About SHRM

The Society for Human Resource Management is the world's largest HR professional society, representing 285,000 members in more than 165 countries. For nearly seven decades, the Society has been the leading provider of resources serving the needs of HR professionals and advancing the practice of human resource management. SHRM has more than 575 affiliated chapter within the United States and subsidiary offices in China, India, and United Arab Emirates. Please visit us at www.shrm.org.

Printing number
10 9 8 7 6 5 4 3 2 1

Acknowledgments

To my dear friends at the American Management Association who have guided, supported, and encouraged my writing and speaking engagements over the years, especially Stephen S. Power, senior acquisitions editor at AMACOM Books; Rosemary Carlough, vice president of marketing; and Nicole Morgenstern, Dave Summers, and Doug Sohn on the training/digital marketing side of the house. Thank you all for your ongoing friendship and partnership. I absolutely love working with you!

And to the finest legal team and legal minds in the business, who helped review select portions of this manuscript as it made its way through the various stages of development: Rich Falcone (no relation to the author), shareholder and employment litigation partner with Littler Mendelson in Costa Mesa, CA; Frank Melton, principal and labor employment attorney in the Los Angeles office of Jackson Lewis P.C.; Jacqueline Cookerly Aguilera, partner, labor and employment, and Kathryn McGuigan, counsel, labor and employment, with Morgan, Lewis & Bockius, LLP in Los Angeles; and Christopher W. Olmsted, shareholder in the San Diego office of Ogletree, Deakins, Nash, Smoak & Stewart, P.C. I consider myself so fortunate to have partnered with you all on this third edition, and I benefitted tremendously from your guidance and counsel.

Contents

Part V: Behavior and Conduct Infractions 287

Ready-to-use materials to help create employee write-ups for your organization
are available to purchasers of this book at: www.amacombooks.org/go/
SampleWriteUps3rdEd.

Introduction

Warning! The traditional negative connotation of *discipline* in the workplace is an outdated vestige of the past. In today's workplace, progressive discipline is going to assume a new role, more positive than anything we've seen up until now. So don't pick up this book thinking that you're about to enter a world of negative strategies to mandate employee compliance by wielding tools of control. Attracting and retaining the best talent has to do with encouraging people to be their best. It's about leadership, fairness, and a willingness to address issues head-on.

Progressive discipline is a means of communicating problems directly and in a timely fashion so that employees can involve themselves in the problem-solving process. But proper communication—both verbal and written—is difficult to accomplish without a framework for structuring your thoughts and sharing your suggestions with your employees. The tools presented in this book offer solutions to one of the most difficult management issues: addressing the inevitable problems that surface in the workplace while maintaining worker loyalty, confidence, and buy-in.

The employee relations system presented here is focused on treating workers with dignity and respect. This simple premise seems easy enough to master, yet many companies have learned the hard way that mishandling disciplinary actions strips people of their dignity and provokes feelings of revenge and anger that all too often find outlet only in the courts.

This book will show you how to:

- Enhance employee performance. Rather than hitting workplace performance problems head-on with negative or punitive measures—or worse, avoiding the problem until it becomes intolerable—you'll learn to address minor infractions before they become major impediments. This book will model a system that will enable you to provide subpar performers with tools, direction, and training to turn unacceptable behavior into positive output.

- Protect your company. This book attempts to incorporate all the legal theory floating around out there into one usable format that simultaneously makes documenting subpar performance easier for managers, makes accepting responsibility for one's actions a primary tenet for employees, and most important, shifts the responsibility for performance improvement away from the company and back toward the worker, where it rightfully belongs. As a result, you'll be able to construct defensible written disciplinary notices that will withstand legal scrutiny.

- Save time and make your life easier. These 101 model write-ups provide real-life samples of how *positive* or *constructive* discipline plays itself out in the workplace. These samples will save you time because they can be customized to fit most disciplinary situations. Simply put, you'll no longer have to guess at what verbiage you should include in a write-up. And at the same time, you'll have a blueprint format that walks you through the verbal discussion with your employee so that you can present positive solutions in addition to clear and unambiguous statements of the consequences of the employee's actions.

Who Should Read This Book?

Written for human resources managers, department heads, first-line supervisors, and business owners, this book is designed as a quick reference for improving employees' behavior and, if necessary, constructing terminations that will withstand legal scrutiny. With very little theory, it provides numerous examples of legally defensible disciplinary actions for practically all types of employee performance problems, such as substandard work quality, absenteeism, tardiness, insubordination, profane language in the workplace, and general misconduct.

Why Is It So Hard to Write Up Employees?

It's simply a fact that in today's legal system, companies that discharge employees will, if challenged, have an obligation to prove that they made affirmative efforts to rehabilitate those employees before reaching the ultimate decision to terminate. When confronted by an arbitrator or scrutinized by a jury, companies need to show that they had no alternative but to separate an individual who refused to accept the organization's invitations to improve his or her performance. Without such proof, the company can find itself liable to the former employee for back pay, job reinstatement, and, potentially, punitive damages. To make matters worse, those punitive damages could in certain circumstances be levied against the manager personally (should that individual be deemed to be working "outside the course and scope of his employment").

This book shows you how to construct documents that are both tough and fair. Traditionally, there are problems that managers face when they confront employees regarding their behavior: How will the employee take the news? Will confrontation make matters worse? What if the employee stays "clean" only long enough to get past the active time frame of the disciplinary write-up?

In addition, because the write-up is a legal document, there is a residual fear that what you put in writing can somehow come back to haunt you. For example, managers typically second-guess themselves when it comes to questions like: Can I write specifics? Am I violating this individual's privacy? Is the employee's problem somehow protected by one of the many worker protection laws like the Family Medical Leave Act (FMLA), the Americans with Disabilities Act (ADA), or workers' comp discrimination rulings? What if there are numerous problems that don't seem to be related to one another—can I move forward in the progressive discipline process by somehow bundling those disparate infractions together?

Managers have come to fear addressing even minor performance shortcomings until they become major impediments. By that time, the problems typically get so out of control that managers reactively initiate the disciplinary process in order to build a "paper trail" for a case against an employee as rapidly as possible. What magnificent advantages lie ahead for managers armed with the tools to proactively address minor concerns before they become major ones!

As an HR practitioner and university instructor, I've seen firsthand how companies go through the agony of reinstating poor performers with back wages and reintegrating those individuals into departments that have long since "healed" from the original terminations. And although no system can guarantee that a company will win every wrongful termination challenge, a write-up template that invites employees to involve themselves in their own improvement game plan and that clearly outlines the company's affirmative efforts to help those employees better themselves will go a long way toward fending off litigators' attacks.

What Are the Benefits of Reading This Book?

This book provides a structured format that ensures that all the legal theory steps contained in other books on employee relations get carried out consistently in daily practice. That consistent application will build your confidence in the documentation process, save time, and minimize the liability inherent in one of the hottest topics in business today: employee performance management and termination.

It is important to build a foundation upon which communication can thrive. That constant focus on opening the lines of communication is what makes this approach different. So what will the employee warnings in our proposed format accomplish?

First, they will structure disciplinary meetings in a way that forces bilateral communication between you, the supervisor, and your subordinate. Discipline will no longer be a one-sided prejudgment in which the employee steps into the room, "takes his whacks" after having been determined guilty, and then returns to work disgruntled and disheartened. In addition, the language and tone of our samples are personal and concise, making it easier for you to deliver difficult news in a fair and direct way.

Second, they will prompt managers and supervisors to involve themselves in their employees' rehabilitation by indicating positive (as well as the traditional negative) consequences and by providing training, resource materials, and a commitment to open communication.

Third, they will encourage employees to involve themselves in their own performance improvement. To this end, the write-up paradigm in our samples includes a personal improvement plan (PIP) so that employees can assume responsibility for their own actions; this shifts the responsibility for performance improvement to the employee and away from the company.

Could this proactive and optimistic approach of ours still end with employee termination? Of course. But only if the employees themselves willfully and repeatedly refuse to adhere to established and reasonable standards of performance and conduct. This disciplinary system has two equally important goals: to rehabilitate poor performers and to terminate problem employees legally.

How the Book Is Structured

This book has been designed for easy reference so that you can pull it from your shelf right before or immediately after a disciplinary meeting with one of your employees in order to construct a well-written disciplinary notice. The initial five chapters address the structure and format of the write-up template that's used in all the samples. Consequently, you can refer back to Chapters 1 through 5 when you're looking for that right word, expression, or phrase while composing one of your own disciplinary memos.

The online link contains the complete write-ups for all the examples in this book. To highlight for you the critical areas that differ from write-up to write-up, we've shortened the sections of the write-ups in the book that remain the same. You can view or print the full write-up at any time from the online resource. In addition, to save you the time of re-creating the template from scratch, Figure 6-1, a blank template, has been included in the online resource so you can download it to your computer immediately.

Disclaimer

The disciplinary modules in this book are based on the tenets of federal law and, in a general way, the requirements of state law. However, state laws covering the various aspects of employee relations and workplace due process differ from state to state. Furthermore, state courts, and in some cases regional courts within states, often differ in their application of basic legal principles that apply to the employment relationship. It is up to you to determine the laws in your state or even in your particular city before administering discipline for workplace offenses.

Please bear in mind at all times that this book is not intended as a legal guide to the complex issues surrounding progressive discipline, termination, and other aspects of your employment practices. Because the book does not purport to render legal advice, it should not be used in place of a licensed practicing attorney when proper legal counsel and guidance become necessary. You must rely on your attorney to render a legal opinion that is related to actual fact situations.

PART I
Mastering the Write-Up Tool

1 Progressive Discipline and Its Legal Considerations

Documenting poor performance and progressive discipline is as much an art as it is a science. Unfortunately, most human resources professionals and line managers don't have the time to study the nuances of progressive discipline, workplace due process, summary dismissal, discharge for cause, and the like. Even when that theory is mastered, however, there remains the challenge of incorporating all those ideas into a written memo that adequately documents subpar job performance or workplace conduct.

So it's not surprising that many managers avoid writing up employees like the plague. And without a template to follow and samples to emulate, it's also no wonder that many managers create memos that cannot withstand legal scrutiny.

If the objective of any disciplinary system is to create and maintain a productive and responsive workforce, then disciplinary actions, when they occur, should focus on rehabilitating employees by deterring them from repeating past problem behaviors. It is simply a fact of the modern workplace that you as a manager are charged with this responsibility.

Terminated employees who are successful at winning wrongful discharge claims, on the other hand, typically can prove that they were denied *due process*—what we call progressive discipline. They successfully argue, with the help of their attorneys, that your company breached its de facto obligation of *good faith and fair dealing* in managing its employees and in following its own policies. So if you've ever scratched your head about losing a case to an employee who flagrantly disregarded work responsibilities, it's probably because an arbitrator concluded that due process was denied.

In other words, if the step formula outlined in your company's progressive discipline policy is violated, or if you fail to properly notify an employee that her job is in jeopardy, then you may end up on the losing end of a wrongful termination suit. Ditto if you dole out punishment (i.e., termination) that doesn't appear to fit the offense. In such cases, arbitrators may conclude that the misuse of your managerial discretion warrants the substitution of their judgment for yours in the handling of a specific worker. Frequently, that results in a lesser penalty (such as *reinstatement plus a written warning* instead of termination).

But what about your rights? Shouldn't workers be held accountable for their actions? Don't you retain any discretion in determining who should play on your team? After all, whose company is it? Well, don't despair. The program outlined in this book is aimed at giving those rights back to you.

With the help of this system, here's how discharge hearings should play out in the future: An arbitrator asks a former employee/plaintiff in a wrongful discharge action, "I see that your former company offered you an opportunity to take part in an EAP program. Did you contact the EAP?" The former employee's flat response is, "No." The arbitrator then asks, "I see that you were encouraged to fill out a section of this write-up regarding your own performance improvement. It's blank, though. Why is that?" The apologetic response is, "Well, I guess I didn't have time."

The arbitrator continues: "I see. Hmm. Your company paid to send you to a one-day off-site training program on conflict resolution in the workplace. Did you attend that workshop?" The employee responds, "Yes, I did." Finally, the arbitrator closes: "So you attended the workshop that was paid for. Yet you did little else to invest in your own personal improvement. And you signed a document showing that you agreed that if you didn't meet the conditions of the agreement, you would resign or be terminated regardless of the reasons for your failure . . . I see no merit in your argument that you were denied due process or that your organization failed to make reasonable attempts to rehabilitate you. This case is dismissed."

You'll immediately notice how the burden was shifted to the employee in terms of proving that he made a good-faith effort to become a better worker. To make this fundamental paradigm shift occur, however, you have to provide the employee with resources he can use to improve himself: coaching and commitment, training, and material resources. And that's a win for both sides, since you, the employer, focus on helping your workers and they, in turn, are charged with accepting your invitations to improve.

It all begins with due process—your efforts to ensure that the employee understands what the problem is, what she needs to do correct the problem, what will happen if she doesn't, and how much time she has to demonstrate improvement.

The Elements of Due Process

A legal theory called the *job as property doctrine* states that employment is a fundamental right of American workers and that the loss of employment has such a serious impact on a person's life that individuals should not lose their jobs without the protection of due process as later codified under the Fourteenth Amendment to the Constitution.[1] Affording due process means recognizing the employee's right to be informed of unsatisfactory performance and to have a chance to defend himself and improve before an adverse employment action (such as discharge) is taken.

---

1 Arthur W. Sherman, Jr., George W. Bohlander, and Herbert J. Chruden, *Managing Human Resources*, 8th Edition (Cincinnati, OH: South-Western Publishing Company, 1988), p. 442.

This *property right* protection places on management an obligation to deal in good faith with employees and to take corrective action measures based on *just cause* (i.e., good reason). This just cause requirement, in turn, mandates that businesses take corrective action measures only for clear, compelling, and justifiable reasons.

But what exactly are the elements of due process?

First, the employee must understand your expectations and the consequences of failing to meet your performance standards. If a write-up merely documents a performance problem without pointing to the consequences of failure to improve, the write-up will lack the "teeth" necessary to meet due process guidelines.

Second, you've got to be consistent in your application of your own rules. Workers have the right to consistent and predictable employer responses when a rule is violated. In other words, problems cannot be corrected on an ad hoc basis without the employer being perceived as arbitrary, unreasonable, or even discriminatory. Bear in mind as well that, generally speaking, practice trumps policy. In other words, regardless of what your handbook or policy and procedure manual says, your past practices will be scrutinized for consistency.

In addition, failure to follow through on threatened consequences damages the credibility of your disciplinary system and sets an unintended precedent: If Employee A, for example, was forgiven for making certain mistakes, Employees B through Z may arguably have to be forgiven for making those same or similar errors.

Third, the discipline must be appropriate for the offense. Occasional poor performance or a minor transgression (known as a *de minimis* infraction) is certainly actionable but probably not cause for termination. An employee's performance track record and prior disciplinary history must certainly be taken into account.

Fourth, the employee should be given an opportunity to respond. Administering discipline without allowing employees to give their side of the story is begging for trouble. Unfortunately, of all the elements of due process that should be incorporated in any write-up blueprint, this self-defense principle is the one that's most often lacking.

Fifth, you need to allow the employee a reasonable period of time to improve her performance. Otherwise, your disciplinary actions will appear to be an artificial excuse to get the employee out of the organization. We'll talk more about acceptable probationary time frames in Chapter 4.

Several other rules of thumb are important to bear in mind as well when dealing with workplace due process:

- As an employer, you have the right to change your policies at any time. Simply give your employees advance notice of the change, along with its effective date, so that all workers can ready themselves to meet your newly defined expectations.

- Infractions need not be treated identically but should be treated consistently. For example, occasional versus habitual tardiness will typically invoke a different response from the company. In other words, you're not precluded from disciplining Susan who reports to work late on a regular basis just because you didn't discipline Fred who came in late one day last week. Likewise, sleeping on the job can be a significant infraction, but it's certainly less of an issue for a secretary (who may receive a written warning for a first offense) than for a night shift nurse (whose first offense results in a final written warning) or for an anesthesiologist (who is terminated for falling asleep during a medical procedure).

▪ The *final incident* plays a very significant role in determining how to best respond to any employee infraction: A clean and compelling final incident, in breach of previous documented warnings, makes for a much safer termination should you company later be challenged. Therefore, look especially to the nature of the final incident when considering termination.

The Traditional Progressive Discipline Paradigm

(1) verbal correction ➡ (2) written warning ➡
(3) final written warning ➡ discharge

The traditional paradigm is used to prove, via documentation, that you made a good-faith effort to lead the employee down the right path. Your affirmative efforts to improve your employee's performance must have been willfully rebuffed despite repeated warnings so that you, as a reasonable employer, were left with no choice other than termination. Keep in mind that you may be required to demonstrate that the discipline was meted out in a fair manner that was consistent with your own policies so that any worker could reasonably expect to be terminated under similar circumstances.

Repeated Violations Trigger Disciplinary Progression

But how exactly does *progressive discipline* progress? Usually the impetus that moves the process from one stage to the next is a repeated violation of the same rule or type of rule (for example, repeated tardiness or unexcused absence). In essence, there must be a link or nexus between events in order to move to the next stage. Without an interrelationship between events, you will end up with a series of independent verbal warnings rather than a progression from a verbal to a written to a final written warning.

For example, an employee who violates your organization's attendance policy and one week later fails to meet a deadline may receive two separate verbal warnings for independent and unrelated transgressions. On the other hand, an employee who violates your company's attendance policy and then develops a tardiness problem will indeed progress through the discipline system because both transgressions are intrinsically connected: Unauthorized absence and tardiness both have a negative effect on the work flow of your office.

It is by no means uncommon to have an employee on separate paths of discipline. A shipping clerk who is already on final written warning for insubordination shouldn't necessarily be terminated if a tardiness problem begins. Tardiness, an event unrelated to insubordination, would not typically be used as the proverbial "straw that breaks the camel's back" to justify termination. That's because there is no nexus or interrelationship between the events: Tardiness interferes with work flow, whereas insubordination relates to individual behavior and conduct—a separate business issue altogether.

On the other hand, because insubordination is a conduct infraction, any other behavior or conduct infractions during the active period of the write-up may indeed result in dismissal. For example, if this shipping clerk on final written warning for insubordination suddenly engages in antagonistic behavior toward his coworkers, insults a customer, or refuses to follow a supervisor's instructions, then a discharge determination could be warranted (barring any significant mitigating circumstances, of course).

Summary Discharges

With all this emphasis on progressive discipline, whatever happened to your right to fire someone on the spot? Well, it's still there: You can fire anyone at any time. However, you may have difficulty defending your actions in a wrongful termination claim. If you've denied an employee due process, the technical merits of your arguments may be largely ignored.

On the other hand, you don't have to offer progressive discipline to someone who breaks the law. Progressive discipline is an employee benefit. If an employee engages in illegal activity or other egregious conduct (such as gross insubordination, gross negligence, theft, embezzlement, time card fraud, or drug use on company premises), you've probably got a clear shot at a quick and defensible termination (known as a *summary dismissal*).

To be on the safe side, though, speak with a labor attorney to fully explore the ramifications of such a dismissal. It's always worth getting a professional legal opinion to ensure that you haven't overlooked anything. If you need to buy yourself some extra time, you can always place the worker on investigatory leave with pay pending further review and a final decision.

Employment at Will

Of course, when it comes to summarily discharging employees, that will also be influenced by the employment status of your workers. If they are hired at will, you will have more leeway in determining whether to retain or terminate. *Employment-at-will* status is employment that does not provide an employee with job security, since the person can be fired on a moment's notice with or without cause. The employment-at-will relationship is created when an employee agrees to work for an employer for an unspecified period of time. It holds that an employer can terminate a worker at any time for any legitimate reason or for no reason at all. Likewise, the employee may leave the organization at any time, with or without notice.[2]

---

2 Most states, but not all, allow at-will employment relationships. For example, the state of Montana has enacted a statute that completely abrogates employment at will. As a result, Montana employers are prohibited from discharging employees without good cause.

On the other hand, the rule is littered with statutory exceptions. That means that you cannot terminate workers if the discharge infringes upon a protected right or goes against public policy. Specifically, there are five exceptions to the employment-at-will doctrine:

1. Employment contracts. If a contract exists, you must adhere to its terms and conditions, including notice requirements, or else you breach the contract. When an employment contract covers a fixed period of time (for example, three years) and is silent concerning grounds for terminating the contract, courts in many states have held that employers have an implied obligation to discharge only for just cause.

2. Statutory considerations. Dismissals are illegal if they are based on age, sex, national origin, religion, union membership, or any other category established in Title VII of the 1964 Civil Rights Act or other legislation. Discrimination is consequently one of the exceptions to the employment-at-will rule, and charges may arise any time you fire someone in a protected class.

3. Public policy exceptions. You cannot terminate an employee for filing a worker's compensation claim, for whistle-blowing, for engaging in group activities that protest unsafe work conditions, or for refusing to commit an unlawful act on the employer's behalf.

4. Implied covenants of good faith and fair dealing. You are prohibited from discharging long-term employees just before they are due to receive anticipated financial benefits.

5. Implied contract exceptions. You may be bound by promises published in your employee handbook or oral promises made at the hiring interview requiring just cause to terminate.

Because of these limitations, you must attempt to protect the at-will employment status at all costs.

Employment-at-will language is typically found at only three critical junctures in the employer-employee relationship: (1) the employment application, (2) the offer letter, and (3) the employee handbook.[3] The at-will language certainly belongs there, but numerous court cases have found that if a long-term employee hasn't seen an application or offer letter

---

3 If you are in an employment-at-will state, you can establish an employment-at-will policy in your employee handbook (or, if you don't have an employee handbook, in a separate memo included in the employee's new hire packet) by expressly stating:

Violation of company policies and rules may warrant disciplinary action. Forms of discipline that the company may elect to use include verbal corrections, written warnings, final written warnings, and/or suspensions. The system is not formal, and the company may, at its sole and absolute discretion, deviate from any order of progressive disciplinary actions and utilize whatever form of discipline is deemed appropriate under the circumstances, up to and including immediate termination of employment. The company's discipline policy in no way limits or alters the at-will employment relationship.

since the date of hire ten or twenty years ago, then she may not necessarily be subject to an at-will employment relationship. Courts have held that it has simply been too long since that message was communicated to the employee. Therefore, communicating your company's employment-at-will policy during the disciplinary process helps protect that policy.

Does employment at will fly in the face of progressive discipline and due process? After all, if you have to take employees through a series of disciplinary actions before you can terminate *for cause*, does that naturally erode your ability to terminate at whim? Well, the two concepts are not mutually exclusive; rather, they are among the complicated, and oftentimes contradictory, issues that make up employment law today. By making the at-will nature of employment known *expressly* (i.e., in writing), you should be better able to successfully argue that an employee did not have a reasonable expectation that discharge could be only for cause.

The Employment-at-Will Affirmative Defense

Remember that your defense attorney will initially attempt to gain a summary judgment— an immediate dismissal—of a wrongful termination claim by employing the at-will defense at the hearing stage. If your defense attorney successfully argues that the ex-worker was employed at-will, understood that she was at-will, and had not had the at-will relationship abrogated during her tenure with your company by any manager's actions or verbal assurances, then the case could simply be dismissed during the hearing (i.e., before the trial stage). The reasons for the termination need not be considered.

However, discrimination is an exception to employment at will. If a plaintiff attorney can show that you discriminated against the employee, retaliated against her for filing a workers' compensation claim, or verbally implied (in front of witnesses) that people "don't get fired around here unless they deserve it," then the employment-at-will affirmative defense may not be sustained.

As a result, if a summary dismissal is not initially granted at the hearing stage by the court or arbitrator, then you will have to justify your decision to terminate at trial by proving that you had just cause. And the way that most employers successfully prove that they had just cause is by presenting the court or the arbitrator with documentation in the form of progressive discipline.

Although much is said about the erosion of the employment-at-will doctrine, "Were you hired at-will?" is still one of the first questions a plaintiff's attorney will ask your ex-employee when deciding whether to take on the case. The attorney knows that if the employee was hired at will, chances of obtaining damages from the company—including damages for wrongful discharge and breach of contract—may be dramatically reduced (assuming the at-will defense is affirmed by the court).[4]

This statement is borne out by employment law case history over the past eighty years. At-will employment came about in the early 1930s. Since then, employees who were

---

4 In other words, for those employees whose rights are not protected by a labor agreement, employment contract, or legal statute (i.e., regarding age, race, or gender), their protection against wrongful discharge is minimal.

dissatisfied with the reasons given for their dismissal have tried to sue their employers, claiming that the companies had to have good cause to fire them. And for many years, courts typically supported employers because of the at-will employment relationship.

That all ended in the early 1980s when a California court held that although the law, as it was written, created a presumption of an at-will employment relationship, that presumption could be challenged by evidence that both parties entered into an employment contract that allowed only termination for cause. Specifically in the 1980 *Tameny v. Atlantic Richfield Co.* case, then California Chief Justice Rose Bird ruled that a long-term employee couldn't be fired under the employment-at-will affirmative defense for refusing to engage in unlawful activities on the company's behalf (in this case, price fixing). Once the employment-at-will veil was pierced, the public policy exception was born, and tort law became a prominent part of the legal landscape.

What was also significant in the California decision was the court's further ruling that the contract could be implied (rather than written or oral) based on a company's past practices. In addition, if language in employee handbooks seemed to suggest that employees could be fired only after some form of due process was provided, then the company was barred from exercising its right to terminate at will. As a result, reaffirming your at-will employment relationship during the disciplinary process gives you the chance to strengthen your defense against a plaintiff's attorney who alleges that an implied promise existed requiring for cause justification.

Implied contract legal theory presents a serious threat to your right to fire an employee on a moment's notice with or without cause. If you inadvertently transform the employment-at-will relationship into an *employment with termination for cause only* relationship, you will unnecessarily expose your organization to increased liability by eliminating your company's first line of defense: the summary judgment.

Without a crystal ball, you can't know in advance what kind of a spin a plaintiff's attorney will place on a case. Therefore, you also can't know if your company will be successful in asserting the employment-at-will affirmative defense (and thereby winning a summary judgment at the hearing stage). Therefore, you should always assume that you'll have to do both: (1) Protect the employment-at-will relationship via your company documentation, but (2) always be prepared to defend your decision to terminate on the merits of the employee's performance (i.e., by showing cause in the form of progressive discipline). In other words, regardless of the employment-at-will relationship, always be prepared to demonstrate just cause to justify a dismissal via documentation. That's fair to your employees and healthy for your company.

Relying on employment at will as a sole defense in terminating workers provides far too many employers with a false sense of security. To avoid falling into that trap, you should protect the employment-at-will relationship with your workers by documenting its existence whenever possible. However, you shouldn't rely on it to make wrongful termination charges magically disappear.

Legal Implications of Probationary Periods

Some labor experts discourage the use of probationary periods for employees who are either newly hired by a company or newly transferred into another position. Their logic stems from the fact that some courts have ruled that the mere completion of such an initial evaluation period suggests express or implied contract obligations that make it more difficult for companies to discharge at will.

Specifically, the completion of a probationary period could be construed to mean that the company can no longer discharge the employee without good cause. Proponents of doing away with probationary periods argue that employees are subject to the same standards of performance and conduct throughout their employment; consequently, no probationary period is necessary, and no implications of job security will arise for employees once their probationary periods are over.

Other labor experts favor retaining traditional probationary periods but abolishing that outdated term, which has been unfavorably interpreted by the courts. They recommend using terms like *introductory, evaluation, training, initiation, eligibility,* or *orientation* periods. True, these designations may help avoid the undesired implications and assurances that the term *probation* has historically carried with it. However, an employee might still infer from these alternative names that the employer has a policy of not discharging without good cause once the period is completed. You, the employer, could consequently find yourself fighting a legal battle over an allegation that you had an obligation to accord due process once a worker passed probation.

Of course, the mere use of the word *probation* rather than *introduction* isn't the whole issue. In interpreting probationary periods, courts look for some reason that they exist—specifically, the employee must receive some form of benefit upon completion of the period. Therefore, to establish a formal probationary period, you need to ensure that there is some difference between your workers' status during the probationary period and after it. Typically, this is done by allowing employees to enjoy some benefit (like accrued vacation or sick leave or 401(k) enrollment) that they did not have before completing the probationary period.[5]

The pros and cons of probationary or introductory periods are well beyond the scope of this book and are prime fodder for legal debate. Still, the ultimate significance of employing such an initiation period will be determined by the laws of your state. Of course, if you're governed by a union contract (AKA collective bargaining agreement) that stipulates that "employees in their probationary period may be discharged without cause and without notice," you'll gain a significant advantage in the whole matter. In essence, such language provides you, the employer, with a contractual right to terminate union workers at whim while in their probationary period. Don't be surprised to learn, however, that the union will

---

5 To establish that the probationary period is a point when performance is evaluated before full benefits begin, create a written policy in your handbook that states: "Completion of the trial period does not entitle you to remain employed by the company for any definite period of time. Both you and the company are free, at any time, with or without notice and with or without cause, to end the employment relationship. After completion of the trial period, eligible employees will receive the benefits described in this handbook."

argue strongly that once that probation period is over, its members (i.e., your employers) cannot be terminated without showing cause.

Generally speaking, it makes total sense to arm yourself with as much flexibility as possible when elevating new employees, without the obligations of due process. And in states that recognize an employment-at-will relationship, probationary periods may be of less significance anyway, since they may not provide your company with any additional flexibility or discretion.

Since most organizations employ some kind of formal initiation period in which to judge employee performance before elevating new hires to "regular" employee status, we'll address disciplining the probationary employee in our samples. Remember that although most employers use probationary time frames of sixty or ninety days, you generally have substantial discretion in setting a period from thirty days to one year. Shorter time frames (thirty to ninety days) are normally used for more junior types of positions; longer windows, like six months or one year, are usually reserved for director and vice presidential–level roles. Practicality will dictate what the reasonable duration should be for the various positions in your organization.

In an effort to diminish the implied interpretation that completing the probationary period guarantees greater job security, your handbook language should expressly state that "the employment relationship is terminable at will, either with or without cause and with or without notice, *at any time* during the employment relationship."

In addition, you should expressly state that the probationary period can be extended more than once at the company's sole discretion and that it also becomes effective at the time of transfer, reassignment, or promotion. Finally, remember to calculate this period in calendar days rather than weeks or months. Any ambiguity in your policy language will most likely be interpreted against you in a court of law. To learn more about the suitability of a probationary period in your company, consult your labor attorney.

2 | Disciplinary Levels, Subjects, and Prior Notifications

The Golden Rule of Progressive Discipline is simply this: It's not enough for a company to merely document discipline; managers have to be able to demonstrate their affirmative efforts at rehabilitating their employees. Here's how it's done.

To begin our venture into the world of progressive discipline, we've got to look at the anatomy of the proposed format. If an infraction of company rules has occurred, performance has fallen below an expected minimum level of output, or the work flow has been impeded as a result of unauthorized absence or tardiness, it may be time to prepare a disciplinary notice. In this chapter, we'll discuss the first four parts of the write-up template: the heading, disciplinary levels, subject, and prior notifications sections.

The Heading

PERFORMANCE CORRECTION NOTICE

Employee Name: *Paul Smith*   **Department:** *Warehouse*

Date Presented: *Friday, May 10, 2017*   **Supervisor:** *Jane Doe*

First, you'll notice that the *customizable narrative* (the part that you write) is shown in italics, while the template document (which does not change from sample to sample) is printed in roman. This will make it easier for you to quickly identify which part of the form you need to fill in for each situation.

In addition, note that the date in the heading should be the date on which the document is shared with the employee, rather than the date on which the incident occurred. You will normally refer to the date of the occurrence in the Incident Description portion of the text. (For example, *On April 29, 2017, you engaged in inappropriate conduct with a coworker . . .*) The active date of the write-up begins the day the employee is made aware of the transgression. Of course, the time of the write-up should coincide with the time of the incident as closely as possible.

Disciplinary Level

DISCIPLINARY LEVEL	PURPOSE OF WRITE-UP
☐ Verbal Correction	(To memorialize the conversation.)
☐ Written Warning	(State nature of offense, method of correction, and action to be taken if offense is repeated.)
☐ Investigatory Leave	(Include length of time and nature of review.)
☐ Final Written Warning	
☐ Without decision-making leave	
☐ With decision-making leave	(Attach memo of instructions.)
☐ With unpaid suspension	

A progressive disciplinary system must show itself to be rehabilitative. The system typically moves through a series of one or more notices that an employee's performance is not meeting standards. So if at any time after a progressive disciplinary intervention, the employee fails to alter behaviors or improve performance, then the next logical step in the process is taken, ultimately resulting in termination for cause.

Each step in the process typically contains some added element to impress upon the employee the growing sense of urgency that the company is attempting to communicate. For example, when an employee fails to render appropriate customer service after having received a verbal warning, then the written warning clearly states that the employee "may have failed to take the previous warning seriously and is consequently receiving this more aggressive form of discipline." The Consequences section of the written warning will then reflect a more severe penalty should an infraction occur again.

The Verbal Correction (AKA First Written Warning)

The verbal correction is the first step in the formal disciplinary process. In contrast to coaching or counseling sessions, which are informal (and are not documented or placed in the employee's personnel file[1]), the verbal correction must document the nature of the current problem and point to future disciplinary action if improvement doesn't occur.

---

1 Any notes you generate during a coaching or counseling session may be placed in your critical incidents diary in your office, but not in the employee's personnel file.

Consequently, it's common to end verbal corrections with the caveat phrase "failure to demonstrate immediate and sustained improvement may result in further disciplinary action up to and including dismissal."

Must every infraction begin with a verbal correction? No. More aggressive disciplinary levels may be appropriate if the employee engages in conduct that in the employer's opinion is more serious than a verbal correction would indicate. For example, an employee might state to a customer over the phone, "You know, I really don't care which loan program you go with. Don't ask me to make that decision for you. Geez!" If this is a first offense, you might not wish to discharge the employee outright; however, you may decide to immediately place the employee on final written notice (even for a first-time offense) that "if you ever again make a derogatory, insulting, or demeaning statement to a customer, you will be immediately discharged."

Similarly, if an accounts receivable clerk leaves a $10,000 check sitting on his desk for thirty days when turnaround time should be within twenty-four hours, then more severe discipline than a verbal correction would be warranted. The litmus test for determining if a verbal correction or more aggressive disciplinary action would be appropriate is simply this: Follow the verbal $\longrightarrow$ written $\longrightarrow$ final written paradigm *unless* starting with the verbal correction would make you, as an employer, appear irresponsible.

You're obligated to match the discipline to the offense. A slap on the hand isn't always appropriate when egregious misconduct or serious performance problems occur. That's why sexual harassment or discrimination findings typically start at the written or final written stage of discipline—even for a first offense.

Note as well that a verbal correction should always be documented. Although "writing down a verbal" may seem contradictory on its face, it is safest to have the employee sign the verbal corrective action notice for two reasons: First, it documents that the employee indeed received the verbal warning, and second, when people sign their names to documents, they tend to take responsibility for the results more readily.

Some labor experts believe that having an employee sign a verbal correction is unnecessary, since it's only a verbal communication. "If the employee signs it," they reason, "then you've in essence given that employee a first written reprimand rather than a verbal warning." Logical? Sure, but what's the harm in trying to increase the individual's commitment? None. So ask for that extra level of insurance. It never hurts to be overly thorough in these matters.

The Written Warning

The written warning is the second step in the formal discipline process and is obviously more serious than the verbal correction. A written warning serves as formal notice that a serious infraction has occurred or that the directives outlined in a previous verbal correction were breached. Its purpose is to inform the employee that her job may now be in jeopardy. The written warning also aims to gain the worker's agreement that this will be the last time that a problem should need to be addressed.

A written warning typically affects an employee's annual performance evaluation as well by preventing the employee from receiving an *exceeds expectations* score as an overall grade. Verbal corrections, in contrast, typically do not have this level of influence over the annual performance grade. You should share this information with employees who receive verbal corrections because, in dollars-and-cents terms, written warnings may indeed affect their pocketbooks.

Let's look at an example. An employee receives a verbal correction for three occurrences of unauthorized absence in a rolling calendar year. The verbal clearly states that five incidents will lead to a written warning, six incidents to a final written warning, and seven incidents to a termination. When the employee has a fifth incident, the written warning states:

> You have breached the terms of the verbal correction you received on April 10. It appears that you may not have taken that warning seriously. The purpose of this written warning is to impress on you the seriousness of this issue and the fact that your position is now in jeopardy of being lost. More significantly, if you incur one more incident of unscheduled, unauthorized absence in the rolling calendar year, you will be immediately placed in final written warning status. A seventh incident will result in immediate discharge for cause.

Because of your clear and concise communication, your instructions and the consequences are undeniable. You will have provided the employee with due process. More importantly, you will have shifted the burden of responsibility for improvement away from your company and to your employee.

Investigatory Leave

Investigatory leave (sometimes referred to as administrative leave) occurs when you suspect a worker of some severe violation or infraction of company rules, but you need to conduct an investigation to confirm your suspicions. Before you interview witnesses or audit company records, you remove the employee from the premises so that an unbiased investigation can occur.

For example, when several female employees make a formal complaint to you that a male supervisor is making lewd comments and sexual innuendos to a point that the workplace feels unfriendly or hostile, you decide to conduct an investigation. You take the female employees' statements and then meet with the accused male supervisor to gain his version of the events.

Assuming that the two sides do not agree, you then decide to meet with witnesses named by both parties. To conduct these witness interviews most effectively, you may remove the male supervisor from the premises for a few days so that an unbiased investigation can occur. In this case, you find that the witnesses confirm the female employees' statements, so you then call the male supervisor at home and invite him back to your office to take the appropriate disciplinary action. Let's assume you choose to place the supervisor on final written warning. You will then check two boxes in this section of the write-up template: (1) investigatory leave and (2) final written warning.

If the witnesses do not bear out the facts as outlined by the female workers, for whatever reason, you would not take any formal action against the supervisor. Therefore, this disciplinary form would not be used, and nothing would be placed into the supervisor's file. You would pay the supervisor for the two days he spent at home while you conducted your internal investigation, and the matter would be closed.

Final Written Warning

The final written warning is just that—a last-chance agreement between employer and employee regarding sustainable, improved performance or conduct. A breached final written warning normally should result in discharge; otherwise, you sabotage the integrity of your entire discipline system. In addition, at this point, any further infractions will result in the employee's firing himself via his refusal to reform.

Whereas written warnings provide one more chance should a further infraction occur, final written warnings offer fewer alternatives. As a result, typical language used throughout this book will state: "This is your last chance, and your position is now in immediate jeopardy of being lost. Failure to demonstrate immediate and sustained improvement may result in further disciplinary action, up to and including dismissal."

Choosing Not to Discharge

There can be an exception to this rule, however. If the employee breaches the terms of a final written warning, but you don't feel that you're on solid legal ground to terminate, you may give the employee another chance. This typically occurs when the final incident is not clear and convincing or when the employee has so much tenure with the company that providing him with another chance is reasonable. Let's briefly look at an illustration.

In our previous example about the supervisor who is accused of making sexual innuendos and creating a hostile work environment, suppose that you found that certain witnesses agreed with the supervisor that no harassment occurred. Indeed, some of these witnesses attest that the female employees not only engaged in but also initiated sexually oriented jokes and comments.

If the supervisor has already received a written warning for violating your company's sexual harassment policy, could you opt to terminate him based on this investigation? Probably not, since the conflicting and contradictory testimony from those witnesses muddies the waters. Without a clean final incident, it might be difficult to justify termination.

Still, the supervisor shouldn't have engaged in or allowed such discussions in the workplace, so discipline is certainly appropriate. Therefore, you might opt to state the following in the new disciplinary notice to the supervisor:

On October 11, 2017, you received a written notice stating that should you ever again engage in conduct that violates our company's sexual harassment policy, you could face further disciplinary action, up to and including dismissal. Our recent investigation reveals that you may have engaged in and allowed conversations that could have potentially created an unfriendly work environment. However, because there is no agreement as to who began or encouraged the conversations that occurred on January 15, 2018, we are not terminating you at this time. We are, instead, giving you another chance.

Be advised that this is your last chance. No future transgressions of this critical company policy will be permitted under any circumstances. You will be held responsible for any such complaints that arise under your purview, and immediate termination may result. In addition, I remind you that our company has zero tolerance for violations of its antidiscrimination and harassment policies. Furthermore, no form of retaliation will be allowed against those employees who come forward to human resources with a good faith complaint.

In taking this action against the supervisor, you would neither violate the terms and conditions of the final warning nor set a dangerous precedent. You would, instead, fit the discipline to the offense, protect the employees who made the original complaint, and accord the supervisor due process. You would also avoid a wrongful discharge claim stemming from controversial witness statements—just the type of confusion and inconsistency that plaintiffs' attorneys love. It would also be appropriate in this case to discipline the female employees for engaging in or instigating inappropriate conversations.

Last-Step Options

Next, a note on semantics in this book: A final written warning is a *last-step option*. Different companies use different last-step options, and which one they use depends on their culture, history, and philosophy of discipline. Following are the five most common forms of last-step options, along with my recommendations concerning their use:

1. Final Written Warning

Recommended. The benefit of using this term is that it's very clear and logically follows the verbal and written disciplinary actions that precede it.

2. Probation

Acceptable. Some companies prefer not to use the term *final written warning* and instead imply it by stating: "If you fail to follow established departmental policies and procedures at any time in the next ninety days, you will be placed on a *formal ninety-day probation*. If you fail to follow procedures or meet minimum performance standards in that probationary period, you will be dismissed." That formal ninety-day probation is actually equivalent to the final written warning.

3. Last-Chance Agreement

Recommended. However, some companies use last-chance agreements as separate, freestanding documents. I recommend including last-chance agreement language in the disciplinary document itself. Therefore, we won't use last-chance agreements *as* the final step of discipline but *in* the final steps of discipline.

4. Unpaid Suspension

Suspensions without pay are recommended only in cases involving willful misconduct or actions with malicious intent. In practice, disciplinary suspension is usually used to punish the employee for seriously unacceptable behavior. By "hitting him in the pocketbook," so to speak, the message is more pointedly brought home that the employee has committed a serious violation that, because of mitigating circumstances, is not currently leading to immediate discharge.

- **Disadvantages of suspension without pay:** This punitive measure has a number of serious disadvantages. First, by its nature, this action is negative, not affirmative. Therefore, it will fly in the face of your company's mission statement or belief about treating employees with dignity and respect. Second, unpaid suspension places an economic burden on the employee's family. In a sense, the family pays for the worker's performance and/or conduct problems, since pay is withheld. And third, placing an employee on unpaid suspension tends to create a martyr syndrome when employees share their woes with one another. The "bad" company takes advantage of the "helpless" employee by humiliating him in front of his family and causing him to lose face. Therefore, I recommend that you typically avoid traditional unpaid disciplinary suspensions whenever possible.

- **Appropriate use of suspension without pay:** On the other hand, if an employee engages in willful misconduct or egregious behavior that smacks of retaliation or harassment, then a traditional unpaid suspension may be appropriate. In such cases, the malicious intent of the employee's actions may dictate that you take a harsh disciplinary posture.

  For example, when a disgruntled dishwasher unloads a stack of new dishes from the box, holds them out in front of his chest, drops them, and then says, "Oops, I guess that was an accident," you might not want to impose a summary discharge because of mitigating circumstances (e.g., this may be the first and only display of improper conduct in his twenty years of employment). However, you could very well place him on an unpaid three-day suspension (assuming your policy and past practices allow for that) so that the disciplinary measure fits the infraction.

  As another example, suppose a telephone company installer crashed a brand new $40,000 vehicle on Monday but failed to inform his supervisor until Friday. Company policy clearly states that any accidents must be reported immediately to supervisors. The employee's willful breach of this clearly established policy allows the supervisor to impose on the twenty-year employee the strictest discipline allowed by the company: a thirty-day unpaid suspension.

Similarly, suppose a warehouse manager asked his boss for three vacation days, Thursday, Friday, and Monday, and his director informed him in advance that Thursday and Friday were okay to take off, but the following Monday was not. The manager promptly told his secretary to mark him down for Thursday and Friday as vacation days and Monday as a sick day. This employee willfully violated his director's immediate instructions (i.e., not to take Monday off) and the company's sick leave policy (i.e., that sick time can be used only for the employee's or family member's actual illness). Again, if this was a first-time offense for a ten-year employee, termination might not be appropriate in the company's eyes. A five-day suspension without pay,[2] however, may be appropriate because of the worker's flagrant disregard of his supervisor's directive and the intentional abuse of company policy.

5. Decision-Making Leave

Decision-making leave is the fifth kind of last-step option and is highly recommended. Organizations that want to achieve best practices in their employee relations activities place employees on one-day *paid* disciplinary leaves, also known as *decision-making leaves* or *days of contemplation*.

In stark contrast to the historical and punitive suspension without pay, the decision-making leave removes the "defacing" mechanism from the discipline process and helps employees focus on their behaviors rather than on yours. (Guilt is always a more effective motivator than anger.) It is most often used when willful misconduct and malice do not come into play; instead, there is either (a) a performance or conduct problem that has recurred and that simply must stop or (b) a demonstrated serious lack of judgment.

For example, an electrician left work promptly at his clock-out time despite the fact that the hospital where he worked was experiencing a brownout. Going home when emergency conditions dictated that he should have remained at the work site in order to repair broken generators jeopardized patient safety. His supervisor immediately placed him on a final written warning and one-day paid suspension so that he could rethink his role as an electrician and as a valuable asset to the hospital. The employee returned two days later with a written commitment letter confirming his role in emergencies and his responsibility to the institution.

In another example, a secretary who was known for "stirring the pot" and feeding the

---

2 A special note about docking pay for exempt workers (like managers) for disciplinary reasons: Unpaid disciplinary suspensions of one or more full days may be imposed in good faith for infractions of workplace conduct rules. Such suspensions must be imposed pursuant to a written policy applicable to all employees.

In contrast, if you were to deduct a partial day's pay for a disciplinary suspension, that could result in the manager's exempt status being negated, and you could be left vulnerable to overtime charges for an FLSA (Fair Labor Standards Act) violation. In other words, the exempt manager could be considered a nonexempt employee who is entitled to overtime pay. The Department of Labor's Wage and Hour Division could end up sticking you with a massive "back wages" assessment in that case for overtime due to your manager!

corporate grapevine was found to have begun a false rumor about a coworker in her department. She stated to others that she was aware that a male employee in her department was gay. Another worker in the unit believed this and brought news of the employee's homosexuality to the employee's mother—a long-time family friend. When it was found that the original rumor, although untrue, had been started by the secretary, it was too late for the damage to be undone—confusion, hurt feelings, and unnecessary drama resulted.

Management placed the secretary on a final written warning plus a one-day paid suspension to rethink her commitment to the institution and the unforeseen damage that false rumors could cause. The secretary, in turn, returned two days later with a written statement confirming her intention never again to engage in rumor mongering. Letters of apology were also composed and delivered in person to her colleague.

You should consider paid decision-making leaves a cheap insurance contract. By sending someone home for one day with pay to impress upon him the seriousness of the problem, you'll pass one of the EEOC's due process tests with flying colors. The Equal Employment Opportunity Commission (EEOC) is the federal government body that investigates and prosecutes claims of discrimination, harassment, and wrongful discharge. The EEOC tends to look favorably on an employer's willingness to pay for an employee's "time out" period.

Besides, by paying for the time off, you retain your right to give your worker a mandatory written homework assignment detailing how he will improve his behavior. You'll consequently get a concrete work product that documents, in the employee's own handwriting, how he will recommit himself to following workplace rules. Here's how you would present the situation to the worker:

> Jeff, in addition to placing you on a final written warning for this repeated violation, I'm giving you a day off with pay tomorrow to rethink your commitment to this organization. The purpose of this administrative leave is to impress upon you the seriousness of your actions. If you choose not to return to work the day after tomorrow, I'll respect your decision. I'll support you in any way I can in finding another position outside the company.
>
> But remember that I'm paying you for the day. If you decide to return to work the day after next, then you'll need to provide me with a one-page written action plan that outlines the concrete steps that you're going to take to correct the problem. Without that written game plan, you won't be admitted back to work. You'll need to present that letter to me first thing Thursday morning in my office and clearly convince me that you're committed to making this work. You'll also need to convince me that this will be the last time that we have to talk about this problem. Finally, understand that if you violate the terms of your own agreement, you'll be terminating yourself. Do you have any questions about that?

That signed commitment letter in the employee's personnel file should go a long way toward getting the employee to buy into his own improvement. More importantly, it provides you with a powerful piece of ammunition should you later terminate the employee for cause and face an arbitrator's challenge. Figure 2–1 provides a sample decision-making leave handout that you can give the employee as he walks out of your office and heads home to ruminate about his future with your company.

Make it clear to the employee during your conversation that this is a once-in-a-career benefit. If you raise the bar in terms of individual responsibility, you'll soon find that people either politely bow out of your firm or recommit, reinvent their jobs, and lose that sense of entitlement that unfortunately plagues so many workers.

The choice of including decision-making leaves in tandem with final written corrections is ultimately yours. These leaves work best with long-term employees, who, because of their tenure, deserve more of a chance to correct performance problems. They can be used with all employees, though, since wrongful discharge claims are not limited to long-term workers. Bear in mind, however, that investing one day's pay can shield your institution from liability while improving morale and having a positive effect on the corporate culture

Figure 2–1. Decision-making leave.

You have received counseling and coaching regarding meeting company standards of performance and conduct. You have also received formal disciplinary documentation, which included a Performance Improvement Plan. However, because your performance still does not meet organizational standards, you are now formally being placed on a one-day decision-making leave with pay.

The purpose of this leave is to impress upon you the fact that your job is now in serious jeopardy of being lost. It will allow you the time necessary to contemplate how you will improve your performance to meet company expectations. In addition, you are required to provide me with a written commitment letter when you report back to work. This letter will be permanently attached to your personnel file. Without this commitment letter, you will not be entitled to return to work.

This commitment letter should address the specific behavior changes that you will make in order to perform at an acceptable level. It will also include suggestions you have for me regarding areas in which you need added direction and support. In addition, it will address the length of the "maintenance period" that you pledge to adhere to and the consequences that you believe are fair if you don't meet your self-imposed goals.

Finally, be advised that this decision-making leave is a once-in-a-career employee benefit. You will not be granted another such leave with pay for a performance/conduct matter again.

I have read these instructions, and I understand the purpose of this one-day paid leave.

_____   _____
Employee Signature   Date

_____
Print Name

```
_____        _____
Supervisor's Signature                 Date


_____
Print Name
```

Caution Regarding Decision-Making Leaves and Unpaid Suspensions

The decision-making leave and suspension without pay should be used not in place of, but as a part of, the final warning. That's why we've placed both under "Final Written Warning" in the disciplinary template. If you don't attach these leaves to the final written warning notice, then employees may assume that they have a right to a suspension or decision-making leave before they can be discharged. In practice, you could end up changing your disciplinary paradigm to look like this:

(1) verbal warning ➜ (2) written warning ➜
(3) final written warning ➜ (4) suspension/decision-making leave ➜ discharge

Adding that suspension or decision-making leave could change the traditional three-tier system to a four-tier system *if* you administer these types of disciplinary actions on their own. That would certainly weaken your ability to discharge employees for cause because you will have inadvertently created a new hoop to jump through.

The purpose of these leaves, however, is not to burden you with even greater due process requirements. Instead, it is to prove your good-faith efforts to bring to employees' attention the seriousness of their offenses. By linking these actions to the final written warning, therefore, you'll retain more flexibility in determining the format of the last-step option without burdening your progressive discipline system.

Classifying the Infraction

SUBJECT: _____

☐ Policy/Procedure Violation

☐ Performance Transgression

☐ Behavior/Conduct Infraction

☐ Absenteeism/Tardiness

Classifying violations is critical lest you end up with a third verbal warning rather than with a progression of disciplinary actions for three *related* incidents. Even if three errors were committed, if the infractions are not linked somehow, you're still at the first stage of discipline. You've simply doled out separate verbal warnings three times. On the other hand, when you can link the incidents, you can progress from a verbal to a written to a final written correction—obviously a much more aggressive and serious approach to repeated violations of company rules or subpar performance.

Many managers mistakenly document isolated events without tying them to a broader theme. The line to the right of the word *Subject* allows you to specifically document the particular problem at hand. For example, you might write something specific like:

Substandard work performance

Pattern of unscheduled absence

Failure to follow your supervisor's reasonable instructions

Substandard customer service

Violation of policy 2.1 on maintaining a friendly and inclusive work environment

Failure to meet minimum sales production standards

However, you then need to tie these individual transgressions to a broader theme of workplace transgressions in order to create an interrelationship among events.

There are four broad categories of performance issues: policy violations, performance transgressions, conduct infractions, and absenteeism and tardiness. You can use these categories to link seemingly unrelated events. You will then be able to successfully progress through the disciplinary system even when transgressions aren't identical. It is also possible for an act to fall into more than one category.

Policy/Procedure Violations

Policy or procedure violations occur when a written company standard or understood rule is broken. For example, a worker who violates a safety policy may be subject to discipline. Likewise, two coworkers engaging in horseplay who end up damaging company equipment should be disciplined even if there is no company rule specifically addressing horseplay in the workplace. In that case, a certain level of common sense regarding workplace behavior can be imputed to the employee.

Some critical issues when applying rules, regulations, policies, and procedures to employee conduct are:

- You will be required to abide by them consistently.

- They must be reasonably related to achieving a legitimate business purpose.

- They must be nondiscriminatory in purpose and application.

- They must not be designed or applied to harass or punish employees.

- They must not infringe upon any of your employees' rights.

Remember that you have the right to set the rules of the game in your company. Legal challenges will occur, however, when you deviate from your own rules, and plaintiffs will win lawsuits if your inconsistency can be proved. Proper documentation is your only defense!

Performance Transgressions

Performance transgressions occur when employees fail to meet established production or output guidelines. Underperforming salespeople, analysts with high error ratios in their calculations, and construction workers who are negligent with their materials and cause unnecessary property damage would be disciplined for unacceptable performance.

Behavior and Conduct Infractions

Behavior and conduct infractions come about when an individual's personal actions violate accepted corporate rules and norms. An employee, for example, who refuses to follow a supervisor's reasonable directive or who attempts to undermine the supervisor's authority by openly challenging her in front of others commits insubordination. Similarly, alcohol-related conduct, profane language, and retaliation all violate behavioral standards.

Absenteeism and Tardiness

The individual's failure to adhere to attendance or timeliness guidelines causes unplanned overtime and work flow redistribution, as others must cover for the absent worker. As a result, the work flow is negatively affected.

Bundling Unrelated Items

What do you do with an employee with violations in separate classifications? In other words, if she receives a verbal warning for a policy infraction one week, a verbal for a performance transgression the next, a verbal for a conduct infraction a week later, and then has a series of unauthorized absences, what can you do to drive home the message that her job is in jeopardy?

Bundling allows violations that are fundamentally unrelated to be lumped together for purposes of documenting poor performance. This accumulation factor often plays an important role in justifying terminations because it documents that workers are not rehabilitating themselves or taking prior warnings seriously. You may consequently advance to a higher disciplinary level by stating:

> You are now receiving a verbal warning for tardiness. This is your fourth verbal warning in as many weeks. As a result, you are not meeting company standards of performance and conduct, and a special probation with more stringent requirements is necessary. In addition, because this is your fourth verbal warning in as many weeks, you are now receiving a written warning for multiple violations of company policies and for unacceptable performance. If you violate any standards of performance and conduct within the next ninety days, you will be placed in a formal ninety-day final written warning period. If you violate any standards of performance and conduct while in that final written warning period, you will be dismissed.

Arbitrators will generally uphold more aggressive disciplinary measures when numerous performance problems—even if unrelated—have accumulated over short time periods.

Prior Notifications

Level of Discipline	Date	Subject
Verbal	_____	_____
Written	_____	_____
Final Written	_____	_____

This section of the write-up is a fail-safe measure to ensure that you, as a manager, have properly notified the employee of past performance issues. Bear in mind that, if your action is challenged, the completeness and thoroughness of your documentation will be taken into consideration. Over time, consistently well-documented interventions will provide your company with clear and logical progressive attempts to rehabilitate your staff members. Simply put, you'll sleep better at night knowing that all the managers in your company are following the same guidelines.

All prior discipline should be noted here, not just discipline related to the current transgression. In other words, although you may be disciplining the employee right now for a breach related to unscheduled absence, last month's disciplinary warning regarding substandard sales production should be captured here as well. In essence, you want to impress upon the employee the totality of events that prove substandard performance.

How far back you go in listing prior disciplinary notifications is up to you. It's most practical to go back one year. A three-year-old problem regarding insubordination won't necessarily add any merit to your current argument that the individual's unscheduled absence is having a negative effect on everyone in the department. However, if you're currently writing up the employee for insubordination, then mentioning that three-year-old transgression might make sense.

It's important to remember to review the worker's personnel file before administering discipline. Discipline can't be administered in a vacuum: It must logically be tied to the employee's prior warnings and performance evaluations. Therefore, you're better off documenting any prior disciplinary actions that, in the fairly recent past, have caused you to avert your efforts away from the workplace in order to address the employee's individual needs.

3 Incident Descriptions and Performance Improvement

"Document, document, document!" That's what you hear all the time as a manager and business owner. The logical need for documentation is clear: It not only helps you recollect specific details that you can later use to justify your actions, but also lends a layer of insulation to the corporation by demonstrating that your decisions were based on sound business fundamentals. In addition, many arbitrators adhere to the adage, "If it isn't documented, it didn't happen." Therefore, you'll need to rely on signed employee disciplinary notices and performance evaluations to mount a defense.

Knowing *how* to document, however, is a different story. That issue will be clearly discussed in this chapter along with the structure of the employee improvement plan. Following is a typical description of events that led a company to take disciplinary action against an employee who had received prior warnings (both verbal and written) regarding substandard job performance.

Incident Descriptions

Incident Description and Supporting Details: Include the following information: Time, Place, Date of Occurrence, and Persons Present as well as Organizational Impact.

Paul,

To date you have had a number of serious performance issues in the Warehouse. Now today, on May 1, 2017, you have again failed to perform one of your essential job functions—the timely delivery of supplies. Specifically, you delivered an incomplete order of medical supplies to Nursing Wing A and also failed to provide the proper paperwork to the charge nurse. As a result, there was a delay in the delivery of supplies, and the work flow was disrupted. This violates our hospital's standards of performance and conduct and also shows a further breach of your responsibilities as outlined in your previous warnings.

This customized narrative section needs to be composed on a case-by-case basis. There are many examples of narratives in this book. Obviously, no one description could fit everything that is going on in your office or work environment at any given time. On the other hand, it helps to see what other employers have written in describing similar employee transgressions. You must describe as accurately as possible the specifics of the problematic performance or conduct.

Incident Description Dos and Don'ts

There are several key rules that will help you compose accurate and legally defensible incident descriptions. First, you must use the traditional who-what-where-when-why-how paradigm when creating the correspondence. For example, you might write:

> On Friday, May 30, at 2:00 P.M. [*when*], you engaged in disrespectful and inappropriate conduct and provided substandard customer service when you told a call-in borrower that you shouldn't be asked to make the decision about selecting an appropriate loan program. You then told the customer that you didn't care what program he selected. You ended that statement with the disrespectful remark "Geez!" [*what*]

> When I later questioned you as to how such a conversation could have come about or why you chose to use a sarcastic and demeaning tone, you told me that you didn't know. You told me you just must have been tired or having a bad day. [*why/how*].

A second rule that will help you compose adequate incident descriptions is to use your senses in describing the events. For example, if you are writing up a secretary for insubordination and for displaying a bad attitude, paint a picture with words by describing the employee's specific actions and behaviors that created that perception in your mind:

> On Wednesday, May 13, at 4:00 in the afternoon, you walked into my office and loudly complained that the work that I left on your desk should have been done by the other secretary. I *saw* you place your hand on your hip, cock your head, and point your finger at me when you delivered your message. Others *heard* you raise your voice and speak rudely to me when you said "So what?" and "Big deal." When you sat down, you leaned over my desk from the edge of your chair, and I *sensed* that you were attempting to intimidate me.

A third rule of thumb is to take any subjective evaluations and make them objective by adding concrete objects or facts to substantiate your claim. For example:

> ***Don't state***
> "You were hostile toward a customer." [*subjective*]

Do state

"You were rude and abrupt with a customer when you told him you didn't care which loan program he picked." [*objective*]

Don't state

"You left your work area untidy again." [*subjective*]

Do state

"An eight-inch stack of incoming work orders was piled on your desk, your trash can was overflowing, and air conditioning parts were lying on your typing table." [*objective*]

Don't state

"You appeared at the client's office under the influence of alcohol." [*subjective*]

Do state

"The client reported that he heard you slurring your words and laughing uncontrollably. He reported that he saw that your eyes were glassy and that you tripped over your own feet when walking across the room. He also smelled alcohol on your breath." [*objective*]

Any time you can describe your observations in behavioral terms, you will strengthen your case.

Fourth, in addition to the facts surrounding the individual's problematic performance, you need to include the negative organizational impact that resulted from the employee's actions. For example, you might conclude the incident description section with one of the following "tags":

- Consequently, you have violated company standards of performance and conduct.

- As a result, you have violated policy 2.10, Timekeeping Procedures.

- I found inconsistencies throughout your calculations and had to correct them myself before they could be processed. This interfered with the work flow in our unit and caused other staff members to work unplanned overtime. A temp was also necessary to complete the project, incurring additional expense. Your repeated abuse of the sick leave system shows that you may not have taken your former warnings seriously. As a result, you are now being placed on a special probation with more stringent requirements.

- This constitutes a further breach of your responsibilities as outlined in your previous warnings.

- Because your manner could have been perceived as belittling, antagonistic, and intimidating, you violated policy 3.2, Respect in the Workplace.[1]

- The failure to actively collect these accounts receivable will reduce our company's cash flow. In addition, I will need to work late for the remainder of the week to ensure that we close our books on time by the month-end deadline.

That element of negative organizational impact is an important part of the disciplinary process because it justifies your actions.

Fifth, whenever possible, write down the employee's response to your questions in this section of the write-up. By documenting "When I asked you how this occurred, you told me . . .," you demonstrate that you have listened and considered the individual's side of the story before reaching a conclusion. It also reduces the risk that the employee's story will change later.

Performance Improvement Plan (PIP)

The Performance Improvement Plan is the next part of our model correction notice. There are five key elements in the improvement plan (outlined below) for a particular employee:

Performance Improvement Plan

1. Measurable/Tangible Improvement Goals: Paul, I expect that no further incidents of misplaced or misdelivered packages or orders will occur in your area. In addition, I expect that you will proactively communicate with us concerning the status of your work and anything that prevents you from completing your assignments in a timely manner.

2. Training or Special Direction to Be Provided: For the next five days, please meet with Dave Wilson daily before you begin your rounds to discuss your delivery agenda.

3. Interim Performance Evaluation Necessary? No

4. Our **Employee Assistance Program** (EAP) provider, Prime Behavioral Health Group, can be confidentially reached to assist you at (800) 555-5555. This is strictly voluntary. A booklet regarding the EAP's services is available from Human Resources.

5. In addition, I recognize that you may have certain ideas to improve the situation at hand. Therefore, I encourage you to provide your own **Personal Improvement Plan Input and Suggestions:**

_____

_____

_____

(Attach additional sheets if needed.)

---

1 I don't recommend writing that an employee "created a hostile working environment" or "sexually harassed" a coworker. Such absolute statements are dangerous because if the harassed employee sues, your own documentation will be used against you. It is better to state "your actions might suggest" or "could be perceived as hostility."

1. Measurable/Tangible Improvement Goals

For progressive discipline to work, it has to have a concrete outcome. That outcome may take the form of increased production numbers, decreased errors, improved interpersonal communications, or a tardiness-free attendance record. In addition to the previous sample, the following examples demonstrate measurable outcomes:

> Our organization has an established history of developing people's skills and valuing the individual. When you told your coworker that she was "incapable of learning" and "never would amount to anything," your remarks about her inability to improve violate our philosophy and culture. I expect you to support your coworkers and encourage them to develop their skills and to find new ways of contributing to our organization.

> I expect that you will meet our organization's guidelines regarding attendance and punctuality from this point forward.

> In the future, I expect you to complete your recruitment statistics report by the first of the month and to tell me in advance if you will be unable to collect the data from your recruiters or the HRIS team to meet this goal.

Notice that each of these statements includes the phrase *I expect* . . . Remember that under the rules of workplace due process, you are obliged to inform the employee of what he has to do in order to correct his problematic performance. This statement should be written in a constructive manner so that it can clearly establish what is expected of the employee in terms of future behavior. By doing so, it demonstrates that you are communicating with the employee to help him succeed on the job.

2. Training or Special Direction to Be Provided

Whenever possible, it's best to address a problem with positive tools as opposed to negative methods. Training is therefore a better alternative than punishment. This important section of the correction notice further documents your attempts to help the employee succeed on her job. Even if discipline must be administered in the form of a warning, it should still be delivered hand in hand with training and other affirmative employer efforts.

Keep in mind as well that training is the glue that binds people to a company: Everyone likes learning new things and developing new skills. And training, more than anything, helps people reinvent their jobs in light of their companies' changing needs. Although motivation is internal and not external, nothing drives an employee to renewed commitment more than being challenged and stimulated by a new learning curve. Here are samples of things you might include:

> On Friday, May 30, you are scheduled to attend a four-hour seminar on PowerPoint that will be taught by our Information Technology department. Two weeks later, you are scheduled to attend another workshop on Excel in order to increase your level of computer competence.

> In an effort to sensitize you about how your behavior affects others, we will arrange for you to attend, on company time and at company expense, a one-day, off-site workshop on dealing with interpersonal conflict in the workplace.
>
> I suggest you take a time management course at a local college.
>
> I am sending you a book on spreadsheet basics. Please familiarize yourself with the essential functions that you need on a day-to-day basis. Then follow up with me three weeks later regarding your progress.
>
> A copy of our attendance policy is attached. Please reread the policy and ask me any questions to help you to understand it.

As you can see, the training or special direction can be as simple as providing the employee with a copy of a policy that was violated, or it can be a matter of heightened feedback, hands-on training, and off-site workshops. The cost of an off-site workshop is a fairly small investment that simultaneously increases worker productivity and minimizes the company's potential liability should the employee later be discharged and file a lawsuit.

Note, however, that the goal here is not to burden yourself or the company with being responsible for assuring the employee's success. Instead, shift the responsibility to the employee to research the necessary workshops, read the appropriate policies, and otherwise follow up with you regarding his progress. And here's why: In a typical wrongful termination lawsuit, the judge will ask what the company, as a good corporate citizen, did to help the employee improve.

If the company created hurdles for itself by promising one-on-one training time or outside workshops that it never ended up offering, then the burden is on the company for not following through and acting irresponsibly. In comparison, if the company provided opportunities to the employee that he never took advantage of or followed up on, then the worker comes across as the irresponsible party.

Here's a common example to keep in mind: In our previous example, we stated, "For the next five days, please meet with Dave Wilson daily before you begin your rounds to discuss your delivery agenda." First, you'll note the qualifier "for the next five days." It's always better to cap time commitments rather than keep them open-ended. So meetings should be scheduled "once a day *for five days*" or "once a week *for three weeks,*" but never just "once a day" or "once a week." In the written warning, "once a week" may appear to a third party to mean "once a week forever" because there was no cap placed on the commitment.

Second, notice that the burden was placed on the employee to meet with Dave, and not vice versa. The employee has to gain trust by meeting with his lead once a day for five days. Therefore, it shouldn't be the lead's or management's responsibility to ensure that the employee indeed shows up. If and when the worker fails to show up, then he is seen as irresponsible for not upholding his end of the bargain. Again, the reasonable employer may have no choice but to terminate an employee who is not acting responsibly toward his job and toward management in light of the performance problems he's experiencing.

Enlightened leadership is all about looking for opportunities to combat problem performance with positive training. You'll find that the problems disappear and commitment goes way up. After all, when it comes to treating others with dignity and respect, people will respond in kind. All you have to do is raise their expectations of themselves.

3. Interim Performance Evaluation Necessary?

The interim performance evaluation is an interesting concept. When you're challenged in court for wrongful discharge, the arbitrator, judge, or plaintiff's attorney will look at the totality of events leading up to your former employee's termination. Disciplinary write-ups alone won't tell the whole story.

When a long-term employee suddenly spirals downward in performance, you may want to issue an interim performance evaluation to break the chain of previous positive evaluations. If there is inconsistency between an employee's annual performance evaluations and progressive disciplinary notices, the ambiguity may be interpreted against your company when you try to support your decision to terminate.

You normally won't have to perform an interim evaluation unless you are dealing with a more senior employee with a very positive history of performance evaluations whose performance has recently nosedived. However, a long, productive work history evidenced by a collection of positive annual reviews may indicate that the current problem stems from something you haven't identified.

After all, juries tend to side with employees, not employers, in judging wrongful discharge claims. Juries will reason that annual reviews cover years of time; progressive disciplinary notices, in contrast, may only represent one bad day in the office. Consequently, the historical annual reviews will be given more weight than your specific discipline. You'll have to justify any inconsistencies between performance reviews and disciplinary actions to demonstrate that you are dealing fairly and equitably with a longer-term employee.

For example, perhaps you've recently assumed responsibility for a new unit, and you find that a particular employee's performance is unacceptable and critically in need of improvement. In that case, what you may have is an underperforming employee whose scores on past annual evaluations were acceptable because the former manager was afraid to confront the employee concerning her behavior for fear of upsetting her. This is a textbook case for an interim performance appraisal.

You must be sure to account for the current behavior or performance problems during that evaluation. Tell the employee that this out-of-cycle review is necessary because you don't feel that her prior evaluations accurately reflect her overall job performance. Inform the employee as well that you intend to give her an overall rating of "not meeting expectations." You may, however, review her again in ninety days (or whatever you deem to be an appropriate period) in order to objectively evaluate her performance progress.

Is this a confrontational meeting? Yes. The employee will sense that you are thoroughly and carefully going about documenting her performance transgressions. Still, you may be doing the individual a big favor by identifying performance areas that require immediate improvement for her own job security and for the good of her career. It's tough but fair. And it holds the employee to exacting standards that keep you in control of the situation.

This process will ensure congruity with your disciplinary write-ups. The end result will be progressive disciplinary notices plus an unacceptable performance evaluation: just the kind of consistency you need to make a termination stick if necessary.

4. Employee Assistance Programs (EAPs)

EAPs are highly recommended because they are one of the most effective "hidden" benefits available today. According to the Department of Labor, up to 12 million people nation-wide—8 percent of all employees—use illicit drugs while working; an additional 13 million full-time workers, or 8 percent of the U.S. workforce, are heavy drinkers. The costs to you are obvious: Absenteeism, increased accidents resulting from compromised safety, theft, lower productivity, and lower morale contribute to losses estimated in excess of $30 billion annually.

How can an EAP help? EAPs provide confidential professional support for employees and their families to help them solve problems that affect their work performance and personal lives. Through an EAP, your employees can voluntarily get help before their personal problems become job performance problems. Your company will benefit directly by reducing your insurance claims, minimizing unauthorized absenteeism, and allowing your managers to focus on productivity and performance—not personal counseling.

In addition to alcohol and drug abuse, EAPs provide education on a variety of wellness issues and offer work-life programs that help organizations broaden the scope of their family-friendly policies. They also assist in the identification and resolution of productivity problems associated with marital, financial, legal, stress, and emotional difficulties that may affect employees' job performance.

Remember, you don't want your managers inquiring about their staff's personal problems. That could open up a whole can of worms because once managers acquire information that may protect an employee from discipline under the Americans with Disabilities Act or other law, your organization may be obligated to reasonably accommodate the employee's need. It's much easier to manage performance than to have to accommodate problems in employees' personal lives.

The premium cost of an EAP typically ranges from $1 to $2 per employee per month for a core program. (It can cost more, however, depending on the benefit level that you choose, and the addition of work-life and wellness programs typically adds $0.25 to $1.00 per employee per month on top of the EAP cost.) So if your company has 200 employees, the EAP could cost you between $200 and $400 a month. If you've got 20,000 employees, you'd have to negotiate a volume discount! But the low cost per capita is quite reasonable considering the value of the benefits available.

In addition, you'll have the option of making formal referrals (as opposed to voluntary referrals) when an employee's performance or behavior disrupts the workplace. For example, if you've got an employee who keeps blowing up at coworkers or verbally harassing subordinates, then you can firmly request that the employee attend an EAP assessment session that you set up.[2] You would inform the intake counselor of the nature of the problem, and the EAP practitioner would then specifically address those issues in the evaluation.

Neither form of referral—voluntary or formal—should be mandatory.[3] The employee always has the choice of attending. The only difference is that with a formal referral, you become involved in the process. You discuss your perception of the work performance problem on the front end and receive limited feedback about the employee's attendance, compliance, and prognosis via the employee's signed release. At the minimum level of service, employees typically receive three counseling sessions per problem for free; they may elect to use their own health care insurance for further treatment.

Furthermore, if an employee with flagging performance appears mentally depressed, under the influence of alcohol, or potentially hostile, you can formally refer the employee to the EAP and then not permit him to continue at his job without a "return to work" release from a licensed health care practitioner. Such leaves are typically paid through the period of initial evaluation. Beyond that, the employee must use accrued time off for any further treatment. These measures simultaneously balance the needs of the particular employee with the safety of others in the workplace.

For these reasons, our write-up paradigm will include a section for EAP referrals. Most of the sample write-ups will include voluntary referral language, but some will include a formal referral, using language such as the following:

> I strongly recommend that you contact the Prime Behavioral Health Group, our Employee Assistance Program (EAP) provider, within 24 hours for further assistance and guidance with this matter. To coordinate this formal referral, please call (800) 555-5555.

One last note on EAPs: You can strongly suggest that an employee contact the EAP, but you shouldn't mandate that he attend by threatening termination. After all, the employer-employee relationship blurs when you mandate that a worker see a mental health professional, for example, outside of the workplace. As a matter of fact, in certain states, that could even give rise to a claim of invasion of privacy. You'll probably be better off making a note in your log of the employee's refusal to cooperate with this outside provider and leaving it at that.

Although you can lead a horse to water, you can't necessarily make it drink. But you sure can document your affirmative efforts to aid an individual. If and when a judge evaluates the employee's wrongful discharge claim, she'll clearly see the merit in your efforts and the unreasonableness of an obstinate employee who refused to get help for himself.

---

2 This is a matter of contention among labor lawyers and employment experts. Some argue that formal referrals are appropriate only in cases where you suspect suicide or violence. They feel that the voluntary, no risk, and confidential nature of the EAP is compromised if you, the employer, make it an extension of your disciplinary authority. That's a point you should discuss with your labor attorney and EAP consultant before reaching a decision about making formal versus voluntary referrals.

3 However, some employers do require a referral; the employee must contact the EAP as a condition of employment. I don't recommend this, but you could discuss this option with your labor attorney and EAP provider.

5. Employee's Personal Improvement Plan Input and Suggestions

A key part of the overall performance improvement plan is the individual's personal input into the process. In the age of the knowledge worker, where the value of intellectual capital far outweighs the value of machinery, formulas, or any other assets, it becomes critical to have an educated workforce buy into your plans. That's what open book management and motivation theory are all about. And it's what enlightened leadership thrives on.

An appeal to your workers to join with you in fixing problems is the ultimate goal of the entire disciplinary process. By showing your commitment to making employees successful and proving to them that they're still part of the team, you provide them with recognition and open communication even when the relationship is strained. Little else need be said about your values and priorities in terms of respecting employees and treating them with dignity. Besides, it's just the right thing to do.

Don't be surprised, though, if not all employees accept your olive branch. Some people just can't get past the insult of being disciplined; others simply won't be committed enough to invest themselves in the process. Once again, however, should you be challenged by an arbitrator regarding your efforts to willfully rehabilitate a worker, you'll more readily pass the test. Simply put, if this section of the write-up is left blank, it reflects poorly on the employee. Like other sections of the write-up, this section shifts the responsibility for success or failure to the individual and away from your organization.

4 Consequences, Rebuttals, and Employee Acknowledgments

As an employer conducting an internal investigation, you're not bound by legal hurdles like proving that the employee is guilty "beyond a reasonable doubt" or "by a preponderance of the evidence." Instead, your burden lies in:

1. Conducting a good-faith investigation in a timely manner

2. Reaching a fair and reasonable conclusion

Therefore, in all that you do, you must pass a test of *predictability* and *consistency*. Predictability in discipline requires that you respond in the same fashion to all similar employee offenses. Consistency in discipline requires that all employees be treated in a similar manner. The best place to demonstrate your predictability and consistency is the Consequences section of the write-up because it must, by definition, be clear, concise, and unequivocal. Let's look at an example.

Consequences

Positive: I will remain available to help you and discuss areas where you require additional support. If you meet your performance goals, no further disciplinary action will be taken regarding this issue. *In addition, you will develop a greater sense of accomplishment in helping our hospital to meet its production goals and in providing direct support to our patient care areas.*

Negative: *The main purpose of this corrective action is to identify, correct, and prevent a future recurrence of a performance problem and to prepare you for satisfactory service in the future. You are now being placed on final written warning. Failure to demonstrate immediate and sustained improvement may result in further disciplinary action up to and including dismissal.* A copy of this document will be placed in your personnel file.

Scheduled Review Date: *Ninety days (August 1, 2017)*

If it's easier to engage in a dialogue about performance problems, then supervisors (even supervisors who typically avoid confrontation at all costs) will be more willing to address problems early on before they get out of control. That's why positive consequences always precede negative ones. They point the way to future solutions by rewarding good behavior.

Positive Consequences

> I will remain available to help you and discuss areas where you require additional support. If you meet the performance goals, no further disciplinary action will be taken regarding this issue.

This statement offers a positive motivation to change behavior or improve performance. Assuming that the employee is being disciplined for the first time, you can hope that she'll latch onto this one statement above all others.

The next sentence, *In addition, you will develop a greater sense of accomplishment in helping our hospital to meet its production goals and in providing direct support to our patient care areas*, is in italics because it serves as an optional, customizable statement to further encourage the employee to improve performance. Other such sample statements include:

- In addition, you will develop a sense of accomplishment in helping our company collect on outstanding receivables and meet its cash flow goals.

- In addition, you will successfully complete your six-month training period and gain more independence and autonomy on your job.

- By correcting your tardiness problem, you will help our department meet its production goals while minimizing last-minute overtime costs and staff rescheduling.

- In addition, you will enjoy more positive interpersonal relationships with your peers and gain more satisfaction at work.

- By communicating more openly with me when something bothers you or makes you feel singled out, you will be less inclined to deny your feelings or to lash out at others who are unaware of your concerns. You will also be less likely to jump to conclusions in the absence of facts. You will consequently establish better rapport with your coworkers and learn to address smaller issues before they become larger problems.

- In addition, by maintaining a work space that is free from clutter, you will gain a better sense of your priorities and manage your time more effectively.

- In addition, by confronting performance and conduct problems early on while they're still small challenges, you'll minimize the chance that they will become major impediments in your working relationship with your subordinates. You will likewise strengthen your perception as a fair and communicative leader.

Negative Consequences

It is critical that every disciplinary write-up include clear, specific, and unambiguous Consequences of an employee's failure to improve performance. Unfortunately, many managers either leave out this Consequences section altogether or paint vague pictures of what can happen if employees don't change their performance or behavior immediately.

Poor Examples of Negative Consequences

Following are examples of weak negative consequences that can leave an employee feeling unsure of your intentions:

- If you do not meet the performance objectives outlined in this disciplinary memo, you will be subject to serious discipline.

- In the future, please don't forget to lock the cash drawer at night before you leave the office.

- Tony, you must stop your habitual lateness and assume responsibility for your actions from this point on. Otherwise, I will be forced to take further action against you.

- The employee is to immediately increase her number of daily outbound collection calls. Otherwise, she will continue to fail to meet minimum performance benchmarks.

The obvious weakness in these examples comes from their ambiguous consequences. Appeals to assume responsibility for one's actions, generic terms such as "serious discipline," and hollow threats of "further action" will be interpreted against you if you are challenged in court to define what you meant.

Properly Written Negative Consequences

Some employers use very specific time windows when doling out consequences, while others use a generic catchall phrase for almost all situations. There's no right or wrong answer in these instances: It's simply a matter of your company's philosophy, culture, union status, and the employment laws of your state. Generally speaking, I recommend the following phrase in the Negative Consequences section of the disciplinary warning template:

> Failure to demonstrate immediate and sustained improvement may result in further disciplinary action, up to and including dismissal.

The reasons for this are simple:

- It buys you the most discretion possible.

- "Further disciplinary action up to and including dismissal" certainly places the employee on notice that his job may be in serious jeopardy of being lost, which fulfills your due process obligations.

- "Immediate and sustained improvement" is a simple enough phrase, indicating that the turnaround can't just be for thirty or sixty days. In short, you retain the discretion to determine what's considered "immediate" and "sustained" and what level of discipline should follow if there is a repeat occurrence of the violation or infraction.

- Most important, judges and arbitrators recognize this common language, and the majority of employment defense lawyers (i.e., those who represent companies like yours and mine) recommend this catchall phrase in most disciplinary situations, especially those involving at-will workers.

Active Time Windows May Also Be Used to Clearly Describe Negative Consequences

In addition to (or instead of) the catchall phrase, active time windows (requiring, for example, thirty, sixty, and ninety-day "stay clean" periods) may be used in the Negative Consequences section of your write-up template. Again, this may be a matter of style, culture, or your senior management team's philosophy about what progressive discipline is meant to do and how it is to be used.

Keeping that in mind, there are certain times and circumstances where active time windows may be preferable:

- In union environments where collective bargaining agreements tend to spell out specific provisions and time frames that govern its members' work schedules, seniority rights, and grievance procedures, specific disciplinary time windows may be the norm.

- In high-risk situations where you may be terminating someone in multiple protected classes or protected activities, time-specific windows may be a more suitable alternative. In such cases, the clearer the notice is in terms of what the problem is, how the individual must correct it, and by when, the better. Your written message might read: "The failure to sell 14 widget systems by March 15, 2017 will result in your termination at that time."

Is there a caveat to be aware of when employing active time windows? Sure: Don't allow your documentation to appear to serve as a guaranteed employment period for the duration of the disciplinary time window. In other words, use the phrase "if at any time within" in the documentation itself. For example, your language might read: If at any time within the next sixty days you fail to . . ., further disciplinary action up to and including dismissal may result." This will make it clear to employees that they're not guaranteed sixty days of work before they can be terminated.

Let's look more specifically at disciplinary time windows. The length of the active time window depends on the nature of the offense and on how long it takes an employee to complete a full cycle of work or to show concrete results:

- *Thirty days.* To closely monitor a poor performer's work, use a short window such as thirty days. If the individual is having difficulty performing the essential functions of the job, then that should be enough time to observe results.

  Example of a well-written verbal warning:

  > I know from your past performance that you are capable of executing all aspects of the clerical specialist position. However, your failure to process incoming records over the past three weeks is unacceptable. If at any time in the next thirty days you fail to meet the performance standards outlined in the disciplinary memo, further discipline up to and including dismissal may occur.

- *Sixty days.* Salespeople in many professions who aren't cutting the mustard typically get sixty-day windows. It takes about that long to make a sale, close the deal, and wait for the receivables to be paid.[1]

  Example of a well-written written warning:

  > You are currently not meeting our company's sales production standards. If you fail to meet established production benchmarks at any time within the next sixty days, you may be placed on a sixty-day final written warning. If you fail to meet sales production standards in that sixty-day final written warning period, you may be dismissed.

- *Ninety days.* To keep employees "clean" for the longest period of time (for example, with tardiness and absenteeism problems), use a ninety-day window. Remember, you're not married to the employee for a guaranteed ninety days; if anything goes wrong within those ninety days, you can automatically move to the next step of discipline. It's just easier for employees to remain tardiness-free for thirty days than it is for ninety days, so why not hold them to a higher standard?

  Example of a well-written final written warning:

  > You are now being placed on a final ninety-day warning. If at any time

---

1 This is true of mortgage bankers and other account executives in the financial services arena. Of course, other types of sales may be measured in longer cycles than sixty days. This will have to be dictated by your company's line of business and performance expectations.

within this ninety-day period you incur two more incidents[2] of unscheduled absence, you may be immediately dismissed.

- *Six months.* It's also not uncommon for middle and senior managers to be placed on probationary notice for six months because that tends to be a reasonable amount of time to measure performance that requires discretion and judgment.

Example of a well-written final written warning:

> The current level of sales in your Western U.S. region is not acceptable. The next six months will consequently serve as a probationary period for you. If you do not meet the production goals and specific benchmark measurements outlined in this memo at any time within that period, you may be dismissed.

Such windows usually cannot be much longer than 180 days because courts or arbitrators may rule that the "stay clean" period was onerous. For example, a warning that "one more unexcused absence in the next year will result in immediate dismissal" may allow you to terminate an employee for cause. However, it's likely that an arbitrator would rule that your active window was unreasonable because it was simply too long. And voilà—your decision to terminate may be reversed, or you may risk exposing your company to unwanted litigation.

Consequences Without Time Limits

There is an important exception, however. If an employee is disciplined for egregious actions such as sexually or verbally harassing a coworker, sleeping on the job, attempting to undermine a supervisor's authority, or demonstrating gross negligence in job performance, then your Consequences section may simply read:

> We are not terminating you at this time. We are, instead, giving you another chance. However, if you *ever again* engage in conduct with a supervisor, coworker, or vendor that could be considered hostile or offensive, you will be immediately discharged.

No time frame is necessary because the employee is given fair warning that any further demonstrations of egregious misconduct will be met with immediate dismissal.

Following are additional samples of well-written negative consequences that you'll see outlined in this book:

- Verbal warning:

> If at any time within the next thirty days you fail to meet departmental performance expectations or any other standards of performance and conduct, disciplinary action up to and including termination may occur.

---

2 An incident is not necessarily one day; rather, it is typically defined as a continuous period of time related to one particular illness or injury.

- Written warning:

> You have violated the terms of your verbal warning issued last month. You are consequently being given this formal written disciplinary warning. If at any time within the next ninety days you fail to meet production standards, you may be placed on a ninety-day final written warning. Failure to meet established production guidelines at any time during that ninety-day final written warning period may result in your dismissal.

- Final written warning:

> You are now being placed on a sixty-day final written warning. If your incoming call volume, scheduled client appointments, and/or recorded loans do not meet company production standards or if you fail to demonstrate specific knowledge of our bank's loan programs when speaking with borrowers at any time within this period, you may be discharged.

- Combination final written warning and written warning for multiple transgressions:

> Because of your flagrant misuse of company property, if you make one more outbound, nonemergency personal phone call at any time within the next ninety days, you may be immediately dismissed.

> In addition, if at any time within the next ninety days you fail to meet any established departmental productivity standards, you may be placed in final written warning status. If you then fail to meet production quotas or any other performance and conduct standards while in that ninety-day final written warning period, you may be dismissed.

Protect yourself from being locked into any one particular transgression by employing the generic phrase "or any other performance and conduct standards." That's the catchall equivalent of "other duties as assigned" in a job description. You're always better off buying yourself the most flexibility and discretion possible.

Extending a New Hire's Probationary Period

As a general rule, workers in their probationary (better referred to as *introductory*) periods should generally be given at least one documented warning before they are discharged. (However, a collective bargaining agreement may override this caution if it clearly states that a probationary employee is not entitled to progressive discipline.) New employees who are discharged while still on probation have the right to seek legal counsel for wrongful termination. The question is whether a plaintiff's attorney will see enough merit in the case to bring a cause of action against the plaintiff's former company. Written proof that the plaintiff was warned may be enough to persuade an attorney to look elsewhere for more favorable cases.

A new employee on the job for ten days has a long way to go before the end of a ninety-day probationary threshold. In that case, if the individual appears to be unable or unwilling to meet the minimum performance expectations of the job, then the Negative Consequences section of your written disciplinary memo should state:

> If at any time *throughout the remainder of your introductory period* you fail to
> . . . or to meet any other standards of performance and conduct, you may be
> discharged.

However, what if the employee is eighty days into a ninety-day probationary period? In that case, there are only ten days until her introductory period is over, and that probably won't be enough time for you to evaluate her performance objectively. Therefore, it's best to extend the introductory period as follows:

> Your initial introductory period will be extended from ninety to one hundred
> and twenty days (through November 25). If at any time within this introductory
> period, you address a manager, coworker, or vendor in an argumentative or
> disrespectful manner, you may be immediately dismissed.

As a rule of thumb, you can extend initial probationary time frames by roughly one-half to one-third of the original period. For example:

- Thirty-day probationary periods can be extended by two weeks.

- Sixty-day probationary periods can be extended by an additional thirty days.

- Ninety-day probationary periods can be extended by thirty days.

- One hundred eighty–day probationary periods can be extended by sixty days, although this is less common since the six-month window is already so long.

Buy yourself that extra time whenever you feel unsure about a new hire's long-term prospects with your company.[3]

Scheduled Review Dates

Performance-related issues should always receive a timely follow-up. It's as easy as jotting down a date on your calendar. Besides, when an employee knows that he'll be held account-able on that day of reckoning, then preparing to meet your expectations becomes all the more important. This is a chance to add positive feedback to a difficult situation, and the opportunity shouldn't be overlooked.

---

3 Many organizations routinely provide performance evaluations at the conclusion of new hires' probationary periods to ensure that performance and conduct are acceptable before the worker attains "regular" employment status.

Performance-related transgressions, including those involving sales production, customer service follow-through, and interactions with coworkers, necessarily deserve follow-up. By observing and rewarding performance achievements, you'll provide poorer performers with the structure, feedback, and direction they need in order to perform at a higher level.

On the other hand, it isn't typically necessary to meet thirty, sixty, or ninety days out regarding a conduct problem or an absenteeism issue. Why not? Because the absence of repeated behaviors is proof enough that the warning has been heeded. For example, if the employee was disciplined for insubordination, violation of company policies regarding sexual harassment, or improper documentation of company records, then he won't need to have a reminder meeting to verify that he's not harassing anyone anymore. Simply stated, you shouldn't have to readdress unacceptable conduct issues because it can appear to add salt to the wound.

One more caveat about performance follow-ups. Documenting that you are scheduling a meeting with the employee three months in advance certainly puts an added burden on you to keep the meeting. If you travel a lot or have difficulty keeping regularly scheduled meetings, skip this step. It will look a lot worse if you fail to keep your promise because it's demoralizing for the employee, who will reason that you're quick to find fault but slow to give warranted praise. It can also be looked down upon by an arbitrator, who may reason that you're inconsistent in your follow-through. After all, our goal in this process is to shift responsibility to the employee—not to find ways of shifting the responsibility back to management!

The Employee Rebuttal

We mentioned earlier that allowing the employee to defend herself is often a key concept that is seriously lacking in workplace due process. The *day in court* principle says that people need to feel that they are being objectively heard, not unilaterally prejudged. After all, an employee may not like being disciplined, but if she feels it's fair, she'll be able to come to terms with it over time. If she feels that the whole thing was a predetermined setup, then feelings of anger, victimization, and revenge will likely remain.

Before discipline is meted out, it makes most sense to meet with the employee to discuss your findings and to learn of any mitigating circumstances. Of course, if a clear company policy like "five tardies equals a verbal correction" is breached, and you have a "no fault" attendance control system, then meeting with the employee in advance is not required. It still is recommended, though, since meeting in person before dispensing discipline gives you and your staff member a chance to talk about improving performance. When the discipline comes, it won't be a shock because you will already have discussed it.

Meeting in advance to discuss your findings regarding an employee's transgression may not lead to agreement, however. Once you've determined that discipline is appropriate, explain to your subordinate the reasons for your findings. Inform the employee as well that there is a formal response mechanism on the write-up that he can use to provide his side of the story.

This rebuttal section of the write-up allows the employee the opportunity to set the record straight and provide a different perspective on the supervisor's allegations. Although it doesn't change your findings, it certainly adds critical balance. And that, above all else, makes things fairer by establishing a more even playing field. Disciplinary documents that don't allow room for the employee to rebut invite resentment and disenchantment. Encourage feedback at all stages of the communications process—formal or otherwise.

Note that there is a signature line in the Rebuttal section of the write-up template. Some employees may refuse to sign a disciplinary warning in the Acknowledgment section, fearing that by signing, they are agreeing with the supervisor's allegations. When that is the case, encourage the employee to write a rebuttal and sign her name to the rebuttal. Failure to sign in the Acknowledgment section in no way weakens your case; signing in the Rebuttal section serves the same purpose in terms of proving the employee's receipt of the document.

The Employee Acknowledgment

The Employee Acknowledgment section is critical but unfortunately missing from most disciplinary documents. Asserting your company's at-will employment status, as discussed in Chapter 1, will go a long way toward protecting your company from third-party legal challenges.

Bear in mind, however, that this clause should be struck from the template (1) if your state does recognize an employment-at-will relationship or (2) when disciplining union employees. Unionized workers are governed by collective bargaining agreements and are not employed at will because they cannot be discharged "for any reason or no reason at all."

The Employee Acknowledgment

I understand that XYZ Company is an at-will employer, meaning that my employment has no specified term and that the employment relationship may be terminated any time at the will of either party on notice to the other. I also realize that XYZ is opting to provide me with corrective action measures and can terminate such corrective measures at any time, solely at its own discretion, and that the use of progressive discipline will not change my at-will employment status.

I have received a copy of this notification. It has been discussed with me, and I have been advised to take time to consider it before I sign it. I have freely chosen to agree to it, and I accept full responsibility for my actions. By signing this, I commit to following the company's standards of performance and conduct.

| _____ | _____ | _____ | _____ |
| Employee Signature | Date | Supervisor's Signature | Date |

Please note that in the 101 write-ups in this book, I have eliminated the Employee Acknowledgment in order to save space, because the same wording is used in almost every case. When the language in the Employee Acknowledgment section changes (which occurs more frequently in final written warnings), a special note has been added to the end of the sample in the book. However, the online link contains all 101 full write-up samples, including this Employee Acknowledgment section, so please refer to the online version for the full documentation in each scenario.

Personal Commitment Agreement

The personal commitment agreement can take on various forms. It places the burden for improvement squarely on the employee's shoulders, and that's why it's saved for last. Most disciplinary actions simply end with the statement: "I have received a copy of this notification." The employee is then to sign the document without committing herself one way or the other. Her signature confirms nothing more than the fact that she received a copy of the disciplinary notice.

Now it's time to reinvent that standard line in light of corporate America's changing needs. Even at the earliest stages of discipline, it's critical to confirm both orally and in writing that the employee assumes responsibility for success or failure on the job. The most effective way to end a coaching session or disciplinary meeting is to gain an oral commitment from the employee like this: "Janet, I'd like a commitment from you that we won't have to discuss this issue again and that you'll assume responsibility for the outcome of all this. Will you make that commitment to me?"

Similarly, if you want to make the personal assumption of responsibility stronger on the written document, you can add the statement:

> In addition, I accept full responsibility for my actions and commit to following all company standards of performance and conduct.

> or

> I understand that this is my last chance. If I fail to achieve the goals agreed to in this document, I will resign or be terminated for cause.[4]

> or

> I understand that my position is now in serious jeopardy of being lost and that I must immediately make substantial improvements in my performance in order to remain employed.

This sends the undeniable message that you are holding the employee accountable for his own success and that you are serious about your intentions. It also may clearly indicate that the employee's position is in jeopardy.

---

4 This particular phraseology is recommended by Lee Paterson, senior partner and labor law expert at the Los Angeles office of Sonnenschein, Nath, and Rosenthal.

Although it may sound harsh, this additional language is unequivocal and incontestable in its intent. At the final stages of discipline, this clarity will work only in your favor.[5] Use this language liberally in final written warnings to prove your intentions of imparting to the employee how serious the problem has become.

Signature Requirements

When the meeting is concluding and the various issues outlined in this write-up have been discussed with the employee, he may do one of four things: (1) Sign the document in the Employee Acknowledgment section, (2) sign it in the Employee Rebuttal section along with his version of the events, (3) refuse to sign anything, or (4) ask for time to consider and reread it before signing it. All options are acceptable.

In the ideal scenario, the individual signs the Employee Acknowledgment. That in effect shows agreement with your findings and the course of action you've outlined. If, on the other hand, the employee wishes to write a rebuttal and sign it in the Employee Rebuttal section, that's absolutely acceptable as well. The purpose of progressive discipline is to communicate problem issues. Problem issues, by nature, have two sides, and there is neither a guarantee nor a necessity that the two sides see eye to eye. What is critical is the documentation of the event—not necessarily the agreement.

If the employee refuses to sign the document at all at the time of the meeting, encourage him to take the document home, reread it, and formulate a rebuttal. The obvious benefit to the employee is that he has a chance to provide his side of the story on paper, and this is obviously better than remaining totally silent. If the employee still refuses to sign the document within the next few days, you should indicate that in the signature area of the write-up by writing, "Employee refused to sign. Notified the employee that these are our findings of what occurred and that she will be expected to meet the standards of performance and conduct outlined."

Witness Acknowledgment

In addition, call a witness (preferably another supervisor or member of your company's management team) into the room and state that the employee has refused to sign the write-up or to rebut it. The witness should sign the document with a clear understanding that she is simply attesting to the fact that she is aware that the employee was given the write-up and has elected not to sign it. Witnesses need not be apprised of all the circumstances surrounding the disciplinary action; they must, however, be in the room with the employee present, and

---

5 Be advised, however, that this language will not eliminate an employee's right to challenge your decision if you terminate. For example, the employee will still have a right to prove in court that she was a victim of wrongful discharge or other unlawful conduct.

they must receive verbal instructions to sign the document in the employee's place. Witness acknowledgment will then be complete, and the employee will not be able to claim later that she never received the document.

The matter can be concluded by providing the employee with a copy of the disciplinary memo, posting the original to the personnel file, and then distributing any other copies as appropriate.

5 Commonly Asked Questions and Practical Answers to Tricky Employee Relations

Following are twenty responses to the most common questions asked by managers when implementing this system of progressive discipline. These responses will help you to better understand important issues that surface in typical progressive disciplinary or discharge meetings.

1. Now that we've dissected the various elements of our write-up model, how do I best deliver my message to the employee when conducting a face-to-face meeting?

There are a few simple rules to follow.

First, when meeting with your employee, explain the nature of the problem as you see it, and then ask the employee for feedback. In a spirit of full transparency, explain up front that disciplinary action may be involved, depending on the feedback you receive. Unless you give workers a verbal recounting of your perception of the events, you won't know if you've missed any extenuating circumstances.

More important, by bringing someone into your office who's already been "judged," so to speak, you make that person feel that she has already been tried and found guilty. That will cut off open communication right from the start of the dialogue, so talk before you address anything on paper, whenever possible.

Second, you may already have prepared a written performance correction before the meeting begins, or you may opt to wait until after the meeting is concluded to prepare the document. That's your choice. In the first case, keep the paperwork concealed until your suspicions are confirmed. Once you are confident that your write-up is an accurate reflection of your version of the events, pull it out to show the employee.

On the other hand, if you wait until after your meeting to compose the write-up, invite the employee back into your office to review what you've written. Don't make a blind delivery where you simply place it on the employee's desk or email it. That will appear cold and heartless, and no one should have such a serious document handled so inconsiderately.

Third, and most significant, read your disciplinary write-up out loud to the employee before handing it to her. When managers and supervisors are first introduced to this system of progressive disciplinary write-ups, their first response is always, "Wow, this is really long!" And that's exactly what we want it to be because the length, in and of itself, is a deterrent factor. A long, detailed document lets the employee know in no uncertain terms that you're very serious about the whole matter. (In contrast, a half-page memo with little content or discussion of consequences or action plans shows that you've made very little investment in the whole process.)

Therefore, you don't want to shock the individual by handing over a two-page single-spaced write-up and forcing her to evaluate its various elements on the spot. It makes a lot more sense for you to read the document out loud first, emphasize the important elements in each section, gain agreement orally, and then, after you find out that the person has no further questions, turn the document over to her.

In essence, that two- or three-page write-up will then confirm your serious intentions as you've discussed them. You'll have treated the person with dignity and respect by not embarrassing her with a litany of documented problems, and you'll find that the entire communication will typically yield much more positive results. Besides, you'll have discussed the positive consequences of improving performance, your commitment to support the individual, and possibly outside training and an EAP referral. Few employees will walk out of such a meeting feeling that they have not been treated fairly or considerately.

2. Is there a way to communicate my dissatisfaction with an employee's performance or conduct without resorting to formal discipline?

Of course! Formal discipline is only one method of proactively rehabilitating workers by focusing their efforts on changed behaviors or heightened performance. It's often the case that an informal "counseling session"—typically the first natural step in the communication process—will work wonders and fix the problem right from the start.

On the other hand, if the initial verbal counseling session doesn't bring about the desired results, a letter of clarification may be just what the doctor ordered. Let's say, for example, that several weeks after verbally notifying a hospital orderly, who's responsible for pulling patients' charts and transporting patients in wheelchairs, you're not satisfied with the level of commitment and patient focus that she appears to be exercising. You notice the same apathetic behaviors setting in again: Janet's not returning medical files, she's not using the department's magnetic scoreboard to show when she's out of the office, and then a patient complains about Janet sitting her in a wheelchair wet from the rain.

Is it time for a formal written warning, or are you afraid that might be too harsh since the infractions are fairly minor? Well, fear not. You no longer have only the two modes available of verbal counseling or formal progressive discipline. A letter of clarification might be just the right tool to impress upon Janet the seriousness of her infractions. Letters of clarification are presented to the employee in written format and require the employee's signature. Logically, when things are written down, they are perceived to be more serious.

In addition, when employees sign their names to documents related to their performance or conduct, they develop a healthy sense of paranoia that those documents may be used later down the line to establish some pattern of past history in their actions. That's what progressive discipline is all about:

- Showing employees what is wrong with their performance or conduct

- Telling them what they need to do to fix the problem at hand

- Giving them a reasonable amount of time to fix the problem

- Clearly documenting the consequences of failing to meet your expectations

The letter of clarification will accomplish the first three (positive) goals of progressive discipline without having the sting of the fourth element of consequences—language along the lines of "further disciplinary action, up to and including termination."

In fact, letters of clarification should specifically state that they are not disciplinary documents. As such, they don't carry the heavy stigma of "being written up." Here's what Janet's letter of confirmation looks like:

> Janet, over the past three weeks, I've shared with you my concerns regarding your performance and conduct. Specifically, I've told you that you are not handling patients' files correctly because items are being misfiled and files are being left in the offices without being returned to the central filing area. In addition, a patient complained that you delivered a wheelchair that was still wet from the rain to the patient pick-up area. Finally, you have failed on several occasions to use the magnetic location board to show when you were on break or lunch. As a result, the schedulers were not able to locate you in a timely fashion.
>
> This isn't a disciplinary document, Janet. It will not be placed in your formal personnel file and will not be shared with other members of management at this time. However, *I have put my concerns in writing to impress upon you the seriousness of these multiple smaller errors.* My greatest concern lies in the fact you appear less focused on your work now than at any time in the past five years. You also appear to be apathetic about the outcome of your assignments, and several of your coworkers have asked me if you were feeling okay because they too noticed a change in your work.
>
> I want you to know that I'm here to help you in any way I can. On the other hand, I am holding you fully accountable for meeting all hospital expectations regarding performance and conduct. I recognize that you may have certain ideas to improve your performance. Therefore, I encourage you to provide your own personal improvement plan suggestions.
>
> Please sign this document to evidence not only that you received it, but also that you agree to accept full responsibility for fixing these problems and changing the perception problems that exist. I know you can do it, and I'm here to support you. Thank you.
>
> X _____   _____
> Employee Signature   Date

Could this document later be used to justify formal disciplinary action if the employee doesn't clean up her act? Absolutely! Indeed, a written warning will make more sense after this informal written clarification letter is given to the employee. Consequently, this letter could help strengthen a future case since you would have provided the employee with ample notification—both informally and formally—that her performance was substandard. As such, it would be much harder for a plaintiff attorney to successfully argue that you've denied the employee workplace due process.

So when's the best time to use such informal letters? Either when individual infractions are repetitive and fairly minor in nature (like Janet's case above) or when group infractions need to be remedied quickly. In another example, if you learn that several of your line managers are sharing employment-related references regarding past workers, then a verbal announcement to the staff may not be enough to show how serious you are about fixing the problem. Still, writing everyone up wouldn't make sense since following the "no references" policy hasn't been formally enforced in the past. Your best bet? Try a letter of clarification like this:

TO ALL ENGINEERING STAFF:

Company policy strictly prohibits providing prospective employers with reference information on past workers. All requests for references must be forwarded to Human Resources. Human Resources will then provide the former workers' dates of employment and last title held.

Subjective references that reveal information about past workers' performance, character, or work habits—especially if negative—could expose our organization to lost wages litigation and claims of defamation. Since any managers who provide such references could be named individually in a lawsuit arising from a claim of defamation, it is critical that you all conform to this existing policy. Thank you.

I agree not to release any reference checking information to any outside employers, employment agencies, or search firms, and I will forward all future calls to Human Resources.

X _____   _____
Employee Signature   Date

When issuing such group confirmation letters, always require that employees individually sign separate documents. Advise them that you will keep their signed letters in your department file for future reference. That should cement in their minds the commitment you've made and they've now made to following company procedures and placing a particular rule "back on the front burner." If further violations occur, however, that signed document will also establish clear grounds for further disciplinary measures.

Letters of clarification, viewed by many employees as precursors to formal discipline, have the same prophylactic effect as formal discipline without the negative trappings. Added to your performance management toolbox, this alternative could strengthen communications by clarifying your expectations and, more importantly, involving employees in their own rehabilitation by treating them with dignity and respect.

3. If an employee goes out on leave of absence after receiving a progressive disciplinary document, will the active windows of discipline be frozen for the period of time that the employee remains out?

Yes. The "stop the clock rule" says that an employee who goes out on extended leave after receiving discipline will have his active window suspended until he returns. In other words, if the employee is placed on a thirty-day warning but then goes out sick for thirty days, he will return to work with the original thirty-day warning still in place. The clock, in essence, stops ticking until the employee returns.

4. How do I determine what level of discipline is appropriate for a given offense?

Remember that while you are responsible for treating like cases alike, this doesn't mean that you will necessarily treat everyone the same way. For example, an employee caught sleeping at his desk may receive a verbal warning if he's a long-term worker with an excellent track record. A new hire in his probationary period might be given a written or even a final written warning for that same offense.

In addition, an accountant sleeping at his desk may be disciplined via a written warning. A nurse on the night shift who is responsible for ensuring patient care and safety may be placed on final written warning for the same offense. And an anesthesiologist sleeping in the operating room may be summarily discharged. Sleeping is not the only issue—the circumstances surrounding the act of sleeping also play a crucial role when determining how to ensure that the behavior isn't repeated.

Therefore, the four criteria that will help you determine the most appropriate level of discipline to employ in any particular instance will be:

- The severity of the offense

- The employee's past performance record

- The employee's length of service with your organization

- Your past practice in dealing with similar infractions

5. Should I remove disciplinary documents from employees' files after a certain amount of time free of any infractions?

This is a subject of debate among employers and labor experts and must be decided on a case-by-case basis. It is optional to include a statement in the Positive Consequences section of the write-up template that states:

> This write-up will be removed from your personnel file one year after the active period expires.

Dick Grote, in his book *Discipline Without Punishment* (AMACOM, 2013), reasons that having the opportunity to remove an unfortunate incident, mistake, or judgment call from an otherwise clean record is reason enough for an employee not to repeat a problem behavior. It's also just the type of carrot, argues Grote, that today's worker strives for. "No one's perfect," reasons the employee, "so just give me the chance to erase that unfortunate exception to my work record, and I'll be sure it doesn't happen again."

This is certainly a noble sentiment, but many labor attorneys quickly point out the practical dangers of such "corporate amnesia." Once a disciplinary document has been removed from a worker's personnel file and placed in some other holding area, your own policy may preclude you from resurrecting the expunged document if the problem surfaces again in the future. In addition, unless you're still around a few years down the line and you happen to remember that an employee was previously disciplined for a given infraction, the new transgression will be treated like a first-time offense.

For example, if an employee in your department store was engaged in the inappropriate discounting of merchandise at the point of sale two years ago, and you are now disciplining her for that very same offense, you will have lost an important historical link to the current problem if you forget about—or are not allowed to consider—the prior violation. It's certainly a lot easier to forget when the historical document is missing from the worker's personnel file. It's also very frustrating to miss an opportunity to demonstrate an ongoing behavior pattern because of your own policy of wiping the slate clean.

Of course, personnel records management goes beyond the scope of this book. However, you should discuss with your labor attorney the positive and negative ramifications of employing this methodology in your disciplinary write-ups. Your decision to adopt such a measure should be based on your company's disciplinary history, mission statement, and corporate culture, and on the state laws that govern your organization.[1]

One special caveat about the removal of disciplinary documents from a personnel file: Although removing disciplinary warning notices one or two years after the incident usually has a motivational effect on employees, this isn't ever appropriate in cases involving sexual harassment, workplace violence, or discrimination. These types of workplace issues have a tendency to repeat themselves over time, especially if they are part of an individual's intrinsic beliefs or way of doing business.

Therefore, in order to wipe out institutional discrimination and to protect the safety of all workers, this one-year removal clause should be discarded when dealing with sexual harassment, violence, and discrimination. The law has a long memory, and your deliberate

---

1 Realize that if you add this incentive to your write-up template, you'll be providing your employees with rights that have historically been offered only to union employees through the collective bargaining process. Namely, many union contracts provide provisions like this:

> Any written discipline report for behavior that is subject to progressive discipline shall be transferred from the employee's file to a confidential file in the department of human resources after a period of twenty-four months free from any documentation of progressive discipline. Such reports shall not be part of the record for use in future progressive disciplinary actions.

The question you'll need to ask yourself is: Will the morale upside of removing records of disciplinary actions from the personnel file after a certain period of time outweigh the potential legal costs?

erasure of historical records that codify prejudice and intolerance can be seen as irresponsible or incriminating.

6. If an employee writes a rebuttal to a progressive disciplinary document, should I, as supervisor, rebut the employee's rebuttal?

Typically not unless there is new information that has surfaced since the original disciplinary notice was constructed. The employee may have the last word in the write-up, since the disciplinary notice can have serious negative effects on her future with the company. What you don't want is a continuous "grudge match" in which both parties continue to challenge the other's allegations. Simply stated, supervisors are responsible for stopping any merry-go-rounds of rebuttals that might ensue. Therefore, generally speaking, allow the employee to have the last word.

7. What happens when an employee survives an initial probationary period (for example, after a written warning for performance), only to fail after the active period expires? How many times must I grant progressive discipline for the same or a similar offense when the employee stays clean only long enough to squeak by the probationary time window?

You have the right to add a mechanism to your write-up that stops this proverbial merry-go-round. The only caveat here is that you must let the employee know very clearly that this is your intended plan of action.

Here's how one company handled it: An employee was given an oral correction in September for excessive absenteeism and failure to notify her supervisor directly that she was going to be out. (This employee simply continued to leave messages on the department's answering machine or to instruct her coworkers to tell the supervisor that she was going to be out.) The oral correction was followed by written corrections in November and December. In April, when the employee reported that she was sick via the departmental answering machine, here was the human resource manager's direct response in the Negative Consequences section of the write-up:

> Mary, you must understand that failure to follow proper procedures in reporting your absences will result in disciplinary *action* up to and including dismissal. In addition, you are now being placed on ninety-day probation *again* for excessive absenteeism. If you incur an unauthorized absence again at any time during the next ninety days, you will be dismissed.
>
> In addition, if you successfully complete this probation and your absenteeism becomes excessive again within six months after this probation period ends, you will not be placed on probation again. Instead, you will be subject to immediate dismissal, since this is your second probationary period in the last six months.

In this case, the employer is totally within her rights to end the cycle. Still, the employer has an obligation to pinpoint the exact consequences of a repeated violation so that the employee can't later claim that she was unaware of the seriousness of the problem.

Remember, one of the critical elements of employee due process is that the worker has a clear understanding of the consequences of his actions. If your termination blindsides the employee because you arbitrarily determined that her repeated problems were excessive, you may end up convincing an arbitrator that you denied due process. As a result, you could easily find yourself on the losing end of a wrongful termination charge.

8. How does the Family and Medical Leave Act (FMLA) limit my right to discipline employees with attendance problems?

The FMLA substantially limits your right to discipline employees with attendance problems. The FMLA was enacted in 1993 by Congress in an attempt to protect workers faced with certain life circumstances from losing their jobs. As an employer, you are governed by the FMLA if you have more than fifty full-time, part-time, and temporary employees.

The FMLA states that if an employee (a) develops a chronic or serious health condition, (b) needs time away from work to care for an ailing spouse, parent, or child, or (c) requires time off to care for a newborn or newly adopted child, then the employee's job should be protected. You, the employer, have the right to obtain medical certification from an authorized health care provider to prove that the employee has a legitimate illness, for example, or is required to take time off to care for an ailing parent. However, once the claim is legitimized by the appropriate medical certification, you cannot take adverse disciplinary action against the person.

FMLA allows employees twelve weeks per year off without pay to care for themselves or their loved ones. To qualify, employees need to have worked for your organization for at least one year and have worked a minimum of 1,250 hours (about twenty-four weeks) preceding the leave. Time can be taken off consecutively ("block" FMLA leave) or incrementally ("intermittent" FMLA leave), say, for doctors' appointments.[2]

A typical intermittent leave scenario looks like this: A doctor certifies that one of your plant engineers is subject to migraine headaches and that they may occur unexpectedly once a month and usually last a day. If the plant engineer calls in and announces that she's home because of a migraine, then this absence is protected by the FMLA and may not be subject to discipline.

FMLA designation and authorization go well beyond the scope of this book. Simply remember to check and see if the worker's time off qualifies as FMLA by contacting your company's human resources department before documenting discipline for unscheduled absence. The FMLA Abuse bonus samples in Part VI of the book may be especially helpful in terms of providing guidance.

---

2 Generally, FMLA leave is unpaid. However, under certain circumstances, employees may be required or permitted by the employer's policy to use paid time off during FMLA leave. Consult a labor specialist for more information regarding requiring employees to use their vacation, holiday, or sick leave accruals to care for their own chronic health conditions or to care for sick family members.

9. Is it acceptable to incorporate progressive disciplinary language into an employee's annual performance evaluation?

Sure. Rather than handing an employee a performance evaluation plus a separate written warning, it's better to incorporate the information into one combined document. There's no rule that states that discipline must occur on a Performance Correction Notice letterhead. Besides, having all the information in one place allows you to connect the specific discipline to the worker's overall performance.

To do this, simply add an addendum to the end of the performance appraisal. Be sure to include the key elements of our write-up paradigm in your narrative text. Figure 5–1 shows how it looks.

Note, however, that it isn't acceptable to document discipline on an annual evaluation if the incident in question is old. In other words, you can't state, "Because of your inability to provide acceptable customer service to John Doe six months ago, this performance evaluation also serves as a disciplinary write-up." That simply wouldn't be fair. Just as you can't discipline an employee for something that's old and long forgotten using a Performance Correction Notice, you shouldn't include disciplinary measures for stale issues in an annual performance appraisal.

10. When I've got multiple disciplinary issues to document, is it better to give the employee separate write-ups or to include the various transgressions in one written communication?

It's always best to include as much information in one written communication as possible. Otherwise, it will appear that you're creating a barrage of paperwork to excessively punish the employee.

The example above, like others throughout this book, demonstrates how multiple infractions can be incorporated into one disciplinary write-up. As long as you clearly outline the issues in the Incident Description portion of the template, putting multiple infractions together in one document is perfectly acceptable. At that point, you will have differing Disciplinary Levels, Subjects, and Consequences for each individual transgression. As long as the employee clearly understands how each consequence relates to each separate infraction, you will have accorded the employee due process.

11. Does an employee have the right to appeal my disciplinary action?

Yes, but how this is handled depends on whether you're governed by a collective bargaining agreement or not. If you're unionized, you must follow the grievance procedure outlined in your collective bargaining agreement. This process typically begins with a "step one" grievance between the employee and the supervisor with a union steward present. If the employee and the union steward believe that the issue was not properly resolved at that initial level, further steps in the grievance process will follow, up to and including binding arbitration.

As a matter of fact, it is very important for employees to challenge discipline early in the process; if the time limit for grieving disciplinary action (typically ten days after the event) is not observed, employees may be precluded from challenging that disciplinary action later on should further disciplinary measures be taken. In other words, employees may have a difficult time grieving a current written warning by arguing that their previous verbal warnings were unjustifiable.

Figure 5–1. Addendum to performance appraisal.

Sylvia,

In addition to your overall score for this annual performance review showing that your performance does not currently meet company expectations, this annual review will also serve as a formal written warning. This addendum serves as a disciplinary document to impress on you the urgency of immediately improving your performance. There are two primary issues of concern:

Issue 1: Unscheduled absence. My audit in preparation for this review shows that you have incurred ten incidents of unscheduled absence in the rolling calendar year. Company policy states that ten incidents of unscheduled absence in a rolling calendar year will result in a final written warning. However, because of a clerical oversight, these incidents were not brought to your attention earlier. Therefore, we must start the disciplinary process with a verbal correction.

The dates of these ten incidents follow:

-
-
-

This number of incidents has impeded the work flow in our unit and could have caused our department to incur unscheduled overtime because others have had to carry an extra workload. Our company's attendance policy is attached. You are now formally warned that any further occurrences of sick leave must be substantiated by a doctor's note. Without the appropriate medical release, you will not be permitted to return to work.

Issue 2: Sleeping on the job. On September 2, the wife of patient #54321 requested that you be reassigned from caring for her husband. She stated to the charge nurse on duty that she saw you sitting at your desk sleeping two times the night before. When questioned, the wife specifically stated that at 3:00 A.M. she saw you sitting in your chair with your head down on the desk and with your eyes closed. When she returned from her husband's room approximately 15 minutes later, she saw you in the same position.

When the charge nurse approached you, she called your name two times, but you did not respond. When she tapped you on the shoulder, you appeared to jump up in a state of surprise and stated, "What is it? What's the matter?" The charge nurse noticed that it took a moment for your eyes to adjust to the light. She asked you if you were sleeping, and you told her that you were indeed sitting down with your head on the desk and with your eyes closed, but you deny having been asleep. I expect that your will never again sit with your head on the desk with your eyes closed. You must not engage in any activity or assume any position that gives the appearance that you are sleeping. Therefore, you are now being placed on final written warning that should you ever again sleep or appear to be sleeping at your workstation, you may be immediately dismissed.

Our **Employee Assistance Program** (EAP) provider, Prime Behavioral Health Group, can be confidentially reached to assist you at (800) 555-5555. A booklet regarding the EAP's services is available in Human Resources.

Sylvia, if you would like to provide your own input regarding this addendum, please provide it here:

_____

_____

_____

Please understand that failure to demonstrate immediate and sustained improvement may result in further disciplinary action up to and including dismissal.

I have received a copy of this notification. It has been discussed with me as part of my annual performance review, and I have been advised to take time to consider it before I sign it. I have freely chosen to agree to it. By signing this document, I commit to following the hospital's standards of performance and conduct.

_____	_____	_____	_____
Employee Signature	Date	Supervisor's Signature	Date

If your unit or organization is not unionized, on the other hand, you would typically follow a conventional step-review appeal procedure as outlined in your policy manual. In such organizations, unlike unionized settings, there is usually no neutral third party (such as an arbitrator) to serve as a judge or arbiter of last resort. Instead, a corporate officer such as the president, plant manager, or director of labor relations will act as the final authority and have final decision-making authority.

12. What if I fear that an employee might become violent during a progressive disciplinary meeting?

Violence in the workplace is a major concern throughout corporate America. Statistics paint a very scary picture of violence on the rise on factory floors and in corporate suites. Disgruntled workers returning to the office after having been discharged or disciplined is a common scenario.

If you expect a worker to react violently to your message, invite an undercover armed security officer to the meeting. Large security firms have personnel available on a moment's notice for such interventions. Post the security agent within earshot, but be sure that he or she remains unseen (for example, right outside the closed door of your office). The security and safety you'll provide for yourself and other members of your staff should your suspicions prove true are well worth the extra expense.

If you're terminating the employee, inform him that he is not to return to company property without your (and only your) express permission. State that this policy is uniformly implemented in all cases of employment separation and that corporate security or building security (if available) will be made aware that he is not to enter the property without a pass.

Finally, if you suspect that this worker may indeed return to the workplace with a weapon, hire armed security officers for an appropriate amount of time to ensure your workers' safety. Statistically, workplace violence often occurs on Mondays, since most workers are terminated on Fridays. Buy yourself added security by ensuring that armed staff is in place to deter such aggression.[3]

13. How long do I have to terminate an employee after an egregious offense like gross misconduct occurs?

Typically not more than a few days. If you fail to terminate an employee very soon after an offense like gross misconduct occurs, your failure to act may be interpreted by a court as an acceptance of the employee's conduct. The plaintiff's attorney will argue that you condoned the behavior by failing to act on it within a reasonable amount of time and that you should consequently be precluded from changing your mind at a later, more convenient date.

Since any delay of more than a few days could imply an acceptance of the misconduct, your subsequent discharge of the employee could be challenged. Remember that you can be held to have violated the implied promise of good faith and fair dealing if your decision to summarily discharge the worker appears to be pretext, capricious, or unrelated to business goals or needs.

14. If I have to terminate an employee, when is the best time to do it?

The best time to terminate a worker is early in the day and early in the week. "Early in the day" makes sense, since you want to remain accessible to the individual if questions arise regarding benefits continuation, unemployment insurance, outstanding 401(k) loans, and the like. More important, people often feel the need for more explanation regarding the company's decision, and your availability is critically important to ensure that the individual has his questions answered and needs met.

"Early in the week" is also an optimum time because, for the very same reason, you'll want to give the employee immediate access to you the next day, after she's "slept on it." Violent tendencies usually increase if the ex-employee goes over the story again and again in her mind without facts to balance her judgment. Violent tendencies decrease in the face of information and open communication.

For example, if an employee is terminated on Tuesday, she can call you on Wednesday and receive clarification or justification of your actions. On the other hand, if she is terminated on Friday and is all alone on Saturday and Sunday, she may develop a "vacuum

---

3 You may also want to look into filing for a temporary restraining order and an injunction against unlawful violence or credible threats of violence by an employee. State laws differ on how this can be done, so consult with legal counsel for guidance.

mentality" in which anger grows unchecked. By Monday, a deranged mind may justify doing damage to a former boss or previous coworkers (which is why workplace violence often occurs on Mondays). As a result, you should avoid Friday terminations whenever possible.

15. This book maintains that accurate and specific termination letters are my best bet because they dissuade plaintiffs' attorneys from taking on a case. However, I've heard defense counsel recommend that generic letters with little or no detail are preferable. Which style is better?

It depends on your writing style. Most defense lawyers will tell you that a well-written, accurate, and firmly founded letter of termination is a true feather in your cap when it comes to warding off lawsuits. They will also argue that documenting your arguments is a very healthy exercise that helps you ensure that termination is the correct remedy for the situation. Besides, that documentation will come in very handy if you're challenged later down the road to reconstruct the circumstances surrounding the discharge.

On the other hand, if the termination letter is poorly written and includes wrong facts or incomplete facts, then you could really damage your case. When in doubt, write a vague letter that simply states, "You are being terminated for violation of company standards of performance and conduct," and leave it at that. There's nothing wrong with a one- or two-sentence termination letter. This way, if your lawyer has to defend your company against this action some time in the future, she'll be able to start with a clean slate and not have to dig herself out of a hole.

And remember, of all the decisions managers make, termination decisions are the ones most likely to get them sued. As we've stated throughout the book, reviewing termination decisions with an attorney prior to taking any adverse action against an employee is a worthwhile investment. However, remember that billable hours add up quickly. To minimize the amount of time it takes to convey the facts to your lawyer, you're better off emailing the termination letter rather than trying to explain everything from scratch.

In addition, some companies choose not to employ termination letters of any kind. Instead, they limit termination meetings to verbal discussions only. This is clearly a matter of style and choice and should be determined in advance by speaking with outside counsel.

16. What are the two biggest mistakes that employers make when documenting discipline?

First, many employers give themselves extra hurdles to jump through by documenting "state of mind" offenses. In an attempt to demonstrate an employee's carelessness or lack of discretion, employers will use qualifying terms like *willfully, deliberately, recklessly, purposely,* and *intentionally.* This may help them communicate the depth of their dissatisfaction with the employee's substandard performance; however, it may create an additional burden of proof if they are forced to substantiate their contentions. Therefore, you should avoid mental element qualifiers as much as possible so that you don't have to prove an employee's state of mind at the time a particular offense was committed.

Second, many employers fail to realize that disciplinary documentation is legally discoverable and may be used against them by a current or former employee. For example, if you state, "Your failure to properly . . . *has compromised* an entire pool of loans," then you are codifying the damage done to the banking institution. That disciplinary document, in the wrong hands, could very easily become a leveraging point to substantiate a plaintiff's claim for damages.

This becomes even more important in sexual harassment claims. Of course, if an employee engages in activities that, in your opinion, create a hostile or offensive working environment, then you'll want to impress upon him the seriousness of his actions. However, if you state, "You have created a hostile and offensive working environment," that discoverable document could be used by a plaintiff's attorney as clear evidence that harassment did indeed occur.

To remedy these potential pitfalls, you're best off stating, "Your failure to properly . . . could have compromised an entire pool of loans" or "Your actions suggest that a hostile and offensive working environment *could have* been created." This way, the responsible disciplinary action that you took won't as easily be misinterpreted as confirmation that wrongdoing actually occurred. Be careful not to let your own documentation incriminate you.

17. How do I make a document or an email attorney-client privileged?

While undertaking an internal investigation, you may want to protect certain communications or recommendations from being discoverable in later litigation. The attorney-client privilege, if utilized properly, should help you accomplish that goal.

The attorney-client privilege may be used when a complaint involves potentially serious concerns (including potential criminal claims), may develop into a lawsuit, or involves a large number of employees, therefore having class action potential. Under such circumstances, you can do your best to invoke the attorney-client privilege to protect documents from a plaintiff attorney's future discovery efforts (although it's not guaranteed: a judge will determine if the attorney-client privilege stands or is revoked due to a failure to follow appropriate legal procedure).

Generally speaking, invoking the attorney-client privilege successfully will entail the following steps:

1. Address the communication directly to your attorney (either in-house or outside counsel).

2. Ask the attorney in the body of your correspondence for a legal analysis and recommendation (i.e., legal opinion) based on the facts outlined.

3. If you need to copy anyone in the memorandum or email, limit copies to all but those who have a legitimate business need to know. For example, if your boss is copied in an email to your attorney, that's logical. However, if fifteen people are copied instead, it may be difficult for a judge to conclude that the document was strictly confidential in nature, and the privilege may be lost. To be on the safe side,

don't forward privileged email messages unless you're sure they would remain within the zone of confidentiality.

4. Label the top of the communication itself (and the subject line in an email): "Privileged and Confidential: Attorney-Client Communication."

Finally, keep in mind the following caveats:

- The privilege does not protect communications between people where no attorney is present and no legal analysis or opinion is sought.

- Simply labeling a document "Privileged and Confidential" does not invoke the legal privilege or make that communication confidential.

- Do not communicate the information discussed with the attorney with others unless instructed to do so. Loose lips can overturn the privilege.

- Remember that, despite your best efforts, a judge may not grant the privilege, even if you've followed all of the steps above. Therefore, always assume that your communication may be used as evidence against your company in court someday. Similarly, never vent your feelings about a claim or a person in an email just because you believe the communication may be privileged. Without a crystal ball to tell the future, you won't know if the privilege will ultimately be granted, and that email record could be blown up in front of a jury on a large easel with your condemning words highlighted in yellow. Then you'll really have some explaining to do!

As the saying goes, the *e* in *email* stands for *evidence*. Don't make an electronic record of any communication that you wouldn't expect to be blasted across the front page of the *New York Times*—attorney-client privileged or not!

18. I've heard that certain employment experts recommend doing away with progressive discipline all together in order to protect a company's employment-at-will relationship with its workers. If that's true, wouldn't all these self-imposed due process obligations and written warnings simply place extra burdens on my company without providing much benefit in return?

A small number of employment lawyers and experts do indeed recommend that companies do away with progressive discipline of any kind. In theory, if a company provides no progressive discipline to anyone, then it should be able to maintain a pure employment-at-will relationship with all of its workers who can be terminated at whim.

Although a company may opt to follow this advice, there are several serious shortcomings to this strategy that need to be kept in mind: First, employment-at-will has a number of exceptions, including discrimination, public policy exceptions (like retaliation), breach of an implied covenant of good faith and fair dealing, and implied contract exceptions.

Therefore, without a crystal ball, a company won't know for sure if it will be able to win a summary judgment (AKA immediate dismissal of the case) at the hearing stage based on the employment-at-will affirmative defense. Put another way, you can't know what kind of spin a plaintiff attorney will place on a case six months to a year from now, and a judge may or may not grant an immediate dismissal of the case. That's especially difficult to second-guess in cases of high-risk situations (i.e., terminating someone in multiple protected classes plus protected activity). So if there's no progressive discipline on file at the time of the trial, your company risks not being able to defend itself, prevail, or even mitigate damages if the judge asks you to demonstrate good cause to justify the termination.

Second, and equally important, even if you could insulate your company from liability by denying anyone notice of substandard job performance before moving to termination, would you really want to? It may sound tempting, but think of some of the unintended consequences:

- Employees may work for you to earn a paycheck, but they'll probably only give so much when they know that they could be terminated at whim, for any reason or for no reason at all—especially if they've seen that happen to some of their coworkers.

- Providing no prior notice of substandard job performance before firing someone may significantly damage your corporate culture and worker motivation. In short, although such a program may benefit your employee relations practice, it will wreak havoc on your recruitment activities. After all, few people will want to join a company that's known for treating its workers unfairly or not considering their needs before doing something as significant as terminating them.

- Without a properly documented disciplinary record, it could be more difficult for your organization to contest unemployment insurance claims.

Remember that the number one reason workers originally organized and joined unions after World War II wasn't to collectively bargain for wages and benefits (as is commonly thought). Although that was certainly an important reason, what they wanted even more was to be engaged in a "termination for just cause only" type of employment relationship. Employment at will, most workers argued, was inherently unfair because they had no control over their futures. Union contracts would at least give them a fair shot at keeping their jobs because they'd have to be warned before being terminated.

It wasn't until employment at will was challenged by a California court in 1980 and exceptions to the employment-at-will relationship were established that workers felt more secure without a collective bargaining agreement behind them. In short, in a knowledge-based economy where your most important assets walk out the door every night, there's little need to create an antagonistic relationship with your "human capital" by pulling any modicum of job security out from underneath them.

19. What are my options for separating an employee who has not been granted progressive discipline? How do you go about terminating someone whose presence poses a problem but who has no progressive disciplinary actions or unacceptable performance evaluations on file?

This is the toughest question of all. You may have the right to terminate employees at will. Even so, if you're challenged, you will have to prove that you followed your organization's policies and past practices in arriving at that decision. If your defense isn't adequate and the employee's attorney can prove that the employment relationship was indeed not at will and that termination required good-cause justification, then you will most likely have to settle out of court.

When you are faced with this predicament, consider meeting with the employee and explaining the situation openly. If you are fair with the person and allow for a transitional period, then you will likely increase your chances for an amicable parting. Perks that you can offer to entice an employee to agree to a "separation by mutual consent" or a "negotiated termination" include:

- Separation packages[4]

- Outplacement (career transition) services

- Uncontested unemployment benefits

- A neutral letter of recommendation strictly based on historical performance evaluation feedback[5]

Hopefully, your cooperation in focusing the individual on a future career in a different company will be viewed as realistic and fair. That path of least resistance may give the worker an easy way out that simultaneously allows her to save face. And once again, you'll maintain a workplace that fosters respect, dignity, fairness, and open communications.

On the other hand, be sure to let the employee know this will be her choice and that you'll respect whatever decision she makes. (After all, you're paying now for some other

---

4 Separation payouts should be awarded only after signed releases have been obtained. The separation money is the legal consideration in exchange for the release. And remember that the Older Workers Benefit Protection Act (OWBPA), which amended the Age Discrimination in Employment Act (ADEA) of 1967, mandates that workers over forty be given a minimum twenty-one days of notice and an additional seven days in which to rescind the agreement.

5 Be very wary of stilted letters of recommendation that portray only positive attributes. You have a moral and legal obligation to provide both positive and negative information in the assessment. In addition, you're obliged to provide truthful, objective information in good faith and without malice to a prospective employer who requests the information and has a need to know. If the material you provide the prospective employer is false or misrepresentative and the company relies on your recommendation and hires the individual, you could be named in a negligent hiring lawsuit further down the road if that employee later becomes violent, sexually harasses another person, or commits a similar substantial breach of conduct (assuming that you're separating the employee for one of those reasons). On the other hand, the employee can sue you for defamation if your characterization in the letter appears biased. It's not hard to see why providing references on past employees is a Catch-22, no-win situation for most employers.

supervisor's failure to document performance problems clearly both in annual performance reviews and written warnings.) For example, you might say:

> Heidi, I'm guessing that you're not totally happy with our working relationship, and truth be told, I'm not either. I've discussed this with our division head and also with human resources, and I've asked Ashley from human resources to join us in this meeting so that we could discuss some options.
>
> In fairness, I want you to know that I told Ashley that I need to begin the progressive discipline process and draft a written warning for you based on the events that occurred yesterday. Still, I feel like there's a bigger issue at hand: You're not happy, I'm not happy, and to start initiating progressive disciplinary measures that could lead to your termination may not do either of us much good.
>
> Ashley thought that it might be better for us to sit down with her and lay our cards on the table. In short, if you're not happy in this role and want to avoid blemishing your record with written warnings and substandard performance reviews that could ultimately lead to a termination for cause, maybe we could work out some terms that will allow you to remain in control of the situation and walk out with your head held high.
>
> I've gotten approval to offer you a three-month separation package that will allow you to continue paying for your medical benefits at your current rate. If you choose to accept that package, you'd need to sign a release absolving the company from liability. And you don't have to answer us now: You could think about this and sleep on it and let us know later this week if it's an option you'd like to pursue.
>
> I don't want to discount the years that you've worked for us. And I figure that if it were me, I would prefer that my boss had enough respect for me to tell me openly and honestly that it might be better for me to pursue different teams in other leagues.
>
> If you choose to accept the package, we won't contest your unemployment. You can tell everyone on the team that you're leaving for whatever reason you deem fit, and of course when you apply at other companies and fill in that "Reason for Leaving" line on the employment application, you could show that you left us rather than vice versa.
>
> If you choose not to take this offer, that's fine, too. At that point, though, I'll ask Ashley to help me draft the written warning that we were going to prepare before we started this meeting today. Again, I'll respect whatever decision you make. Just let me know in the next few days how you're feeling about all of this, okay?

It's important that you have a third-party witness (in this case, human resources) at a meeting like this; otherwise, the employee could argue that you forced her to quit by threatening termination if she didn't. That could lead to a "constructive discharge" claim, which looks for similar remedies under the law as a wrongful discharge claim. If it's just one word against the other, it may make it very difficult for you, as the employer, to defend yourself against the employee's allegations.

For the same reason, it's important that the employee realize that if she doesn't agree to accept the separation package, she'll receive a written warning. Heidi needs to know that up front before she makes her decision. Otherwise, it will appear as if you're giving her a warning after she decides not to resign, and in a judge's or arbitrator's eyes, that could easily appear to be retaliatory behavior on your part. It goes without saying that your strategy session with human resources or outside counsel in a situation like this is critical *before* you engage in any conversations with the employee.

Finally, your offer doesn't have to not include a separation package in exchange for a release. Instead, you may simply opt to allow the employee to look for another full-time job while employed with your firm:

> Heidi, I'm guessing that you're not totally happy with our working relationship, and truth be told, neither am I. I've discussed this with our division head and also with human resources, and I've asked Ashley from human resources to join us in this meeting so that we could discuss some options.
>
> If you'd like to pursue looking for a full-time position elsewhere, I could support that. I'd rather we be honest and up front with one another right from the start so that you don't have to feel like you have to walk on eggshells or make up an excuse every time you land an interview.
>
> If you'd like to pursue this option, though, please keep two things in mind: First, we still come first. You'd need to give me 24 hours' advance notice whenever you'd have an interview planned so that we could divvy up the workload and reassign responsibilities as appropriate. Second, it's time that we put our concerns down in writing in the form of a formal written warning. This has been necessary for quite some time now, and your choosing to launch a job search, if that's indeed what you choose to do, really can't get in the way of the written record that we need to create.
>
> For now, we'll prepare the written warning. Please give some thought to the option of initiating a job search, and I'll be as flexible for you as I can. What are your thoughts about that?

The written warning at this point is important because Heidi's willingness to launch a job search shouldn't hold you back from managing her performance and holding her to high expectations. Many an unsuspecting employer have allowed individuals to begin interviews elsewhere, only later to find that they have taken advantage of the situation and not kept their word. If that's the case with Heidi, then having that written warning on file now gives you a lot more leverage to move through the progressive discipline system a month or two from now if you learn that she's not keeping her end of the bargain. In short, protect yourself and your company by placing a stake in the ground the day you hold this conversation so that you don't lose a few months in the progressive discipline process by having to start from scratch—after you've been taken advantage of.

20. How does progressive discipline contribute to the overall written record established by the employer?

It's critical that you understand the role of progressive discipline relative to the overall written record that governs a worker's employment or otherwise helps to justify termination. Consistency between annual performance reviews and documented corrective action is necessary to prevail in the courtroom, but it's also fairest to your employees who require clear and reliable feedback regarding their performance and/or conduct in order to course-correct and make the appropriate adjustments to keep their jobs.

Yet a lack of consistency plagues many employers, who often fail to give appropriate feedback while the worker is employed and then have difficulty justifying their termination decision after the worker is dismissed. For example, far too many leaders in corporate America engage in "grade inflation" when it comes to issuing performance review overall scores. They'll either avoid disciplining an employee totally or else they'll issue corrective action, even through the final written warning level, only to issue a "meets expectations" score on the annual performance appraisal.

Why? Avoidance and unwillingness to confront a problem head on are typically the key culprits. Also, there can be feelings of guilt—they feel bad that the worker won't receive a merit increase or bonus if they receive a failed annual performance review score. Or more likely, they don't understand how the two subsystems of performance management—annual reviews and progressive disciplinary warnings—intertwine and play similar and complementary roles in the eyes of the law.

Think of it this way: Annual performance reviews are like battleships. They make lots of waves, cover an entire year's performance, and validate or invalidate that year's contributions with the box at the very end of the review that reads, "Exceeds, meets, or fails to meet expectations."

Documented disciplinary warnings, in comparison, are like PT boats. They zip in and around the personnel file to capture one bad day of conduct or several weeks or months of substandard job performance. From a purely functional standard, they serve to break the chain of positive performance reviews that exist in the worker's personnel file.

If an employer takes the step of documenting corrective action—even through the final written warning stage—but then issues an annual performance appraisal documenting that the employee "met expectations" despite all the problems that occurred during the review period, then the annual performance review—the battleship—validates the entire year. This is because, all else being equal, battleships trump PT boats.

It's best when there's consistency between the battleships and the PT boats and the corrective action throughout the review year is captured accurately and fairly in the annual performance review. If the employee's overall contribution is a net negative for the performance year, then the review must capture the essence of those issues in the form with a "does not meet expectations" overall score. In those cases, the consistency between the battleships (annual performance reviews) and PT boats (documented progressive discipline) provides you, the employer, with maximum discretion to retain the employee or move forward with separation (assuming there is a clean final incident that breaches the terms of the final written warning).

In comparison, if the supervisor inflates the grade on the annual review for whatever reason, then that battleship will trump all those PT boats if the supervisor is looking to terminate the individual later down the road. This can cause a major roadblock and breakdown in the individual's official employment record. The easiest rule of thumb to apply in these circumstances is as follows: If a supervisor believes that a member of the team probably won't be around a year from now due to ongoing performance or conduct problems, then issue a failing annual review that is consistent with the progressive discipline that's been communicated.

On the other hand, if the progressive discipline that's been issued isn't all that serious or doesn't rise to the level where the supervisor is considering termination at some point in the near future, then issuing a "meets expectations" score on the annual performance review makes sense—although making mention of the disciplinary incidents throughout the review period would be warranted on the performance appraisal document itself since it captures an entire year's feedback.

Always look for consistency between the overall score on your performance appraisal document and the progressive discipline involved in any employee's situation. It's fair because it informs the worker of the company's expectations and holds the individual accountable to a higher level of output and productivity. In the eyes of the law, it accords the employee workplace due process, which is the legal standard that courts employ to see if a wrongful termination claim can be substantiated.

6 About the Sample Write-Ups

The remainder of this book consists of the 101 sample write-ups. They are organized according to the kind of problem behavior involved, and in general the write-ups deal with more serious charges as you go through the book. Some of the write-ups are connected by a story line involving the same employees and managers, so you can follow the progression from first infraction to final dismissal (when necessary) of an employee.

The format of the write-ups is the same throughout, except for the termination notices, which are in letter format. The standard elements in the document template appear in roman type, while the narrative (which would vary from case to case) is shown in italics. Figure 6-1 shows a complete blank template. The template is also included in the online resource that you can find at: **www.amacombooks.org/go/SampleWriteUps3rdEd.**

One of the most important parts of the template is the Employee Acknowledgment, which comes at the end of the write-up. As I explained in Chapter 4, owing to space limitations and since it doesn't vary in most write-ups, the Employee Acknowledgment section is not actually shown in the following samples in the book. It is shown only here in Figure 6–1 and at the end of Write-Up #1, but it should be part of any write-up you do. When the acknowledgment does vary in wording because of special circumstances (for example, in final written warnings), the change is indicated in a note at the end of the write-up sample in the book.

So be sure to review the Employee Acknowledgment section every time you include it in an actual written warning that you create. After all, you won't necessarily see this section on the pages that follow, but you can rest assured that it does appear in each write-up in the online version.

Figure 6–1. Performance correction notice template.

PERFORMANCE CORRECTION NOTICE

Employee Name: _____   Department: _____

Date Presented: _____   Supervisor: _____

DISCIPLINARY LEVEL

☐ **Verbal Correction**—(To memorialize the conversation.)

☐ **Written Warning**—(State nature of offense, method of correction, and action to be taken if offense is repeated.)

☐ **Investigatory Leave**—(Include length of time and nature of review.)

☐ **Final Written Warning**

    ☐ Without decision-making leave

    ☐ With decision-making leave (Attach memo of instructions.)

    ☐ With unpaid suspension

SUBJECT: _____

☐ Policy/Procedure Violation

☐ Performance Transgression

☐ Behavior/Conduct Infraction

☐ Absenteeism/Tardiness

PRIOR NOTIFICATIONS

Level of Discipline	Date	Subject
Verbal	_____	_____
Written	_____	_____
Final Written	_____	_____

Incident Description and Supporting Details: Include the following information: Time, Place, Date of Occurrence, and Persons Present as well as Organizational Impact.

PERFORMANCE IMPROVEMENT PLAN

1. Measurable/Tangible Improvement Goals:

2. Training or Special Direction to Be Provided:

3. Interim Performance Evaluation Necessary?

4. Our **Employee Assistance Program** (EAP) provider, Prime Behavioral Health Group, can be confidentially reached to assist you at (800) 555-5555. This is strictly voluntary. A booklet regarding the EAP's services is available from Human Resources.

5. In addition, I recognize that you may have certain ideas to improve your performance. Therefore, I encourage you to provide your own **Personal Improvement Plan Input and Suggestions**:

_____

_____

(Attach additional sheets if needed.)

OUTCOMES AND CONSEQUENCES

Positive:

Negative:

Scheduled Review Date:

EMPLOYEE COMMENTS AND/OR REBUTTAL

_____

_____

_____

(Attach additional sheets if needed.)

X _____
Employee Signature

EMPLOYEE ACKNOWLEDGMENT

I understand that XYZ company is an at-will employer, meaning that my employment has no specified term and that the employment relationship may be terminated any time at the will of either party on notice to the other. I also realize that XYZ is opting to provide me with corrective action measures and can terminate such corrective measures at any time, solely at its own discretion, and that the use of progressive discipline will not change my at-will employment status.

I have received a copy of this notification. It has been discussed with me, and I have been advised to take time to consider it before I sign it. I have freely chosen to agree to it, and I accept full responsibility for my actions. By signing this, I commit to follow the company's standards of performance and conduct.

_____   _____   _____   _____
Employee Signature   Date   Supervisor's Signature   Date

Witness: (if employee refuses to sign)

_____   _____   _____
Name   Date   Time

Distribution of copies: ☐ Employer ☐ Supervisor ☐ Department Head ☐ Human Resources

PART II

Disciplining the Probationary Employee

#1 Disciplining the Probationary Employee

Secretary with a sixty-day introductory period is having serious difficulty meeting the performance expectations of the job.

PERFORMANCE CORRECTION NOTICE

Employee Name: *Sid Carpenter*   **Department:** *Administration*

Date Presented: *December 1, 2017*   **Supervisor:** *Patricia Charlier*

DISCIPLINARY LEVEL

☐ **Verbal Correction**—(To memorialize the conversation.)

☒ **Written Warning**—(State nature of offense, method of correction, and action to be taken if offense is repeated.)

☐ **Investigatory Leave**—(Include length of time and nature of review.)

☐ **Final Written Warning**

  ☐ Without decision-making leave

  ☐ With decision-making leave (Attach memo of instructions.)

  ☐ With unpaid suspension

SUBJECT: *Substandard work*

☐ Policy/Procedure Violation

☒ Performance Transgression

☒ Behavior/Conduct Infraction

☐ Absenteeism/Tardiness

PRIOR NOTIFICATIONS

Level of Discipline	Date	Subject
Verbal	_____	_____
Written	_____	_____
Final Written	_____	_____

Incident Description and Supporting Details: Include the following information: Time, Place, Date of Occurrence, and Persons Present as well as Organizational Impact.

Sid,

You are leaving your work unfinished by not following the checklists that we established as guidelines for you during group orientation last Monday. I have commented to you that I did not feel that you were taking accurate notes regarding the information I gave you over the past two weeks, and I also shared my concern when you got up in the middle of a training session to refill your coffee down the hall without asking permission. You missed five minutes of a twenty-minute presentation, and you seemed unconcerned about the material you missed. I have seen that your eyes wander when we are in group training, and I have heard you ask questions that showed me that you were not listening to what you were told. As a result, you are not catching on to your new work assignments, and your performance is not meeting company standards.

PERFORMANCE IMPROVEMENT PLAN

1. Measurable/Tangible Improvement Goals: *Sid, I expect you to make every effort to master all the new information that you have learned over the past two weeks. I expect you to take accurate and detailed notes and to follow the checklists that will walk you through each assignment. Furthermore, I expect you to listen attentively and share with me any time that you do not understand something that you were told.*

2. Training or Special Direction to Be Provided: *I am providing you with another copy of your job description. Please read it immediately and see me tomorrow if you have any questions. I will also make myself available to you each day at 4:30 to see if you have any questions about your work assignments. I would like you to bring your checklists and any notes that you have taken regarding a particular question so that when I answer questions for you, you will have the resources to master those issues in the future.*

3. Interim Performance Evaluation Necessary? *No*

4. Our **Employee Assistance Program** (EAP) provider, Prime Behavioral Health Group, can be confidentially reached to assist you at (800) 555-5555. This is strictly voluntary. A booklet regarding the EAP's services is available from Human Resources.

5. In addition, I recognize that you may have certain ideas to improve your performance. Therefore, I encourage you to provide your own **Personal Improvement Plan Input and Suggestions:**

_____

_____

_____

(Attach additional sheets if needed.)

OUTCOMES AND CONSEQUENCES

Positive: *I will remain available to help you and discuss areas where you require additional support. If you meet your performance goals, no further disciplinary action will be taken regarding this issue. In addition, you will successfully complete the terms of your introductory period and gain more independence on your job.*

Negative: *You are not currently meeting company work performance standards. If you are unable to meet company performance requirements at any time within the remainder of your introductory period (through January 21, 2017), you will be dismissed. A copy of this document will be placed in your personnel file.*

Scheduled Review Date: *One week (December 8, 2017)*

EMPLOYEE COMMENTS AND/OR REBUTTAL

_____

_____

_____

(Attach additional sheets if needed.)

X _____
   Employee Signature

EMPLOYEE ACKNOWLEDGMENT

I understand that XYZ company is an at-will employer, meaning that my employment has no specified term and that the employment relationship may be terminated any time at the will of either party on notice to the other. I also realize that XYZ is opting to provide me with corrective action measures and can terminate such corrective measures at any time, solely at its own discretion, and that the use of progressive discipline will not change my at-will employment status.

I have received a copy of this notification. It has been discussed with me, and I have been advised to take time to consider it before I sign it. I have freely chosen to agree to it, and I accept full responsibility for my actions. *I understand that my position is now in jeopardy of being lost and that I must make substantial improvements in my performance in order to remain employed.* By signing this, I commit to follow the company's standards of performance and conduct.

_____ _____ _____ _____
Employee Signature   Date   Supervisor's Signature   Date

Witness: (if employee refuses to sign)

_____ _____ _____
Name   Date   Time

Distribution of copies: ☐ Employer ☐ Supervisor ☐ Department Head ☐ Human Resources

#2 Disciplining the Probationary Employee

Receptionist with a forty-five-day introductory period is having serious difficulty meeting the performance expectations of the job.

PERFORMANCE CORRECTION NOTICE

Employee Name: *Vicki Turnier*   **Department:** *Operating Room*

Date Presented: *November 10, 2017*   **Supervisor:** *Karen Forrest*

DISCIPLINARY LEVEL

☐ **Verbal Correction**—(To memorialize the conversation.)

☒ **Written Warning**—(State nature of offense, method of correction, and action to be taken if offense is repeated.)

☐ **Investigatory Leave**—(Include length of time and nature of review.)

☐ **Final Written Warning**

    ☐ Without decision-making leave

    ☐ With decision-making leave (Attach memo of instructions.)

    ☐ With unpaid suspension

SUBJECT: *Substandard work performance and failure to follow departmental policies and procedures*

☒ Policy/Procedure Violation

☒ Performance Transgression

☐ Behavior/Conduct Infraction

☐ Absenteeism/Tardiness

PRIOR NOTIFICATIONS

Level of Discipline	Date	Subject
Verbal	_____	_____
Written	_____	_____
Final Written	_____	_____

Incident Description and Supporting Details: Include the following information: Time, Place, Date of Occurrence, and Persons Present as well as Organizational Impact.

Vicki,

Two weeks ago, I met with you to discuss the following issues regarding your performance:

- *You had worked overtime without approval on two occasions even though you knew that overtime needed advance approval. This violates departmental standards of performance and conduct.*

- *On many occasions, your phones were not answered promptly. Physicians have complained that they were left on hold for an unreasonable amount of time. The staff has complained that the phones and comm. lines were left ringing because you were not at your workstation or because you were talking to someone else on another line and ignoring incoming calls.*

- *I also instructed you to leave specific instructions regarding your whereabouts when leaving your workstation so that a designated person could answer your phones in your absence and know specifically when you would return. Leaving the workstation without proper phone-forwarding instructions has disrupted the work flow in our unit.*

Yesterday, we had a critically ill patient in OR #1. The patient's condition deteriorated rapidly, and an additional surgeon was summoned. Prior to leaving for the day, I explained the critical nature of the situation to you and asked you to be available at the phones through the end of your shift and to answer the phones promptly. I also approved in advance any overtime if needed.

When I arrived at home at 6:10 P.M., I called the OR at extension 5555 to check on the situation. The phone rang twenty-five times without being answered. This prompted me to page the nursing supervisor, Janet Faraci. I called back at 6:35 P.M., and when you answered the phone, you told me that you never heard the phone ring and that you were in the area at all times. However, the nursing supervisor reported to your workstation at approximately 6:15 P.M. and stated that no one was at the desk. She waited there for five minutes and left when she was paged to go elsewhere. The lack of phone coverage during that critical period could have compromised patient safety. Furthermore, your dishonesty regarding your whereabouts has placed your job in serious jeopardy of being lost.

PERFORMANCE IMPROVEMENT PLAN

1. Measurable/Tangible Improvement Goals: *Vicki, I expect that you will always answer the telephone promptly, and acknowledge all incoming calls and place them on hold accordingly. I also expect you to be specific when requesting phone coverage from others: Explain to the recovery room and OR nurses when you will be gone for break or lunch, when you will return, and the status of any important messages or issues on your desk. If you have any difficulties meeting your workload deadlines, please page me immediately. Finally, I expect you to honestly address all questions regarding your performance or whereabouts, even if the answer is uncomfortable. In short, I expect you to assume responsibility for all your actions.*

2. Training or Special Direction to Be Provided: *Please review your job description tonight, and meet with me tomorrow if you have any questions about your job responsibilities. I will also make myself available to you (at your request) to sit at your workstation with you to answer questions or observe your work.*

3. Interim Performance Evaluation Necessary? *No*

4. Our **Employee Assistance Program** (EAP) provider, Prime Behavioral Health Group, can be confidentially reached to assist you at (800) 555-5555. This is strictly voluntary. A booklet regarding the EAP's services is available from Human Resources.

5. In addition, I recognize that you may have certain ideas to improve your performance. Therefore, I encourage you to provide your own **Personal Improvement Plan Input and Suggestions:**

_____

_____

_____

(Attach additional sheets if needed.)

OUTCOMES AND CONSEQUENCES

Positive: I will remain available to help you and discuss areas where you require additional support. If you meet your performance goals, no further disciplinary action will be taken regarding this issue. *In addition, you will successfully complete the terms of your introductory period and gain more independence on your job.*

Negative: *You are not currently meeting company work performance standards. If you again leave your workstation without proper notification or coverage, if you fail to answer phones in a timely manner, or if you are unable to meet company performance requirements at any time within the remainder of your introductory period (through December 5), you will be dismissed.* A copy of this document will be placed in your personnel file.

Scheduled Review Date: One week (November 17th)

EMPLOYEE COMMENTS AND/OR REBUTTAL

_____

_____

_____

(Attach additional sheets if needed.)

X _____

Employee Signature

EMPLOYEE ACKNOWLEDGMENT GOES HERE

Note: Since the employee's job is in jeopardy, add this sentence to the Employee Acknowledgment: "I understand that my position is now in jeopardy of being lost and that I must make substantial improvements in my performance in order to remain employed."

#3 Disciplining the Probationary Employee

Recently hired branch administrator fails to process necessary loan paperwork on time; the paperwork is found sitting on the administrator's desk by the branch manager.

PERFORMANCE CORRECTION NOTICE

Employee Name: *Meredith Parker*   **Department:** *Denver branch*

Date Presented: *December 29, 2017*   **Supervisor:** *Conrad Elliott*

DISCIPLINARY LEVEL

☐ **Verbal Correction**—(To memorialize the conversation.)

☒ **Written Warning**—(State nature of offense, method of correction, and action to be taken if offense is repeated.)

☐ **Investigatory Leave**—(Include length of time and nature of review.)

☐ **Final Written Warning**

    ☐ Without decision-making leave

    ☐ With decision-making leave (Attach memo of instructions.)

    ☐ With unpaid suspension

SUBJECT: *Substandard work performance*

☒ Policy/Procedure Violation

☒ Performance Transgression

☐ Behavior/Conduct Infraction

☐ Absenteeism/Tardiness

PRIOR NOTIFICATIONS

Level of Discipline	Date	Subject
Verbal	_____	_____
Written	_____	_____
Final Written	_____	_____

Incident Description and Supporting Details: Include the following information: Time, Place, Date of Occurrence, and Persons Present as well as Organizational Impact.

Meredith,

I found the Panico $97,000 loan file sitting on your desk one and a half weeks after the borrowers signed all appropriate paperwork. Your failure to process their loan paperwork in a timely manner could have potentially affected the loan's final interest rate and jeopardized the entire transaction.

Regarding the Verucchi file, you stated that you mailed an affidavit to the borrower on December 24 via FedEx priority overnight. You insisted that you left the completed FedEx on the mail-out table in the mailroom. The borrower called me on the night of December 26 to tell me that he hadn't received the letter yet. You confirmed for the borrower at that time over the telephone in my presence that you had indeed FedExed the letter on December 24. After that conversation, I checked with our mailroom staff and found that no record of such a mailing exists. I also contacted FedEx myself, and they likewise had no record of the file. Clearly, the facts that you presented to me do not agree with our mailroom's or FedEx's records.

PERFORMANCE IMPROVEMENT PLAN

1. Measurable/Tangible Improvement Goals: *Meredith, because of the timely nature of the loans we process, I expect you to pay very close attention to all time-related deadlines. I also expect you to follow the exacting standards that you were trained on when learning our company's procedures for loan processing. Finally, I expect you to conduct daily audits of your desk work to ensure that no projects or loans are sitting idly when they should be forwarded to someone else or some other department for proper handling.*

2. Training or Special Direction to Be Provided: *As we discussed in training, I remind you to always ask, What's the next logical step in this loan's processing? or Who else needs to be involved in this loan's handling in order to successfully close it? In addition, I would like you to present your training notes to me tomorrow with the points highlighted that would have averted these two mishaps. Finally, please review your job description, and see me tomorrow if you have any questions related to your position's key responsibilities, essential job functions, or secondary accountabilities.*

3. Interim Performance Evaluation Necessary? *No*

4. Our **Employee Assistance Program** (EAP) provider, Prime Behavioral Health Group, can be confidentially reached to assist you at (800) 555-5555. This is strictly voluntary. A booklet regarding the EAP's services is available from Human Resources.

5. In addition, I recognize that you may have certain ideas to improve your performance. Therefore, I encourage you to provide your own **Personal Improvement Plan Input and Suggestions:**

_____

_____

_____

(Attach additional sheets if needed.)

OUTCOMES AND CONSEQUENCES

Positive: I will remain available to help you and discuss areas where you require additional support. If you meet your performance goals, no further disciplinary action will be taken regarding this issue. *In addition, you will successfully complete the terms of your introductory period and gain more independence and satisfaction on your job.*

Negative: *You are not currently meeting company work performance standards. If you again leave loan files that have active time deadlines unattended on your desk, if you fail to properly mail, FedEx, or otherwise distribute material that will help close that loan, or if you are unable to meet company performance requirements at any time within the remainder of your introductory period (through February 16, 2017), you will be dismissed.* A copy of this document will be placed in your personnel file.

Scheduled Review Date: *One week (January 3, 2017)*

EMPLOYEE COMMENTS AND/OR REBUTTAL

_____

_____

_____

(Attach additional sheets if needed.)

X _____

Employee Signature

EMPLOYEE ACKNOWLEDGMENT GOES HERE

Note: Since the employee's job is in jeopardy, add this sentence to the Employee Acknowledgment: "I understand that my position is now in jeopardy of being lost and that I must make substantial improvements in my performance in order to remain employed."

#4 Disciplining the Probationary Employee: Extending the Length of Probation

Insurance claims adjuster has difficulty managing claims files and fails to cooperate when instructed to assist a coworker. Her sixty-day introductory period will be increased by thirty days to a total of ninety days.

PERFORMANCE CORRECTION NOTICE

Employee Name: *Barbara Maguire*

Date Presented: *August 18, 2017*

Department: *Personal Lines Claims*

Supervisor: *Floyd Richards*

DISCIPLINARY LEVEL

☐ **Verbal Correction**—(To memorialize the conversation.)

☒ **Written Warning**—(State nature of offense, method of correction, and action to be taken if offense is repeated.)

☐ **Investigatory Leave**—(Include length of time and nature of review.)

☐ **Final Written Warning**

    ☐ Without decision-making leave

    ☐ With decision-making leave (Attach memo of instructions.)

    ☐ With unpaid suspension

SUBJECT: *Substandard work performance; lack of cooperation*

☒ Policy/Procedure Violation

☒ Performance Transgression

☒ Behavior/Conduct Infraction

☐ Absenteeism/Tardiness

PRIOR NOTIFICATIONS

Level of Discipline	Date	Subject
Verbal	_____	_____
Written	_____	_____
Final Written	_____	_____

Incident Description and Supporting Details: Include the following information: Time, Place, Date of Occurrence, and Persons Present as well as Organizational Impact.

Barbara,

Your job performance has not been satisfactory for the period of time that you have been employed. In the six weeks that you have been aboard, the following problems have occurred:

- *Your job duties have not been completed in a timely or accurate manner. I have returned six files to you that you had marked "Closed" but that actually had outstanding issues in them. Of those six, three should have been forwarded to the Subrogation Department for further company action rather than retired in our unit. In addition, you checked off that two of those files had completed information when, in fact, materials were missing. For example, in the Michael Saunders file, you indicated that the plaintiff attorney's summons and complaint were included in the file when they weren't.*

- *You have stated to me on several occasions that your job functions and instructions were understood, and then you failed to remember them the next day. For example, when I instructed you on how to close out a file via computer database, you explained everything back to me. The next day, you failed to close out open coverages spending on four separate files. Worse, when Ana Orrick, supervisor, questioned you about those open entries, you told her that you were never shown how to close them.*

- *Two days ago, I instructed you to assist Angel Jones with computer database closeouts. You were reluctant to do so, told her you were too busy after agreeing with me that you would help her, and, in Angel's words, "bitched" the whole time after I again instructed you to help her. This behavior fails to meet company conduct standards.*

PERFORMANCE IMPROVEMENT PLAN

1. Measurable/Tangible Improvement Goals: *Barbara, I expect you to immediately improve your performance and conduct to meet company standards. I expect you to thoroughly audit your files to ensure that before you mark them "Closed," they are indeed fully prepared and documented. I expect you to admit when you've made a mistake and not to place the blame on others or on the system. I expect you to cooperate with your coworkers at all times and follow all my directives. Finally, if you cannot comply with my directives or feel that they are not reasonable, I want you to share your concerns with me so that we can mutually resolve the problem.*

2. Training or Special Direction to Be Provided: *Policy 15.6, Standards of Performance and Conduct, is attached from our company's policies and procedures manual. Please review the policy to ensure that you understand our company's expectations of your performance. Also, please review your job description and the company handbook, and see me tomorrow if you have any questions about your performance expectations. For the next two weeks, I will more closely monitor your closed files to ensure that you fully understand our company's processes for adjusting bodily injury and property damage claims.*

3. Interim Performance Evaluation Necessary? *No*

4. Our **Employee Assistance Program** (EAP) provider, Prime Behavioral Health Group, can be confidentially reached to assist you at (800) 555-5555. This is strictly voluntary. A booklet regarding the EAP's services is available from Human Resources.

5. In addition, I recognize that you may have certain ideas to improve your performance. Therefore, I encourage you to provide your own **Personal Improvement Plan Input and Suggestions:**

_____

_____

_____

(Attach additional sheets if needed.)

OUTCOMES AND CONSEQUENCES

Positive: I will remain available to help you and discuss areas where you require additional support. If you meet your performance goals, no further disciplinary action will be taken regarding this issue. *In addition, you will successfully complete the terms of your introductory period and gain more independence on your job.*

Negative: *You are not currently meeting company work performance standards. We are consequently extending your initial sixty-day introductory period by an additional thirty days (a total of ninety) through October 1, 2017. If you again fail to process your claims files in an accurate or timely manner, if you deny that you were trained to perform a certain task or forget how to perform a particular job function, if you fail to cooperate with your coworkers or follow my directives, or if you are unable to meet company performance requirements at any time within the remainder of your extended introductory period, you will be dismissed.* A copy of this document will be placed in your personnel file.

Scheduled Review Date: *Three days (August 21)*

EMPLOYEE COMMENTS AND/OR REBUTTAL

_____

_____

_____

(Attach additional sheets if needed.)

X _____

Employee Signature

EMPLOYEE ACKNOWLEDGMENT GOES HERE

Note: Since the employee's job is in jeopardy, add this sentence to the Employee Acknowledgment: "I understand that my position is now in jeopardy of being lost and that I must make substantial improvements in my performance in order to remain employed."

#5 Disciplining the Probationary Employee: Extending the Length of Probation

Computer operator returns to work late at night with little reason to be there and is later found using the company PC to update her résumé. Her 90-day introductory period will be increased by 30 days, to a total of 120 days.

PERFORMANCE CORRECTION NOTICE

Employee Name: *Iris Avery*　　　　**Department:** *Information Systems*

Date Presented: *July 14, 2017*　　　**Supervisor:** *Barbara Lauder*

DISCIPLINARY LEVEL

☐ **Verbal Correction**—(To memorialize the conversation.)

☒ **Written Warning**—(State nature of offense, method of correction, and action to be taken if offense is repeated.)

☐ **Investigatory Leave**—(Include length of time and nature of review.)

☐ **Final Written Warning**

    ☐ Without decision-making leave

    ☐ With decision-making leave (Attach memo of instructions.)

    ☐ With unpaid suspension

SUBJECT: *Improper use of company equipment; unauthorized return to work late at night*

☒ Policy/Procedure Violation

☒ Performance Transgression

☒ Behavior/Conduct Infraction

☐ Absenteeism/Tardiness

PRIOR NOTIFICATIONS

Level of Discipline	Date	Subject
Verbal	_____	_____
Written	_____	_____
Final Written	_____	_____

Incident Description and Supporting Details: Include the following information: Time, Place, Date of Occurrence, and Persons Present as well as Organizational Impact.

Iris,

On July 9, you returned to work from 10:00 P.M. to 11:00 P.M. and entered the main client/server room at 10:30 P.M. Laura Wallace, supervisor of microcomputer systems, complained to me the next day about your entering the client/server room late at night. She told me that when she asked you why you were there at 10:30 at night, you stated that you needed to install a CD-ROM on the server. However, the only reason you would have needed to be in the client/server room late at night would have been to install software on the server.

You had no business returning to work late at night and entering the client/server room. When you left work at 5:30 P.M. that Friday night, the end of your regularly scheduled shift, you waved good night to everyone. When you returned to work on Monday morning at 8:30 A.M., you told no one of your late-night return to the office that Friday. Therefore, I find very little merit in your argument and question why you entered the client/server room late at night.

A second issue has arisen that concerns me. You know that personal use of company equipment is not permitted and that I uniformly enforce this rule. Two weeks ago at a staff meeting, I reminded everyone that the use of company equipment for personal needs would subject employees to disciplinary measures. On Monday, July 12, however, I found that you had opened your personal résumé file on the A drive. Although the diskette was not in the PC at the time, MS Word shows the last four files opened. When I asked you if "resume_ia.doc" was your personal file, you admitted it was. Your actions consequently violate a department policy and a direct instruction.

PERFORMANCE IMPROVEMENT PLAN

1. Measurable/Tangible Improvement Goals: *Iris, I expect you not to return to work late at night without my prior approval for safety and security reasons. In addition, you are not to use any company property (including PCs, facsimiles, or telephones) for personal use under any circumstances, including during your break time or after hours.*

2. Training or Special Direction to Be Provided: *Handouts on "Department Telephone and Equipment Usage" are attached. Please read them and see me if any issues need further clarification.*

3. Interim Performance Evaluation Necessary? *No*

4. Our **Employee Assistance Program** (EAP) provider, Prime Behavioral Health Group, can be confidentially reached to assist you at (800) 555-5555. This is strictly voluntary. A booklet regarding the EAP's services is available from Human Resources.

5. In addition, I recognize that you may have certain ideas to improve your performance. Therefore, I encourage you to provide your own **Personal Improvement Plan Input and Suggestions:**

_____

_____

_____

(Attach additional sheets if needed.)

OUTCOMES AND CONSEQUENCES

Positive: I will remain available to help you and discuss areas where you require additional support. If you meet your performance goals, no further disciplinary action will be taken regarding this issue. _In addition, you will successfully complete the terms of your introductory period and gain more independence on your job._

Negative: _In your first two and a half months, you have not met company work performance standards. We are consequently extending your initial 90-day introductory period by an additional 30 days (for a total of 120), through September 3, 2017. If you again enter corporate property without prior authorization or inappropriately use company equipment, or if you are unable to meet company performance requirements at any time within the remainder of your extended introductory period, you will be dismissed._ A copy of this document will be placed in your personnel file.

Scheduled Review Date: _None_

EMPLOYEE COMMENTS AND/OR REBUTTAL

_____

_____

_____

(Attach additional sheets if needed.)

X _____

Employee Signature

EMPLOYEE ACKNOWLEDGMENT GOES HERE

#6 Disciplining the Probationary Employee: Extending the Length of Probation

Programmer/analyst with a 180-day initial introductory period is having difficulty from both a technical and an interpersonal standpoint: He makes excuses for his shortcomings and consistently fails to listen to his customers' needs. His initial introductory period will be increased by an additional 60 days, to a total of 240 days (eight months).

PERFORMANCE CORRECTION NOTICE

Employee Name: *Dick Diller*   **Department:** *Research & Development*

Date Presented: *February 14, 2017*   **Supervisor:** *Marsha Branson*

DISCIPLINARY LEVEL

☐ **Verbal Correction**—(To memorialize the conversation.)

☒ **Written Warning**—(State nature of offense, method of correction, and action to be taken if offense is repeated.)

☐ **Investigatory Leave**—(Include length of time and nature of review.)

☐ **Final Written Warning**

    ☐ Without decision-making leave

    ☐ With decision-making leave (Attach memo of instructions.)

    ☐ With unpaid suspension

SUBJECT: *Substandard work performance and customer service*

☐ Policy/Procedure Violation

☒ Performance Transgression

☒ Behavior/Conduct Infraction

☐ Absenteeism/Tardiness

PRIOR NOTIFICATIONS

Level of Discipline	Date	Subject
Verbal	_____	_____
Written	_____	_____
Final Written	_____	_____

Incident Description and Supporting Details: Include the following information: Time, Place, Date of Occurrence, and Persons Present as well as Organizational Impact.

Dick,

Over the past five months, we've discussed shortcomings in your performance from both a technical and an interpersonal standpoint. I feel it's time that these issues receive formal written documentation because the problems do not appear to be getting any better. I've discussed your performance with a number of internal customers, and I've learned that you fail to listen to customers' needs and that you jump to conclusions that wouldn't necessarily mesh with our company's systems or programs. For example, even though you're new to our structure at this point, you've voiced forceful opinions to a number of people about the need to do away with Macs.

Several of your customers have complained that you asked them for their opinion and then turned around and did things your own way anyway. Furthermore, you continue to see strong barriers between your job and the jobs of others in terms of what work you will do and what work is "below" you or "too menial" for you. Finally, I received a complaint just a few days ago about your losing your temper and acting rudely with a customer in the finance department. This behavior violates company standards of performance and conduct.

PERFORMANCE IMPROVEMENT PLAN

1. Measurable/Tangible Improvement Goals: *Dick, I expect you to provide excellent customer service companywide. I expect you to listen carefully to customers' needs and to allow them to finish their thoughts before interrupting them. I expect you to never again lose your temper with others or to dismiss their requests as "below" you. And I hold you fully accountable for meeting the project guidelines that we established when you first began working here.*

2. Training or Special Direction to Be Provided: *I would like you to spend time seriously considering your role in this organization, the impact you'd like to have from both a technical and an interpersonal standpoint, and the reputation you would like to see developed. Once you have considered these issues, I would like to meet with you to discuss how to best achieve your goals. I would like you to set another meeting within the next two weeks to hear your feedback. Please contact my secretary to schedule the appointment.*

3. Interim Performance Evaluation Necessary? *No*

4. Our **Employee Assistance Program** (EAP) provider, Prime Behavioral Health Group, can be confidentially reached to assist you at (800) 555-5555. This is strictly voluntary. A booklet regarding the EAP's services is available from Human Resources.

5. In addition, I recognize that you may have certain ideas to improve your performance. Therefore, I encourage to you provide your own **Personal Improvement Plan Input and Suggestions:**

_____

_____

(Attach additional sheets if needed.)

OUTCOMES AND CONSEQUENCES

Positive: I will remain available to help you and discuss areas where you require additional support. If you meet your performance goals, no further disciplinary action will be taken regarding this issue. *In addition, you will successfully complete the terms of your introductory period and gain more independence on your job.*

Negative: *In your first five months of employment, you have not met company work performance standards. We are consequently extending your initial 180-day introductory period by an additional 60 days for a total of 240 days (eight months), through June 3, 2017. You are now formally warned that any further incidents of interpersonal problems with coworkers, including rudeness, loss of your temper, or failure to reasonably listen to customers' complaints without jumping to conclusions, will result in your immediate dismissal. Similarly, from a technical standpoint, if you fail to work within the confines of existing company systems (rather than trying to change the whole system), if you fail to produce a meaningful product within pre-established deadlines, or if you take an exceptionally long time to perform a simple task like a basic computer conversion, you may likewise be dismissed.* A copy of this document will be placed in your personnel file.

Scheduled Review Date: *Two weeks (February 28)*

EMPLOYEE COMMENTS AND/OR REBUTTAL

_____

_____

_____

(Attach additional sheets if needed.)

X _____
Employee Signature

EMPLOYEE ACKNOWLEDGMENT GOES HERE

Note: Since the employee's job is in jeopardy, add this sentence to the Employee Acknowledgment: "I understand that my position is now in jeopardy of being lost and that I must make substantial improvements in my performance in order to remain employed."

#7 Performance Problems That Arise Right After the New Hire's Probationary Period Ends

Telephone sales representative launches a unilateral character attack against coworkers by badmouthing them to other coworkers.

PERFORMANCE CORRECTION NOTICE

Employee Name: *Sarah Orozco*   **Department:** *Telemarketing*

Date Presented: *October 11, 2017*   **Supervisor:** *Mary Scoridinski*

DISCIPLINARY LEVEL

☐ **Verbal Correction**—(To memorialize the conversation.)

☒ **Written Warning**—(State nature of offense, method of correction, and action to be taken if offense is repeated.)

☐ **Investigatory Leave**—(Include length of time and nature of review.)

☐ **Final Written Warning**

    ☐ Without decision-making leave

    ☐ With decision-making leave (Attach memo of instructions.)

    ☐ With unpaid suspension

SUBJECT: *Inappropriate communication about coworkers*

☒ Policy/Procedure Violation

☒ Performance Transgression

☒ Behavior/Conduct Infraction

☐ Absenteeism/Tardiness

PRIOR NOTIFICATIONS

Level of Discipline	Date	Subject
Verbal	_____	_____
Written	_____	_____
Final Written	_____	_____

Incident Description and Supporting Details: Include the following information: Time, Place, Date of Occurrence, and Persons Present as well as Organizational Impact.

Sarah,

On September 26, you circulated a formal complaint letter to your coworkers in the telephone room about loan officers and appraisers that was inappropriate. First, your actions were viewed by your coworkers as a unilateral attack on other employees, and it consequently de-motivated and insulted other staff members who were not aware of your issues with them. It is unacceptable to vent your frustrations with coworkers without first (a) going to them to find a mutual solution or (b) bringing the matter to your supervisor's attention. Second, you did not have your facts straight. You assumed that home appraisals were not being conducted because the appraisers were "too slow, lazy, and uncaring," when, in fact, appraisers typically schedule meetings up to a week in advance. Your comment about branch managers "not having the guts to do what they're paid for—namely manage" likewise shows that your opinions were not well founded. Indeed, your actions made you appear to be whiny and immature in the eyes of your coworkers and disrupted production and camaraderie in your unit.

PERFORMANCE IMPROVEMENT PLAN

1.Measurable/Tangible Improvement Goals: *Sarah, I expect you to refrain from voicing personal opinions that are aimed at wearing down morale or producing negativity. I also expect you to take your problem issues to the source in an effort to resolve them rather than merely complain about them. You are responsible for making this company a better and more effective organization, and I expect you to hold yourself accountable to that standard.*

2. Training or Special Direction to Be Provided: *Please review your employee handbook regarding "corporate communications" and "grievance and dispute resolution." Please see me the next time you feel a need to communicate a problem concerning company procedures or your coworkers' performance.*

3. Interim Performance Evaluation Necessary? *No*

4. Our **Employee Assistance Program** (EAP) provider, Prime Behavioral Health Group, can be confidentially reached to assist you at (800) 555-5555. This is strictly voluntary. A booklet regarding the EAP's services is available from Human Resources.

5. In addition, I recognize that you may have certain ideas to improve your performance. Therefore, I encourage you to provide your own **Personal Improvement Plan Input and Suggestions:**

_____

_____

_____

(Attach additional sheets if needed.)

OUTCOMES AND CONSEQUENCES

Positive: I will remain available to help you and discuss areas where you require additional support. If you meet your performance goals, no further disciplinary action will be taken regarding this issue. *In addition, you will develop more positive interpersonal relationships with your coworkers by developing a reputation for an open communication style.*

Negative: *I am concerned by what appears to be an apparent lack of judgment and an anger that did not express itself while you were in your initial sixty-day introductory period. Now that your formal probation is over, you appear to be presenting another side of your persona that has been hidden so far. Understand, Sarah, that any further unilateral attacks against coworkers, supervisors, or customers will not be tolerated and may lead to further disciplinary action up to and including immediate dismissal.* A copy of this document will be placed in your personnel file.

Scheduled Review Date: *None*

EMPLOYEE COMMENTS AND/OR REBUTTAL

_____

_____

_____

(Attach additional sheets if needed.)

X _____
  Employee Signature

EMPLOYEE ACKNOWLEDGMENT GOES HERE

#8 Performance Problems That Arise Right After the New Hire's Probationary Period Ends

Paralegal's interest in his position appears to wane soon after his ninety-day introductory period ends. He begins playing solitaire on his PC and appears defensive and overly sensitive when he's questioned about his performance.

PERFORMANCE CORRECTION NOTICE

Employee Name: *Mark Gonzales*   **Department:** *Trademarks/Patents*

Date Presented: *November 23, 2017*   **Supervisor:** *Gordon Hondo*

DISCIPLINARY LEVEL

☐ **Verbal Correction**—(To memorialize the conversation.)

☒ **Written Warning**—(State nature of offense, method of correction, and action to be taken if offense is repeated.)

☐ **Investigatory Leave**—(Include length of time and nature of review.)

☐ **Final Written Warning**

     ☐ Without decision-making leave

     ☐ With decision-making leave (Attach memo of instructions.)

     ☐ With unpaid suspension

SUBJECT: *Substandard work; oversensitivity to constructive criticism*

☒ Policy/Procedure Violation

☒ Performance Transgression

☒ Behavior/Conduct Infraction

☐ Absenteeism/Tardiness

PRIOR NOTIFICATIONS

Level of Discipline	Date	Subject
Verbal	_____	_____
Written	_____	_____
Final Written	_____	_____

Incident Description and Supporting Details: Include the following information: Time, Place, Date of Occurrence, and Persons Present as well as Organizational Impact.

Mark,

Less than two weeks ago, I congratulated you on completing your initial training period at our firm. I remarked on how much you appeared to me to be enjoying your work, and you stated that you indeed felt very involved in your position and felt like you were making a difference. However, in the past week I have received two complaints about your performance. First, two fellow attorneys brought to my attention the fact that they witnessed you playing solitaire on your PC throughout the day. They noticed this because your PC faces out into the hallway, and although you have your back to the door, others who pass by and glance into the room can see your computer desktop very clearly.

When I brought this issue to your attention, you reacted by immediately defending yourself. You stated that no one had any business looking at your computer desktop and that as long as the work was getting done, no one had the right to criticize you. Understand that I would expect my peers to bring issues such as this to my immediate attention, just as I would serve as an extra set of eyes and ears for them. Therefore, it was totally appropriate for them to bring this matter to me. Your overreaction and inappropriate sensitivity are not what I expected, however, especially seeing that you were indeed playing computer games while we're under deadline.

Second, it appears that you are not as up to date on your desk as I originally believed. Client attorney Charles Stone called me to say that the Vanguard file is not prepared for litigation because several pieces of information are missing: Namely, the subpoena duces tecum was not properly served on Chandler Corporation, so the records are not available; the deposition subpoena for John Roscoe is missing; and your litigation checklist has not been properly completed. You have been working on this case for a month, and these omissions could seriously jeopardize the time limits that we're facing.

PERFORMANCE IMPROVEMENT PLAN

1. Measurable/Tangible Improvement Goals: *Mark, I expect you to refrain from playing solitaire on your PC. More importantly, I expect you to create and maintain an image that is appropriate for a newly hired paralegal in a large, well-recognized law firm. I expect you to accept constructive criticism in the spirit in which it is meant. And most importantly, I expect you to meet all deadlines on all cases at all times. Should there ever be a time when you can't meet the deadlines established, I expect you to let me know in advance so that I can provide additional resources for you to meet your goal.*

2. Training or Special Direction to Be Provided: *I will meet with you later this week to review all files pending on your desk. I will answer specific questions you have about our firm's administrative practices and work with you on the more challenging files that require added attention. I will then meet with you at weekly intervals for the next month to ensure that you are totally up to speed on your desk.*

3. Interim Performance Evaluation Necessary? *No*

4. Our **Employee Assistance Program** (EAP) provider, Prime Behavioral Health Group, can be confidentially reached to assist you at (800) 555-5555. This is strictly voluntary. A booklet regarding the EAP's services is available from Human Resources.

5. In addition, I recognize that you may have certain ideas to improve your performance. Therefore, I encourage you to provide your own **Personal Improvement Plan Input and Suggestions:**

_____

_____

_____

(Attach additional sheets if needed.)

OUTCOMES AND CONSEQUENCES

Positive: I will remain available to help you and discuss areas where you require additional support. If you meet your performance goals, no further disciplinary action will be taken regarding this issue. _In addition, you will derive greater satisfaction from your work if you feel more confident about what I'm looking for in the files that you handle._

Negative: _I was very busy during your first three months at this firm, and I perhaps jumped to conclusions regarding your performance and potential fit in the organization. This document serves as a written warning for substandard performance. I hope that we will never have to address these issues again—especially the issues regarding your apparent disinterest in your job and your hypersensitivity. However, if at any time in the next ninety days you fail to complete your research and administrative duties in a timely manner, you will be placed on a ninety-day final written warning. Any breaches of this agreement or the firm's standards of performance and conduct during that final warning period may result in your discharge._ A copy of this document will be placed in your personnel file.

Scheduled Review Date: _Three days (November 26)_

EMPLOYEE COMMENTS AND/OR REBUTTAL

_____

_____

_____

(Attach additional sheets if needed.)

X _____

Employee Signature

EMPLOYEE ACKNOWLEDGMENT GOES HERE

#9 Performance Problems That Arise Right After the New Hire's Probationary Period Ends

Important company documents are discovered in a mailroom clerk's empty boxes; the clerk has no idea how the documents got there.

PERFORMANCE CORRECTION NOTICE

Employee Name: *Sean Rourke*   **Department:** *Mailroom*

Date Presented: *May 18, 2017*   **Supervisor:** *Linda Lawrence*

DISCIPLINARY LEVEL

☐ **Verbal Correction**—(To memorialize the conversation.)

☒ **Written Warning**—(State nature of offense, method of correction, and action to be taken if offense is repeated.)

☐ **Investigatory Leave**—(Include length of time and nature of review.)

☐ **Final Written Warning**

    ☐ Without decision-making leave

    ☐ With decision-making leave (Attach memo of instructions.)

    ☐ With unpaid suspension

SUBJECT: *Substandard work performance*

☒ Policy/Procedure Violation

☒ Performance Transgression

☒ Behavior/Conduct Infraction

☐ Absenteeism/Tardiness

PRIOR NOTIFICATIONS

Level of Discipline	Date	Subject
Verbal	_____	_____
Written	_____	_____
Final Written	_____	_____

Incident Description and Supporting Details: Include the following information: Time, Place, Date of Occurrence, and Persons Present as well as Organizational Impact.

Sean,

You completed your sixty-day initial training period approximately one and a half months ago. Two incidents have occurred since then, however, that are of serious concern to me. First, when you were off last Friday, Norma was looking for some empty boxes. She found a box underneath your desk, but it had some "D" purchase order (PO) copies in it. You stated that you didn't know how they got there. You gave Doris a similar response the week before when more than half a stack of POs to be filed had disappeared. No explanation was given at that time either.

Yesterday afternoon, I found a three-quarter-inch stack of scheduled inspection program (SIP) manual sheets on top of binders on the front office filing cabinet. SIP sheets do not belong in the front office at all, and leaving them sitting on top of binders on top of a high filing cabinet could easily lead to their being lost or thrown away.

In addition to finding these papers where they shouldn't be, I noticed signs on the two left drawers of your desk stating "HANDS OFF!" and "KEEP OUT!" This kind of notation is inappropriate and antagonistic. I appreciated your removing them right away.

PERFORMANCE IMPROVEMENT PLAN

1. Measurable/Tangible Improvement Goals: *Sean, I expect you to be much more careful about the filing work that you are responsible for. I expect you to keep your work area organized and your to-be-filed paperwork in the proper storage area. I also expect you to check with me before you post any signs in your office—especially signs with messages that detract from a friendly workplace.*

2. Training or Special Direction to Be Provided: *I am providing you with a copy of your job description along with the department's filing manual. Although you have already studied the manual, I would like you to review it again. Please see me tomorrow, and let me know if there are any aspects of your job or this department's procedures that are unclear to you.*

3. Interim Performance Evaluation Necessary? *No*

4. Our **Employee Assistance Program** (EAP) provider, Prime Behavioral Health Group, can be confidentially reached to assist you at (800) 555-5555. This is strictly voluntary. A booklet regarding the EAP's services is available from Human Resources.

5. In addition, I recognize that you may have certain ideas to improve your performance. Therefore, I encourage you to provide your own **Personal Improvement Plan Input and Suggestions:**

_____

_____

_____

(Attach additional sheets if needed.)

OUTCOMES AND CONSEQUENCES

Positive: I will remain available to help you and discuss areas where you require additional support. If you meet your performance goals, no further disciplinary action will be taken regarding this issue. *In addition, you will sense greater job satisfaction by working in a more organized way and gaining greater control of your filing items.*

Negative: *I was very busy during your first two months in our department, and I perhaps jumped to conclusions regarding your performance and potential fit in the organization. This document serves as a written warning for substandard performance. I hope that we will never have to address these issues again. Understand, however, that I hold you fully accountable for all aspects of PO filing and mail delivery—your essential job functions and primary responsibilities.*

If at any time in the next thirty days you fail to complete your filing or mailroom duties in a timely manner, or if POs are lost or suddenly appear in places that you were unaware of, you will be placed on a sixty-day final written warning. Any breaches of this agreement or the department's standards of performance and conduct in that final warning period may result in your discharge. A copy of this document will be placed in your personnel file.

Scheduled Review Date: *One week (May 25)*

EMPLOYEE COMMENTS AND/OR REBUTTAL

_____

_____

_____

(Attach additional sheets if needed.)

X _____
Employee Signature

EMPLOYEE ACKNOWLEDGMENT GOES HERE

PART III

Policy and Procedure Violations

#10 Inappropriate Interviewing Questions

Supervisor interviews a pregnant and disabled job applicant who complains about the supervisor's questions and argues that she has been discriminated against under the Americans with Disabilities Act.

PERFORMANCE CORRECTION NOTICE

Employee Name: *Sarah von Trapp*   **Department:** *Telecommunications*

Date Presented: *November 1, 2017*   **Supervisor:** *Cary Luipoldt*

DISCIPLINARY LEVEL

☐ **Verbal Correction**—(To memorialize the conversation.)

☒ **Written Warning**—(State nature of offense, method of correction, and action to be taken if offense is repeated.)

☐ **Investigatory Leave**—(Include length of time and nature of review.)

☐ **Final Written Warning**

    ☐ Without decision-making leave

    ☐ With decision-making leave (Attach memo of instructions.)

    ☐ With unpaid suspension

SUBJECT: *Inappropriate interviewing questions*

☒ Policy/Procedure Violation

☒ Performance Transgression

☐ Behavior/Conduct Infraction

☐ Absenteeism/Tardiness

PRIOR NOTIFICATIONS

Level of Discipline	Date	Subject
Verbal	_____	_____
Written	_____	_____
Final Written	_____	_____

Incident Description and Supporting Details: Include the following information: Time, Place, Date of Occurrence, and Persons Present as well as Organizational Impact.

Sarah,

On October 15, you interviewed a pregnant candidate with a partial arm for an installer position. Yesterday, the applicant received a rejection letter from the Human Resources Department, and she called to complain that your line of questioning was discriminatory and violated her rights under the Americans with Disabilities Act. When I spoke with you, you admitted that you asked her the following questions:

"What current or past medical problems might limit your ability to do the job?"

"Don't you think your arm might hinder your ability to do the installer job?"

"What are your career plans after you have the baby?"

"Will you be able to make adequate child care arrangements once the baby is born?"

These questions might suggest an indifference to federally protected rights, which, of course, would violate our company's policies and past practices.[1] We must also now reinterview this candidate to ensure that she was properly evaluated. Your lack of discretion and judgment violate our company's standards of performance and conduct.

PERFORMANCE IMPROVEMENT PLAN

1. Improvement Goals: *Sarah, I expect you to strictly adhere to our company's Equal Employment Opportunity policy. I also expect you to master the material that you learned in our annual recruitment workshop regarding allowable interviewing questions. Finally, I expect you to never again unnecessarily expose our firm to liability associated with the hiring process or any other employment-related procedure.*

2. Training or Special Direction to Be Provided: *Attached is a copy of policies 2.95, Equal Employment Opportunity, and 2.99, Recruitment and Selection Procedures. Recall that no questions regarding a candidate's pregnancy or child care plans are allowable under the law. Pregnancy discrimination is regarded as a form of sexual harassment.*

In addition, you may ask, "Are you able to perform the essential functions of the job with or without a reasonable accommodation?" (Hand the applicant a copy of the job description before requiring a response.) However, you may not ask the following questions:

- *Will you need a reasonable accommodation to perform the job?*

- *What type of accommodation will you need to perform the job?*

- *How will you perform the job?*

---

1 It's critical to remember that your audience is not just Sarah, your employee; it is also a potential judge, arbitrator, or jury! That's because disciplinary documents are discoverable, meaning that a plaintiff's attorney could subpoena this write-up and use it against you to prove that you indeed discriminated against the job candidate. On the one hand, you want to impart to Sarah how serious her error was. On the other hand, you don't want to make a case for a plaintiff's attorney by codifying your findings of employee wrongdoing. That's why it's so important to include a disclaimer that states that "such actions would violate our company's policies and past practices." This same caveat applies to sexual harassment, retaliation, and negligence issues.

As you should be aware, questions like these may be appropriate only after the candidate receives a contingent job offer. The matters are not the concern of line management in the interviewing process, however, and will be appropriately handled by Human Resources and Employee Health Services.

3. Interim Performance Evaluation Necessary? *No*

4. Our **Employee Assistance Program** (EAP) provider, Prime Behavioral Health Group, can be confidentially reached to assist you at (800) 555-5555. This is strictly voluntary. A booklet regarding the EAP's services is available from Human Resources.

5. In addition, I recognize that you may have certain ideas to improve your performance. Therefore, I encourage you to provide your own **Personal Improvement Plan Input and Suggestions:**

_____

_____

_____

(Attach additional sheets if needed.)

OUTCOMES AND CONSEQUENCES

Positive: I will remain available to help you and discuss areas where you require additional support. If you meet your performance goals, no further disciplinary action will be taken regarding this issue.

Negative: *Sarah, if you ever again inappropriately question job applicants about their physical or mental disabilities, histories of workers' compensation or health insurance claims, past treatment for alcohol or drug use, medical history, record of job absenteeism, or any other federally protected right, further disciplinary action up to and including dismissal will result.* A copy of this document will be placed in your personnel file.

Scheduled Review Date: *None*

EMPLOYEE COMMENTS AND/OR REBUTTAL

_____

_____

_____

(Attach additional sheets if needed.)

X _____

Employee Signature

EMPLOYEE ACKNOWLEDGMENT GOES HERE

#11 Failure to Follow Departmental Policies and Procedures

Technician fails to follow clearly established guidelines for calling in sick and, consequently, borders on job abandonment.

PERFORMANCE CORRECTION NOTICE

Employee Name: *Furley Luperini*   **Department:** *Marketing*

Date Presented: *January 18, 2017*   **Supervisor:** *Laura Rollins*

DISCIPLINARY LEVEL

☐ **Verbal Correction**—(To memorialize the conversation.)

☒ **Written Warning**—(State nature of offense, method of correction, and action to be taken if offense is repeated.)

☐ **Investigatory Leave**—(Include length of time and nature of review.)

☐ **Final Written Warning**

    ☐ Without decision-making leave

    ☐ With decision-making leave (Attach memo of instructions.)

    ☐ With unpaid suspension

SUBJECT: *Failure to follow departmental policies and procedures*

☒ Policy/Procedure Violation

☐ Performance Transgression

☒ Behavior/Conduct Infraction

☐ Absenteeism/Tardiness

PRIOR NOTIFICATIONS

Level of Discipline	Date	Subject
Verbal		
Written		
Final Written		

Incident Description and Supporting Details: Include the following information: Time, Place, Date of Occurrence, and Persons Present as well as Organizational Impact.

Furley,

On Friday, January 8, you did not come to work or call in at 7:30, your regular start time. Instead, you called at 1:30 P.M. to announce that you had fallen down some steps, hurt your shoulder, and were in the doctor's office all morning. You told me that you would return to work on Monday, January 11. On Monday, however, you did not return to work, nor did you call. You failed to notify me on Tuesday and Wednesday as well. Only on Wednesday afternoon did you speak with me when I reached you at home. In addition, you stated that you had left me a message on Monday, January 11. However, I never received that message. (Note that my answering machine is in fine working order.) Furthermore, departmental policy 2.01 states that you must speak directly with your supervisor when calling in sick.

Although you state that you are not aware of this policy, it is your responsibility to know how to perform within standard departmental operating procedures. The employee handbook clearly defines this protocol, and it also defines job abandonment, which occurs when an employee does not show up or call for three consecutive business days. Had I not reached you on Wednesday, job abandonment would have occurred, and you would have been dismissed.

PERFORMANCE IMPROVEMENT PLAN

1. Measurable/Tangible Improvement Goals: *Furley, I expect that you will familiarize yourself not only with this policy but with all policies and procedures outlined in our company's employee handbook. You must familiarize yourself with all company rules from this point forward.*

2. Training or Special Direction Provided: *I will meet with you in one week to review our organization's policies and procedures as outlined in the employee handbook. Please read the entire handbook and see me immediately if you have any questions.*

3. Interim Performance Evaluation Necessary? *No*

4. Our **Employee Assistance Program** (EAP) provider, Prime Behavioral Health Group, can be confidentially reached to assist you at (800) 555-5555. This is strictly voluntary. A booklet regarding the EAP's services is available from Human Resources.

5. In addition, I recognize that you may have certain ideas to improve your performance. Therefore, I encourage you to provide your own **Personal Improvement Plan Input and Suggestions:**

_____

_____

_____

(Attach additional sheets if needed.)

OUTCOMES AND CONSEQUENCES

Positive: I will remain available to help you and discuss areas where you require additional support. If you meet your performance goals, no further disciplinary action will be taken regarding this issue. *In addition, once you familiarize yourself with our organization's rules of the road, you will increase your confidence in performing according to company expectations.*

Negative: *You are now being placed on notice that if you ever again fail to follow established policies and procedures regarding calling in sick, you may be discharged. In addition, if you abuse any employment privileges, or if you engage in any conduct that indicates a lack of responsibility or that violates any standards of performance and conduct in the next ninety days, you may be placed in final written warning. Failure to follow policies and procedures during that final written warning period may result in your dismissal.* A copy of this document will be placed in your personnel file.

Scheduled Review Date: *One week (January 25, 2017)*

EMPLOYEE COMMENTS AND/OR REBUTTAL

_____

_____

_____

(Attach additional sheets if needed.)

X _____
Employee Signature

EMPLOYEE ACKNOWLEDGMENT

#12 Failure to Follow Departmental Policies and Procedures

Accounting clerk fails to deposit incoming checks the day they are received, and the checks are subsequently lost.

PERFORMANCE CORRECTION NOTICE

Employee Name: *Terry Archer* **Department:** *Central Processing*

Date Presented: *November 21, 2017* **Supervisor:** *Susie Waterman*

DISCIPLINARY LEVEL

☐ **Verbal Correction**—(To memorialize the conversation.)

☒ **Written Warning**—(State nature of offense, method of correction, and action to be taken if offense is repeated.)

☐ **Investigatory Leave**—(Include length of time and nature of review.)

☐ **Final Written Warning**

    ☐ Without decision-making leave

    ☐ With decision-making leave (Attach memo of instructions.)

    ☐ With unpaid suspension

SUBJECT: *Failure to follow departmental procedure for check processing*

☒ Policy/Procedure Violation

☒ Performance Transgression

☐ Behavior/Conduct Infraction

☐ Absenteeism/Tardiness

PRIOR NOTIFICATIONS

Level of Discipline	Date	Subject
Verbal		
Written	Aug 22, 2017	Excessive, unscheduled absenteeism
	Aug 22, 2017	Pattern of unscheduled absenteeism
Final Written		

Incident Description and Supporting Details: Include the following information: Time, Place, Date of Occurrence, and Persons Present as well as Organizational Impact.

Terry,

On November 11, 2017, I sent a letter of apology to fund-raiser Janice Witken because seven donor checks had been misplaced (see my letter to Janice, which is attached). As a result, Janice had to ask the seven donors to place a stop payment on their checks to our organization. Our departmental policy regarding check processing is that all checks must be deposited on the same day on which they are received. There are no exceptions to this rule.

The dates of the seven checks in question range from October 4 to October 15. In none of these cases did you notify me in advance that you had failed to deposit them. These checks were subsequently lost. Although you are not responsible for the checks being lost, your violation of departmental policy surfaced when we tracked the checks down and could have contributed to their being lost.

PERFORMANCE IMPROVEMENT PLAN

1. Measurable/Tangible Improvement Goals: *Terry, because of the timely nature of donation deposits, I expect you to strictly follow all departmental policies and procedures regarding check handling. I also expect you to* immediately *inform me any time you become aware of a problem like this in the future.*

2. Training or Special Direction to Be Provided: *You have been previously instructed on all phases of check handling. However, I am attaching another copy of our departmental policy on check handling, and at your suggestion, I am also redistributing this policy to all members of the staff. Please read the policy today and see me if you have any questions.*

3. Interim Performance Evaluation Necessary? *No*

4. Our **Employee Assistance Program** (EAP) provider, Prime Behavioral Health Group, can be confidentially reached to assist you at (800) 555-5555. This is strictly voluntary. A booklet regarding the EAP's services is available from Human Resources.

5. In addition, I recognize that you may have certain ideas to improve your performance. Therefore, I encourage you to provide your own **Personal Improvement Plan Input and Suggestions:**

_____

_____

_____

(Attach additional sheets if needed.)

OUTCOMES AND CONSEQUENCES

Positive: I will remain available to help you and discuss areas where you require additional support. If you meet your performance goals, no further disciplinary action will be taken regarding this issue.

Negative: *You are now being formally placed on notice that any further violations regarding check handling or any other standard departmental procedures may result in further disciplinary action up to and including dismissal.* A copy of this document will be placed in your personnel file.

Scheduled Review Date: *None*

EMPLOYEE COMMENTS AND/OR REBUTTAL

_____

_____

_____

(Attach additional sheets if needed.)

X _____
Employee Signature

EMPLOYEE ACKNOWLEDGMENT

#13 Excessive Personal Telephone Calls

A telephone audit reveals that a collector is making an unacceptable number of phone calls to her home, thereby violating the terms of her previous annual evaluation and a prior written warning.

PERFORMANCE CORRECTION NOTICE

Employee Name: *Jeannie London*   **Department:** *Collections*

Date Presented: *September 6, 2017*   **Supervisor:** *Albert Burnham*

DISCIPLINARY LEVEL

☐ **Verbal Correction**—(To memorialize the conversation.)

☐ **Written Warning**—(State nature of offense, method of correction, and action to be taken if offense is repeated.)

☐ **Investigatory Leave**—(Include length of time and nature of review.)

☒ **Final Written Warning**

    ☒ Without decision-making leave

    ☐ With decision-making leave (Attach memo of instructions.)

    ☐ With unpaid suspension

SUBJECT: *Excessive personal telephone calls*

☒ Policy/Procedure Violation

☒ Performance Transgression

☒ Behavior/Conduct Infraction

☐ Absenteeism/Tardiness

PRIOR NOTIFICATIONS

Level of Discipline	Date	Subject
Verbal	Apr 16, 2017	Annual evaluation documents excessive personal telephone calls
Written	May 18, 2017	Substandard performance and excessive telephone calls
Final Written	_____	_____

Incident Description and Supporting Details: Include the following information: Time, Place, Date of Occurrence, and Persons Present as well as Organizational Impact.

Jeannie,

In April, you received your annual performance evaluation, which stated that you did not meet departmental performance expectations and that you were making excessive personal telephone calls. On May 18, you received a written correction for excessive telephone usage.

A departmental telephone audit was conducted last week. Despite these two notices of unacceptable conduct, at least 21 of your 68 calls in June, or 31 percent, were personal. And in July, at least 48 of 126 calls, or 39 percent, were personal. These calls were all made to your home phone number. This indicated that you may not have taken your prior warning or your April evaluation as seriously as you should have.

PERFORMANCE IMPROVEMENT PLAN

1. Measurable/Tangible Improvement Goals: *Jeannie, I expect you to follow all rules and regulations at all times regarding personal telephone usage or any of the other standards of performance and conduct outlined in the employee handbook. Furthermore, you are to use a public telephone from now on unless your supervisor approves an exception to that rule in case of emergency.*

2. Training or Special Direction to Be Provided: *You received a copy of the policy regarding personal telephone usage when you were disciplined in May. Reread that policy immediately and tell me if you have any questions.*

3. Interim Performance Evaluation Necessary? *No*

4. Our **Employee Assistance Program** (EAP) provider, Prime Behavioral Health Group, can be confidentially reached to assist you at (800) 555-5555. This is strictly voluntary. A booklet regarding the EAP's services is available from Human Resources.

5. In addition, I recognize that you may have certain ideas to improve your performance. Therefore, I encourage you to provide your own **Personal Improvement Plan Input and Suggestions:**

_____

_____

_____

(Attach additional sheets if needed.)

OUTCOMES AND CONSEQUENCES

Positive: I will remain available to help you and discuss areas where you require additional support. If you meet your performance goals, no further disciplinary action will be taken regarding this issue. *In addition, we will not charge you for the new personal telephone calls you made over the past two months.*

Negative: *You are now being placed on notice that if in the next ninety days you make one additional personal phone call on company time that is not of an emergency nature, you may be immediately dismissed. After that ninety-day period, your calls will continue to be monitored on an ongoing basis. Any further transgressions may subject you to further progressive disciplinary action up to and including dismissal.* A copy of this document will be placed in your personnel file.

Scheduled Review Date: *None*

EMPLOYEE COMMENTS AND/OR REBUTTAL

_____

_____

_____

(Attach additional sheets if needed.)

X _____

Employee Signature

EMPLOYEE ACKNOWLEDGMENT

Note: Since this is a final written warning, add the following sentence to the Employee Acknowledgment: "I understand that this is my last chance. If I fail to abide by the rules established in this memo, I will voluntarily resign or be discharged for cause."

#14 Software Piracy (Unauthorized Installation)

Employee loaded personal software onto his office PC and thereby violated a company rule and jeopardized licensing agreements.

PERFORMANCE CORRECTION NOTICE

Employee Name: *Dennis Pryor*   **Department:** *Manufacturing*

Date Presented: *April 29, 2017*   **Supervisor:** *Larry Connors*

DISCIPLINARY LEVEL

☐ **Verbal Correction**—(To memorialize the conversation.)

☒ **Written Warning**—(State nature of offense, method of correction, and action to be taken if offense is repeated.)

☐ **Investigatory Leave**—(Include length of time and nature of review.)

☐ **Final Written Warning**

　　☐ Without decision-making leave

　　☐ With decision-making leave (Attach memo of instructions.)

　　☐ With unpaid suspension

SUBJECT: *Unauthorized installation of personal software onto company PC*

☒ Policy/Procedure Violation

☐ Performance Transgression

☐ Behavior/Conduct Infraction

☐ Absenteeism/Tardiness

PRIOR NOTIFICATIONS

Level of Discipline	Date	Subject
Verbal	_____	_____
Written	_____	_____
Final Written	_____	_____

Incident Description and Supporting Details: Include the following information: Time, Place, Date of Occurrence, and Persons Present as well as Organizational Impact.

Dennis,

In December of 2016, data security administrator Bill Wright performed a "baseline software audit" and removed programs from your PC that were not authorized for installation. You were told not to load any unauthorized copies of software again.

In a random software audit conducted on April 22, 2017, Bill Wright found programs on your PC that were formally removed from your system back in December and for which there is no proof of ownership. This clearly violates our company's software piracy policies, which state that no unauthorized copies of computer software are to be loaded on an employee's PC under any circumstances. Your actions might violate U.S. copyright law as well.

PERFORMANCE IMPROVEMENT PLAN

1. Measurable/Tangible Improvement Goals: *Dennis, I expect you to uphold all rules and policies regarding software installation and to abide by all of our organization's standards of performance and conduct.*

2. Training or Special Direction Provided: *A copy of the company policy on unauthorized installation of software is attached. Please read it immediately and let me know if you have any questions.*

3. Interim Performance Evaluation Necessary? *No*

4. Our **Employee Assistance Program** (EAP) provider, Prime Behavioral Health Group, can be confidentially reached to assist you at (800) 555-5555. This is strictly voluntary. A booklet regarding the EAP's services is available from Human Resources.

5. In addition, I recognize that you may have certain ideas to improve your performance. Therefore, I encourage you to provide your own **Personal Improvement Plan Input and Suggestions:**

_____

_____

_____

(Attach additional sheets if needed.)

OUTCOMES AND CONSEQUENCES

Positive: I will remain available to help you and discuss areas where you require additional support. If you meet your performance goals, no further disciplinary action will be taken regarding this issue.

Negative: *You are now being placed on notice that if you ever again install or copy unauthorized software on to your workstation, disciplinary action up to and including termination may result.* A copy of this document will be placed in your personnel file.

Scheduled Review Date: *None*

EMPLOYEE COMMENTS AND/OR REBUTTAL

_____

_____

_____

(Attach additional sheets if needed.)

X _____
Employee Signature

EMPLOYEE ACKNOWLEDGMENT GOES HERE

#15 Unauthorized Use of Company Equipment, Time, Materials, or Facilities

Employee faxed a personal opinion from his office to a local radio talk show program.

PERFORMANCE CORRECTION NOTICE

Employee Name: *Michael James*   **Department:** *Administration*

Date Presented: *January 13, 2017*   **Supervisor:** *Richard Cuthbertson*

DISCIPLINARY LEVEL

☐ **Verbal Correction**—(To memorialize the conversation.)

☒ **Written Warning**—(State nature of offense, method of correction, and action to be taken if offense is repeated.)

☐ **Investigatory Leave**—(Include length of time and nature of review.)

☐ **Final Written Warning**

    ☐ Without decision-making leave

    ☐ With decision-making leave (Attach memo of instructions.)

    ☐ With unpaid suspension

SUBJECT: *Unauthorized use of company equipment, time, materials, or facilities*

☒ Policy/Procedure Violation

☒ Performance Transgression

☐ Behavior/Conduct Infraction

☐ Absenteeism/Tardiness

PRIOR NOTIFICATIONS

Level of Discipline	Date	Subject
Verbal	_____	_____
Written	_____	_____
Final Written	_____	_____

Incident Description and Supporting Details: Include the following information: Time, Place, Date of Occurrence, and Persons Present as well as Organizational Impact.

Michael,

The department of human resources received a copy today of the personal correspondence that you faxed to the Jay and Dennis Radio Show yesterday January 12, at 1:09 P.M. This is a corporate communications issue that could have very serious results for our organization. First, you used company property and time to handle a personal issue. Second, and more significantly, your faxed copy to the radio station that showed our company's name, Vanguard Biotech, at the top of the page. That Vanguard Biotech marker could have resulted in Vanguard's being identified as "co-owner" of that opinion. ("Michael from Vanguard Biotech just faxed us his opinion . . .") Vanguard cannot be associated with any public opinions of its employees through radio or any other media. This is consequently a serious violation of corporate communications policy.

PERFORMANCE IMPROVEMENT PLAN

1. Measurable/Tangible Improvement Goals: *Michael, I expect you to become more sensitive to the ramifications of your decisions in terms of how they can affect the name brand or equity of Vanguard in the public's eye. In addition, I expect you to follow all policies regarding use of company equipment during work hours.*

2. Training or Special Direction to Be Provided: *Attached to this document is a copy of policy 2.54 regarding corporate communications and policy 2.99 regarding personal use of company property. Please read these documents thoroughly and see me with any questions.*

3. Interim Performance Evaluation Necessary? *No*

4. Our **Employee Assistance Program** (EAP) provider, Prime Behavioral Health Group, can be confidentially reached to assist you at (800) 555-5555. This is strictly voluntary. A booklet regarding the EAP's services is available from Human Resources.

5. In addition, I recognize that you may have certain ideas to improve your performance. Therefore, I encourage you to provide your own **Personal Improvement Plan Input and Suggestions:**

_____

_____

_____

(Attach additional sheets if needed.)

OUTCOMES AND CONSEQUENCES

Positive: I will remain available to help you and discuss areas where you require additional support. If you meet your performance goals, no further disciplinary action will be taken regarding this issue.

Negative: *You are never again to use company property or company time to voice your personal opinion to any media-related organization. Your personal opinion must remain disassociated from Vanguard Biotech. You are now being placed on notice that if such an instance should happen again, you may be immediately dismissed.*

Furthermore, any further incidents of personal use of company property while on company time—for whatever reason—may lead to disciplinary action up to and including termination. A copy of this document will be placed in your personnel file.

Scheduled Review Date: *None*

EMPLOYEE COMMENTS AND/OR REBUTTAL

_____

_____

_____

(Attach additional sheets if needed.)

X _____
Employee Signature

EMPLOYEE ACKNOWLEDGMENT GOES HERE

Bonus Sample: Lost Equipment

Field technician loses her hard hat while working on an on-site customer project.

PERFORMANCE CORRECTION NOTICE

Employee Name: *Ingrid Nieminen* **Department:** *Field Services*

Date Presented: *October 11, 2017* **Supervisor:** *Philip Khan*

DISCIPLINARY LEVEL

☐ **Verbal Correction**—(To memorialize the conversation.)

☒ **Written Warning**—(State nature of offense, method of correction, and action to be taken if offense is repeated.)

☐ **Investigatory Leave**—(Include length of time and nature of review.)

☐ **Final Written Warning**

   ☐ Without decision-making leave

   ☐ With decision-making leave (Attach memo of instructions.)

   ☐ With unpaid suspension

SUBJECT: *Lost personal protective equipment (hard hat)*

☒ Policy/Procedure Violation

☐ Performance Transgression

☐ Behavior/Conduct Infraction

☐ Absenteeism/Tardiness

PRIOR NOTIFICATIONS

Level of Discipline	Date	Subject
Verbal	_____	_____
Written	_____	_____
Final Written	_____	_____

Incident Description and Supporting Details: Include the following information: Time, Place, Date of Occurrence, and Persons Present as well as Organizational Impact.

Ingrid,

On October 10, you reported that you lost your company hard hart while visiting a customer's premises. This document serves to notify you that you are being issued a written warning for violation of the Company Issued Tools & Equipment policy, which follows:

Employees are required to use company tools, equipment, property, and resources safely and responsibly and to use good judgment in maintaining the security of company-issued equipment. Employees in positions requiring the use of company tools and/or equipment are responsible for their care and safekeeping. Loss or damage to company property many result in corrective action, up to and including termination of employment.

You reported the misplacement/loss of your hard hat to your supervisor in a timely manner and stated that you were working on an electrical outage issue with another technician. You confirmed that the hard hat was not necessary as personal protective equipment (PPE) for the repair you were conducting and that you needed to remove it to fit into the space. However, you also stated that at the time, you did not realize you left your hard hat in the rear of the vehicle. Further, as you proceeded to drive away, you came to a stop sign and realized your hard hat wasn't near the docking station where you normally keep it. You searched your company vehicle but could not find the missing hard hat—you also called the other tech to help search the location where you had been working, but you were unable to find it.

As a result of not following the Company Issued Tools & Equipment policy, you are being issued a written warning, which affords you the opportunity to correct this behavior.

PERFORMANCE IMPROVEMENT PLAN

1. Measurable/Tangible Improvement Goals: *Ingrid, the proper care for your company-issued tools and PPE is an area that you must monitor on a regular and ongoing basis and is an essential function of your job as a field services technician. Be aware of your surroundings and never leave any company property unattended, out of sight, or where damage or theft may occur.*

Remember to properly store/secure your equipment, carry it with you as you go from site to site, and account for it at the completion of every assignment. Likewise, conduct a quick tool/equipment check before and after completing each job and at the beginning and end of each workday, to ensure you have all of your tools and equipment accounted for.

2. Training or Special Direction Provided: *To emphasize the importance in handling company tools and/or equipment, please refamiliarize yourself with our company's "Issued Tools & Equipment" policy. Further, please review our policy on Personal Protective Equipment immediately. You are required to review all company policies and make yourself familiar with them on a regular, ongoing basis. Please ask your supervisor, manager, or HR support person any questions if you are in need of any clarification on this or any other policy.*

3. Interim Performance Evaluation Necessary? *No*

4. Our **Employee Assistance Program** (EAP) provider, Prime Behavioral Health Group, can be confidentially reached to assist you at (800) 555-5555. This is strictly voluntary. A booklet regarding the EAP's services is available from Human Resources.

5. In addition, I recognize that you may have certain ideas to improve your performance. Therefore, I encourage you to provide your own **Personal Improvement Plan Input and Suggestions:**

_____

_____

_____

(Attach additional sheets if needed.)

OUTCOMES AND CONSEQUENCES

Positive: I will remain available to help you and discuss areas where you require additional support. If you meet your performance goals, no further disciplinary action will be taken regarding this issue.

Negative: *You must clearly understand that failure to demonstrate immediate and sustained improvement may result in further disciplinary action up to and including dismissal.* A copy of this document will be placed in your personnel file.

Scheduled Review Date: N/A

EMPLOYEE COMMENTS AND/OR REBUTTAL

_____

_____

_____

(Attach additional sheets if needed.)

X _____
Employee Signature

EMPLOYEE ACKNOWLEDGMENT GOES HERE

#16 Unauthorized Removal of Company Files

Social worker takes confidential client files home to work on them over the weekend and then forgets to bring them back to the office on Monday.

PERFORMANCE CORRECTION NOTICE

Employee Name: *Patricia Morrow*   **Department:** *Social Work*

Date Presented: *January 20, 2017*   **Supervisor:** *Matt Finneran*

DISCIPLINARY LEVEL

☐ **Verbal Correction**—(To memorialize the conversation.)

☒ **Written Warning**—(State nature of offense, method of correction, and action to be taken if offense is repeated.)

☐ **Investigatory Leave**—(Include length of time and nature of review.)

☐ **Final Written Warning**

  ☐ Without decision-making leave

  ☐ With decision-making leave (Attach memo of instructions.)

  ☐ With unpaid suspension

SUBJECT: *Inappropriate removal of company property; breach of confidentiality policy*

☒ Policy/Procedure Violation

☒ Performance Transgression

☐ Behavior/Conduct Infraction

☐ Absenteeism/Tardiness

PRIOR NOTIFICATIONS

Level of Discipline	Date	Subject
Verbal	_____	_____
Written	_____	_____
Final Written	_____	_____

Incident Description and Supporting Details: Include the following information: Time, Place, Date of Occurrence, and Persons Present as well as Organizational Impact.

Patricia,

Yesterday State Care Licensing (SCL) audited Rogers Family Services. The auditor performed a random check of our client files. The auditor discovered that seven client files from your caseload were not in the file cabinet. When I asked you if you knew where they were, you stated, "I know I shouldn't have, but I brought them home over the weekend to catch up on my progress notes. I've been having some personal problems and have fallen behind in my work." You then stated that had you known an audit was occurring on Monday, you would not have removed the files from the cabinet.

Because I was unable to produce the requested files for the auditor during her spot check, our agency received a citation. It is strictly against company policy to remove client files from the premises. As a social worker at Rogers Family Services, it is your responsibility to adhere to confidentiality mandates. Your actions directly violated client confidentiality and have also jeopardized our agency's SCL audit.

PERFORMANCE IMPROVEMENT PLAN

1. Measurable/Tangible Improvement Goals: *Patricia, I expect you to never again remove client files from the premises. Similarly, I expect you to uphold all standards of confidentiality as found in the Employee Confidentiality Agreement and policy 6.1, Confidential Information. In addition, if you again fall behind in your work, I expect you to inform me of that fact so that we can work together to manage your workload.*

2. Training or Special Direction to Be Provided: *Attached is a copy of policy 6.1. Please read it immediately and see me if you have any questions. Please review your Employee Confidentiality Agreement as well to ensure that you understand your responsibilities to our patients.*

3. Interim Performance Evaluation Necessary? *No*

4. Our Employee Assistance Program (EAP) provider, Prime Behavioral Health Group, can be confidentially reached to assist you at (800) 555-5555. This is strictly voluntary. A booklet regarding the EAP's services is available from Human Resources.

5. In addition, I recognize that you may have certain ideas to improve your performance. Therefore, I encourage you to provide your own **Personal Improvement Plan Input and Suggestions:**

_____

_____

_____

(Attach additional sheets if needed.)

OUTCOMES AND CONSEQUENCES

Positive: I will remain available to help you and discuss areas where you require additional support. If you meet your performance goals, no further disciplinary action will be taken regarding this issue.

Negative: *Failure to meet company confidentiality standards is a serious offense. If you ever again fail to abide by our organization's Client Confidentiality policy in any way or if you remove company property from the premises without prior approval, further disciplinary action up to and including dismissal may result.* A copy of this document will be placed in your personnel file.

Scheduled Review Date: *None*

EMPLOYEE COMMENTS AND/OR REBUTTAL

_____

_____

_____

(Attach additional sheets if needed.)

X _____

Employee Signature

EMPLOYEE ACKNOWLEDGMENT GOES HERE

Bonus Sample: Employee Time Card Falsification[2]

Long-term exempt employee was recently reclassified as nonexempt and demonstrates apathy toward tracking and reporting his time correctly on his time card.

PERFORMANCE CORRECTION NOTICE

Employee Name: *Santosh Patel*   **Department:** *Field Services*

Date Presented: *June 20, 2017*   **Supervisor:** *Joaquin Sousa*

DISCIPLINARY LEVEL

☐ **Verbal Correction**—(To memorialize the conversation.)

☒ **Written Warning**—(State nature of offense, method of correction, and action to be taken if offense is repeated.)

☐ **Investigatory Leave**—(Include length of time and nature of review.)

☐ **Final Written Warning**

    ☐ Without decision-making leave

    ☐ With decision-making leave (Attach memo of instructions.)

    ☐ With unpaid suspension

SUBJECT: *Failure to follow proper timekeeping guidelines*

☒ Policy/Procedure Violation

☐ Performance Transgression

☒ Behavior/Conduct Infraction

☐ Absenteeism/Tardiness

---

2 Time card falsification may be subject to progressive discipline or be treated as a summary dismissal/ immediate termination, depending on the circumstances. Time is a proxy for money in the workplace, and stealing time is akin to stealing money because the end result is the same: Unearned money ends up in the employee's pocket at the company's expense. In this example, a long-term employee who was historically exempt was recently reclassified as nonexempt. As such, he is still getting used to the new time card system, and the company opts not to terminate.

In Termination Notice 88, in comparison, a short-term employee manipulates the system to show that he worked more hours on paper than he actually did, which resulted in a termination decision—even for a first offense. Always discuss with qualified legal counsel whether the appropriate action surrounding time card manipulation warrants corrective action or termination.

PRIOR NOTIFICATIONS

Level of Discipline	Date	Subject
Verbal	_____	_____
Written	_____	_____
Final Written	_____	_____

Incident Description and Supporting Details: Include the following information: Time, Place, Date of Occurrence, and Persons Present as well as Organizational Impact.

Santosh,

This document serves to notify you that you are being issued a written warning for violating our Effective Timekeeping Rules policy.

On April 25, I trained you and the rest of team on how to complete time cards accurately in light of your recent reclassification to nonexempt status. However, last week I noticed a pattern of your arriving late to your first job but clocking in prior to your start time. We sat together so that I could instruct you one-on-one on the company policy and clock-in procedures.

On May 16, I noticed once again that you clocked into Kronos before you arrived at your first job, so I conducted a two-week look-back audit of your Kronos timekeeping records. Research confirmed that you continued to make errors on your time card submissions, specifically clocking into Kronos before you arrived at your first field location. We likewise sat and discussed this, and you assured me that you understood how to clock in properly and how important it was that the electronic record reflects your physical whereabouts.

Over the past two weeks, I conducted a random audit of your clock-in times relative to your actual start times and found the following:

Date	Clock-In Time	Actual Start Time	Overage
June 3	7:56 A.M.	8:06 A.M.	10 minutes
June 4	1:14 P.M.	1:23 P.M.	9 minutes
June 6	8:00 A.M.	8:06 A.M.	6 minutes
June 7	1:04 P.M.	1:09 P.M.	5 minutes
June 8	1:23 P.M.	1:34 P.M.	11 minutes
June 9	8:01 A.M.	8:09 A.M.	8 minutes
June 11	8:01 A.M.	8:07 A.M.	6 minutes
June 15	8:01 A.M.	8:20 A.M.	19 minutes

TOTAL OVERAGE = 74 minutes

When I discussed this with you, Santosh, you stated that you're still upset about having been reclassified to hourly status and do not agree with the company's decision for this change in your classification. However, as we discussed, this change is a direct result of recent changes in the law regarding wage and hour classification, and as such, it is critical that you assume responsibility for managing this task accurately from this point forward.

Further, as a result of your ongoing incorrect start/stop submissions into Kronos, you are being issued this corrective action memo, which is intended to make you aware of the seriousness of your actions and to afford you the opportunity to correct this issue.

PERFORMANCE IMPROVEMENT PLAN

1. Measurable/Tangible Improvement Goals: *I have coached you individually and the team as a whole on the importance of arriving at your workstation or at your first field appointment on time and clocking in and out of Kronos accurately. I have reiterated the importance of accurate timekeeping during our weekly staff meetings. I also have mentioned in past meetings that occasionally I will be conducting audits on employees to ensure that this is being done correctly.*

Moving forward and at all times you are expected to:

- *Adhere to department and company policies, guidelines, and requirements.*

- *Ensure that you are taking lunch no later than five hours after the start of your shift begins and that your lunch break is no longer than sixty minutes.*

- *Ensure that you are clocking into Kronos when you arrive to the job (expected time is 8:00 A.M.) and clocking out of Kronos upon completion of your last job—NOT while driving to the job or when returning home.*

- *Notify your supervisor immediately if you find that you may need to work additional hours to complete your work. You are likewise required to notify your supervisor prior to reporting to work/work areas that you are not assigned to and assisting other technicians.*

- *Status yourself correctly and accurately in Kronos when on lunch and breaks.*

2. Training or Special Direction Provided: *Please familiarize yourself with Kronos time card reporting procedures and other equipment or policies that you need to report to work and record your time accurately. You may reach out to Payroll with specific questions that go beyond my training sessions.*

3. Interim Performance Evaluation Necessary? *No*

4. Our **Employee Assistance Program** (EAP) provider, Prime Behavioral Health Group, can be confidentially reached to assist you at (800) 555-5555. This is strictly voluntary. A booklet regarding the EAP's services is available from Human Resources.

5. In addition, I recognize that you may have certain ideas to improve your performance. Therefore, I encourage you to provide your own **Personal Improvement Plan Input and Suggestions:**

_____

_____

_____

(Attach additional sheets if needed.)

OUTCOMES AND CONSEQUENCES

Positive: I will remain available to help you and discuss areas where you require additional support. _Your accurate time card submissions will help us account for and assign resources appropriately and manage our budget efficiently._

Negative: _Immediate and sustained improvement is required. Future violations of this or any company policy, whether or not specifically outlined above, may result in further corrective action up to and including termination._ A copy of this document will be placed in your personnel file.

Scheduled Review Date: _None_

EMPLOYEE COMMENTS AND/OR REBUTTAL

_____

_____

_____

(Attach additional sheets if needed.)

X _____

Employee Signature

EMPLOYEE ACKNOWLEDGMENT GOES HERE

#17 Leaving the Work Site During a Regularly Scheduled Shift

Printer leaves the shop floor unannounced and takes unscheduled and extended breaks.

PERFORMANCE CORRECTION NOTICE

Employee Name: *Danny Fontaine*   **Department:** *Print Shop*

Date Presented: *April 25, 2017*   **Supervisor:** *Rosalind Libretto*

DISCIPLINARY LEVEL

☐ **Verbal Correction**—(To memorialize the conversation.)

☒ **Written Warning**—(State nature of offense, method of correction, and action to be taken if offense is repeated.)

☐ **Investigatory Leave**—(Include length of time and nature of review.)

☐ **Final Written Warning**

　☐ Without decision-making leave

　☐ With decision-making leave (Attach memo of instructions.)

　☐ With unpaid suspension

SUBJECT: *Leaving the work site during a regularly scheduled shift*

☒ Policy/Procedure Violation

☒ Performance Transgression

☐ Behavior/Conduct Infraction

☐ Absenteeism/Tardiness

PRIOR NOTIFICATIONS

Level of Discipline	Date	Subject
Verbal	*May 17, 2017*	*Unauthorized, unscheduled absence*
	Nov 15, 2016	*Unauthorized, unscheduled absence*
	June 17, 2016	*Substandard production*
Written	_____	_____
Final Written	_____	_____

Incident Description and Supporting Details: Include the following information: Time, Place, Date of Occurrence, and Persons Present as well as Organizational Impact.

Danny,

On Friday, April 18, you clocked out for your one-hour lunch period at 1:01 P.M. and clocked back in at 2:04. However, you were later seen leaving the building at around 2:30 and returning at approximately 3:40. You did not inform your supervisor of your where-abouts during this absence, and you were away from your workstation for over an hour. Your absence was witnessed by security officer Brenda Nettleton and your late return by your two coworkers. This issue was not brought to your immediate attention because I was away for one week on business.

On Tuesday, April 22, you were observed taking your ten-minute morning break and leaving the premises at 9:45 A.M. However, you did not return to your workstation until 10:18. You are entitled to a ten-minute break, yet you remained away from the workplace for over a half hour. This likewise violates company policy.

PERFORMANCE IMPROVEMENT PLAN

1. Measurable/Tangible Improvement Goals: *Danny, I expect you to never again leave your workstation without prior approval from your immediate supervisor. You are to limit your breaks to no more and no less than ten minutes at all times.*

2. Training or Special Direction to Be Provided: *Please review your employee handbook to familiarize yourself with company expectations of your day-to-day performance. A copy of your job description is attached to this document for the same purpose.*

3. Interim Performance Evaluation Necessary? *Yes. Because your recent attendance issues and time away from your workstation have recurred, I will reissue a performance evaluation that addresses your overall performance, although it is not time for your regularly scheduled review. We will meet next week to review this performance appraisal.*

4. Our **Employee Assistance Program** (EAP) provider, Prime Behavioral Health Group, can be confidentially reached to assist you at (800) 555-5555. This is strictly voluntary. A booklet regarding the EAP's services is available from Human Resources.

5. In addition, I recognize that you may have certain ideas to improve your performance. Therefore, I encourage you to provide your own **Personal Improvement Plan Input and Suggestions:**

_____

_____

_____

(Attach additional sheets if needed.)

OUTCOMES AND CONSEQUENCES

Positive: I will remain available to help you and discuss areas where you require additional support. If you meet your performance goals, no further disciplinary action will be taken regarding this issue.

Negative: *You are now being placed on notice that if you ever again leave your workstation during your normally scheduled work hours without informing your supervisor and gaining her permission, you may be dismissed. In addition, if you fail to adhere to your ten-minute break period, further disciplinary action up to and including termination may result.* A copy of this document will be placed in your personnel file.

Scheduled Review Date: *One week (May 2)*

EMPLOYEE COMMENTS AND/OR REBUTTAL

_____

_____

_____

(Attach additional sheets if needed.)

X _____
Employee Signature

EMPLOYEE ACKNOWLEDGMENT GOES HERE

#18 Working Unauthorized Overtime

An administrative assistant punches out at 5:00 P.M., the end of her regularly scheduled work shift, and then returns to the office to continue working (thereby violating instructions given at a previous coaching session that she not work unauthorized overtime). The supervisor fears that the employee will burn out under stress that could be related to her long hours and failure to take appropriate breaks.

PERFORMANCE CORRECTION NOTICE

Employee Name: *Gail Gleason*   **Department:** *Human Resources*

Date Presented: *July 7, 2017*   **Supervisor:** *Eileen Bernards*

DISCIPLINARY LEVEL

☒ **Verbal Correction**—(To memorialize the conversation.)

☐ **Written Warning**—(State nature of offense, method of correction, and action to be taken if offense is repeated.)

☐ **Investigatory Leave**—(Include length of time and nature of review.)

☐ **Final Written Warning**

    ☐ Without decision-making leave

    ☐ With decision-making leave (Attach memo of instructions.)

    ☐ With unpaid suspension

SUBJECT: *Working unauthorized overtime*

☒ Policy/Procedure Violation

☐ Performance Transgression

☐ Behavior/Conduct Infraction

☐ Absenteeism/Tardiness

PRIOR NOTIFICATIONS

Level of Discipline	Date	Subject
Verbal	_____	_____
Written	_____	_____
Final Written	_____	_____

Incident Description and Supporting Details: Include the following information: Time, Place, Date of Occurrence, and Persons Present as well as Organizational Impact.

Dear Gail,

Yesterday you clocked out at 5:00 P.M., your regularly scheduled time off, and then returned to the office to continue working. Janet Sorensen, a supervisor working late that night, observed you working until 8:00 and commented to me on what a diligent and responsible employee you are. As much as I appreciate your dedication to this job, Gail, I need to formalize my feelings about working overtime without proper credit.

Just one month ago I met with you and asked you not to work through your breaks and lunches. I explained that you are entitled by law to two ten-minute breaks during the day: one in the morning and one in the afternoon. Your lunch period lasts from 12:00 to 12:30. I also explained that your working past 5:00 without being on the clock places the company at risk of violating the Fair Labor Standards Act. The fact that you were not authorized to work those hours might not protect the company from violating the law. I specifically told you that any further occurrences would have to be handled as discipline, and you agreed to this.

Therefore, to protect the company, I must formally document that we are committed to protecting our organization's exemption status. As a human resources professional, I know that you'll take this action in the spirit in which it was meant. In addition, the three hours you worked last night will be credited toward your overtime this week.

PERFORMANCE IMPROVEMENT PLAN

1. Measurable/Tangible Improvement Goals: *Gail, I expect that you will communicate with me if you project that you will have difficulty meeting your work goals. I want you to inform me as well if I'm putting too much work on your desk at any given time. Finally, I expect you to work overtime only when you are properly clocked in and receiving overtime credit.*

2. Training or Special Direction Provided: *Attached is a copy of the firm's Working Hours policy. Please pay special attention to the section entitled Nonexempt Employees, and let me know if you have any questions.*

3. Interim Performance Evaluation Necessary? *No*

4. Our **Employee Assistance Program** (EAP) provider, Prime Behavioral Health Group, can be confidentially reached to assist you at (800) 555-5555. This is strictly voluntary. A booklet regarding the EAP's services is available from Human Resources.

5. In addition, I recognize that you may have certain ideas to improve your performance. Therefore, I encourage you to provide your own **Personal Improvement Plan Input and Suggestions:**

_____

_____

_____

(Attach additional sheets if needed.)

OUTCOMES AND CONSEQUENCES

Positive: I will remain available to help you and discuss areas where you require additional support. If you meet your performance goals, no further disciplinary action will be taken regarding this issue.

Negative: *Gail, please do not engage in unauthorized overtime again.*[3] *Failure to abide by this agreement may lead to further disciplinary action.* A copy of this document will be placed in your personnel file.

Scheduled Review Date: *None*

EMPLOYEE COMMENTS AND/OR REBUTTAL

_____

_____

_____

(Attach additional sheets if needed.)

X _____
Employee Signature

EMPLOYEE ACKNOWLEDGMENT GOES HERE

---

3 This is a lightly stated negative consequence because the supervisor appreciated the good will and extra effort that the employee put forth in working overtime. Nevertheless, the employee violated a clear directive and certainly exposed the company to a wage and hour claim for overtime—even if that overtime wasn't authorized by management. Remember, the wage and hour board will not consider whether overtime was authorized; the fact that the employee worked is all that counts to substantiate a claim for back wages.

#19 Disclosure of Confidential Information About the Company or Its Customers

Buyer discloses information about a bidding price to a competitor and loses a sale.

PERFORMANCE CORRECTION NOTICE

Employee Name: *Brent Goldman*   **Department:** *Purchasing*

Date Presented: *August 8, 2017*   **Supervisor:** *Raul Reisman*

DISCIPLINARY LEVEL

☐ **Verbal Correction**—(To memorialize the conversation.)

☒ **Written Warning**—(State nature of offense, method of correction, and action to be taken if offense is repeated.)

☐ **Investigatory Leave**—(Include length of time and nature of review.)

☐ **Final Written Warning**

    ☐ Without decision-making leave

    ☐ With decision-making leave (Attach memo of instructions.)

    ☐ With unpaid suspension

SUBJECT: *Disclosure of confidential information*

☒ Policy/Procedure Violation

☒ Performance Transgression

☐ Behavior/Conduct Infraction

☐ Absenteeism/Tardiness

PRIOR NOTIFICATIONS

Level of Discipline	Date	Subject
Verbal	_____	_____
Written	_____	_____
Final Written	_____	_____

Incident Description and Supporting Details: Include the following information: Time, Place, Date of Occurrence, and Persons Present as well as Organizational Impact.

Brent,

On August 1, you conducted a telephone conversation with Morris Kirschenbaum, a wholesaler, regarding the price of switch plates for an upcoming sale. Specifically, you told Mr. Kirschenbaum that the best bid that you currently had was $0.20 each for a lot. Another wholesaler, Fred Schiller, whom we've worked with for the past two and a half years, learned of your disclosure to Mr. Kirschenbaum. Mr. Schiller later refused to honor our original bid and consequently severed our working relationship because you disclosed confidential information to a third party.

This disclosure of confidential pricing information violates policy 3.01, Confidential Information, which states: "All sales price bids are to be kept strictly confidential. Release of prior sales or present bids is strictly prohibited."

PERFORMANCE IMPROVEMENT PLAN

1. Measurable/Tangible Improvement Goals: *Brent, I expect you to abide by all established policies and procedures. I also expect that you will never again display such a serious lack of judgment or discretion by sharing bid prices in advance of a sale.*

2. Training or Special Direction to Be Provided: *Policy 3.01 is attached. Please read this policy immediately and see me with any questions that you may have.*

3. Interim Performance Evaluation Necessary? *No*

4. Our **Employee Assistance Program** (EAP) provider, Prime Behavioral Health Group, can be confidentially reached to assist you at (800) 555-5555. This is strictly voluntary. A booklet regarding the EAP's services is available from Human Resources.

5. In addition, I recognize that you may have certain ideas to improve your performance. Therefore, I encourage you to provide your own **Personal Improvement Plan Input and Suggestions:**

_____

_____

_____

(Attach additional sheets if needed.)

OUTCOMES AND CONSEQUENCES

Positive: I will remain available to help you and discuss areas where you require additional support. If you meet your performance goals, no further disciplinary action will be taken regarding this issue. *In addition, you will help our company remain profitable by ensuring that our bids are competitive and that our relationships with our vendors remain solid.*

Negative: *If you ever again divulge confidential company information regarding pricing, bids, or any other protected areas of information, disciplinary action up to and including dismissal may result.* A copy of this document will be placed in your personnel file.

Scheduled Review Date: *None*

EMPLOYEE COMMENTS AND/OR REBUTTAL

_____

_____

_____

(Attach additional sheets if needed.)

X _____
Employee Signature

EMPLOYEE ACKNOWLEDGMENT GOES HERE

#20 Failure to Follow Company Dress Code

Receptionist arrives at work in blue jeans after having previously been sent home for the same infraction.

PERFORMANCE CORRECTION NOTICE

Employee Name: *Carol Smith*   **Department:** *Commercial Claims*

Date Presented: *June 30, 2017*   **Supervisor:** *Sue O'Connor*

DISCIPLINARY LEVEL

☒ **Verbal Correction**—(To memorialize the conversation.)

☐ **Written Warning**—(State nature of offense, method of correction, and action to be taken if offense is repeated.)

☐ **Investigatory Leave**—(Include length of time and nature of review.)

☐ **Final Written Warning**

    ☐ Without decision-making leave

    ☐ With decision-making leave (Attach memo of instructions.)

    ☐ With unpaid suspension

SUBJECT: *Failure to follow company dress code*

☒ Policy/Procedure Violation

☐ Performance Transgression

☒ Behavior/Conduct Infraction

☐ Absenteeism/Tardiness

PRIOR NOTIFICATIONS

Level of Discipline	Date	Subject
Verbal	_____	_____
Written	_____	_____
Final Written	_____	_____

Incident Description and Supporting Details: Include the following information: Time, Place, Date of Occurrence, and Persons Present as well as Organizational Impact.

Carol,

Two months ago, on April 18, you were sent home for wearing inappropriate clothing to work. At that time, you appeared at work in blue jeans, and this violates company policy. I sent you home to change, and you were not compensated for time away from work. You returned to work in appropriate business attire and confirmed for me that you understood the dress code policy and that you agreed to abide by it. I chose not to formally document your inappropriate dress because I believed we would not have to address this issue again.

Earlier today you again arrived at work in blue jeans. You stated that you were wearing "designer jeans," that the rest of your outfit was appropriate for work, and that your other clothes were all in the laundry. It is also important to note that I was not scheduled to be in the office today, and you might have taken advantage of that. Because of your repeated transgression of this company policy, you are now formally receiving a verbal warning regarding your dress.

PERFORMANCE IMPROVEMENT PLAN

1. Measurable/Tangible Improvement Goals: *Carol, I expect you to abide by all company standards of performance and conduct, especially the company dress code. Because we work in an insurance claims center, all employees are expected to adhere to a more formal code of dress, as outlined in company policy 6.04:*

> *Our professional atmosphere is maintained in part by the image that our employees present to customers and vendors. Employees should, therefore, utilize good judgment in determining their dress and appearance. Employees who are inappropriately dressed will be sent home and directed to return to work in proper attire. Such employees will not be compensated for the time away from work.*

> *Specific guidelines for female employees are: Skirt lengths should be appropriate for a business office. Jeans, tennis shoes, slippers, sweatshirts, jogging suits, and backless halter-type tops are prohibited.*

2. Training or Special Direction to Be Provided: *Attached to this document is a copy of Dress Code policy 6.04. Please read this policy immediately and see me if you have any questions.*

3. Interim Performance Evaluation Necessary? *No*

4. Our **Employee Assistance Program** (EAP) provider, Prime Behavioral Health Group, can be confidentially reached to assist you at (800) 555-5555. This is strictly voluntary. A booklet regarding the EAP's services is available from Human Resources.

5. In addition, I recognize that you may have certain ideas to improve your performance. Therefore, I encourage you to provide your own **Personal Improvement Plan Input and Suggestions:**

_____

_____

_____

(Attach additional sheets if needed.)

OUTCOMES AND CONSEQUENCES

Positive: I will remain available to help you and discuss areas where you require additional support. If you meet your performance goals, no further disciplinary action will be taken regarding this issue. _In addition, you will help our department achieve the desired level of professionalism to conduct our business._

Negative: _You were once again sent home today without pay to change into more professional attire. However, because this is the second time that this has happened, your actions have caused an unnecessary interruption in our department's work flow. Consequently, you are now receiving this verbal warning confirming that if you ever again appear at work in jeans or other inappropriate attire as outlined in policy 6.04, further disciplinary action up to and including dismissal may result._ A copy of this document will be placed in your personnel file.

Scheduled Review Date: _None_

EMPLOYEE COMMENTS AND/OR REBUTTAL

_____

_____

_____

(Attach additional sheets if needed.)

X _____
Employee Signature

EMPLOYEE ACKNOWLEDGMENT GOES HERE

#21 Smoking on Company Grounds

Janitor is found smoking in a restroom even though the company maintains a tobacco-free environment.

PERFORMANCE CORRECTION NOTICE

Employee Name: *Karl Nielsen*   **Department:** *Environmental Services*

Date Presented: *May 1, 2017*   **Supervisor:** *Steve Goldman*

DISCIPLINARY LEVEL

☒ **Verbal Correction**—(To memorialize the conversation.)

☐ **Written Warning**—(State nature of offense, method of correction, and action to be taken if offense is repeated.)

☐ **Investigatory Leave**—(Include length of time and nature of review.)

☐ **Final Written Warning**

    ☐ Without decision-making leave

    ☐ With decision-making leave (Attach memo of instructions.)

    ☐ With unpaid suspension

SUBJECT: *Smoking on company grounds*

☒ Policy/Procedure Violation

☐ Performance Transgression

☒ Behavior/Conduct Infraction

☐ Absenteeism/Tardiness

PRIOR NOTIFICATIONS

Level of Discipline	Date	Subject
Verbal	_____	_____
Written	_____	_____
Final Written	_____	_____

Incident Description and Supporting Details: Include the following information: Time, Place, Date of Occurrence, and Persons Present as well as Organizational Impact.

Karl,

Earlier today, a member of our security department reported that you were smoking a cigarette in the men's restroom on the 27th floor. When I asked you if this was true, you confirmed for me that it was. Specifically, you told me that you were taking your ten-minute morning break and didn't want to take the elevator to the ground level in order to smoke outside. You also told me that you are aware that smoking on company premises is a violation of standard operating procedures.

PERFORMANCE IMPROVEMENT PLAN

1. Measurable/Tangible Improvement Goals: *Karl, I expect you to follow all company standards of performance and conduct, especially a rule that could jeopardize the health or safety of your coworkers. This rule is established not only by our company but by city ordinance. Consequently, I expect you to protect our company from outside legal challenges resulting from breaches of this policy.*

2. Training or Special Direction to Be Provided: *Attached is policy 1.21, Smoking (Tobacco and Tobacco Products). Please read the policy immediately and confirm with me tomorrow that you have read it, understand it, and agree to abide by it.*

3. Interim Performance Evaluation Necessary? *No*

4. Our **Employee Assistance Program** (EAP) provider, Prime Behavioral Health Group, can be confidentially reached to assist you at (800) 555-5555. This is strictly voluntary. A booklet regarding the EAP's services is available from Human Resources.

5. In addition, I recognize that you may have certain ideas to improve your performance. Therefore, I encourage you to provide your own **Personal Improvement Plan Input and Suggestions:**

_____

_____

_____

(Attach additional sheets if needed.)

OUTCOMES AND CONSEQUENCES

Positive: I will remain available to help you and discuss areas where you require additional support. If you meet your performance goals, no further disciplinary action will be taken regarding this issue.

Negative: *Company policy states the following: Smoking and the use of all tobacco products are prohibited inside and on all properties owned and/or operated by Johnson Oil and all of its corporate facilities . . . Employees in violation of this policy shall (1) receive a verbal warning notice for the first violation of this policy, (2) receive a written warning for a second violation, and (3) be subject to termination for a third offense.* A copy of this document will be placed in your personnel file.

Scheduled Review Date: *None*

EMPLOYEE COMMENTS AND/OR REBUTTAL

_____

_____

_____

(Attach additional sheets if needed.)

X _____

Employee Signature

EMPLOYEE ACKNOWLEDGMENT GOES HERE

#22 Unauthorized Release of References
to Prospective Employers

PERFORMANCE CORRECTION NOTICE

Employee Name: *Dave Winterfeld*   **Department:** *Corporate Finance*

Date Presented: *December 9, 2017*   **Supervisor:** *Dave Collins*

DISCIPLINARY LEVEL

☐ **Verbal Correction**—(To memorialize the conversation.)

☒ **Written Warning**—(State nature of offense, method of correction, and action to be taken if offense is repeated.)

☐ **Investigatory Leave**—(Include length of time and nature of review.)

☐ **Final Written Warning**

    ☐ Without decision-making leave

    ☐ With decision-making leave (Attach memo of instructions.)

    ☐ With unpaid suspension

SUBJECT: *Unauthorized release of references to prospective employers*

☒ Policy/Procedure Violation

☐ Performance Transgression

☐ Behavior/Conduct Infraction

☐ Absenteeism/Tardiness

PRIOR NOTIFICATIONS

Level of Discipline	Date	Subject
Verbal	_____	_____
Written	_____	_____
Final Written	_____	_____

Incident Description and Supporting Details: Include the following information: Time, Place, Date of Occurrence, and Persons Present as well as Organizational Impact.

Dave,

Our organization maintains a strict corporate policy that no information is to be shared with prospective employers regarding current or past workers' performance records. However, Laura Faraci, a former financial analyst who reported to you for three years and who left the company two months ago, complained to Human Resources yesterday that you provided information about her performance to a prospective employer. This information may preclude her from attaining that position, and she has consequently threatened to retain an attorney to protect her rights.

You subsequently admitted to sharing subjective information about Laura's performance with a peer in another organization. Regardless of the existing relationship that you have with this peer, the liability exposure to our organization remains the same. As such, you have violated our organization's standards of performance and conduct. You have, however, accepted full responsibility for your actions. I expect that we will never again have to broach this issue.

PERFORMANCE IMPROVEMENT PLAN

1. Measurable/Tangible Improvement Goals: *Dave, I expect you, as a corporate controller and officer of this company, to follow duly established rules and regulations. I expect you to equally enforce these very same rules.*

2. Training or Special Direction to Be Provided: *You attended a management training workshop this past summer that specifically addressed the liabilities inherent in providing subjective references, including defamation and invasion of privacy. In addition, you signed an agreement stipulating that no information may be given out on an informal basis to other organizations, as this could be interpreted as subjective performance feedback on our company's part. See me if you ever again question how certain rules apply to the workplace or if exceptions can be made.*

3. Interim Performance Evaluation Necessary? *Yes. Because this incident is now the third occurrence of problematic performance that we have informally discussed in the last two months (the other two include excessive, unauthorized absence and the inappropriate use of upgraded rental cars while on business travel), I have decided that an interim performance evaluation is necessary. I will meet with you in one week to review your performance. Please complete a self-evaluation of your strengths, areas in need of improvement, and first-quarter goals by December 16. I will meet with you to evaluate your self-evaluation at that time. I will then compose my own evaluation of your overall performance considering your input.4*

4. Our **Employee Assistance Program** (EAP) provider, Prime Behavioral Health Group, can be confidentially reached to assist you at (800) 555-5555. This is strictly voluntary. A booklet regarding the EAP's services is available from Human Resources.

---

4 When an out-of-cycle performance review is administered, it should show that the employee is not meeting company expectations. Therefore, there is agreement between the progressive discipline documentation and the performance evaluation.

5. In addition, I recognize that you may have certain ideas to improve your performance. Therefore, I encourage you to provide your own **Personal Improvement Plan Input and Suggestions:**

_____

_____

_____

(Attach additional sheets if needed.)

OUTCOMES AND CONSEQUENCES

Positive: I will remain available to help you and discuss areas where you require additional support. If you meet your performance goals, no further disciplinary action will be taken regarding this issue.

Negative: *You are now being placed on notice that if you again engage in conduct of this nature, you may be dismissed.* A copy of this document will be placed in your personnel file.

Scheduled Review Date: *December 16, 2017*

EMPLOYEE COMMENTS AND/OR REBUTTAL

_____

_____

_____

(Attach additional sheets if needed.)

X _____
Employee Signature

EMPLOYEE ACKNOWLEDGMENT GOES HERE

#23 Email Misuse (Nonwork-Related Usage)

Company newsletter editor posts personal information on the company's email system, thereby violating the company's communication policy. Note that this employee has violated multiple rules and patently disobeyed his supervisor's direct instructions over several months; moreover, the employee has misrepresented his actions to his boss. The supervisor wished to terminate the employee for dishonesty, insubordination, and multiple policy infractions. However, since the employee had never been given any previous written warnings, Human Resources placed the worker on final written warning.

PERFORMANCE CORRECTION NOTICE

Employee Name: *Irwin Mann*   **Department:** *Information Systems*

Date Presented: *February 4, 2017*   **Supervisor:** *Bill Culligan*

DISCIPLINARY LEVEL

☐ **Verbal Correction**—(To memorialize the conversation.)

☐ **Written Warning**—(State nature of offense, method of correction, and action to be taken if offense is repeated.)

☐ **Investigatory Leave**—(Include length of time and nature of review.)

☒ **Final Written Warning**

   ☒ Without decision-making leave

   ☐ With decision-making leave (Attach memo of instructions.)

   ☐ With unpaid suspension

SUBJECT: *Violation of company policy 6.05, Voice and Electronic Mail; insubordination; failure to follow reasonable directives; dishonesty*

☒ Policy/Procedure Violation

☒ Performance Transgression

☒ Behavior/Conduct Infraction

☐ Absenteeism/Tardiness

PRIOR NOTIFICATIONS

Level of Discipline	Date	Subject
Verbal	_____	_____
Written	_____	_____
Final Written	_____	_____

Incident Description and Supporting Details: Include the following information: Time, Place, Date of Occurrence, and Persons Present as well as Organizational Impact.

Irwin,

On December 15, 2017, while I was scanning the company's email printout, I came across a document that was apparently a sexually oriented and offensive joke titled, "Forbidden Zone." I brought this immediately to your attention and told you that I didn't find it appropriate that you, our company's newsletter editor, would poke fun at our organization and its key management members. I told you that I found your humor sarcastic and offensive. You made a sardonic remark about gay people and their workplace preferences. I told you, "You've got to stop running these inappropriate email missives. Got it?" You responded reluctantly, "Got it." I assumed that we would no longer have to address this issue.

On January 7, 2017, I witnessed you abusing the company's email system for a second time. I walked up behind you and saw you posting horse racing results from the night before. I asked you what you were doing, and you responded, "I just had some personal business to attend to." I explained to you that you had committed that you would no longer abuse the company's email system. You responded, "You told me to stop writing inappropriate jokes in the newsletter. I didn't know that included racing results." I stated, "I'm reminding you again: Stop abusing the company email system."

On February 1, 2017, I conducted a standard email review for the most recent two-week period. I was surprised and disappointed to learn that you had ignored my prior warnings and continued to send racing results. As a matter of fact, less than half of the messages you sent were work-related; the majority were personal. I asked you later that day if you had any problems with the issues we had discussed previously regarding email misuse. You told me everything was "fine and dandy." I asked you if there was anything else you wanted or needed to share with me. You said, "No." I called you into my office at day's end to share the email log results that I had acquired. When I showed you the email entries you made regarding horse races and the list of nonbusiness emails you had sent, you replied, "Look, I guess I'm not the model employee these days. Please cut me some slack. I'm under a lot of pressure."

This third violation of the company's email policy and my direct requests reveals that you did not take your former warnings as seriously as you should have. Consequently, you are now being placed on a special probation with stringent requirements.

PERFORMANCE IMPROVEMENT PLAN

1. Measurable/Tangible Improvement Goals: *Irwin, I expect you to follow all company policies and procedures, especially those relating to email, Internet, and Intranet usage. As the editor of the company newsletter, I expect you to conduct yourself in a respectful way and to maintain all confidentiality. I expect you to represent yourself and your actions honestly, and I expect you to heed my directions. I hold you fully accountable for all the responsibilities and duties outlined in your job description.*

2. Training or Special Direction to Be Provided: *A copy of policy 6.05 is attached. Note that it says that the following uses of the company's email system are prohibited:*

- *Nonbusiness-related chatter*

- *Use of profanity or suggestive material*

- *Private consulting, commercial enterprises, or any use for personal financial gain*

3. Interim Performance Evaluation Necessary? *No*

4. Our **Employee Assistance Program** (EAP) provider, Prime Behavioral Health Group, can be confidentially reached to assist you at (800) 555-5555. This is strictly voluntary. A booklet regarding the EAP's services is available from Human Resources.

5. In addition, I recognize that you may have certain ideas to improve your performance. Therefore, I encourage you to provide your own **Personal Improvement Plan Input and Suggestions:**

_____

_____

_____

(Attach additional sheets if needed.)

OUTCOMES AND CONSEQUENCES

Positive: I will remain available to help you and discuss areas where you require additional support. If you meet your performance goals, no further disciplinary action will be taken regarding this issue.

Negative: *Working with the company's email system is your essential job function. Because of your lack of discretion, you have now placed your position in serious jeopardy. We are not terminating you at this time. We are, instead, giving you another chance. If you ever again engage in the creation of inappropriate email entries that potentially violate elements of our antidiscrimination policy, especially regarding employees' sexuality or sexual preferences, post horse racing results, or violate any other aspects of the company's email policy, you may be immediately discharged for cause. Furthermore, if you engage in dishonest behavior, send any personal, nonwork-related emails without my prior approval, or violate any other standards of performance and conduct, disciplinary action up to and including dismissal may result.* A copy of this document will be placed in your personnel file.

Scheduled Review Date: *None*

EMPLOYEE COMMENTS AND/OR REBUTTAL

_____

_____

_____

(Attach additional sheets if needed.)

X _____
Employee Signature

EMPLOYEE ACKNOWLEDGMENT GOES HERE

Note: Since this is a special probation with stringent requirements, add the following sentence to the Employee Acknowledgment: "I understand that this is my last chance. If I fail to abide by the tenets of this memo, I will voluntarily resign or be discharged for cause.

Bonus Sample: Email Misuse (Racially Influenced and Distasteful Messaging)

Employee accidentally forwards inappropriate emails to a director in another division, who in turn reports the abuse to the employee's HR department.

PERFORMANCE CORRECTION NOTICE

Employee Name: *Ari Waldman*　　　　　**Department:** *Procurement*

Date Presented: *April 18, 2017*　　　　　**Supervisor:** *Zhang Hsiao*

DISCIPLINARY LEVEL

☐ **Verbal Correction**—(To memorialize the conversation.)

☐ **Written Warning**—(State nature of offense, method of correction, and action to be taken if offense is repeated.)

☐ **Investigatory Leave**—(Include length of time and nature of review.)

☒ **Final Written Warning**

　　☒ Without decision-making leave

　　☐ With decision-making leave (Attach memo of instructions.)

　　☐ With unpaid suspension

SUBJECT: *Misuse of electronic information resources/nonwork-related emails; lack of professional discretion*

☒ Policy/Procedure Violation

☐ Performance Transgression

☒ Behavior/Conduct Infraction

☐ Absenteeism/Tardiness

PRIOR NOTIFICATIONS

Level of Discipline	Date	Subject
Verbal	_____	_____
Written	_____	_____
Final Written	_____	_____

Incident Description and Supporting Details: Include the following information: Time, Place, Date of Occurrence, and Persons Present as well as Organizational Impact.

Ari,

This document serves as a Final Written Warning for violation of our company's Use of Electronic Information Resources policy.

On April 16, you forwarded three emails to six coworkers that were nonwork-related and furthermore were racially/culturally insensitive and distasteful. This lack of judgment on your part caused you to be in direct violation of our Use of Electronic Information Resources policy as well as our company's expectations around professionalism in the workplace.

By your own admission during our meeting, you intended to forward the emails to a select group of coworker friends; however, you mistakenly forwarded them on to a director in our Texas office with a similar name. Upon receiving your emails, the director in Texas promptly replied: "I'm not sure why I'm included in these emails. In the future, please do not forward any questionable nonwork-related emails to me." That individual then forwarded the distasteful emails to our head of Human Resources here in New Hampshire.

The use of company email should be used for company-related communication. Likewise, all other forms of electronic communication (e.g., instant messaging, facsimile, and voice mail) must be utilized for work-related needs. The company population is very diverse, and every employee may have different ideas about what's offensive and what's not offensive. Any employee can easily be offended by such an email or questionable nonwork-related communication (in passing or a mistaken forward, for example), such that feelings can be hurt, trust undermined, relationships damaged, and more. Also, the legal ramifications of a perceived racial slur or sexual innuendo, as demonstrated in the email you sent, can put you and the company at risk.

PERFORMANCE IMPROVEMENT PLAN

1. Measurable/Tangible Improvement Goals: *I expect you to adhere to the Use of Electronic Information Resources policy as well as all professionalism standards outlined in our employee handbook and code of conduct.*

Moreover, email, facsimile, voice mail, texts, and any other electronic information resources are not to be used in a way that is disruptive or offensive to others. Electronic information resources are not to be used for communications that may inadvertently offend others, detract from our inclusive and employee-centric work environment, or otherwise violate our organization's respect in the workplace policy.

2. Training or Special Direction Provided: *You must reacquaint yourself immediately with all policies and procedures as outlined in the employee handbook and code of conduct, especially the Use of Electronic Information Resources policy. If you have any questions, please contact me, another member of management, or Human Resources.*

3. Interim Performance Evaluation Necessary? *No*

4. Our **Employee Assistance Program** (EAP) provider, Prime Behavioral Health Group, can be confidentially reached to assist you at (800) 555-5555. This is strictly voluntary. A booklet regarding the EAP's services is available from Human Resources.

5. In addition, I recognize that you may have certain ideas to improve your performance. Therefore, I encourage you to provide your own **Personal Improvement Plan Input and Suggestions:**

_____

_____

_____

(Attach additional sheets if needed.)

OUTCOMES AND CONSEQUENCES

Positive: I will remain available to help you and discuss areas where you require additional support. If you meet your performance goals and avoid similar indiscretions in the future, no further disciplinary action will be taken regarding this issue.

Negative: *Immediate and sustained improvement is required. Future violations of this or any policy, whether or not specifically outlined above, may result in further disciplinary action, up to and including dismissal.* A copy of this document will be placed in your personnel file.

Scheduled Review Date: *None*

EMPLOYEE COMMENTS AND/OR REBUTTAL

_____

_____

(Attach additional sheets if needed.)

X _____

Employee Signature

EMPLOYEE ACKNOWLEDGMENT GOES HERE

Bonus Sample: Personal Cell Phone Use

Retail sales representative uses his personal cell phone on the sales floor while customers are present, which violates company policy.

PERFORMANCE CORRECTION NOTICE

Employee Name: *Roberto Silva*　　　　**Department:** *Retail Sales*

Date Presented: *April 15, 2017*　　　　**Supervisor:** *Lisa Leibowitz*

DISCIPLINARY LEVEL

☒ **Verbal Correction**—(To memorialize the conversation.)

☐ **Written Warning**—(State nature of offense, method of correction, and action to be taken if offense is repeated.)

☐ **Investigatory Leave**—(Include length of time and nature of review.)

☐ **Final Written Warning**

　☐ Without decision-making leave

　☐ With decision-making leave (Attach memo of instructions.)

　☐ With unpaid suspension

SUBJECT: *Personal cell phone use on the sales floor*

☒ Policy/Procedure Violation

☒ Performance Transgression

☒ Behavior/Conduct Infraction

☐ Absenteeism/Tardiness

PRIOR NOTIFICATIONS

Level of Discipline	Date	Subject
Verbal	_____	_____
Written	_____	_____
Final Written	_____	_____

Incident Description and Supporting Details: Include the following information: Time, Place, Date of Occurrence, and Persons Present as well as Organizational Impact.

Roberto,

On April 14, you were observed using your personal cell phone for nonwork-related reasons while on the sales floor, which violates our company's Cellular Phone/PDA Usage policy. Personal cell phones and personal digital assistants are not permitted on the sales floor at any time during a retail representative's shift. You were instructed and informed about this policy when you went through new hire orientation, and as you are aware, this policy is consistently enforced in our store. The cellular phone policy states the following:

It is the policy in Retail Sales Stores that usage of cellular phones and personal digital assistants (PDAs), while on the clock, is not allowed in the work area. The use of such devices must not disrupt business operations or hinder an employee's ability to focus on performing work. It is the policy of the Retail Sales Department that all employees are to refrain from using their personal cell phones on the floor while working.

Further, as we discussed, personal cell phone usage on company premises during working hours is disruptive to your customer service responsibilities and a distraction to other employees. If you need to make a personal call outside of prescheduled breaks, you are to notify your supervisor (or, if not available, another leader on the floor), status yourself correctly, and utilize the break room or anywhere where your phone calls will not be distracting to others—but never on the sales floor itself. This document subsequently serves as a documented verbal warning for violation of this company policy.

PERFORMANCE IMPROVEMENT PLAN

1. Measurable/Tangible Improvement Goals: *Roberto, you are not to use your personal cell phone during business hours unless there is an emergency, which should be communicated to your supervisor in advance, if possible. In exceptional cases of emergency, any calls must be taken outside the retail sales area. Immediate and sustained improvement is required.*

2. Training or Special Direction Provided: *You are required to reacquaint yourself with the Cellular Phone/PDA Usage policy. If you have any questions, please contact me, any other member of the retail management team, or your Human Resources Business Partner.*

3. Interim Performance Evaluation Necessary? *No*

4. Our **Employee Assistance Program** (EAP) provider, Prime Behavioral Health Group, can be confidentially reached to assist you at (800) 555-5555. This is strictly voluntary. A booklet regarding the EAP's services is available from Human Resources.

5. In addition, I recognize that you may have certain ideas to improve your performance. Therefore, I encourage you to provide your own **Personal Improvement Plan Input and Suggestions:**

_____

_____

_____

(Attach additional sheets if needed.)

OUTCOMES AND CONSEQUENCES

Positive: I will remain available to help you and discuss areas where you require additional support. If you meet your performance goals, no further disciplinary action will be taken regarding this issue.

Negative: *You must clearly understand, however, that failure to demonstrate immediate and sustained improvement may result in further disciplinary action up to and including dismissal.* A copy of this document will be placed in your personnel file.

Scheduled Review Date: *None*

EMPLOYEE COMMENTS AND/OR REBUTTAL

_____

_____

_____

(Attach additional sheets if needed.)

X _____
Employee Signature

EMPLOYEE ACKNOWLEDGMENT GOES HERE

#24 Off-Duty Conduct and "Moonlighting"

Company electrician works three nights a week for an outside contractor; she reports to work tired, is limited in her ability to work overtime, and makes follow-up phone calls for her side business while in the primary employer's office.

PERFORMANCE CORRECTION NOTICE

Employee Name: *Jacqueline Lawrence*   **Department:** *Engineering*

Date Presented: *May 15, 2017*   **Supervisor:** *Jack Gregory*

DISCIPLINARY LEVEL

☐ **Verbal Correction**—(To memorialize the conversation.)

☒ **Written Warning**—(State nature of offense, method of correction, and action to be taken if offense is repeated.)

☐ **Investigatory Leave**—(Include length of time and nature of review.)

☐ **Final Written Warning**

    ☐ Without decision-making leave

    ☐ With decision-making leave (Attach memo of instructions.)

    ☐ With unpaid suspension

SUBJECT: *Off-duty conduct/moonlighting affecting your performance*

☒ Policy/Procedure Violation

☒ Performance Transgression

☒ Behavior/Conduct Infraction

☐ Absenteeism/Tardiness

PRIOR NOTIFICATIONS

Level of Discipline	Date	Subject
Verbal	_____	_____
Written	_____	_____
Final Written	_____	_____

Incident Description and Supporting Details: Include the following information: Time, Place, Date of Occurrence, and Persons Present as well as Organizational Impact.

Jacqueline,

It has recently come to my attention that you are working three nights a week for our contracting service, Vanguard Electrical. Specifically, you work Monday, Tuesday, and Thursday nights from 6:00 P.M. to 12:30 A.M. As a result, you have appeared at work tired and unfocused on the days following your late-night side job. In addition, you have been unable to perform overtime when I have asked you to volunteer over the past month. Although I have not made overtime mandatory to this point, it will be mandatory for the next month as we prepare for our upcoming summer company reunion. Finally, I audited your telephone bills for the past two months and found that a significant number of calls—up to thirty per month—were placed to Vanguard Electrical or to customers of Vanguard Electrical.

Our company's policy on outside employment is stated this way in the employee hand-book:

> *While employed at our firm, employees are expected to devote their energies to their jobs. For this reason, second jobs are strongly discouraged. Strictly prohibited is outside employment that:*
>
> - *Conflicts with an employee's work schedule, duties, and responsibilities*
>
> - *Impairs or has a detrimental effect on the employee's work performance*
>
> - *Requires the employee to conduct outside work or related activities on company property during the employer's working hours or using the employer's facilities and/ or equipment*

When asked about this, you stated that you limited all calls to your lunch periods and breaks. However, your current outside employment is interfering with our organization's legitimate business interests in violation of our policy.

PERFORMANCE IMPROVEMENT PLAN

1. Measurable/Tangible Improvement Goals: *Jacque, while our company doesn't seek to interfere with the off-duty and personal conduct of its employees, your current activities are interfering with our organization's legitimate business interests. Although I will not mandate that you give up your nighttime work with our vendor, you will very likely need to change your schedule immediately so that you will no longer violate our policy. I expect you to report to work in the proper physical and mental condition to perform your job. I expect you and your coworkers to be available for overtime at all times, whether planned in advance or scheduled the same day. And I expect you never again to conduct outside business on company time, on company premises, or using company equipment like telephones, faxes, or computers. You have indicated your agreement to follow these requirements going forward, and for that reason we are not terminating your employment or issuing you a final written warning.*

2. Training or Special Direction to Be Provided: *I am attaching a copy of our Outside Employment policy with this memo. I expect you to abide by its rules at all times. Please pay special attention to the sections on Prohibited Employment and Remedial Action. See me if you have any questions regarding the policy.*

3. Interim Performance Evaluation Necessary? *No*

4. Our **Employee Assistance Program** (EAP) provider, Prime Behavioral Health Group, can be confidentially reached to assist you at (800) 555-5555. This is strictly voluntary. A booklet regarding the EAP's services is available from Human Resources.

5. In addition, I recognize that you may have certain ideas to improve your performance. Therefore, I encourage you to provide your own **Personal Improvement Plan Input and Suggestions:**

_____

_____

_____

(Attach additional sheets if needed.)

OUTCOMES AND CONSEQUENCES

Positive: I will remain available to help you and discuss areas where you require additional support. If you meet your performance goals, no further disciplinary action will be taken regarding this issue. *In addition, I believe that you will gain greater job satisfaction by focusing on one position, reporting to work in fit condition, and relieving the stress that comes with performing outside work on company time. You will also increase your earning potential by working overtime here, which will be paid at time-and-a-half under certain circumstances.*[5]

Negative: *You are now formally notified that if you again report to work in a tired or unfit condition, or if your work suffers because of improper judgment or careless errors, disciplinary action up to and including dismissal may occur. Similarly, if you make even one more phone call, fax, or computer entry dealing with your outside business, you will be subject to immediate dismissal.* A copy of this document will be placed in your personnel file.

Scheduled Review Date: *None*

---

5 The time-and-a-half payment for overtime depends on the state that you reside in. In most states, overtime is governed by a weekly threshold of forty hours. (If the employee works over forty hours in a workweek, all hours over forty are paid at time-and-a-half.) In certain states, overtime is governed by a daily threshold of eight hours in addition to the weekly threshold. (If the employee works over eight hours in a day, regardless of the number of weekly hours worked, she will be entitled to overtime for all hours worked in excess of eight.)

EMPLOYEE COMMENTS AND/OR REBUTTAL

_____

_____

_____

(Attach additional sheets if needed.)

X _____

Employee Signature

EMPLOYEE ACKNOWLEDGMENT GOES HERE

PART IV

Performance Transgressions

#25 Substandard Work Performance

Warehouse worker consistently fails to deliver products to departments in a timely fashion. Paperwork is lost. As a result, the work flow is disrupted.

PERFORMANCE CORRECTION NOTICE

Employee Name: *Paul Smith*   **Department:** *Warehouse*

Date Presented: *Friday, May 1, 2017*   **Supervisor:** *Jane Doe*

DISCIPLINARY LEVEL

☐ **Verbal Correction**—(To memorialize the conversation.)

☐ **Written Warning**—(State nature of offense, method of correction, and action to be taken if offense is repeated.)

☐ **Investigatory Leave**—(Include length of time and nature of review.)

☒ **Final Written Warning**

    ☒ Without decision-making leave

    ☐ With decision-making leave (Attach memo of instructions.)

    ☐ With unpaid suspension

SUBJECT: *Substandard work performance*

☒ Policy/Procedure Violation

☒ Performance Transgression

☐ Behavior/Conduct Infraction

☐ Absenteeism/Tardiness

PRIOR NOTIFICATIONS

Level of Discipline	Date	Subject
Verbal	*Jan 13, 2017*	*Substandard work performance*
Written	*Apr 1, 2017*	*Substandard work performance*
Final Written	_____	_____

Incident Description and Supporting Details: Include the following information: Time, Place, Date of Occurrence, and Persons Present as well as Organizational Impact.

Paul,

To date you have had a number of serious performance issues in the warehouse. Now today, on May 1, 2017, you have again failed to perform one of your essential job functions—the timely delivery of supplies. Specifically, you delivered an incomplete order of medical supplies to Nursing Wing A and also failed to provide the proper paperwork to the charge nurse. As a result, there was a delay in the delivery of supplies, and patient care and the work flow were disrupted. This violates our hospital's standards of performance and conduct and also shows a further breach of your responsibilities as outlined in your previous warnings.

PERFORMANCE IMPROVEMENT PLAN

1. Measurable/Tangible Improvement Goals: *Paul, I expect that no further incidents of misplaced or misdelivered packages or orders will occur in the next ninety days. In addition, I require that you communicate both openly and on a timely basis with us concerning the status of your work and anything that prevents you from completing your assignments in a timely manner.*

2. Training or Special Direction Provided: *Dave Wilson and I will commit to spending more time with you providing clear and concise direction and feedback. For the next five days, Dave will meet with you daily before you begin rounds to discuss your delivery agenda.*

3. Interim Performance Evaluation Necessary? *No*

4. Our **Employee Assistance Program** (EAP) provider, Prime Behavioral Health Group, can be confidentially reached to assist you at (800) 555-5555. This is strictly voluntary. A booklet regarding the EAP's services is available from Human Resources.

5. In addition, I recognize that you may have certain ideas to improve your performance. Therefore, I encourage you to provide your own **Personal Improvement Plan Input and Suggestions:**

_____

_____

_____

(Attach additional sheets if needed.)

OUTCOMES AND CONSEQUENCES

Positive: I will remain available to help you and discuss areas where you require additional support. If you meet your performance goals, no further disciplinary action will be taken regarding this issue. *In addition, you will develop a greater sense of accomplishment in helping our hospital to meet its production goals and in providing direct support to our patient care areas.*

Negative: *You are now being placed on final written warning. If at any time in the next ninety days you fail to meet the guidelines established in this disciplinary write-up in terms of the timely delivery of supplies or completed paperwork, or if you violate any other organizational standards of performance and conduct, you may be discharged.* A copy of this document will be placed in your personnel file.

Scheduled Review Date: *Ninety days (August 1, 2017)*

EMPLOYEE COMMENTS AND/OR REBUTTAL

_____
_____
_____

(Attach additional sheets if needed.)

X _____
Employee Signature

EMPLOYEE ACKNOWLEDGMENT GOES HERE

Note: Because this is a final written warning, add this sentence to the end of the Employee Acknowledgment: "In addition, I understand that this is my last chance and that I am in serious jeopardy of losing my job. If I breach any of the performance standards established in this notice, I will voluntarily resign or be discharged for cause."

#26 Substandard Work Performance

Human resources recruitment coordinator provided incorrect information when reporting monthly production results and failed to update company records.

PERFORMANCE CORRECTION NOTICE

Employee Name: *Don Wolcinski*   **Department:** *Human Resources*

Date Presented: *May 1, 2017*   **Supervisor:** *Roger Wyndham*

DISCIPLINARY LEVEL

☐ **Verbal Correction**—(To memorialize the conversation.)

☒ **Written Warning**—(State nature of offense, method of correction, and action to be taken if offense is repeated.)

☐ **Investigatory Leave**—(Include length of time and nature of review.)

☐ **Final Written Warning**

    ☐ Without decision-making leave

    ☐ With decision-making leave (Attach memo of instructions.)

    ☐ With unpaid suspension

SUBJECT: *Substandard work performance*

☒ Policy/Procedure Violation

☒ Performance Transgression

☐ Behavior/Conduct Infraction

☐ Absenteeism/Tardiness

PRIOR NOTIFICATIONS

Level of Discipline	Date	Subject
Verbal	*Apr 2, 2017*	*Substandard performance*
Written	_____	_____
Final Written	_____	_____

Incident Description and Supporting Details: Include the following information: Time, Place, Date of Occurrence, and Persons Present as well as Organizational Impact.

Don,

One month ago, you were given a verbal correction regarding your work performance. That followed an informal coaching session the month before that. Currently, you are not meeting departmental performance standards. Following are some of the outstanding issues that occurred in the past month:

Issue 1: On April 11, I inquired about the status of the March monthly recruitment report. You sent me an email that day with information regarding two of our six divisions. However, both of those reports contained inaccurate information (which I have attached to this document).[1] I double-checked your work by contacting the recruiters whom you support and found that their numbers were different. On April 4, 2017, therefore, I asked you to recheck your figures. However, I received no response to my email. When I emailed you again on April 23 requesting that same information, only then did you bring me the reports with corrections. As a result, you didn't provide me with the information I requested in a timely fashion. Second, the corrected reports that you gave me did not specifically address the inaccuracies in the first report. I would have expected you to point out any inaccurate information.

Issue 2: On April 28 at a monthly department quality assurance meeting, you presented a progress report on quarterly recruitment and turnover results. However, you had not adequately prepared your report, and you subsequently confused the numbers and percentages in front of the group. This further demonstrates a lack of understanding in one of your essential job function areas. As a result, I had to interrupt your presentation and complete your presentation for you.

PERFORMANCE IMPROVEMENT PLAN

1. Measurable/Tangible Improvement Goals: *Don, I expect you to meet the goals that were outlined in your previous warning. Namely, you must clearly communicate any time you have a question about the information given to you by the recruiters whom you support. I expect you to double-check your work against actual company records before presenting me with a final report. I also expect you to clearly account for any discrepancies in your calculations versus the company's final numbers. Finally, I expect you to review your job description to ensure that you are familiar with your primary and secondary job responsibilities.*

2. Training or Special Direction to Be Provided: *I recommend reviewing the textbooks that you used to pass your certification as a Professional in Human Resources from the Society of Human Resources Management. I will meet with you in the next seventy-two hours to review how you calculate our company's cost-per-hire, turnover, and time-to-start ratios.*

3. Interim Performance Evaluation Necessary? *No*

---

1 Whenever possible, always attach original documentation to the warning as evidence.

4. Our **Employee Assistance Program** (EAP) provider, Prime Behavioral Health Group, can be confidentially reached to assist you at (800) 555-5555. This is strictly voluntary. A booklet regarding the EAP's services is available from Human Resources.

5. In addition, I recognize that you may have certain ideas to improve your performance. Therefore, I encourage you to provide your own **Personal Improvement Plan Input and Suggestions:**

_____

_____

_____

(Attach additional sheets if needed.)

OUTCOMES AND CONSEQUENCES

Positive: I will remain available to help you and discuss areas where you require additional support. If you meet your performance goals, no further disciplinary action will be taken regarding this issue. *In addition, you will gain more confidence in performing your job and quantifying the success of the recruitment unit.*

Negative: *You are now being placed on notice that if you fail to meet any standards of performance and conduct at any time in the next ninety days, you will be placed on final written warning. If you fail to meet any goals and objectives outlined in this memo while you are in that final warning period, you may be dismissed.* A copy of this document will be placed in your personnel file.

Scheduled Review Date: *Thirty days (June 1)*

EMPLOYEE COMMENTS AND/OR REBUTTAL

_____

_____

_____

(Attach additional sheets if needed.)

X _____
Employee Signature

EMPLOYEE ACKNOWLEDGMENT GOES HERE

#27 Substandard Work Performance

Secretary continuously mixes up scheduled appointments and fails to complete tasks by deadline.

PERFORMANCE CORRECTION NOTICE

Employee Name: *Theresa Dresher*   **Department:** *R&D*

Date Presented: *April 8, 2017*   **Supervisor:** *Hans Bahr*

DISCIPLINARY LEVEL

☐ **Verbal Correction**—(To memorialize the conversation.)

☒ **Written Warning**—(State nature of offense, method of correction, and action to be taken if offense is repeated.)

☐ **Investigatory Leave**—(Include length of time and nature of review.)

☐ **Final Written Warning**

    ☐ Without decision-making leave

    ☐ With decision-making leave (Attach memo of instructions.)

    ☐ With unpaid suspension

SUBJECT: *Substandard work performance*

☒ Policy/Procedure Violation

☒ Performance Transgression

☐ Behavior/Conduct Infraction

☐ Absenteeism/Tardiness

PRIOR NOTIFICATIONS

Level of Discipline	Date	Subject
Verbal	*Mar 26, 2017*	*Unacceptable work performance*
Written	_____	_____
Final Written	_____	_____

Incident Description and Supporting Details: Include the following information: Time, Place, Date of Occurrence, and Persons Present as well as Organizational Impact.

Theresa,

Over the past two months, you and I have discussed issues regarding your work performance. Specifically, we talked about improving your organizational skills and your ability to get things back to me by deadline. I also brought to your attention that your lack of follow-up has caused confusion regarding my meeting schedule and has impeded my ability to return phone calls in a timely manner.

In addition, I have had to follow up with you on a number of occasions to ensure that your work was getting done. On three different occasions, you had fallen seriously behind in your work and failed to notify me. This occurred with the Hamby, Palmer, and Dollinger accounts. Your filing activities related to my meetings need to be more consistent and timely so that important records are updated on a daily basis. To date, you are still allowing three to five days of filing to accumulate before you place the materials in the appropriate files. All these issues have forced me to divert my time from other business matters.

PERFORMANCE IMPROVEMENT PLAN

1. Measurable/Tangible Improvement Goals: *Theresa, I expect you to be more proactive in managing your workload and my schedule on a day-to-day basis. I expect you to concentrate on your work so that minor and thoughtless errors don't lead to more serious problems down the road.*

2. Training or Special Direction to Be Provided: *Theresa, for the next week, I need to meet with you every day between 4:00 and 4:30 regarding the status of the various projects that you're working on. This added structure should help you meet your performance goals. I encourage you to research time management training workshops that would benefit you; I will be willing to send you to such a workshop on company time and at company expense.*

3. Interim Performance Evaluation Necessary? *No*

4. Our **Employee Assistance Program** (EAP) provider, Prime Behavioral Health Group, can be confidentially reached to assist you at (800) 555-5555. This is strictly voluntary. A booklet regarding the EAP's services is available from Human Resources.

5. In addition, I recognize that you may have certain ideas to improve your performance. Therefore, I encourage you to provide your own **Personal Improvement Plan Input and Suggestions:**

_____

_____

(Attach additional sheets if needed.)

OUTCOMES AND CONSEQUENCES

Positive: I will remain available to help you and discuss areas where you require additional support. If you meet your performance goals, no further disciplinary action will be taken regarding this issue. *In addition, you will develop a greater sense of independence and autonomy on your job.*

Negative: *You are now being placed on notice that you are not meeting departmental performance standards. If at any time in the next thirty days you fail to demonstrate that you are capable of managing my administrative calendar or completing tasks in a timely manner, you will be placed in a thirty-day final warning period. If you fail to meet performance expectations during that final warning period, you may be dismissed.* A copy of this document will be placed in your personnel file.

Scheduled Review Date: *Thirty days (May 8)*

EMPLOYEE COMMENTS AND/OR REBUTTAL

_____

_____

_____

(Attach additional sheets if needed.)

X _____
Employee Signature

EMPLOYEE ACKNOWLEDGMENT GOES HERE

#28 Substandard Work Performance

Accounting clerk with a five-year history of progressive disciplinary measures resumes poor work habits that have been documented in the past. Note as well that the last two years' evaluations have not met standards and that opportunities to discharge this individual were missed on several occasions. However, in this case, the last written disciplinary action is over one year old. Therefore, the company chooses not to terminate at this time and places her on a final written warning plus decision-making leave for excessive telephone calls and substandard performance. The letter of termination is located in Part VII, Termination Notices (Write-Up #85).

PERFORMANCE CORRECTION NOTICE

Employee Name: *Mary Wellington*   **Department:** *Accounting*

Date Presented: *August 31, 2017*   **Supervisor:** *Linda Huntley*

DISCIPLINARY LEVEL

☐ **Verbal Correction**—(To memorialize the conversation.)

☐ **Written Warning**—(State nature of offense, method of correction, and action to be taken if offense is repeated.)

☐ **Investigatory Leave**—(Include length of time and nature of review.)

☒ **Final Written Warning**

    ☐ Without decision-making leave

    ☒ With decision-making leave (Attach memo of instructions.)

    ☐ With unpaid suspension

SUBJECT: *Substandard work performance, excessive telephone usage, unwillingness to perform properly assigned work, refusal to follow proper work instructions, persistent infraction of properly established work rules*

☒ Policy/Procedure Violation

☒ Performance Transgression

☒ Behavior/Conduct Infraction

☐ Absenteeism/Tardiness

PRIOR NOTIFICATIONS

Level of Discipline	Date	Subject
Final Written Warning	Nov 14, 2016	Unsatisfactory performance: substandard productivity
Written Warning	Apr 12, 2016	Excessive personal telephone calls (overall annual performance evaluation score = does not meet expectations)
Written Warning	May 4, 2015	Substandard performance (overall annual performance evaluation score = does not meet expectations)
Final Written Warning	Nov 19, 2014	Substandard performance: lack of follow-through, failure to follow instructions, substandard productivity, careless errors causing a financial loss to the company
Written Warning	Oct 28, 2014	Taking extended breaks
Verbal Warning	Oct 8, 2014	Taking extended breaks
Written Warning	Dec 15, 2012	Excessive absenteeism

Incident Description and Supporting Details: Include the following information: Time, Place, Date of Occurrence, and Persons Present as well as Organizational Impact.

Mary,

There are multiple, serious performance transgressions that you have committed over the past three months that have recently come to our attention as a result of a departmental audit.

They are as follows:

• Issue 1: You were instructed to follow up on two special cases that were greater than $10,000 and to make first-level appeals to Medicare. We were already over the ninety-day guideline to file an appeal. You ignored that fact and filed the appeal anyway. This is a consistent oversight on your part and is one of your essential job responsibilities. Because you failed to meet those requirements, the case will not be considered on its merits, as the timeliness requirements were not met. In two particular cases (Scozzaro, Account #11236, and Seidman, Account #91423), your lack of judgment in taking the next appropriate step to "save the claim" caused our company to lose the right to collect moneys due. The direct loss of income equals approximately 20 percent of $14,200 ($10,000 + $4,200), or $2,840.

• Issue 2: Descanso, Account #91355. Your supervisor, Debbie Gaertner, instructed you in November of 2017 to follow up on this post-ninety-day claim in order to remove it from your books. To date, you have taken no action on this claim. Note that you were placed on a final written warning for this very claim in November of 2014 when it was discovered that your lack of follow-through had barred our company from collecting $1,578.

You changed supervisors in January and in April, so this file was not audited until this month. When I asked you why you hadn't taken care of it or reported to management that it was still open, you admitted that, for various reasons, you "just didn't do it." It is evident that you did not take your former warning seriously.

• Issue 3: Personal phone calls. Following is a list of frequently called personal telephone numbers:

Month	Destination	Number of Personal Calls
June	Home phone 767-6715	7
	Husband's work phone 815-3000	18
	Husband's car phone 451-2921	4
Month total		**29 (31 total; 94% were personal calls)**
July	Home phone 767-6715	7
	Husband's work phone 815-3000	15
	Husband's car phone 451-2921	11
Month total		**33 (45 total; 73% were personal calls)**

In May, you made only one phone call to Medicare for the entire month. Medicare is the only payer you deal with, and this is your primary job responsibility. June's and July's numbers above reveal an excessive number of personal phone calls on company time. This clearly violates numerous warnings that you received for improper telephone usage in the past. It likewise reveals that you did not take your prior warnings as seriously as you should have.

• Issue 4: Failure to follow instructions. On Wednesday morning, August 26, at approximately 9:00, your supervisor, Linda Huntley, instructed you to stop your billing and to begin your Invoice Activity Report (IAR) project. At 11:00, Linda asked you how you were doing. You told her that you were not doing that assigned work but were preparing billing for a coworker. That violated your supervisor's immediate instruction. Linda told you that she needed the IAR by 1:00, but she left the office until 3:00. When she returned at 3:00, you still had not completed the project. You became angry at that point and were rude to her, stating, "Why don't you stop riding me about this already?" You also complained to your coworkers about your supervisor's "hostility" toward you, and they, in turn, complained to Linda about how difficult it is to work with you. Failure to meet deadlines and to communicate appropriately with your peers are ongoing problems that are thoroughly documented in prior performance evaluations and disciplinary write-ups.

PERFORMANCE IMPROVEMENT PLAN

1. Measurable/Tangible Improvement Goals: *Mary, I expect you to adhere strictly to your job duties from this point forward. I expect you to meet all deadlines, and I expect you to inform your supervisor if, for whatever reason, you will not be able to meet a deadline. You are not to make any more personal telephone calls without your supervisor's approval; if emergency calls become necessary, you must inform your supervisor immediately after the call about the nature of the emergency. You must meet all company productivity standards and follow all instructions. You must follow all properly established work rules. Finally, I expect you to complete all the necessary paperwork on the long-overdue Descanso account so as to remove it from our books. This must be completed within four weeks (by September 30).*

2. Training or Special Direction to Be Provided: *Linda will meet with you twice a week for the next month to ensure that your desk activities meet departmental production standards. Each meeting will last from 15 to 30 minutes and will occur as close to the beginning of your shift as possible. Please take advantage of this one-on-one instruction time by preparing questions that you have on your most difficult files.*

In addition, a copy of your job description is attached. Please review it immediately and discuss any questions you have about it with Linda.

Finally, you are now being placed on a one-day paid "day of contemplation" to consider your future with our company. A handout is attached explaining your instructions for this day off and the assignment that will be due should you choose to return to work.

3. Interim Performance Evaluation Necessary? *No. Your past two annual performance reviews show that you have not met performance expectations. I believe that you are not currently meeting performance expectations.*

4. Our **Employee Assistance Program** (EAP) provider, Prime Behavioral Health Group, can be confidentially reached to assist you at (800) 555-5555. This is strictly voluntary. A booklet regarding the EAP's services is available from Human Resources.

5. In addition, I recognize that you may have certain ideas to improve your performance. Therefore, I encourage you to provide your own **Personal Improvement Plan Input and Suggestions:**

_____

_____

_____

(Attach additional sheets if needed.)

OUTCOMES AND CONSEQUENCES

Positive: I will remain available to help you and discuss areas where you require additional support. If you meet your performance goals, no further disciplinary action will be taken regarding this issue.

Negative: *We are choosing not to terminate you at this time, but are, instead, giving you another chance. If in the next ninety days you fail to follow properly established operational procedures, if you make one more personal phone call on company time without my advance approval, if you fail to follow through on your case load, if you fail to follow immediate instructions, or if you fail to meet any other established company policies on performance and conduct, you may be immediately dismissed. Finally, if you fail to complete the Descanso paperwork by September 30, you may likewise be dismissed.* A copy of this document will be placed in your personnel file.

Scheduled Review Date: *Thirty days (September 30)*

EMPLOYEE COMMENTS AND/OR REBUTTAL

_____

_____

_____

(Attach additional sheets if needed.)

X _____

Employee Signature

EMPLOYEE ACKNOWLEDGMENT GOES HERE

Note: Since this is a final written warning with decision-making leave, add the following sentences to the Employee Acknowledgment: "I have also been advised to discuss this with a union steward or any other person that I deem appropriate. I understand that my position is now in jeopardy of being lost and that this is my last chance. Should I fail to abide by the terms and conditions of this agreement, I will voluntarily resign or be discharged for cause."

#29 Substandard Work Performance

Programmer analyst snaps at his internal customers (department heads), refuses to listen, and blows up at others when he's asked to change his schedule on short notice. He also barges into people's meetings when he needs something done and refuses to wait his turn.

PERFORMANCE CORRECTION NOTICE

Employee Name: *Henry Higgins*   **Department:** *Research*

Date Presented: *October 24, 2017*   **Supervisor:** *Gail Monroe*

DISCIPLINARY LEVEL

☐ **Verbal Correction**—(To memorialize the conversation.)

☐ **Written Warning**—(State nature of offense, method of correction, and action to be taken if offense is repeated.)

☐ **Investigatory Leave**—(Include length of time and nature of review.)

☒ **Final Written Warning**

    ☒ Without decision-making leave

    ☐ With decision-making leave (Attach memo of instructions.)

    ☐ With unpaid suspension

SUBJECT: *Substandard work performance and customer service*

☒ Policy/Procedure Violation

☒ Performance Transgression

☒ Behavior/Conduct Infraction

☐ Absenteeism/Tardiness

PRIOR NOTIFICATIONS

Level of Discipline	Date	Subject
Verbal	*Jan 3, 2017*	*Substandard work performance*
Written	*Apr 1, 2017*	*Substandard work performance*
Final Written	_____	_____

Incident Description and Supporting Details: Include the following information: Time, Place, Date of Occurrence, and Persons Present as well as Organizational Impact.

Henry,

Today Rae Mauro (VP, Research Administration), Paula Spellman (Director of Human Resources), and I met with you to discuss problem performance areas brought to our attention by your customers in the departments of Information Systems, Finance, and Purchasing. Namely, your customers have complained that you have demonstrated "explosive anger" on occasion and that your performance has been unpredictable and erratic. The managerial heads of these departments have personally witnessed your voice get louder and your face turn red and have noted your inability or unwillingness to listen to their concerns when you became frustrated during a discussion.

You have been characterized as having demonstrated "overwhelming negativity" and rigidity, which have caused your customers to prefer to "do without" rather than to engage your services. For example, on various occasions you have mentioned that our company is "technically in the Dark Ages," "unwilling to invest money where it's needed most," and "obstinate in its refusal to join the rest of the civilized world." Your lack of service orientation has hurt our department's image and its ability to provide adequate customer service.

PERFORMANCE IMPROVEMENT PLAN

1. Measurable/Tangible Improvement Goals: *Henry, I expect that you will always place your customers' needs first in order to demonstrate our department's commitment to providing our customers with timely solutions. I expect that you will always treat others with dignity and respect and refrain from appearing to talk down to them, to chastise them for their lack of technical knowledge, or to interrupt them before they have completed their thoughts. I expect that you will never again lose your temper under any circumstances.*

In addition, Henry, I want to again further emphasize that you develop a respect for other employees' and my time schedules, requests, and priorities. It is critical that you become more attuned to this immediately and that you ask for a convenient time to meet, giving some estimate of how much time is needed, rather than coming in unannounced without regard for the amount of time that you'll need to solve a problem. Of course, in an emergency, you can interrupt me at any time. Otherwise, please sensitize yourself to my needs and others' needs in this regard.

Finally, I expect you to assume total responsibility for the outcomes of your behavior and interaction with others. I expect that we will never again have to discuss the issue of interpersonal conflict in the workplace or lack of customer service support.

2. Training or Special Direction to Be Provided: *The Human Resources department is currently holding customer service training workshops that are aimed at sensitizing employees about the way they come across and how they can improve their overall customer service presentations. It is mandatory that you sign up for this class this week and attend a workshop in the next two weeks.*

In addition, the Human Resources training and development department is looking into outside training workshops that would benefit you in terms of (a) dealing with interper-

sonal conflict in the workplace and (b) increasing your listening skills. Please contact Paula Spellman by November 1 regarding training opportunities that our organization will pay for in order to increase your skills in these areas.

Also, Paula Spellman and I will set up meetings with Information Services, Finance, and Purchasing in order to rebuild bridges of communication with you. These meetings will occur in the next two weeks.

3. Interim Performance Evaluation Necessary? *No*

4. Our **Employee Assistance Program** (EAP) provider, Prime Behavioral Health Group, can be confidentially reached to assist you at (800) 555-5555. This is strictly voluntary. A booklet regarding the EAP's services is available from Human Resources.

5. In addition, I recognize that you may have certain ideas to improve your performance. Therefore, I encourage you to provide your own **Personal Improvement Plan Input and Suggestions:**

_____

_____

_____

(Attach additional sheets if needed.)

OUTCOMES AND CONSEQUENCES

Positive: I will remain available to help you and discuss areas where you require additional support. If you meet your performance goals, no further disciplinary action will be taken regarding this issue. *In addition, you will develop a greater sense of teamwork and camaraderie as you foster stronger relationships with your customers while enhancing our department's image and capabilities.*

Negative: *You are now being placed on notice that if you ever again engage in behavior that demonstrates "explosive anger" or extreme rudeness or abruptness, if your actions strip people of their respect and dignity, or if you violate our company's policy on harassment by demonstrating hostility toward others, you will be immediately dismissed. Furthermore, Henry, if you continue to receive complaints about substandard customer service or failure to appropriately listen to a customer's needs, further disciplinary action up to and including termination may result.* A copy of this document will be placed in your personnel file.

Scheduled Review Date: *None*

EMPLOYEE COMMENTS AND/OR REBUTTAL

_____

_____

_____

(Attach additional sheets if needed.)

X _____
          Employee Signature

EMPLOYEE ACKNOWLEDGMENT GOES HERE

Note: Because this is a final written warning, add this sentence to the end of the Employee Acknowledgment: "In addition, I understand that this is my last chance and that I am in serious jeopardy of losing my job. If I breach any of the performance standards established in this notice, I will voluntarily resign or be discharged for cause."

#30 Substandard Work Performance

Plant engineer is sloppy, loses paperwork, fails to inform his supervisor of the status of back-logged work on his desk, and demonstrates poor judgment in performing his job.

PERFORMANCE CORRECTION NOTICE

Employee Name: *Jim Farad*   **Department:** *Technical Support Services*

Date Presented: *April 1, 2017*   **Supervisor:** *Al Sommer*

DISCIPLINARY LEVEL

☐ **Verbal Correction**—(To memorialize the conversation.)

☒ **Written Warning**—(State nature of offense, method of correction, and action to be taken if offense is repeated.)

☐ **Investigatory Leave**—(Include length of time and nature of review.)

☐ **Final Written Warning**

   ☐ Without decision-making leave

   ☐ With decision-making leave (Attach memo of instructions.)

   ☐ With unpaid suspension

SUBJECT: *Failure to follow departmental policies and procedures; substandard work performance*

☒ Policy/Procedure Violation

☒ Performance Transgression

☒ Behavior/Conduct Infraction

☐ Absenteeism/Tardiness

PRIOR NOTIFICATIONS

Level of Discipline	Date	Subject
Verbal	_____	_____
Written	_____	_____
Final Written	_____	_____

Incident Description and Supporting Details: Include the following information: Time, Place, Date of Occurrence, and Persons Present as well as Organizational Impact.

Jim,

Your overall performance does not currently meet organizational performance standards. The fact that you have too many work orders open and are not finishing up your work in a timely manner has caused your customers to request that you not be assigned to service their equipment.

Furthermore, as we have discussed numerous times in the past six months, your work area is cluttered with unrepaired equipment. As a result, work orders and equipment are getting misplaced and backlogged. For example, on Monday, February 16, an unrelated Repair Work Order was found inside an incoming folder. The repair order was obviously lost.

You consistently fail to complete scheduled inspection work orders within a reasonable time frame. For example, this year you were again late in completing the research lab's scheduled inspections despite your commitment to the lab manager last year. This jeopardized the lab's license renewal. In addition, because you failed to inform me of the status of your late projects and specific problems in meeting deadlines, I was unaware of the problems until they blew up. This reduces our unit's credibility among our customers as well as my own reputation as an effective manager.

Finally, from a technical standpoint, you are not meeting performance standards. It is not uncommon that I have to repair work that you have attempted—unsuccessfully—to repair. This leads to inefficiency and rework. For example, we purchased a new Forma C02 incubator this year. While it was still under warranty, you took it upon yourself to make inappropriate humidity calibration adjustments. You did more than you should have with a new product under warranty. This reveals poor judgment on your part and could have jeopardized the warranty.

PERFORMANCE IMPROVEMENT PLAN

1. Measurable/Tangible Improvement Goals: *Jim, I expect that you will make an immediate commitment to meeting the performance and conduct standards outlined in this memo. I expect you to openly communicate with me regarding the status of work on your desk— especially work that is behind schedule. I expect you to keep your work area organized by filling all new work orders by the end of the day and by storing unrepaired equipment and parts in an organized manner. I hold you accountable for making timely repairs like everyone else in the department.*

2. Training or Special Direction to Be Provided: *I will personally meet with you three times next week—on Monday, Wednesday, and Friday at 8:00 A.M.—to review the status of the work on your desk. In those meetings, you will need to discuss the status of each project, your progress in meeting deadlines, and your plans to tidy up your work area.*

3. Interim Performance Evaluation Necessary? *Yes. We have privately discussed these issues in my office on three separate occasions over the past six months. Therefore, I will now formally review your performance and issue you an interim evaluation regarding your track record in meeting the essential functions of your job.*

4. Our **Employee Assistance Program** (EAP) provider, Prime Behavioral Health Group, can be confidentially reached to assist you at (800) 555-5555. This is strictly voluntary. A booklet regarding the EAP's services is available from Human Resources.

5. In addition, I recognize that you may have certain ideas to improve your performance. Therefore, I encourage you to provide your own **Personal Improvement Plan Input and Suggestions:**

_____

_____

_____

(Attach additional sheets if needed.)

OUTCOMES AND CONSEQUENCES

Positive: I will remain available to help you and discuss areas where you require additional support. If you meet your performance goals, no further disciplinary action will be taken regarding this issue.

Negative: *You are currently not meeting organizational standards of performance and conduct. If you fail to perform at an acceptable level at any time in the next ninety days, you will be placed in a formal ninety-day probationary period. If you fail to meet performance standards during that ninety-day probationary period, you will be subject to further disciplinary action up to and including dismissal.* A copy of this document will be placed in your personnel file.

Scheduled Review Date: *Two weeks (April 15)*

EMPLOYEE COMMENTS AND/OR REBUTTAL

_____

_____

_____

(Attach additional sheets if needed.)

X _____

Employee Signature

EMPLOYEE ACKNOWLEDGMENT GOES HERE

#31 Substandard Work Performance

Mortgage banking property review appraiser uses inappropriate comps to determine the market value of two properties and thereby disrupts the sale of those properties.

PERFORMANCE CORRECTION NOTICE

Employee Name: *Harry Heffner*   **Department:** *Appraisal*

Date Presented: *March 28, 2017*   **Supervisor:** *Bill Lundquist*

DISCIPLINARY LEVEL

☐ **Verbal Correction**—(To memorialize the conversation.)

☒ **Written Warning**—(State nature of offense, method of correction, and action to be taken if offense is repeated.)

☐ **Investigatory Leave**—(Include length of time and nature of review.)

☐ **Final Written Warning**

   ☐ Without decision-making leave

   ☐ With decision-making leave (Attach memo of instructions.)

   ☐ With unpaid suspension

SUBJECT: *Substandard work performance*

☒ Policy/Procedure Violation

☒ Performance Transgression

☐ Behavior/Conduct Infraction

☐ Absenteeism/Tardiness

PRIOR NOTIFICATIONS

Level of Discipline	Date	Subject
Verbal	_____	_____
Written	_____	_____
Final Written	_____	_____

Incident Description and Supporting Details: Include the following information: Time, Place, Date of Occurrence, and Persons Present as well as Organizational Impact.

Harry,

The Edgar Rabinowitz loan (original review date October 22, 2017) was rejected from the loan pool because the pool reappraisal found your appraised value very out of line. You agreed with the outside appraiser of this wholesale loan that the Rabinowitz property was worth $830,000. The pool, however, appraised this property at $635,000. Your failure to pull and review comps for this property and confirm the outside evaluator's appraisal resulted in the loan being rejected from the pool.

The company also missed the opportunity to sell the Ronald McGlone property (December 16, 2017, review date) because you raised our retail appraiser's original estimate of $86,000 to $103,000. As a desk review appraiser, you must receive my sign-off before altering an in-house appraiser's original estimate. In reviewing your work, I found that the comps that you used to rebut our in-house appraiser's valuation were not appropriate for that specific property because you failed to adjust for certain devaluing factors. For example, the McGlone property was located next to a railroad track and in a brush area.

Both of these examples violate our department's established appraisal review policies and procedures and have had considerable negative financial impact on our business operations.

PERFORMANCE IMPROVEMENT PLAN

1. Measurable/Tangible Improvement Goals: *Harry, I expect you to always clear with me in advance any time you wish to readjust an in-house appraiser's value upward. I also expect you to follow departmental guidelines regarding desk review protocol.*

2. Training or Special Direction to Be Provided: *I will meet with you for one hour per week for the next three weeks to randomly audit your current cases. Please take advantage of that hour time slot to bring up any questions you have regarding more challenging and unconventional appraisals.*

3. Interim Performance Evaluation Necessary? *No*

4. Our **Employee Assistance Program** (EAP) provider, Prime Behavioral Health Group, can be confidentially reached to assist you at (800) 555-5555. This is strictly voluntary. A booklet regarding the EAP's services is available from Human Resources.

5. In addition, I recognize that you may have certain ideas to improve your performance. Therefore, I encourage you to provide your own **Personal Improvement Plan Input and Suggestions:**

_____

_____

_____

(Attach additional sheets if needed.)

OUTCOMES AND CONSEQUENCES

Positive: I will remain available to help you and discuss areas where you require additional support. If you meet your performance goals, no further disciplinary action will be taken regarding this issue. *In addition, you will gain a greater sense of job satisfaction as your confidence and expertise build.*

Negative: *Harry, I know that as a four-year employee with a consistent performance record, you can master the task at hand. For that reason, I am holding you fully accountable for the end result of your evaluations and desk reviews. However, I now have no choice but to place you on a formal ninety-day written warning. If at any time during this period you are unable to perform at an acceptable level or if you fail to follow any company policies or procedures, you may be placed on a ninety-day final written warning. Any transgressions in that final written warning period may result in your dismissal.* **A copy of this document will be placed in your personnel file.**

Scheduled Review Date: *One week (April 4)*

EMPLOYEE COMMENTS AND/OR REBUTTAL

_____

_____

_____

(Attach additional sheets if needed.)

X _____
Employee Signature

EMPLOYEE ACKNOWLEDGMENT GOES HERE

#32 Substandard Customer Service

Maintenance mechanic fails to follow up with customers after repairs are done and often leaves the scene as soon as someone else from his department arrives to help him repair a broken item.

PERFORMANCE CORRECTION NOTICE

Employee Name: *Frank Walters*   **Department:** *Engineering*

Date Presented: *November 27, 2017*   **Supervisor:** *Albert D'Amico*

DISCIPLINARY LEVEL

☒ **Verbal Correction**—(To memorialize the conversation.)

☐ **Written Warning**—(State nature of offense, method of correction, and action to be taken if offense is repeated.)

☐ **Investigatory Leave**—(Include length of time and nature of review.)

☐ **Final Written Warning**

    ☐ Without decision-making leave

    ☐ With decision-making leave (Attach memo of instructions.)

    ☐ With unpaid suspension

SUBJECT: *Substandard customer service*

☒ Policy/Procedure Violation

☒ Performance Transgression

☒ Behavior/Conduct Infraction

☐ Absenteeism/Tardiness

PRIOR NOTIFICATIONS

Level of Discipline	Date	Subject
Verbal	_____	_____
Written	_____	_____
Final Written	_____	_____

Incident Description and Supporting Details: Include the following information: Time, Place, Date of Occurrence, and Persons Present as well as Organizational Impact.

Frank,

On November 20, you failed to complete an air conditioning assignment that you were responsible for as an HVAC engineer. Specifically, you needed to wait for one part from the warehouse to complete the job, yet you went home without completing the work. The HVAC lead engineer on the next shift had to finish your work for you when he was paged to complete the repair. This demonstrates my overall concern that you turn over repairs to the lead person too easily without exhausting all remedies yourself. You also failed to communicate the status of that repair on the repair order worksheet; this caused unnecessary confusion.

Furthermore, you do not follow through with your customers to ensure that a repair was completed adequately. You are expected to make follow-up phone calls or visits after you have completed a repair. You also fail to inform customers that you're there once you arrive to fix something. When you don't announce your presence, customers are not made aware of the repair and assume that it has not been taken care of. This violates departmental policy.

On November 22, when attempting to repair the ventilation in the finance director's office, you requested support from another HVAC engineer. When your coworker arrived to help you, you simply left the area without saying anything. Air conditioning is your specialty, and your arbitrary delegation of the work to your peer was inappropriate and disrupted his schedule.

PERFORMANCE IMPROVEMENT PLAN

1. Measurable/Tangible Improvement Goals: *Frank, I expect you to assume responsibility for the work that is delegated to you via repair orders. I expect you to communicate clearly with your customers once you arrive on the scene and to follow up with them after the fact to ensure their satisfaction. I expect you to communicate any problem areas to your coworkers up front so that they are not blindsided by customer complaints after you have supposedly resolved the situation. And I expect you to appreciate your coworkers' support and to learn from them while they assist you. You are not to leave a work area once a peer arrives to help you, nor are you to leave unfinished work for the next shift.*

2. Training or Special Direction to Be Provided: *I will assign lead Jeff Gardner to oversee your work for three "runs." You are to explain clearly to him your understanding of the repair order, announce yourself to customers when you arrive, make the repairs yourself, and follow up with customers to ensure their satisfaction.*

3. Interim Performance Evaluation Necessary? *No*

4. Our **Employee Assistance Program** (EAP) provider, Prime Behavioral Health Group, can be confidentially reached to assist you at (800) 555-5555. This is strictly voluntary. A booklet regarding the EAP's services is available from Human Resources.

5. In addition, I recognize that you may have certain ideas to improve your performance. Therefore, I encourage you to provide your own **Personal Improvement Plan Input and Suggestions:**

_____

_____

_____

(Attach additional sheets if needed.)

OUTCOMES AND CONSEQUENCES

Positive: I will remain available to help you and discuss areas where you require additional support. If you meet your performance goals, no further disciplinary action will be taken regarding this issue. _In addition, you will regain the sense of satisfaction that you have had up until recently in knowing that a job is done well and completed to customers' satisfaction. You've been successful in your role until the past three months. I know that you can attain that same level of performance again. I want your commitment that this will be the last time that we have to discuss these issues._

Negative: _You are now being placed on notice that if you fail to improve your job performance, customer service, or communication with your peers, further disciplinary action up to and including dismissal may result._ A copy of this document will be placed in your personnel file.

Scheduled Review Date: _Thirty days (December 27)_

EMPLOYEE COMMENTS AND/OR REBUTTAL

_____

_____

_____

(Attach additional sheets if needed.)

X _____
Employee Signature

EMPLOYEE ACKNOWLEDGMENT GOES HERE

#33 Safety Infractions

Plant engineer who normally drives a golf cart or pickup truck on campus is given a DUI (Driving Under the Influence) conviction for noncompany activities that restricts his ability to drive for the company; the company decides it can reasonably accommodate this limitation by having the employee ride a bicycle to perform his job because he needs only to carry a tool belt.[2]

PERFORMANCE CORRECTION NOTICE

Employee Name: *Kevin Farthington*

Department: *Engineering*

Date Presented: *February 10, 2017*

Supervisor: *Bob Fisk*

DISCIPLINARY LEVEL

☐ **Verbal Correction**—(To memorialize the conversation.)

☒ **Written Warning**—(State nature of offense, method of correction, and action to be taken if offense is repeated.)

☐ **Investigatory Leave**—(Include length of time and nature of review.)

☐ **Final Written Warning**

    ☐ Without decision-making leave

    ☐ With decision-making leave (Attach memo of instructions.)

    ☐ With unpaid suspension

SUBJECT: *Work performance/loss of driver's license*

☒ Policy/Procedure Violation

☒ Performance Transgression

☐ Behavior/Conduct Infraction

☐ Absenteeism/Tardiness

---

2 Disciplining an employee who receives an off-duty drunken driving conviction is generally proper if you, the employer, can show a direct relationship between the conviction and the person's job duties. In this particular case, driving is a necessity for the plant engineer. On the other hand, discipline might not be appropriate if the employee's duties did not involve driving, and you couldn't otherwise demonstrate how the company was uniquely affected by the conviction. Check with qualified legal counsel to ensure that your interpretation of the relevance of the driving conviction meets both federal and state law guidelines.

PRIOR NOTIFICATIONS

Level of Discipline	Date	Subject
Verbal	_____	_____
Written	_____	_____
Final Written	_____	_____

Incident Description and Supporting Details: Include the following information: Time, Place, Date of Occurrence, and Persons Present as well as Organizational Impact.

Kevin,

Because you have had your license restricted and are no longer able to drive a motorized vehicle on company property, you have severely restricted the terms and scope of your employment. As an engineer, it is critical that you satisfy the needs of campus personnel from both a timeliness and a customer service standpoint. The company has agreed to accommodate your request by allowing you to ride a bicycle on campus to reach your job destinations.

You are required to wear a rider's safety helmet at all times when you are bicycling. In addition, this new employment arrangement will be continued at the company's sole discretion. Furthermore, the company reserves the right to periodically evaluate your performance in order to ensure that the standards of timeliness and customer service are not being compromised by your inability to drive.

This accommodation in no way exempts you from meeting any of the essential job functions outlined in your job description.

PERFORMANCE IMPROVEMENT PLAN

1. Measurable/Tangible Improvement Goals: *Kevin, I expect that you will meet all production deadlines and maintain a timely and customer-friendly service to meet line managers' needs. I expect that you will not rely on your inability to drive on campus as an excuse for failure to meet work order deliveries. I expect you to advise me immediately of any difficulties in meeting your work agenda so that I can assist you in developing a workable action plan to keep your customers satisfied.*

2. Training or Special Direction to Be Provided: *Please meet with me weekly for the next month to ensure that you are meeting your production deadlines.*

3. Interim Performance Evaluation Necessary? *No*

4. Our **Employee Assistance Program** (EAP) provider, Prime Behavioral Health Group, can be confidentially reached to assist you at (800) 555-5555. This is strictly voluntary. A booklet regarding the EAP's services is available from Human Resources.

5. In addition, I recognize that you may have certain ideas to improve your performance. Therefore, I encourage you to provide your own **Personal Improvement Plan Input and Suggestions:**

_____

_____

_____

(Attach additional sheets if needed.)

OUTCOMES AND CONSEQUENCES

Positive: I will remain available to help you and discuss areas where you require additional support. If you meet your performance goals, no further disciplinary action will be taken regarding this issue.

Negative: _You are now being placed on notice that if, at any time in the next thirty days, you are unable to meet the essential job functions of your position or if you fail to meet any other standards of performance and conduct, disciplinary action up to and including dismissal will occur._ A copy of this document will be placed in your personnel file.

Scheduled Review Date: _Thirty days (March 12, 2017)_

EMPLOYEE COMMENTS AND/OR REBUTTAL

_____

_____

_____

(Attach additional sheets if needed.)

X _____
Employee Signature

EMPLOYEE ACKNOWLEDGMENT GOES HERE

#34 Safety Infractions

Maintenance mechanic leaves work at the end of his regularly assigned shift even though there is an ongoing emergency situation.

PERFORMANCE CORRECTION NOTICE

Employee Name: *Dan Rolfe*   **Department:** *Engineering*

Date Presented: *September 4, 2017*   **Supervisor:** *Allan Parker*

DISCIPLINARY LEVEL

☐ **Verbal Correction**—(To memorialize the conversation.)

☒ **Written Warning**—(State nature of offense, method of correction, and action to be taken if offense is repeated.)

☐ **Investigatory Leave**—(Include length of time and nature of review.)

☐ **Final Written Warning**

    ☐ Without decision-making leave

    ☐ With decision-making leave (Attach memo of instructions.)

    ☐ With unpaid suspension

SUBJECT: *Refusal to follow legitimate and proper working instructions; unsatisfactory work performance regarding safety*

☒ Policy/Procedure Violation

☒ Performance Transgression

☒ Behavior/Conduct Infraction

☐ Absenteeism/Tardiness

PRIOR NOTIFICATIONS

Level of Discipline	Date	Subject
Verbal	_____	_____
Written	_____	_____
Final Written	_____	_____

Incident Description and Supporting Details: Include the following information: Time, Place, Date of Occurrence, and Persons Present as well as Organizational Impact.

Dan,

On August 10, 2017, at 3:45 P.M., the hospital campus experienced a loss of electrical power. Power was out for approximately two and one-half hours, and this was technically designated a brownout. At that time, the emergency generators came on to supply power to the patient care areas, but the majority of the electrical power remained out of service throughout the campus. This was considered an emergency situation.

Paul Mahoney, your coworker, arrived at approximately 3:45 P.M. when the power went out. Paul could not find you in your office, so he looked for you in the generator building. He located you at 4:00, the end of your regularly assigned shift. Paul updated you on the status of power around campus and asked you to work with him to restore power throughout the campus. You stated, however, that you could not stay because that would result in overtime. Paul asked if you understood that the entire campus had lost power. You stated that you realized this, but you still insisted that you could not stay at work since your overtime had not been preapproved. You consequently left work. Such poor judgment compromised patient care and employee safety and violated Victory Hospital's standards of performance and conduct.

PERFORMANCE IMPROVEMENT PLAN

Measurable/Tangible Improvement Goals: *Dan, I expect you, as a maintenance mechanic, to use judgment based on your knowledge and experience in situations such as this one. Although you were notified in writing the week before that there would be no approved overtime because of budgeting constraints, it is an understood rule that no employee is to leave the hospital during an emergency condition when that employee is capable of helping. The "statement" that you made by leaving was an obvious protest of the rule prohibiting overtime. I expect you, however, to safeguard patient care and employee safety at all times, whether an emergency exists or not.*

Training or Special Direction to Be Provided: *I am enclosing a copy of the hospital's policy on employees' responsibilities during emergencies. Please read this policy immediately and see me with any questions. In any future emergency that requires your assistance, you will be paid overtime for work performed above and beyond your shift.*

Interim Performance Evaluation Necessary? *No*

Our **Employee Assistance Program** (EAP) provider, Prime Behavioral Health Group, can be confidentially reached to assist you at (800) 555-5555. This is strictly voluntary. A booklet regarding the EAP's services is available from Human Resources.

In addition, I recognize that you may have certain ideas to improve your performance. Therefore, I encourage you to provide your own **Personal Improvement Plan Input and Suggestions:**

_____

_____

_____

(Attach additional sheets if needed.)

OUTCOMES AND CONSEQUENCES

Positive: I will remain available to help you and discuss areas where you require additional support. If you meet your performance goals, no further disciplinary action will be taken regarding this issue.

Negative: *You are now being placed on written notice for lack of judgment and failure to perform your essential job functions. If you ever again fail to follow emergency instructions or compromise patient care or employee safety, you may be immediately dismissed.* A copy of this document will be placed in your personnel file.

Scheduled Review Date: *None*

EMPLOYEE COMMENTS AND/OR REBUTTAL

_____

_____

_____

(Attach additional sheets if needed.)

X _____
Employee Signature

EMPLOYEE ACKNOWLEDGMENT GOES HERE

#35 Lack of Sales Production

A mortgage loan officer continues to have difficulty reaching her production numbers after having been notified in a recent performance evaluation that her performance must improve.

PERFORMANCE CORRECTION NOTICE

Employee Name: *Joan Teller*   **Department:** *Loan Information Services*

Date Presented: *November 11, 2017*   **Supervisor:** *Peter Winters*

DISCIPLINARY LEVEL

☐ **Verbal Correction**—(To memorialize the conversation.)

☒ **Written Warning**—(State nature of offense, method of correction, and action to be taken if offense is repeated.)

☐ **Investigatory Leave**—(Include length of time and nature of review.)

☐ **Final Written Warning**

    ☐ Without decision-making leave

    ☐ With decision-making leave (Attach memo of instructions.)

    ☐ With unpaid suspension

SUBJECT: *Substandard work*

☒ Policy/Procedure Violation

☒ Performance Transgression

☐ Behavior/Conduct Infraction

☐ Absenteeism/Tardiness

PRIOR NOTIFICATIONS

Level of Discipline	Date	Subject
Verbal	_____	_____
Written	*Oct 7, 2017*	*Substandard performance*
Final Written	_____	_____

Incident Description and Supporting Details: Include the following information: Time, Place, Date of Occurrence, and Persons Present as well as Organizational Impact.

Joan,

On your six-month performance evaluation, which you received last month, you were notified that you had to "increase the volume of your outbound calls by 20 percent" to reach the minimum daily threshold.

Although you passed your new employee ninety-day introductory period back in July with relative ease, the past few months have shown a decline in your mastery of the basics. To date, you are not making enough outbound calls or scheduling enough property appraisals to meet minimum production requirements. In addition, your production numbers in the area of recorded loans have fallen 15 to 20 percent short of expected minimums in the past two months. Finally, in monitoring your phone calls, I have witnessed that you are not properly determining borrowers' needs in terms of offering the appropriate loan programs. This concerns me because you demonstrated in your first three months of employment that you could reach these production numbers, distinguish among our loan products, and qualify borrowers successfully. As a result, you are currently not meeting sales production standards.

PERFORMANCE IMPROVEMENT PLAN

1. Measurable/Tangible Improvement Goals: *Joan, I expect you to immediately increase your volume of outbound sales calls to reach the minimum established by departmental policy—fifty calls per day. I also expect you to master the details related to our firm's various homeowner loan packages so that you can recommend suitable options to borrowers with authority and confidence.*

2. Training or Special Direction to Be Provided: *I will provide you with our company's sales training manual so that you have an opportunity to review the basic features and benefits of our loan products. I will also ask Rena Stein, sales supervisor, to sit with you at your workstation for half a day to provide you with one-on-one feedback regarding incoming sales calls. Rena will also review with you the key questions to ask in determining borrowers' loan-to-value ratios.*

3. Interim Performance Evaluation Necessary? *No*

4. Our **Employee Assistance Program** (EAP) provider, Prime Behavioral Health Group, can be confidentially reached to assist you at (800) 555-5555. This is strictly voluntary. A booklet regarding the EAP's services is available from Human Resources.

5. In addition, I recognize that you may have certain ideas to improve your performance. Therefore, I encourage you to provide your own **Personal Improvement Plan Input and Suggestions:**

_____

_____

_____

(Attach additional sheets if needed.)

OUTCOMES AND CONSEQUENCES

Positive: I will remain available to help you and discuss areas where you require additional support. If you meet your performance goals, no further disciplinary action will be taken regarding this issue. *In addition, by raising your raw production numbers and reviewing the solutions that our loan options can provide to borrowers, you should increase your output to minimum performance thresholds and establish the groundwork necessary to earn your first commission check.*

Negative: *You are now being placed on a sixty-day written notice that you are not meeting the terms established in your recent performance evaluation. If your incoming call volume, scheduled appointments, and/or recorded loans do not meet company standards, or if you fail to demonstrate an ability to sell our firm's loan programs at any time during that period, you will be subject to additional discipline up to and including termination.* A copy of this document will be placed in your personnel file.

Scheduled Review Date: *Thirty days (December 11)*

EMPLOYEE COMMENTS AND/OR REBUTTAL

_____

_____

_____

(Attach additional sheets if needed.)

X _____

Employee Signature

EMPLOYEE ACKNOWLEDGMENT GOES HERE

Bonus Sample: Substandard Sales Performance (Extension of Final Written Warning)

Sales supervisor's final written warning is extended by an additional thirty days for only meeting certain performance thresholds but not others.

PERFORMANCE CORRECTION NOTICE

Employee Name: *Laura Preminger*   **Department:** *Business Development*

Date Presented: *June 17, 2017*   **Supervisor:** *Heidi Champlin*

DISCIPLINARY LEVEL

☐ **Verbal Correction**—(To memorialize the conversation.)

☐ **Written Warning**—(State nature of offense, method of correction, and action to be taken if offense is repeated.)

☐ **Investigatory Leave**—(Include length of time and nature of review.)

☒ **Final Written Warning**—*Thirty-day extension*

    ☒ Without decision-making leave

    ☐ With decision-making leave (Attach memo of instructions.)

    ☐ With unpaid suspension

SUBJECT: *Substandard job performance*

☐ Policy/Procedure Violation

☒ Performance Transgression

☐ Behavior/Conduct Infraction

☐ Absenteeism/Tardiness

PRIOR NOTIFICATIONS

Level of Discipline	Date	Subject
Verbal	*Nov 17, 2016*	*Substandard performance*
Written	*Jan 17, 2017*	*Substandard performance*
Final Written	*Apr 10, 2017*	*Substandard performance*

Incident Description and Supporting Details: Include the following information: Time, Place, Date of Occurrence, and Persons Present as well as Organizational Impact.

Laura,

This document serves to notify you that you are being issued a thirty-day extension to the final written warning you received on April 10, 2017. This notice will remain in effect from June 17, 2017 to July 17, 2017, and provide you with an opportunity to correct and improve your performance.

In April and May, your team met minimum monthly sales goals; however, ongoing issues are still recurring with regard to following directives, meeting priorities and deadlines, completing training programs, managing your team's performance, and overall following up and responding.

Since you received the final written warning on April 10, 2017, we have held weekly one-on-one sessions to assess your progress on the following dates: April 16, April 21, April 28, May 8, May 12, May 26, and June 2. While your team is now performing at an acceptable level sales-wise, you must demonstrate individual improvement in the following areas:

Issue 1: Failure to Follow Directives

- *On January 17, 2017 (your written warning), and April 10, 2017 (your final written warning), you were instructed to register and complete five training workshops that could provide comprehensive guidance with regard to your organizational skills and leadership development. You were required to register for all five trainings within thirty days from the date that you received the final written warning (April 10, 2017). This was not completed as directed; in fact, you still have not registered or completed any one of the trainings.*

- *On May 27, 2017, I asked you to complete an action plan by May 29, 2017, for meeting our newest national goals for the third quarter. On May 30, 2017, I sent you a follow-up reminder because I had not received your action plan. At that point, you responded that you were working on the proposal with the help of your team. As of today, I still have not received your action plan with the information/revisions I requested—now over two weeks after the due date.*

- *On May 11, 2017, I sent you an email asking you to review your Weekly Comments before they were sent to me because they included the exact same plusses and deltas from the previous weeks. As you are aware, the purpose of the Weekly Comments is to address all new weekly wins and opportunities in your business. I still continue to receive weekly comments from you with the same exact information as the previous weeks, lending to the appearance of a quick copy and paste rather than specific updates and recommendations.*

Issue 2: Timeliness and Accountability

- *I have asked you to ensure that all corrective action for agents that do not meet their sales goals in a given cycle be completed within the first week of the start of the new sales cycle. You continue to submit corrective action documents over two weeks out.*

- *On May 26, 2017, I discussed with you one team member's month-end performance, and we agreed to proceed with a business case for termination due to her continued poor performance and attendance issues. In order to complete the termination paperwork, I needed notes from your meetings with this employee at the junctures where you issued her written and final written warnings. You did not provide the required notes until June 6, 2017, unnecessarily delaying the termination process.*

Laura, the examples above directly reflect a continuous lack of follow-up, timeliness, and accountability. While you have steadied your team's sales performance over the past eight cycles, your commitment and efforts toward these other performance areas need to improve immediately. I will continue to work with you to provide assistance to meet all sales targets, including any other support I can provide regarding the aforementioned performance deficiencies. I am extending the performance improvement process for thirty days with the hopes that the added time will be beneficial to your improvement and help you meet all the terms outlined in your recent final written warning.

PERFORMANCE IMPROVEMENT PLAN

1. Measurable/Tangible Improvement Goals: *As a sales supervisor, you are expected to follow directives and communicate with me in advance if you cannot meet specific deadlines or face any challenges in plans. Further, I expect you to:*

(a) Reply to all emails/communicate with me no later than 24 hours from receipt

(b) Meet with all your agents on a weekly basis and document all coaching sessions

(c) Complete outstanding corrective actions within two days from the date of incident

(d) Complete all pending training workshops within the next four weeks

2. Training or Special Direction Provided: *I will continue to meet with you one-on-one during our weekly sessions. Please let me know what challenges you may be facing during those weekly sessions or anytime in between. From this point forward, however, I will assume that all activities due will be complete, unless I hear otherwise from you.*

3. Interim Performance Evaluation Necessary? *No*

4. Our **Employee Assistance Program** (EAP) provider, Prime Behavioral Health Group, can be confidentially reached to assist you at (800) 555-5555. This is strictly voluntary. A booklet regarding the EAP's services is available from Human Resources.

5. In addition, I recognize that you may have certain ideas to improve your performance. Therefore, I encourage you to provide your own **Personal Improvement Plan Input and Suggestions:**

_____

_____

_____

(Attach additional sheets if needed.)

OUTCOMES AND CONSEQUENCES

Positive: I will remain available to help you and discuss areas where you require additional support. If you meet your performance goals, no further disciplinary action will be taken regarding this issue.

Negative: *However, it is essential moving forward that you focus on areas that remain a concern: following directives, meeting deadlines, and taking initiative (i.e., by completing trainings, communicating proactively, and managing your team's performance). Failure to demonstrate immediate and sustained improvement will result in your dismissal.*

Scheduled Review Date: *Four weeks (July 17)*

EMPLOYEE COMMENTS AND/OR REBUTTAL

_____

_____

_____

(Attach additional sheets if needed.)

X _____
Employee Signature

EMPLOYEE ACKNOWLEDGMENT GOES HERE

#36 Unwillingness to Perform Properly Assigned Work

An operating room (OR) orderly fails to report to work as instructed and fails to complete a work assignment.

PERFORMANCE CORRECTION NOTICE

Employee Name: *Michael Fisler*   **Department:** *Customer Service*

Date Presented: *April 10, 2017*   **Supervisor:** *Wolfgang Bauer*

DISCIPLINARY LEVEL

☐ **Verbal Correction**—(To memorialize the conversation.)

☒ **Written Warning**—(State nature of offense, method of correction, and action to be taken if offense is repeated.)

☐ **Investigatory Leave**—(Include length of time and nature of review.)

☒ **Final Written Warning**

    ☒ Without decision-making leave

    ☐ With decision-making leave (Attach memo of instructions.)

    ☐ With unpaid suspension

SUBJECT: *Written warning: substandard performance; final written warning: insubordination*

☒ Policy/Procedure Violation

☒ Performance Transgression

☒ Behavior/Conduct Infraction

☐ Absenteeism/Tardiness

PRIOR NOTIFICATIONS

Level of Discipline	Date	Subject
Verbal	_____	_____
Written	_____	_____
Final Written	_____	_____

Incident Description and Supporting Details: Include the following information: Time, Place, Date of Occurrence, and Persons Present as well as Organizational Impact.

Michael,

Issue 1: On March 27, 2017, department supervisor Anne Rollins requested that you fill out a "Where Does My Time Go?" report to measure how effectively you manage your time. You told Anne that you refused to do the report because you felt like you were being picked on. Your supervisor responded, "Well, you have to because I'm asking you to."

When your supervisor questioned you at the end of the day regarding your completion of this report, you stated that you hadn't had time to complete the report. Your supervisor requested that you complete the report by your next workday, Monday, March 31. She explained to you that everyone in the department had to complete this form—not just you.

However, on Monday morning, you said nothing to your supervisor about the report. At 4:00 Monday afternoon, your supervisor asked you for the completed report. You responded that you hadn't had an opportunity to complete it. You consequently failed to follow direct instructions and to perform properly assigned work.

Issue 2: On April 8, 2017, supervisor Steffi Falker asked you to come to work the following day at 8:00 A.M. instead of 10:00 A.M., your normally scheduled time. Steffi explained to you that you were needed for staffing reasons, namely that your coworker would not be in that day. You said nothing to your supervisor and only nodded your head. You then turned and walked away.

On April 9, you showed up at work at 10:00, your regularly scheduled time. You said nothing to Steffi about not reporting to work at 8:00 A.M. You consequently breached your duty to inform your supervisor that you weren't planning on coming in. As a result, the work flow was disrupted, and customer service was compromised. Your refusal to follow a reasonable directive constitutes insubordination.

PERFORMANCE IMPROVEMENT PLAN

1. Measurable/Tangible Improvement Goals: *Michael, your behavior must change immediately and your performance must substantially improve if you are to keep your job. You are from this point on to acknowledge your supervisor when you are being addressed, clearly communicate any questions you have regarding your instructions, and complete all assignments as directed in a timely fashion.*

2. Training or Special Direction Provided: *Your job description is attached for your review. Please study your employee handbook as well so that you better understand what the company expects of you.*

3. Interim Performance Evaluation Necessary? *No. Your annual review is due next month; these issues will be reviewed at that time.*

4. Our **Employee Assistance Program** (EAP) provider, Prime Behavioral Health Group, can be confidentially reached to assist you at (800) 555-5555. This is strictly voluntary. A booklet regarding the EAP's services is available from Human Resources.

5. In addition, I recognize that you may have certain ideas to improve your performance. Therefore, I encourage you to provide your own **Personal Improvement Plan Input and Suggestions:**

_____

_____

_____

(Attach additional sheets if needed.)

OUTCOMES AND CONSEQUENCES

Positive: I will remain available to help you and discuss areas where you require additional support. If you meet your performance goals, no further disciplinary action will be taken regarding this issue. _In addition, you will be able to make a more positive impact on the operations of our department and create more open and communicative relations with your supervisors and coworkers._

Negative: _If you ever again fail to follow immediate instructions from your supervisor, you may be discharged. If you ever again fail to inform your supervisor of your inability or unwillingness to report to work at a given time or to complete a given assignment, you may likewise be immediately terminated for cause. In addition, if in the next ninety days you fail to meet any other standards of performance and conduct, you will be placed in a formal ninety-day probationary period. Further transgressions at any time while in that probationary period may result in dismissal._ **A copy of this document will be placed in your personnel file.**

Scheduled Review Date: _Ninety days (July 10, 2017)_

EMPLOYEE COMMENTS AND/OR REBUTTAL

_____

_____

_____

(Attach additional sheets if needed.)

X _____
Employee Signature

EMPLOYEE ACKNOWLEDGMENT GOES HERE

Note: Because this is a final written warning, add this sentence to the end of the Employee Acknowledgment: "In addition, I understand that this is my last chance and that I am in serious jeopardy of losing my job. If I breach any of the performance standards established in this notice, I will voluntarily resign or be discharged for cause."

#37 Unwillingness to Perform Properly Assigned Work

Lab aide with ten years of seniority engages in insubordinate conduct, makes veiled threats and abusive gestures, and generally refuses to take orders from a newly hired supervisor who is half his age. This is the first in a series of three write-ups (see Write-Ups #54 and 55) leading up to dismissal. The letter of termination is located in Part VII, Termination Notices (Write-Up #84).

PERFORMANCE CORRECTION NOTICE

Employee Name: *Rick Ricardo*　　　**Department:** *Research Lab*

Date Presented: *August 7, 2017*　　　**Supervisor:** *John Josephson*

DISCIPLINARY LEVEL

☒ **Verbal Correction**—(To memorialize the conversation.)

☐ **Written Warning**—(State nature of offense, method of correction, and action to be taken if offense is repeated.)

☐ **Investigatory Leave**—(Include length of time and nature of review.)

☐ **Final Written Warning**

　　☐ Without decision-making leave

　　☐ With decision-making leave (Attach memo of instructions.)

　　☐ With unpaid suspension

SUBJECT: *Substandard performance and insubordination; unwillingness to perform properly assigned work*

☒ Policy/Procedure Violation

☒ Performance Transgression

☒ Behavior/Conduct Infraction

☐ Absenteeism/Tardiness

PRIOR NOTIFICATIONS

Level of Discipline	Date	Subject
Verbal	_____	_____
Written	_____	_____
Final Written	_____	_____

Incident Description and Supporting Details: Include the following information: Time, Place, Date of Occurrence, and Persons Present as well as Organizational Impact.

Rick,

On August 4, you failed to unload the contents from a delivery truck when it arrived at the loading dock at 10:00 A.M. Your supervisor, John Josephson, noticed that you were sitting at the edge of the loading dock when the vendor offered to help you unload. You told the vendor to do it himself, since you were "having a bad day." John then asked you to unload the truck immediately and reminded the vendor that you were to unload all heavy materials yourself; the vendor was welcome to help you only if he limited his activities to light lifting.

On August 6, John saw another truck driver unloading the contents of his truck onto our platform. He asked the driver where you were. The driver stated that he had seen you twenty minutes earlier, but that when you saw him, you "ducked into the building" and hadn't been seen since. John unloaded the contents of the truck onto a pallet so that it could be forklifted into the facility. You became angry when you saw John working with the vendor and accused John of trying to make you look like you weren't doing your job. John explained that he was only trying to help you manage your workload, but you refused to listen and then walked away.

I spoke with you, Rick, to learn about your interpretation of these events. You told me that neither issue was serious and that a mountain was being made of a molehill. "Everyone's allowed to have a bad day, and I don't need John doing my job for me. John thinks he's better than me, and I don't care for his arrogance." I am disappointed, Rick, with this sudden change in your behavior and your apparent dissatisfaction with your job since John became your supervisor six weeks ago. I am also disappointed that you refuse to take responsibility for your actions and fail to see any wrongdoing on your part. Your actions demonstrate that you are not performing at an acceptable level.

PERFORMANCE IMPROVEMENT PLAN

1. Measurable/Tangible Improvement Goals: *Rick, I expect you to be ready and willing to unload delivery trucks the moment they pull up to the ramp. I expect you to move all heavy items, since it is not the delivery driver's responsibility to remove the heavy cargo. I expect you to show appreciation when your new supervisor assists you or attempts to make your job easier, and I hold you accountable for communicating with John whenever you disagree with one of his directives so that you can get an immediate response and not allow your perceptions to fester. Finally, I want to meet with you tomorrow after you've read this documentation so that you can convince me that we won't ever have to address these issues again.*

2. Training or Special Direction to Be Provided: *I have instructed John to meet with you daily from 8:00 to 8:10 A.M. to review your work schedule for the day. This will happen for the next two weeks so that John gets a better understanding of your responsibilities and so that you get more comfortable communicating with him. I am also attaching a copy of your signed job description, which details your responsibilities for unloading trucks. Please reread the entire job description and see me if you have any questions about your duties and responsibilities.*

3. Interim Performance Evaluation Necessary? *No*

4. Our **Employee Assistance Program** (EAP) provider, Prime Behavioral Health Group, can be confidentially reached to assist you at (800) 555-5555. This is strictly voluntary. A booklet regarding the EAP's services is available from Human Resources.

5. In addition, I recognize that you may have certain ideas to improve your performance. Therefore, I encourage you to provide your own **Personal Improvement Plan Input and Suggestions:**

_____

_____

_____

(Attach additional sheets if needed.)

OUTCOMES AND CONSEQUENCES

Positive: I will remain available to help you and discuss areas where you require additional support. If you meet your performance goals, no further disciplinary action will be taken regarding this issue. *In addition, Rick, you will contribute to a friendlier work environment and increase the level of camaraderie among staff members in our department as you foster stronger relations with your new supervisor.*

Negative: *I want you to take this verbal warning seriously. If you fail to abide by the terms of this agreement in the next ninety days, further disciplinary action up to and including dismissal will occur. Any future violations beyond this ninety-day period will likewise result in disciplinary action.* A copy of this document will be placed in your personnel file.

Scheduled Review Date: *Two weeks (August 21)*

EMPLOYEE COMMENTS AND/OR REBUTTAL

_____

_____

_____

(Attach additional sheets if needed.)

X _____
Employee Signature

EMPLOYEE ACKNOWLEDGMENT GOES HERE

#38 Recurring Negligence and Thoughtlessness

Food service preparer with fifteen years of tenure continuously fails to handle company equipment properly.

PERFORMANCE CORRECTION NOTICE

Employee Name: *Peter Thorpe*   **Department:** *Food Services*

Date Presented: *April 25, 2018*   **Supervisor:** *Dick Ford*

DISCIPLINARY LEVEL

☐ **Verbal Correction**—(To memorialize the conversation.)

☐ **Written Warning**—(State nature of offense, method of correction, and action to be taken if offense is repeated.)

☐ **Investigatory Leave**—(Include length of time and nature of review.)

☒ **Final Written Warning**

    ☒ Without decision-making leave

    ☐ With decision-making leave (Attach memo of instructions.)

    ☐ With unpaid suspension

SUBJECT: *Recurring negligence and thoughtlessness*

☒ Policy/Procedure Violation

☒ Performance Transgression

☐ Behavior/Conduct Infraction

☐ Absenteeism/Tardiness

PRIOR NOTIFICATIONS

Level of Discipline	Date	Subject
Verbal	July 11, 2017	Substandard performance/misuse of company property
Written	Sept 19, 2017	Substandard performance/misuse of company property
Final Written	Dec 22, 2017	Substandard performance/misuse of company property

Incident Description and Supporting Details: Include the following information: Time, Place, Date of Occurrence, and Persons Present as well as Organizational Impact.

Peter,

Today it was discovered that you placed a food cart on its side against a wall to dry in the sun rather than following standard organizational procedure and wiping it off. This poses a physical hazard to you and to others, and it damages the cart as well. You were specifically warned about mishandling food service equipment in a final written warning, a written warning, and a verbal warning over the past nine months. Turning food carts on their side to dry was one specific action that you were instructed to avoid repeating in the future.[3]

Furthermore, your most recent annual performance review in February addressed this very same issue and graded you as "not meeting expectations" in terms of properly handling equipment and following standard procedures. Such recurring negligence and thoughtlessness involving routine work is unacceptable. In addition, Peter, you have demonstrated a pattern of being told what you need to do and then violating those instructions.

PERFORMANCE IMPROVEMENT PLAN

1. Measurable/Tangible Improvement Goals: *Peter, I expect you to follow all standard departmental policies and procedures at all times. I expect you to be especially mindful of past transgressions in order to avoid repeating them.*

2. Training or Special Direction to Be Provided: *In the past six months, you have received a booklet summarizing key departmental policies and procedures. Your previous warnings and your most recent performance evaluation thoroughly addressed departmental expectations and special instructions for you to follow. You are to review all of those documents again to ensure that you thoroughly understand what is expected of you, and you are to see me tomorrow with any questions regarding what you've read.*

3. Interim Performance Evaluation Necessary? *No. Your most recent performance evaluation documents that you are not meeting the overall performance expectations of your job.*

4. Our **Employee Assistance Program** (EAP) provider, Prime Behavioral Health Group, can be confidentially reached to assist you at (800) 555-5555. This is strictly voluntary. A booklet regarding the EAP's services is available from Human Resources.

5. In addition, I recognize that you may have certain ideas to improve your performance. Therefore, I encourage you to provide your own **Personal Improvement Plan Input and Suggestions:**

_____

_____

_____

(Attach additional sheets if needed.)

---

3 Even though the employee had been specifically warned about placing food carts on their side, the company chose not to terminate for what could be interpreted as a de minimis, or minor, offense.

OUTCOMES AND CONSEQUENCES

Positive: I will remain available to help you and discuss areas where you require additional support. If you meet your performance goals, no further disciplinary action will be taken regarding this issue.

Negative: *Peter, we are not terminating you at this time because of your long tenure with our organization. We are, instead, giving you another chance. If you again fail to handle equipment according to departmental guidelines or violate any other standards of perfor-mance and conduct, you may be immediately dismissed.* A copy of this document will be placed in your personnel file.

Scheduled Review Date: None

EMPLOYEE COMMENTS AND/OR REBUTTAL

_____

_____

_____

(Attach additional sheets if needed.)

X _____
Employee Signature

EMPLOYEE ACKNOWLEDGMENT GOES HERE

Note: Since this is a final written warning, add these sentences to the Employee Acknowledgment: "In addition, I understand that this is my last chance. If I fail to meet the performance standards established in this notice, I will voluntarily resign or be discharged for cause."

Bonus Sample: Improper Cash Handling (Dual Custody Violation)

Employee responsible for closing out the safe at night mistakenly leaves the safe door open with cash and checks exposed.

PERFORMANCE CORRECTION NOTICE

Employee Name: *Katia Kovalenko*

Date Presented: *June 7, 2017*

Department: *Retail Stores*

Supervisor: *Al Gupta*

DISCIPLINARY LEVEL

☐ **Verbal Correction**—(To memorialize the conversation.)

☐ **Written Warning**—(State nature of offense, method of correction, and action to be taken if offense is repeated.)

☐ **Investigatory Leave**—(Include length of time and nature of review.)

☒ **Final Written Warning**

    ☒ Without decision-making leave

    ☐ With decision-making leave (Attach memo of instructions.)

    ☐ With unpaid suspension

SUBJECT: *Misappropriation of funds and failure to follow dual custody policy*

☒ Policy/Procedure Violation

☒ Performance Transgression

☐ Behavior/Conduct Infraction

☐ Absenteeism/Tardiness

PRIOR NOTIFICATIONS

Level of Discipline	Date	Subject
Verbal		
Written	*Dec 18, 2016*	*Substandard customer service*
Final Written		

Incident Description and Supporting Details: Include the following information: Time, Place, Date of Occurrence, and Persons Present as well as Organizational Impact.

Katia,

This document serves to notify you that you are being issued a final written warning for violating our company policy relating to misappropriation of funds and dual custody.

On Monday, June 5, 2017, at 8:45 P.M., a facilities representative emailed me and store supervisor Adele Sumpter to notify us that the safe in your store was found left open by Janitorial Services. Photos of the safe were included in the email.

You and one other employee were closing the store at the end of the business day on June 3, 2017. Security manager Ralph Chang, human resources representative David Otis, and retail store supervisor Adele Sumpter reviewed the security footage provided. The video footage showed that you violated both the Dual Custody procedure and the Retail Store Cash Handling policy, which resulted in the store safe being left open, neglected, and vulnerable.

Contents of the safe exposed:

- *Change Fund $380.00*
- *Drawer $100.00*
- *Drawer $100.00*
- *Deposit $1,507.38*
- *Deposit $1,659.47*

Total Cash $3,746.85

- *Check Deposit $185.00*
- *Check Deposit $299.08*

Total Check $484.08

Katia, you and a coworker were working the closing shift. Upon closing the cable store, you were shown by the video footage to have been negligent by not maintaining 100 percent focus on your cash and the safe. Furthermore, you did not verify that the safe door was locked by attempting to open it before leaving the cash room, and you did not perform as "one unit" with your coworker. The Cash Handling policy on misappropriation of funds and dual custody is clear in terms of the severity of leaving the safe open and unattended at the close of the shift.

During your interview with the store supervisor and with Human Resources, you confirmed that you understood the policy and its key purpose of protecting company assets.

As a result of these serious violations of the Cash Handling and Dual Custody policies and in accordance with those policies, Katia, you are being issued a final written warning. This notice affords you the opportunity to correct this behavior.

PERFORMANCE IMPROVEMENT PLAN

1. Measurable/Tangible Improvement Goals: *Katia, from this point forward, you will follow the Dual Custody procedures consistently and exactly as outlined. Should you have any questions about this policy or anything related to these procedures, you will immediately contact your supervisor, another member of management, or Human Resources.*

Dual Custody: You should stand next to the person you are verifying, and your eyes and attention should be focused on their every action. It is your responsibility to ensure that they do not make a mistake or deviate from any portion of the Cash Handling policy during the dual custody transaction.

Further, when the representative closes out at night and is ready for dual custody verification, they must never leave the presence of the verifier. The representative must not divert their focus or eyes from the verifier as funds are recounted. The representative and the verifier are to perform as one unit, with dual 100 percent focus from the point of receiving the funds to be verified through safe-drop completion. You must verify that the safe door is locked by attempting to open it before leaving the cash room. Each person must be able to say with absolute certainty that funds were accurately counted, recorded, posted, and secured in the safe.

2. Training or Special Direction Provided: *You will repeat Cash Handling training, including re-reviewing the Cash Handling policy in its entirety to prevent further incidents.*

3. Interim Performance Evaluation Necessary? *No.*

4. Our **Employee Assistance Program** (EAP) provider, Prime Behavioral Health Group, can be confidentially reached to assist you at (800) 555-5555. This is strictly voluntary. A booklet regarding the EAP's services is available from Human Resources.

5. In addition, I recognize that you may have certain ideas to improve your performance. Therefore, I encourage you to provide your own **Personal Improvement Plan Input and Suggestions:**

_____

_____

_____

(Attach additional sheets if needed.)

OUTCOMES AND CONSEQUENCES

Positive: I will remain available to help you and discuss areas where you require additional support. If you meet your performance goals, no further disciplinary action will be taken regarding this issue.

Negative: *Immediate and sustained improvement of the stated deficiencies must occur. Future violations of any company policies and/or procedures, whether or not specifically addressed above, may result in further disciplinary action up to and including dismissal.*

Scheduled Review Date: *None*

EMPLOYEE COMMENTS AND/OR REBUTTAL

_____

_____

_____

(Attach additional sheets if needed.)

X _____

Employee Signature

EMPLOYEE ACKNOWLEDGMENT GOES HERE

#39 Acts Resulting in Loss to the Employer

Programmer/analyst failed to complete an important assignment for a program conversion by deadline and also failed to inform his supervisor of this problem; as a result, the company had to hire a contractor to complete the project as quickly as possible.

PERFORMANCE CORRECTION NOTICE

Employee Name: *Mike Assael*   **Department:** *Information Technology*

Date Presented: *January 12, 2017*   **Supervisor:** *Gail Engel*

DISCIPLINARY LEVEL

☐ **Verbal Correction**—(To memorialize the conversation.)

☒ **Written Warning**—(State nature of offense, method of correction, and action to be taken if offense is repeated.)

☐ **Investigatory Leave**—(Include length of time and nature of review.)

☐ **Final Written Warning**

    ☐ Without decision-making leave

    ☐ With decision-making leave (Attach memo of instructions.)

    ☐ With unpaid suspension

SUBJECT: *Acts resulting in loss to the employer*

☒ Policy/Procedure Violation

☒ Performance Transgression

☐ Behavior/Conduct Infraction

☐ Absenteeism/Tardiness

PRIOR NOTIFICATIONS

Level of Discipline	Date	Subject
Verbal	_____	_____
Written	_____	_____
Final Written	_____	_____

Incident Description and Supporting Details: Include the following information: Time, Place, Date of Occurrence, and Persons Present as well as Organizational Impact.

Mike,

There have been numerous occasions on which you failed to properly complete your work and communicate/follow up with your supervisor regarding the status of your work. For example, on September 5, Karen Smith gave you a task on FundPro conversion mapping that was to be completed by September 8. Of the thirty mappings that needed to be completed, twenty-two were finished by September 17—nine days past the deadline. Of the eight remaining conversion assignments, however, you completed only two. As a result, an assignment deadline was not met.

On October 30, Paul Marker and Karen Smith met with you to discuss the lack of progress in your software conversion. You were told at that time that the conversion needed to be ready in two and a half months to meet the January 17 "go live" date. You acknowledged that you understood the critical nature of the conversion deadline and the list of changes that needed to be done since you were falling behind in your work.

In a November 25 meeting with Paul Marker, you were asked to present solutions and suggestions to the final revised list that you were presented with on November 21. However, at that point, you still hadn't reviewed the new list. Also, following that conversation, Paul asked you to present a final plan to him by the close of business on November 27. You didn't present a plan to Paul until December 3.

At this point, you do not appear to be capable of making all the necessary changes in time to meet the conversion deadline. As a result, we will have to hire an outside consultant to complete your work and meet the January 17 "go live" date.

This write-up is based on two issues: first, your failure to meet the conversion deadline, which is your ultimate responsibility; second, your failure to communicate any problems in your work area to your boss. Indeed, the only way your supervisors learned of the delinquency in your work was via their own auditing efforts.

When you were first given this assignment, you were told that it would most likely require long hours. Based on your computerized time logs, however, you have made very little commitment to the hours necessary to meet the deadlines that you originally accepted. Also, because of your failure to communicate, we find ourselves at a deadline for which we are not ready. This violates our organization's standards of performance and conduct.

PERFORMANCE IMPROVEMENT PLAN

1. Measurable/Tangible Improvement Goals: *Mike, I expect you to complete all assignments that you are assigned. I expect you to communicate any time that your work is falling behind—especially if this might potentially affect a large group project or companywide "go live" deadline. Finally, I expect you, as an exempt employee, to work whatever hours are necessary to ensure that your work is complete, accurate, and timely.*

2. Training or Special Direction to Be Provided: *For the next month, I will meet with you every Monday at 4:00 to ensure that your work is caught up and that you are realistically planning your day to meet your projected workload. In addition, I require you to email me every day for the next month outlining what you've done on the projects that we've set. This will help me help you by monitoring the projects on your desk, managing goals, and communicating more openly with your peers, staff, and boundary partners.*

3. Interim Performance Evaluation Necessary? *Yes. Because continuous management follow-up (approximately on a monthly basis for the past four months) has not yielded more positive results, I will reevaluate your overall performance in an effort to monitor the projects on your desk and aid you in setting goals, prioritizing your efforts, and communicating more openly with me and the other managers. This out-of-cycle review will reflect your current level of performance.*

4. Our **Employee Assistance Program** (EAP) provider, Prime Behavioral Health Group, can be confidentially reached to assist you at (800) 555-5555. This is strictly voluntary. A booklet regarding the EAP's services is available from Human Resources.

5. In addition, I recognize that you may have certain ideas to improve your performance. Therefore, I encourage you to provide your own **Personal Improvement Plan Input and Suggestions:**

_____

_____

_____

(Attach additional sheets if needed.)

OUTCOMES AND CONSEQUENCES

Positive: I will remain available to help you and discuss areas where you require additional support. If you meet your performance goals, no further disciplinary action will be taken regarding this issue.

Negative: *You are now being placed on formal written notice that you are not meeting the standards of performance and conduct as outlined in your programmer/analyst job description. If in the next ninety days you fail to meet project deadlines, fail to properly communicate the status of your projects to your supervisors, or fail to meet any other standards of performance and conduct, you will be placed on a final ninety-day probationary period. If you fail to perform to management's expectations during that probationary period, you may be dismissed.* A copy of this document will be placed in your personnel file.

Scheduled Review Date: *One Month (February 12, 2017)*

EMPLOYEE COMMENTS AND/OR REBUTTAL

_____

_____

_____

(Attach additional sheets if needed.)

X _____
Employee Signature

EMPLOYEE ACKNOWLEDGMENT GOES HERE

#40 Acts Resulting in Loss to the Employer

A seasonal food service preparer at an amusement park fails to keep his work area organized. In addition, he opens a new box of dishes by turning it upside down to remove the contents; some of the dishes break.

PERFORMANCE CORRECTION NOTICE

Employee Name: *Michael Shore*   **Department:** *Food Service*

Date Presented: *April 26, 2017*   **Supervisor:** *Ron Sington*

DISCIPLINARY LEVEL

☐ **Verbal Correction**—(To memorialize the conversation.)

☒ **Written Warning**—(State nature of offense, method of correction, and action to be taken if offense is repeated.)

☐ **Investigatory Leave**—(Include length of time and nature of review.)

☐ **Final Written Warning**

    ☐ Without decision-making leave

    ☐ With decision-making leave (Attach memo of instructions.)

    ☐ With unpaid suspension

SUBJECT: *Acts resulting in loss to the employer; poor work performance, poor judgment, and lack of attention*

☒ Policy/Procedure Violation

☒ Performance Transgression

☒ Behavior/Conduct Infraction

☐ Absenteeism/Tardiness

PRIOR NOTIFICATIONS

Level of Discipline	Date	Subject
Verbal	_____	_____
Written	_____	_____
Final Written	_____	_____

Incident Description and Supporting Details: Include the following information: Time, Place, Date of Occurrence, and Persons Present as well as Organizational Impact.

Michael,

On April 21 at 5:30 A.M., I arrived at work and observed the following conditions from the night before:

- *Three racks of coffee mugs and iced tea glasses were still on the tray lid cart and not put away.*

- *The filter at the dish machine catcher station was full of food.*

- *The yellow bin for broken glasses was not empty.*

- *The dish room dustpan was not washed or in its place.*

- *Tray line salad bowls were not organized appropriately on the pushcart. They were piled high and could easily come falling down with a gentle push.*

Leaving your work area in such disarray violates Wonder Mountain's standards of performance and conduct.

In addition, I received a note from the nighttime supervisor in my work area along with two broken dishes from a new shipment that arrived yesterday. The note stated that you had difficulties pulling the new dishes out of the box, so you turned the box upside down and shook it. The new plates fell to the ground, and two of them cracked. This could easily have been avoided had you simply requested someone to hold the box while you pulled the dishes out. The resulting loss of property requires us to order a replacement set of dishes—a cost of $25.

PERFORMANCE IMPROVEMENT PLAN

1. Measurable/Tangible Improvement Goals: *Michael, I expect that you will consistently leave your workstation clean, organized, and ready for the next shift. I expect you to use sounder judgment when it comes to handling company property and to ask for help when you have difficulty completing a physical task like opening boxes and crates. I also expect you to follow all standard policies and procedures at all times.*

2. Training or Special Direction to Be Provided: *You have had sufficient dish room training and continuous guidance on a daily basis throughout the season. Please ask me or another lead float for help if you have any questions or difficulties managing your work. I want you to review the policy handbook that you were given at the beginning of the season during orientation.*

3. Interim Performance Evaluation Necessary? *No*

4. Our **Employee Assistance Program** (EAP) provider, Prime Behavioral Health Group, can be confidentially reached to assist you at (800) 555-5555. This is strictly voluntary. A booklet regarding the EAP's services is available from Human Resources.

5. In addition, I recognize that you may have certain ideas to improve your performance. Therefore, I encourage you to provide your own **Personal Improvement Plan Input and Suggestions:**

_____

_____

_____

(Attach additional sheets if needed.)

OUTCOMES AND CONSEQUENCES

Positive: I will remain available to help you and discuss areas where you require additional support. If you meet your performance goals, no further disciplinary action will be taken regarding this issue. _I anticipate that your cooperation and attention to detail will increase our efficiency as a unit and bring you increased job satisfaction._

Negative: _You are now being placed on notice that if you, at any time during the remainder of the season, leave your work area in disarray or if you damage company property because of negligence or poor judgment, you will be placed on final written warning. If at any time in that final notice period you fail to meet the guidelines established in this memo or if you violate any other park standards of performance and conduct, you may be dismissed._ A copy of this document will be placed in your personnel file.

Scheduled Review Date: _None_

EMPLOYEE COMMENTS AND/OR REBUTTAL

_____

_____

_____

(Attach additional sheets if needed.)

X _____
Employee Signature

EMPLOYEE ACKNOWLEDGMENT GOES HERE

#41 Slow or Inefficient Production

A hospital orderly delivers wet wheelchairs without cleaning them first and fails to deliver bottled water as instructed. Note that this write-up refers to prior "directional notices" that the employee signed outlining his performance expectations.

PERFORMANCE CORRECTION NOTICE

Employee Name: Frank Columbus   **Department:** Operating Room

Date Presented: September 25, 2017   **Supervisor:** Elsa Leuchthand

DISCIPLINARY LEVEL

☐ **Verbal Correction**—(To memorialize the conversation.)

☒ **Written Warning**—(State nature of offense, method of correction, and action to be taken if offense is repeated.)

☐ **Investigatory Leave**—(Include length of time and nature of review.)

☐ **Final Written Warning**

    ☐ Without decision-making leave

    ☐ With decision-making leave (Attach memo of instructions.)

    ☐ With unpaid suspension

SUBJECT: *Substandard work performance: slow or inefficient production*

☐ Policy/Procedure Violation

☒ Performance Transgression

☒ Behavior/Conduct Infraction

☐ Absenteeism/Tardiness

PRIOR NOTIFICATIONS

Level of Discipline	Date	Subject
Verbal	_____	_____
Written	July 21, 2016	Substandard work performance
Final Written	_____	_____

Incident Description and Supporting Details: Include the following information: Time, Place, Date of Occurrence, and Persons Present as well as Organizational Impact.

Frank,

On Thursday, September 24, Dorothy Epifanio, RN, asked you to pick up some wheel-chairs from downstairs. You brought the chairs to the OR, but the chairs were wet and covered with pine needles as a result of the rain. You, however, did not clean the chairs and prepare them for use as required in your job description. As a result, the RNs them-selves were forced to clean and prepare the chairs to transport patients.

On Tuesday, September 22, RN Gail Niceguy paged me because we were out of bottled water. The nurse needed water for patients' oral hygiene. She asked you to bring a bottle back on an empty stretcher from Wing B as you returned from delivering a patient. You responded to this coworker by saying, "I'm not a slave, and it's not in my job description." You returned later without the bottle, and I was paged by the nurse, who wished to file a complaint against you. Your behavior in these two instances violates hospital standards of performance and conduct.

PERFORMANCE IMPROVEMENT PLAN

1. Measurable/Tangible Improvement Goals: *Frank, I expect you to provide excellent customer service to patients and coworkers at all times. I expect you to follow verbal directives and adhere to the duties outlined in your job description. I expect you never again to insult a coworker by stating that you're "not a slave." I also expect you never again to tell a coworker that something is "not in your job description." If indeed you feel that you are being asked to do something that is not your responsibility, you are to contact me immediately.*

2. Training or Special Direction to Be Provided: *On February 26, 2017, June 28, 2016, and March 31, 2015, you and all other orderlies received special written performance expectations to clarify your role and responsibilities. Among these instructions are the following:*

- *You are expected to have a gurney ready for a patient before the patient is transported.*

- *You are expected to follow directions and instructions from the team leaders/RNs.*

- *Be a team player and support the entire team.*

You are to reread these memos as you will be held accountable for the performance expectations described in them. You are also to review your job description for the same reason.

3. Interim Performance Evaluation Necessary? *No*

4. Our **Employee Assistance Program** (EAP) provider, Prime Behavioral Health Group, can be confidentially reached to assist you at (800) 555-5555. This is strictly voluntary. A booklet regarding the EAP's services is available from Human Resources.

5. In addition, I recognize that you may have certain ideas to improve your performance. Therefore, I encourage you to provide your own **Personal Improvement Plan Input and Suggestions:**

_____

_____

_____

(Attach additional sheets if needed.)

OUTCOMES AND CONSEQUENCES

Positive: I will remain available to help you and discuss areas where you require additional support. If you meet your performance goals, no further disciplinary action will be taken regarding this issue.

Negative: _You are now being placed on notice that if at any time within the next ninety days you fail to meet any standards of performance and conduct as outlined in this disciplinary memo, the three instructional memos attached (which you previously signed and pledged to follow), or your job description, you will be placed on a ninety-day final written warning. If at any time within that ninety-day final written warning period you fail to meet established performance standards, you may be dismissed._

In addition, Frank, any further derogatory utterances to your coworkers regarding your "not being a slave" or something "not being in your job description" may lead to disciplinary action up to and including termination. A copy of this document will be placed in your personnel file.

Scheduled Review Date: _None_

EMPLOYEE COMMENTS AND/OR REBUTTAL

_____

_____

_____

(Attach additional sheets if needed.)

X _____
Employee Signature

EMPLOYEE ACKNOWLEDGMENT GOES HERE

#42 Slow or Inefficient Production

Collections clerk's productivity is not acceptable, and her work requires constant rechecking for accuracy.

PERFORMANCE CORRECTION NOTICE

Employee Name: *Summer Vincents*   **Department:** *Accounting*

Date Presented: *May 1, 2017*   **Supervisor:** *John Hurlbutt*

DISCIPLINARY LEVEL

☐ **Verbal Correction**—(To memorialize the conversation.)

☐ **Written Warning**—(State nature of offense, method of correction, and action to be taken if offense is repeated.)

☐ **Investigatory Leave**—(Include length of time and nature of review.)

☒ **Final Written Warning**

  ☒ Without decision-making leave

  ☐ With decision-making leave (Attach memo of instructions.)

  ☐ With unpaid suspension

SUBJECT: *Slow and inefficient production; lack of productivity and quality*

☐ Policy/Procedure Violation

☒ Performance Transgression

☐ Behavior/Conduct Infraction

☐ Absenteeism/Tardiness

PRIOR NOTIFICATIONS

Level of Discipline	Date	Subject
Verbal	*Feb 4, 2017*	*Excessive personal phone calls and sloppy work*
Written	*Apr 18, 2017*	*Productivity and excessive personal phone calls*
Final Written	_____	_____

Incident Description and Supporting Details: Include the following information: Time, Place, Date of Occurrence, and Persons Present as well as Organizational Impact.

Summer,

On January 8, 2017, you and I met for another counseling session regarding your productivity. I clarified that our department's published production standard was fifteen calls per day. However, the total number of calls that you made during the entire month of February was thirty-four—the equivalent of only two days' work. This count was calculated from your weekly reports. However, because you failed to turn in your daily logs (which is mandatory for all collections reps) on five separate instances, I had to take time away from my own work to research and tally these totals. I presented this information to you on April 18, yet you had no excuse for having made such a minimal number of calls.

In addition, on February 25, I took you off calls and had you process the backlog of mail. You processed 151 pieces of mail (which was acceptable) over the next three weeks. In reviewing the mail that you had processed for accuracy, however, I found that your write-ups were very sloppy and sometimes illegible. I reminded you several times that the correct Invoice Number and Detail Number must be recorded on the write-up sheet. I found inconsistencies throughout the write-ups and had to correct them myself before they could be processed. This slowed down the work flow in our unit.

Your inconsistent and erratic performance, Summer, makes double-checking all your work necessary. The time spent reviewing careless errors should be devoted to making calls to collect outstanding balances on accounts due. I remain concerned about your excessive personal conversations with your coworkers and incoming personal phone calls (which cannot be monitored). You are not meeting departmental standards of production. Because of ongoing problems with these same issues, you are now being placed on a special probation with more stringent requirements.

PERFORMANCE IMPROVEMENT PLAN

1. Measurable/Tangible Improvement Goals: *Summer, I expect you to immediately improve the quantity and quality of your work. Your telephone calls must immediately increase to meet the minimum number of daily outbound calls (fifteen). Your work with the mail must be reasonably free from error and careless mistakes. I expect that you will limit inbound calls to emergencies only.*

2. Training or Special Direction to Be Provided: *I will meet with you daily for the next week to ensure that you are meeting your fifteen-call-per-day minimum. I remind you, Summer, that this is a minimum benchmark—not a daily outbound call goal. In addition, I am providing you with copies of (1) your job description, (2) departmental production guidelines, and (3) the corporate policy regarding personal phone calls on company time. Please review these documents immediately, and see me if you have any questions about your essential job functions or what is expected from you.*

3. Interim Performance Evaluation Necessary? *No. However, I remind you that your most recent evaluation in March shows that your overall performance is not meeting performance expectations.*

4. Our **Employee Assistance Program** (EAP) provider, Prime Behavioral Health Group, can be confidentially reached to assist you at (800) 555-5555. This is strictly voluntary. A booklet regarding the EAP's services is available from Human Resources.

5. In addition, I recognize that you may have certain ideas to improve your performance. Therefore, I encourage you to provide your own **Personal Improvement Plan Input and Suggestions:**

_____

_____

_____

(Attach additional sheets if needed.)

OUTCOMES AND CONSEQUENCES

Positive: I will remain available to help you and discuss areas where you require additional support. If you meet your performance goals, no further disciplinary action will be taken regarding this issue. *In addition, you will develop a greater sense of accomplishment in helping our department collect on outstanding receivables and meet its cash flow goals.*

Negative: *You are now being placed on notice that if you are discovered engaging in a personal telephone call of a nonemergency nature at any time in the next ninety days, you may be dismissed.*

In addition, if in the next ninety days you fail to meet any established departmental standards of productivity or performance, you may likewise be dismissed. A copy of this document will be placed in your personnel file.

Scheduled Review Date: *Tomorrow (May 2)*

EMPLOYEE COMMENTS AND/OR REBUTTAL

_____

_____

_____

(Attach additional sheets if needed.)

X _____
   Employee Signature

EMPLOYEE ACKNOWLEDGMENT GOES HERE

Note: Since this is a final written warning with no decision-making leave, add the following sentences to the Employee Acknowledgment: "In addition, I understand that my position is seriously in jeopardy of being lost and that this is my last chance to improve my performance and to meet minimum company expectations. If I fail to meet these expectations or otherwise demonstrate that I am not sufficiently responsible to continue my employment, I will voluntarily resign or be discharged for cause.

#43 Failure to Observe Working Schedule, Including Rest and Lunch Periods

Mailroom clerk is found reading the newspaper during the first half hour of his shift.

PERFORMANCE CORRECTION NOTICE

Employee Name: *Philip Steiner*   **Department:** *Mailroom*

Date Presented: *March 3, 2017*   **Supervisor:** *Jim Halper*

DISCIPLINARY LEVEL

☒ **Verbal Correction**—(To memorialize the conversation.)

☐ **Written Warning**—(State nature of offense, method of correction, and action to be taken if offense is repeated.)

☐ **Investigatory Leave**—(Include length of time and nature of review.)

☐ **Final Written Warning**

    ☐ Without decision-making leave

    ☐ With decision-making leave (Attach memo of instructions.)

    ☐ With unpaid suspension

SUBJECT: *Failure to observe working schedule*

☒ Policy/Procedure Violation

☒ Performance Transgression

☐ Behavior/Conduct Infraction

☐ Absenteeism/Tardiness

PRIOR NOTIFICATIONS

Level of Discipline	Date	Subject
Verbal	_____	_____
Written	_____	_____
Final Written	_____	_____

Incident Description and Supporting Details: Include the following information: Time, Place, Date of Occurrence, and Persons Present as well as Organizational Impact.

Philip,

In the past, I have shared with you the importance of working diligently and offering your services to other supervisors when your own workload slows down. On Tuesday, March 2, I observed you reading the newspaper in the second-floor employee lounge at 9:00, your start time. I didn't say anything because I assumed that you would begin work at that point. When I returned to my office at 9:25, I walked past the employee lounge again, and you were still sitting there reading the same paper. When I addressed you, you admitted that you shouldn't have been taking a break. You stated that there wasn't any work for you to do. You also readily admitted that you had been in the break room since 9:00 (confirming my observations). Still, this is a clear breach of performance standards that cannot be repeated.

PERFORMANCE IMPROVEMENT PLAN

1. Measurable/Tangible Improvement Goals: *Philip, you are expected to work when on the clock. Therefore, I expect you to make yourself available to your coworkers or supervisors by asking for work if there is downtime. In addition, you must become conscious of the negative impression you could give others who see you sitting and reading the paper during work hours.*

2. Training or Special Direction Provided: *None*

3. Interim Performance Evaluation Necessary? *No*

4. Our **Employee Assistance Program** (EAP) provider, Prime Behavioral Health Group, can be confidentially reached to assist you at (800) 555-5555. This is strictly voluntary. A booklet regarding the EAP's services is available from Human Resources.

5. In addition, I recognize that you may have certain ideas to improve your performance. Therefore, I encourage you to provide your own **Personal Improvement Plan Input and Suggestions:**

_____

_____

_____

(Attach additional sheets if needed.)

OUTCOMES AND CONSEQUENCES

Positive: I will remain available to help you and discuss areas where you require additional support. If you meet your performance goals, no further disciplinary action will be taken regarding this issue. *In addition, you'll increase your value to the company if you become known as someone who is always willing to help out when things slow down in your area.*

Negative: *As we agreed, any further incidents of lounging during the workday or failing to offer your services to others when the workload slows down may lead to further disciplinary action up to and including dismissal.* A copy of this document will be placed in your personnel file.

Scheduled Review Date: *None*

EMPLOYEE COMMENTS AND/OR REBUTTAL

_____

_____

_____

(Attach additional sheets if needed.)

X _____
Employee Signature

EMPLOYEE ACKNOWLEDGMENT GOES HERE

#44 Failure to Observe Working Schedule, Including Rest and Lunch Periods

A sales assistant clocks in to work but then immediately returns to the parking lot to park her car; as a result, a customer is kept waiting for an additional twenty-five minutes.

PERFORMANCE CORRECTION NOTICE

Employee Name: *Marlene Gordeeva*   **Department:** *Customer Service*

Date Presented: *August 23, 2017*   **Supervisor:** *Vanessa Jones*

DISCIPLINARY LEVEL

☐ **Verbal Correction**—(To memorialize the conversation.)

☐ **Written Warning**—(State nature of offense, method of correction, and action to be taken if offense is repeated.)

☐ **Investigatory Leave**—(Include length of time and nature of review.)

☒ **Final Written Warning**

    ☒ Without decision-making leave

    ☐ With decision-making leave (Attach memo of instructions.)

    ☐ With unpaid suspension

SUBJECT: *Failure to appear at your workstation in a timely manner; tardiness*

☒ Policy/Procedure Violation

☒ Performance Transgression

☒ Behavior/Conduct Infraction

☒ Absenteeism/Tardiness

PRIOR NOTIFICATIONS

Level of Discipline	Date	Subject
Verbal	*June 13, 2017*	*Tardiness*
Written	*July 13, 2017*	*Tardiness*
Final Written	_____	_____

Incident Description and Supporting Details: Include the following information: Time, Place, Date of Occurrence, and Persons Present as well as Organizational Impact.

Marlene,

On August 14, your supervisor reported that you did not appear at your workstation until 7:25 A.M., twenty-five minutes after the beginning of your shift. A customer with a prearranged appointment had been waiting for you since 7:00 A.M. You were witnessed parking your car in the red zone in front of the building at 7:00. You ran into the main entrance, swiped your ID badge through the Kronos machine, and then ran out to your car to find a parking spot. By the time you returned to the office, it was twenty-five minutes past your start time.

We waited to see the weekly Kronos report to ensure that you in fact swiped in to work at 7:00. This was indeed the case; you did not attempt to manually edit your punch after the fact. As a result, you violated company policy 5.51 on Timekeeping. Understand, Marlene, that this issue is separate from and more serious than the problems you have been experiencing with tardiness. Failing to appear at your workstation for a significant period of time after swiping in falls under the violation "Failure to observe working schedules." In addition, time is "stolen" from the company because of your willful misrepresentation of company records. Work flow was disrupted, and you provided subpar customer service as well.

PERFORMANCE IMPROVEMENT PLAN

1. Measurable/Tangible Improvement Goals: *Marlene, I expect that you will never again jeopardize your employment by swiping in to work without going directly to your work area in order to take care of a personal need. I also expect your tardiness problem to cease; your previous written warning stated that you were to adhere to company policy regarding attendance at all times.*

2. Training or Special Direction to Be Provided: *I am attaching a copy of policy 5.51 on Timekeeping. I am also providing a copy of policy 5.82 on Recordkeeping; this policy describes record falsification and its consequences. You were given a copy of the tardiness policy with your July 13 written warning. Read these policies immediately and bring any questions you have regarding them to me tomorrow. I also recommend that you review your employee handbook to familiarize yourself with company rules and standards of performance and conduct.*

3. Interim Performance Evaluation Necessary? *No*

4. Our **Employee Assistance Program** (EAP) provider, Prime Behavioral Health Group, can be confidentially reached to assist you at (800) 555-5555. This is strictly voluntary. A booklet regarding the EAP's services is available from Human Resources.

5. In addition, I recognize that you may have certain ideas to improve your performance. Therefore, I encourage you to provide your own **Personal Improvement Plan Input and Suggestions:**

_____

_____

_____

(Attach additional sheets if needed.)

OUTCOMES AND CONSEQUENCES

Positive: I will remain available to help you and discuss areas where you require additional support. If you meet your performance goals, no further disciplinary action will be taken regarding this issue. _In addition, by familiarizing yourself with the rules and policies attached to this document and in the employee handbook, you will feel more secure concerning what's expected of you._

Negative: _You are now being placed on notice that if you ever again swipe in without reporting directly to your workstation, or if you leave your workplace unattended while you are officially on the clock, you may be immediately dismissed. In addition, I remind you that according to company policy, if you have two more tardies in the rolling calendar year, you will be placed on final written warning for tardiness. A third incident in the rolling calendar year will result in dismissal._ A copy of this document will be placed in your personnel file.

Scheduled Review Date: _None_

EMPLOYEE COMMENTS AND/OR REBUTTAL

_____

_____

_____

(Attach additional sheets if needed.)

X _____

Employee Signature

EMPLOYEE ACKNOWLEDGMENT GOES HERE

Note: Because this is a final written warning, add this sentence to the end of the Employee Acknowledgment: "In addition, I understand that this is my last chance and that I am in serious jeopardy of losing my job. If I breach any of the performance standards established in this notice, I will voluntarily resign or be discharged for cause."

#45 Sleeping on the Job (Written Warning)

Insurance adjuster falls asleep in his cubicle while reviewing files and is discovered by his supervisor.

PERFORMANCE CORRECTION NOTICE

Employee Name: *Eric Burrows*   **Department:** *Personal Lines Claims*

Date Presented: *October 17, 2017*   **Supervisor:** *Barbara McDonald*

DISCIPLINARY LEVEL

☐ **Verbal Correction**—(To memorialize the conversation.)

☒ **Written Warning**—(State nature of offense, method of correction, and action to be taken if offense is repeated.)

☐ **Investigatory Leave**—(Include length of time and nature of review.)

☐ **Final Written Warning**

    ☐ Without decision-making leave

    ☐ With decision-making leave (Attach memo of instructions.)

    ☐ With unpaid suspension

SUBJECT: *Sleeping on the job*

☒ Policy/Procedure Violation

☒ Performance Transgression

☒ Behavior/Conduct Infraction

☐ Absenteeism/Tardiness

PRIOR NOTIFICATIONS

Level of Discipline	Date	Subject
Verbal	_____	_____
Written	_____	_____
Final Written	_____	_____

Incident Description and Supporting Details: Include the following information: Time, Place, Date of Occurrence, and Persons Present as well as Organizational Impact.

Eric,

Today I walked by your cubicle at approximately 9:00 and saw you sitting in your chair with your head down in your arms. I assumed that you were resting your head because you had a headache. When I walked by again at 9:08, I saw that you were still sitting in the same position and had not moved. I came into your cubicle to see how you were, and when I called your name once, you did not answer. When I tapped your shoulder, you jumped up in alarm because I had awakened you.

We later discussed the fact that you were working late at night and had been busy with personal affairs after work. You apologized for this mishap, assured me that it would not happen again, and committed yourself to getting more sleep at night. Your actions, however, have violated company performance standards.

PERFORMANCE IMPROVEMENT PLAN

1. Measurable/Tangible Improvement Goals: *Eric, I expect you to get enough sleep at night to arrive at work each morning refreshed and eager to begin. I expect you to remain sufficiently responsible to retain your position as claims adjuster.*

2. Training or Special Direction to Be Provided: *Attached to this document is a copy of your job description. Please review the section on Accountabilities to refamiliarize yourself with your performance expectations.*

3. Interim Performance Evaluation Necessary? *No*

4. Our **Employee Assistance Program** (EAP) provider, Prime Behavioral Health Group, can be confidentially reached to assist you at (800) 555-5555. This is strictly voluntary. A booklet regarding the EAP's services is available from Human Resources.

5. In addition, I recognize that you may have certain ideas to improve your performance. Therefore, I encourage you to provide your own **Personal Improvement Plan Input and Suggestions:**

_____

_____

_____

(Attach additional sheets if needed.)

OUTCOMES AND CONSEQUENCES

Positive: I will remain available to help you and discuss areas where you require additional support. If you meet your performance goals, no further disciplinary action will be taken regarding this issue. *In addition, you will increase your productivity and help our department reach its targeted claims processing goals.*

Negative: *You are now being placed on notice that if you again fall asleep on company time and on company premises, further discipline up to and including dismissal will result.* A copy of this document will be placed in your personnel file.

Scheduled Review Date: *None*

EMPLOYEE COMMENTS AND/OR REBUTTAL

_____

_____

_____

(Attach additional sheets if needed.)

X _____
Employee Signature

EMPLOYEE ACKNOWLEDGMENT GOES HERE

Bonus Sample: Sleeping on the Job (Final Written Warning)

Intensive Care Unit nurse on the night shift falls asleep at the patient monitoring board in the Intensive Care Unit (ICU).

PERFORMANCE CORRECTION NOTICE

Employee Name: *Rolf Wenger*   **Department:** *Intensive Care Unit*

Date Presented: *July 1, 2017*   **Supervisor:** *Katie Gore*

DISCIPLINARY LEVEL

☐ **Verbal Correction**—(To memorialize the conversation.)

☐ **Written Warning**—(State nature of offense, method of correction, and action to be taken if offense is repeated.)

☐ **Investigatory Leave**—(Include length of time and nature of review.)

☒ **Final Written Warning**

    ☒ Without decision-making leave

    ☐ With decision-making leave (Attach memo of instructions.)

    ☐ With unpaid suspension

SUBJECT: *Falling asleep at the ICU panel*

☒ Policy/Procedure Violation

☒ Performance Transgression

☒ Behavior/Conduct Infraction

☐ Absenteeism/Tardiness

PRIOR NOTIFICATIONS

Level of Discipline	Date	Subject
Verbal	_____	_____
Written	_____	_____
Final Written	_____	_____

Incident Description and Supporting Details: Include the following information: Time, Place, Date of Occurrence, and Persons Present as well as Organizational Impact.

Rolf,

On June 28 at approximately 2:30 in the morning, patient #11236 pressed on their help button but did not receive a reply. Likewise, the patient light outside their room was activated but had gone unnoticed for almost forty minutes. The patient's family member made a complaint the following morning after your shift had concluded, and it was discovered via video that you were asleep at the ICU desk. Your head was resting on your arms on the desk, and there was little body movement until approximately 3:10 A.M., when you woke up and responded to the patient's request.

When we asked you about this at the beginning of your next shift tonight, you stated that you might have fallen asleep. You stated that you recalled seeing the patient's light and responding to it, but you don't remember seeing it go on. You confirmed that it very likely was the case that you had fallen asleep at your workstation.

Further, you acknowledged the critical nature of remaining vigilant at the ICU desk—especially during the midnight shift—because patients' lives could be in jeopardy. As a result of this transgression, which could have potentially compromised patient care, you are receiving this final written warning, confirming that any similar transgressions in the future could result in termination of employment.

PERFORMANCE IMPROVEMENT PLAN

1. Measurable/Tangible Improvement Goals: *I realize that you recognize the critical nature of patient care at all times, especially during the midnight shift. Likewise, I appreciate your willingness to accept responsibility for this particular occurrence. However, I expect that you will never again compromise patient safety by putting yourself in a situation where you could potentially fall asleep during your shift and especially while monitoring the ICU desk in the late-night hours.*

2. Training or Special Direction Provided: *None*

3. Interim Performance Evaluation Necessary? *No*

4. Our **Employee Assistance Program** (EAP) provider, Prime Behavioral Health Group, can be confidentially reached to assist you at (800) 555-5555. This is strictly voluntary. A booklet regarding the EAP's services is available from Human Resources.

5. In addition, I recognize that you may have certain ideas to improve your performance. Therefore, I encourage you to provide your own **Personal Improvement Plan Input and Suggestions:**

_____

_____

_____

(Attach additional sheets if needed.)

OUTCOMES AND CONSEQUENCES

Positive: I will remain available to help you and discuss areas where you require additional support. If you meet your performance goals, no further disciplinary action will be taken regarding this issue.

Negative: *If you ever again fall asleep on company time and on company premises, further disciplinary action up to and including dismissal will result. In addition, if you ever again fall asleep at the ICU desk while monitoring critical patients, your employment will be terminated.*

Scheduled Review Date: *None*

EMPLOYEE COMMENTS AND/OR REBUTTAL

_____

_____

_____

(Attach additional sheets if needed.)

X _____
Employee Signature

EMPLOYEE ACKNOWLEDGMENT GOES HERE

#46 Failure to Learn New Material During Training

Newly trained employee fails to take notes and acknowledges that she understands things when she really doesn't. This employee gets very nervous whenever her supervisor sits next to her to train her or observe her work, and she spends much of her time asking her coworkers for help, thereby diverting them from their work. The supervisor instructs this employee to retrain herself.

PERFORMANCE CORRECTION NOTICE

Employee Name: *Marge Kingston* **Department:** *Finance*

Date Presented: *December 19, 2017* **Supervisor:** *Shirley Laverne*

DISCIPLINARY LEVEL

☐ **Verbal Correction**—(To memorialize the conversation.)

☒ **Written Warning**—(State nature of offense, method of correction, and action to be taken if offense is repeated.)

☐ **Investigatory Leave**—(Include length of time and nature of review.)

☐ **Final Written Warning**

   ☐ Without decision-making leave

   ☐ With decision-making leave (Attach memo of instructions.)

   ☐ With unpaid suspension

SUBJECT: *Failure to learn new material in training*

☐ Policy/Procedure Violation

☒ Performance Transgression

☒ Behavior/Conduct Infraction

☐ Absenteeism/Tardiness

PRIOR NOTIFICATIONS

Level of Discipline	Date	Subject
Verbal	*Aug 2, 2017*	*Unsatisfactory work performance*
Written	_____	_____
Final Written	_____	_____

Incident Description and Supporting Details: Include the following information: Time, Place, Date of Occurrence, and Persons Present as well as Organizational Impact.

Marge,

As you know, in May of 2017, KRLG's consultants reorganized our department's structure and work procedures to better meet our hospital's needs. At that time, your position was changed from a specialist in Medicare follow-up to a generalist. Namely, you were asked to assume a role in the Large Balance unit ($5,000+ accounts).

In August 2017, you received a verbal warning because of unsatisfactory work performance in that unit. Specifically, you had difficulty in two key areas: (1) telephone contacts with patients and payers (in that you did not know how to appropriately question the status of your accounts) and (2) reading and comprehending the Explanation of Benefits (EOB) statements.

At that time, I committed to meeting with you for one-on-one training to help you gain a mastery of these techniques. I also shared with you that you would be given an appropriate amount of time to learn them. However, in our training sessions, you didn't take notes. Furthermore, on many occasions, when I asked you if you understood what I was explaining to you, you said yes when you apparently didn't understand (as evidenced by your errors and your reliance on your coworkers). In addition, we transferred you to the Medium Balance unit in August because there was less of a need for telephone contact with patients and payers, and we thought this would work to your benefit.

However, to date, you continue to demonstrate a lack of understanding in your role in the Medium Balance unit. Specifically, you still do not understand the processing of EOBs and the calculation of percentages to ensure that insurance was paid correctly. In addition, you continue to request support from your coworkers in areas in which I specifically trained you. This has disrupted the work flow in your area and in our unit.

PERFORMANCE IMPROVEMENT PLAN

1. Measurable/Tangible Improvement Goals: *Marge, I expect you to communicate openly with me any time you don't understand my directions. I also expect you to come to me—not your coworkers—when you have a question about your work. I expect you to follow all departmental policies and procedures for administering and processing EOBs.*

2. Training or Special Direction to Be Provided: *Because you didn't take notes when we sat together for training over the past four months, it is critical that you re-create a system of notes to ensure that you are comfortable handling the thirty or so different types of EOBs. To help you master EOB processing and to increase your confidence in EOB processing, you are to create a thirty-page booklet with specific explanations of each type of EOB that you come across on a day-to-day basis. This booklet should contain specific instructions on how to interpret the explanation of benefits and any variables that normally surface in the administration process.*

I want you to complete your notebook by January 15, 2017. However, I would like you to meet with me each time you've completed one of these examples. I will ensure that your processing notes are correct and answer any questions that surface while you are relearning the system. Understand that I will wait to hear from you regarding the individual completion of these EOB modules, and I will make myself available when you are ready.

3. Interim Performance Evaluation Necessary? *No*

4. Our **Employee Assistance Program** (EAP) provider, Prime Behavioral Health Group, can be confidentially reached to assist you at (800) 555-5555. This is strictly voluntary. A booklet regarding the EAP's services is available from Human Resources.

5. In addition, I recognize that you may have certain ideas to improve your performance. Therefore, I encourage you to provide your own **Personal Improvement Plan Input and Suggestions:**

_____

_____

_____

(Attach additional sheets if needed.)

OUTCOMES AND CONSEQUENCES

Positive: I will remain available to help you and discuss areas where you require additional support. If you meet your performance goals, no further disciplinary action will be taken regarding this issue. *In addition, you will enjoy greater work satisfaction by feeling more confident about your day-to-day responsibilities. You will also help our department meet its financial goals as set by KRLG.*

Negative: *Marge, I hold you responsible for mastering these tasks because I know you can do it. However, if in the next sixty days you fail to meet departmental production procedures as outlined in this memo, you will be placed on a sixty-day final written warning. If you fail to meet standards during that sixty-day final written warning period, you will be subject to further disciplinary action up to and including dismissal.* A copy of this document will be placed in your personnel file.

Scheduled Review Date: *January 15, 2018*

EMPLOYEE COMMENTS AND/OR REBUTTAL

_____

_____

_____
(Attach additional sheets if needed.)

X _____
                Employee Signature

EMPLOYEE ACKNOWLEDGMENT GOES HERE

Bonus Sample: Failure to Retain Information After Training

Aircraft mechanic (union) continues to demonstrate challenges in meeting specific performance targets, quality results, and project delivery dates. The company is very specific in following the progressive disciplinary terms outlined in its collective bargaining agreement.

PERFORMANCE CORRECTION NOTICE

Employee Name: *Claude Mansour*　　　　**Department:** *Warehouse*

Date Presented: *April 2, 2017*　　　　**Supervisor:** *Debbie Suh*

DISCIPLINARY LEVEL

☐ **Verbal Correction**—(To memorialize the conversation.)

☒ **Written Warning**—(State nature of offense, method of correction, and action to be taken if offense is repeated.)

☐ **Investigatory Leave**—(Include length of time and nature of review.)

☐ **Final Written Warning**

　☐ Without decision-making leave

　☐ With decision-making leave (Attach memo of instructions.)

　☐ With unpaid suspension

SUBJECT: *Substandard job performance, inferior quality results, and missed deadlines*

☐ Policy/Procedure Violation

☒ Performance Transgression

☐ Behavior/Conduct Infraction

☐ Absenteeism/Tardiness

PRIOR NOTIFICATIONS

Level of Discipline	Date	Subject
Verbal	*Mar 4, 2017*	*Performance/Quality*
Written	_____	_____
Final Written	_____	_____

Incident Description and Supporting Details: Include the following information: Time, Place, Date of Occurrence, and Persons Present as well as Organizational Impact.

Claude,

As we discussed, your overall productivity, quality results, and timeliness remain a challenge and are not currently meeting acceptable performance standards. Since our discussion on March 4, numerous issues have been brought to your attention regarding these very same issues. Specifically, at the time of occurrence, we addressed the following productivity, quality, and delivery issues with you:

- *You remain unable to differentiate consistently between the blades on visual inspection or by part number, despite having been trained and certified in these areas.*

- *You are not able to demonstrate a clear understanding of how to complete and submit the inventory forms. The number of resubmissions due to errors in the initial inputs has caused unnecessary delays.*

- *You have requested additional training on scanning and rotating, which has been provided. However, you continue to delay or postpone these activities or ask others to help you with them or do them for you.*

- *Despite prior training and certification, you continue to demonstrate challenges with photographing and resizing photos, causing rework and processing delays.*

- *Your administrative ticketing and processing remains uncoordinated and misaligned, especially surrounding the shipping checklist and pick tickets. Backlogs in ticket processing are having further impacts down the line.*

When we discussed this with you last month, you asked for additional computer training, which you received three times a week for two weeks. You informed us that you felt you were given too much responsibility too early when you had no previous aviation experience. However, as you are aware, your position doesn't specifically require prior aviation experience, and you have been trained consistently with your peers since your date of hire and certified in particular areas accordingly.

Retention of the information is at issue. You are responsible for demonstrating mastery of the duties and responsibilities you have been trained and certified in. It is not acceptable to continually ask your supervisor or peers for help in processing orders or working with the tools of your trade, and the delays and postponements we have experienced stem from your inability to master the basics of your craft.

PERFORMANCE IMPROVEMENT PLAN

1. Measurable/Tangible Improvement Goals: *You have agreed, in conjunction with your supervisor and union steward, that the following tasks must be performed on a continuous and consistent basis from this point forward:*

Tasks	Initials
1. Ensure all items are packed as per the packing procedures	
2. Counts should be completed before packaging begins	
3. Counts should be double-checked to ensure accuracy	
4. All shipments require a checklist	
5. Set up a folder in the warehouse drive with photographs showing how parts are packaged, and use this as a future reference tool	
6. Documents are to be scanned correctly; refer to your notes from training for further assistance	
7. Arrive at your place of work on time and ready to begin at the onset of each scheduled shift	
8. Notify me, your supervisor, any time you believe you will not be able to complete a particular task so that alternative support can be provided	

Please initial to the right of each task to demonstrate that you agree with these performance standards. I expect you to study your prep notes from prior training and certification sessions and see me if you are unclear on any of your roles or responsibilities. Likewise, I expect you to be able to work independently in any areas where you are expected to demonstrate competence. Focus on retaining your training materials so that you can work independently without delay and without having to rely on your coworkers to perform tasks that you have already been trained in or that constitute an essential and foundational function of your job.

2. Training or Special Direction Provided: *At this point, you have been trained and certified in all key aspects of your role. You have likewise been retrained in several areas where you requested additional support. However, if after reviewing your instructional materials you develop additional questions about the material content, please meet with me to discuss those areas. We will set aside time for one-on-one hands-on training, but please note that these should be clarification issues—not retraining of basic material that you have already been trained on and certified in.*

3. Interim Performance Evaluation Necessary? *No*

4. Our **Employee Assistance Program** (EAP) provider, Prime Behavioral Health Group, can be confidentially reached to assist you at (800) 555-5555. This is strictly voluntary. A booklet regarding the EAP's services is available from Human Resources.

5. In addition, I recognize that you may have certain ideas to improve your performance. Therefore, I encourage you to provide your own **Personal Improvement Plan Input and Suggestions:**

_____

_____

_____

(Attach additional sheets if needed.)

OUTCOMES AND CONSEQUENCES

Positive: I will remain available to help you and discuss areas where you require additional support. _If you meet your performance, quality, and timeliness goals on an ongoing basis, no further disciplinary action will be taken regarding these specific issues. Further, you will develop greater confidence around your ability to contribute to the team and to our organization's delivery results._

Negative: _The disciplinary process has been escalated to the written warning level because your overall performance needs to improve and be sustained on an ongoing and consistent basis. According to the terms of the union contract, failure to demonstrate immediate and sustained improvement over the next thirty days may require escalation to the final written warning stage or further disciplinary action up to and including dismissal._ A copy of this document will be placed in your personnel file.

Scheduled Review Date: _Tuesday, May 2, 2017_

EMPLOYEE COMMENTS AND/OR REBUTTAL

_____

_____

_____

(Attach additional sheets if needed.)

X _____
Employee Signature

EMPLOYEE ACKNOWLEDGMENT GOES HERE

#47 High Error Factor and Scrap Rate

Printer produces low-volume, low-quality RSVP cards and brochures that must be scrapped and redone. Note that this individual is already in final written warning for unacceptable attendance.

PERFORMANCE CORRECTION NOTICE

Employee Name: *Robert Winger*   **Department:** *Print Shop*

Date Presented: *January 22, 2017*   **Supervisor:** *Jean Sharperson*

DISCIPLINARY LEVEL

☐ **Verbal Correction**—(To memorialize the conversation.)

☒ **Written Warning**—(State nature of offense, method of correction, and action to be taken if offense is repeated.)

☐ **Investigatory Leave**—(Include length of time and nature of review.)

☐ **Final Written Warning**

    ☐ Without decision-making leave

    ☐ With decision-making leave (Attach memo of instructions.)

    ☐ With unpaid suspension

SUBJECT: *High error factor and scrap rate*

☒ Policy/Procedure Violation

☒ Performance Transgression

☐ Behavior/Conduct Infraction

☐ Absenteeism/Tardiness

PRIOR NOTIFICATIONS

Level of Discipline	Date	Subject
Verbal	*Nov 14, 2016*	*Annual review: substandard job performance*
Written	*Aug, 22, 2016*	*Unscheduled absence (UA), pattern of UA*
	Nov 14, 2016	*Excessive tardiness*
Final Written	*Aug 22, 2016*	*Leaving the work area without prior authorization*
	Nov 14, 2016	*Unscheduled absence*

Incident Description and Supporting Details: Include the following information: Time, Place, Date of Occurrence, and Persons Present as well as Organizational Impact.

Robert,

In your November 14, 2016, review, you were informed that you needed to show (a) immediate improvement in the quality and quantity of your work, (b) quicker turnaround time, (c) increased productivity, (d) more efficient planning and time management, and (e) quicker setup time. Since that time, you have not demonstrated sufficient improvement.

I received a complaint about the quality of your work from the R&B Group because the golf invitations and RSVP cards that you produced were inferior. As a result, the documents that you created need to be scrapped, and the project needs to begin again.

In terms of the quantity of your work, I have had to continuously check to make sure that customers' needs are met. It takes you approximately two to three hours to set up for a job. It then takes you an additional two to three hours to run the job. As a result, you are running a total of only one-and-a-half jobs per day. I expect you and other members of the staff to run a minimum of three jobs per day.

Because of this, I have to constantly reschedule jobs and work overtime to ensure that your work meets specified deadlines. In addition, you are expected to make 2,000 impressions per hour on a daily basis. On average, you do not meet this daily requirement three to five times per month. As a result of this, and because you are right now on final written warning for excessive absence, you are not meeting company standards of performance and conduct. As you were informed in your November 14, 2016, disciplinary memo, your position is in serious jeopardy of being lost.

PERFORMANCE IMPROVEMENT PLAN

1. Measurable/Tangible Improvement Goals: *Robert, I expect you to immediately bring both the quality and quantity of your work to an acceptable level and thereby minimize your scrap rate to meet departmental requirements. I expect you to increase your productivity by consistently reaching the minimum production threshold of 2,000 impressions per hour per day, turning your jobs around more quickly, and minimizing your setup time. I expect you to inform me if you need help with meeting any of these goals or if further training is necessary.*

2. Training or Special Direction to Be Provided: *I will make myself available to you to answer any specific questions that arise on a day-to-day basis. If you require any additional technical support from the printing manufacturer, please let me know so that I can set up a one-on-one training session for you.*

3. Interim Performance Evaluation Necessary? *No*

4. Our **Employee Assistance Program** (EAP) provider, Prime Behavioral Health Group, can be confidentially reached to assist you at (800) 555-5555. This is strictly voluntary. A booklet regarding the EAP's services is available from Human Resources.

5. In addition, I recognize that you may have certain ideas to improve your performance. Therefore, I encourage you to provide your own **Personal Improvement Plan Input and Suggestions:**

_____

_____

_____

(Attach additional sheets if needed.)

OUTCOMES AND CONSEQUENCES

Positive: I will remain available to help you and discuss areas where you require additional support. If you meet your performance goals, no further disciplinary action will be taken regarding this issue.

Negative: *If at any time within the next forty-five days you fail to meet the performance guidelines established in this document or if you fail to meet any other company or departmental standards of performance or production, you may be placed on a forty-five-day probation. If you fail to meet the terms of this warning during that probationary period, you may be dismissed. I again remind you that if you have one additional unscheduled, non-qualified absence or tardiness through May 14, 2017, you may likewise be immediately dismissed.* A copy of this document will be placed in your personnel file.

Scheduled Review Date: *Forty-five days (March 9, 2017)*

EMPLOYEE COMMENTS AND/OR REBUTTAL

_____

_____

_____

(Attach additional sheets if needed.)

X _____

Employee Signature

EMPLOYEE ACKNOWLEDGMENT GOES HERE

Note: Since the employee is on final written warning for a separate offense, add this sentence to the second paragraph of the Employee Acknowledgment: "I understand that my position continues to be in serious jeopardy of being lost, and I commit that if I do not abide by the terms of this agreement, I will voluntarily resign or be discharged for cause."

#48 Falsification of Employer Records

A blood donor technician falsely documents the time when a patient's charting was to have taken place. It was determined via investigation that she was not in the room at the time she supposedly completed working with the patient

---

PERFORMANCE CORRECTION NOTICE

Employee Name: *Maryanne Vasquez*   **Department:** *Blood Donor Room*

Date Presented: *June 24, 2017*   **Supervisor:** *Dianne Xavier*

DISCIPLINARY LEVEL

☐ **Verbal Correction**—(To memorialize the conversation.)

☐ **Written Warning**—(State nature of offense, method of correction, and action to be taken if offense is repeated.)

☐ **Investigatory Leave**—(Include length of time and nature of review.)

☒ **Final Written Warning**

   ☒ Without decision-making leave

   ☐ With decision-making leave (Attach memo of instructions.)

   ☐ With unpaid suspension

SUBJECT: *Document falsification*

☒ Policy/Procedure Violation

☒ Performance Transgression

☐ Behavior/Conduct Infraction

☐ Absenteeism/Tardiness

PRIOR NOTIFICATIONS

Level of Discipline	Date	Subject
Verbal		
Written	*Oct 14, 2016*	*Document falsification*
Final Written		

Incident Description and Supporting Details: Include the following information: Time, Place, Date of Occurrence, and Persons Present as well as Organizational Impact.

Maryanne,

You were given a written warning on October 14, 2017, for documenting on a donor chart that venipuncture sites were checked at 1300 and 1315. You were out of the unit at the actual time that the charting was to have taken place.

Today, you are being given a final written warning for repeating the same offense on June 14. I entered the whole blood donor room at 1500 and was told by a floating technician who had just begun working on one of your donors that you had documented that your donor was checked at 1505. This was impossible since 1505 was still five minutes in the future.

When I asked you about this, you first stated that you must have made a mistake in the time. You then admitted that you "knew the patient would be all right," so you left the work site. This repeat transgression violates our institution's standards of performance and conduct.

PERFORMANCE IMPROVEMENT PLAN

1. Measurable/Tangible Improvement Goals: *Maryanne, I expect you to accurately and truthfully reflect patient status in records at all times. There are to be no further exceptions—even for cases that seem routine. I expect you to make a commitment to me and the institution that you will never again engage in behavior that compromises patient safety or activities that falsify company documentation.*

2. Training or Special Direction to Be Provided: *I am providing you with a copy of departmental policies and procedures. Please reread this manual immediately.*

3. Interim Performance Evaluation Necessary? *No*

4. Our **Employee Assistance Program** (EAP) provider, Prime Behavioral Health Group, can be confidentially reached to assist you at (800) 555-5555. This is strictly voluntary. A booklet regarding the EAP's services is available from Human Resources.

5. In addition, I recognize that you may have certain ideas to improve your performance. Therefore, I encourage you to provide your own **Personal Improvement Plan Input and Suggestions:**

_____

_____

_____

(Attach additional sheets if needed.)

OUTCOMES AND CONSEQUENCES

Positive: I will remain available to help you and discuss areas where you require additional support. If you meet your performance goals, no further disciplinary action will be taken regarding this issue.

Negative: *This repeated offense has jeopardized your job and warranted a special probation with more stringent requirements. You are now being placed on notice that if you ever again falsify company documents, you will be immediately dismissed. If you again compromise patient safety, disciplinary action up to and including termination will occur. No other chances will be given.* A copy of this document will be placed in your personnel file.

Scheduled Review Date: *None*

EMPLOYEE COMMENTS AND/OR REBUTTAL

_____

_____

_____

(Attach additional sheets if needed.)

X _____
Employee Signature

EMPLOYEE ACKNOWLEDGMENT GOES HERE

Note: Since this is a final written warning, add this sentence to the Employee Acknowledgment: "Furthermore, I understand that this is my last chance. If I fail to meet the terms and conditions outlined in this agreement, I will voluntarily resign or be discharged for cause."

#49 Lack of Communication with Supervisor

A fund-raising employee falls far behind in his work, yet fails to inform his supervisor until the supervisor learns of the situation on his own.

PERFORMANCE CORRECTION NOTICE

Employee Name: *Bill Carroll*   **Department:** *Fund-raising*

Date Presented: *April 7, 2017*   **Supervisor:** *John Fallon*

DISCIPLINARY LEVEL

☐ **Verbal Correction**—(To memorialize the conversation.)

☒ **Written Warning**—(State nature of offense, method of correction, and action to be taken if offense is repeated.)

☐ **Investigatory Leave**—(Include length of time and nature of review.)

☐ **Final Written Warning**

    ☐ Without decision-making leave

    ☐ With decision-making leave (Attach memo of instructions.)

    ☐ With unpaid suspension

SUBJECT: *Lack of communication with supervisor*

☒ Policy/Procedure Violation

☒ Performance Transgression

☐ Behavior/Conduct Infraction

☐ Absenteeism/Tardiness

PRIOR NOTIFICATIONS

Level of Discipline	Date	Subject
Verbal	*Feb 17, 2017*	*Substandard performance*
Written	_____	_____
Final Written	_____	_____

Incident Description and Supporting Details: Include the following information: Time, Place, Date of Occurrence, and Persons Present as well as Organizational Impact.

Bill,

On February 7, Peter Winters and I discussed with you your responsibility to communicate with us concerning any problems with your work (especially prioritizing your workload and meeting deadlines regarding matching gifts). I stated at that time that your performance must improve and that the meeting served as an official warning.

Yesterday, I asked you where you were on the status of matching gifts because I hadn't seen any matching gifts recently that required my approval. You stated that you had "a couple current," hesitated, and then said that you had older documents that needed research. At that point, I told you that you had to stop everything and bring all documents to me. When you brought your documents to me for review, I found that they were very old—in some cases four months old. When I asked you why you hadn't communicated the status of those documents to me, you vaguely stated that you were busy. In addition, you acknowledged that you knew you had these outdated documents on your desk and that it was important to get them out.

Departmental policy dictates that matching gifts documentation is to be turned around within twenty-four to forty-eight hours. Consequently, you have failed to meet department performance standards on two accounts: First, your work was seriously delinquent, and second, you consciously chose not to communicate the status of your workload and the fact that you needed help.

PERFORMANCE IMPROVEMENT PLAN

1. Measurable/Tangible Improvement Goals: *Bill, I expect you to meet the twenty-four- to forty-eight-hour turnaround time with no exceptions from this point on. More important, I expect you to always clearly communicate the status of work on your desk and to let me know if things are falling behind so that I can assist you personally or redistribute the work to other staff members.*

2. Training or Special Direction Provided: *I want you to check with me once a week for the next three weeks regarding the status of work on your desk. In those meetings, I require that you identify any areas of matching gifts processing that you are having trouble mastering so that I can ensure your thorough understanding of the system.*

3. Interim Performance Evaluation Necessary? *No—your annual review is due in two weeks.*

4. Our **Employee Assistance Program** (EAP) provider, Prime Behavioral Health Group, can be confidentially reached to assist you at (800) 555-5555. This is strictly voluntary. A booklet regarding the EAP's services is available from Human Resources.

5. In addition, I recognize that you may have certain ideas to improve your performance. Therefore, I encourage you to provide your own **Personal Improvement Plan Input and Suggestions:**

_____

_____

_____

(Attach additional sheets if needed.)

OUTCOMES AND CONSEQUENCES

Positive: I will remain available to help you and discuss areas where you require additional support. If you meet your performance goals, no further disciplinary action will be taken regarding this issue.

Negative: *If in the next ninety days you fail to complete the timely turnaround of work on your desk, or if you violate any standards of performance and conduct, you will be placed in a ninety-day probationary period. If you fail to meet performance standards while in that probationary period, you may be dismissed. In addition, if you ever again fail to communicate your needs to me or allow your work to suffer because of that, disciplinary action up to and including dismissal may result.* A copy of this document will be placed in your personnel file.

Scheduled Review Date: *April 14, 2017*

EMPLOYEE COMMENTS AND/OR REBUTTAL

_____

_____

_____

(Attach additional sheets if needed.)

X _____

Employee Signature

EMPLOYEE ACKNOWLEDGMENT GOES HERE

#50 Lack of Communication with Supervisor

Quality assurance specialist fails to communicate work status to supervisor and to share information with coworkers and also misses an important agreed-upon deadline without telling anyone. This is a two-year employee who has been basically unsupervised as a result of a previous reduction in force and who now has a new manager overseeing his work.

PERFORMANCE CORRECTION NOTICE

Employee Name: *Jerry Watkins*   **Department:** *Quality Assurance*

Date Presented: *November 24, 2017*   **Supervisor:** *Roger Mahan*

DISCIPLINARY LEVEL

☐ **Verbal Correction**—(To memorialize the conversation.)

☒ **Written Warning**—(State nature of offense, method of correction, and action to be taken if offense is repeated.)

☐ **Investigatory Leave**—(Include length of time and nature of review.)

☐ **Final Written Warning**

    ☐ Without decision-making leave

    ☐ With decision-making leave (Attach memo of instructions.)

    ☐ With unpaid suspension

SUBJECT: *Lack of communication with supervisor; substandard work performance*

☒ Policy/Procedure Violation

☒ Performance Transgression

☒ Behavior/Conduct Infraction

☐ Absenteeism/Tardiness

PRIOR NOTIFICATIONS

Level of Discipline	Date	Subject
Verbal	_____	_____
Written	_____	_____
Final Written	_____	_____

Incident Description and Supporting Details: Include the following information: Time, Place, Date of Occurrence, and Persons Present as well as Organizational Impact.

Jerry,

On November 20, you and I met with department head Dr. Bennett and Tom Weston in Human Resources to discuss performance problems that you have had over the past six months to one year. Although I have been supervising you for only the past six weeks, I have noticed the following issues, and this is what we discussed:

- *You didn't complete the evaluation and revision of ISO procedures on time as outlined in the May 6, 2017, memo (see attached); you also didn't ensure that procedures were approved by the department director or by Compliance prior to implementation. The target date by which you agreed to complete these tasks was September 29, 2016. However, you completed neither of these tasks by the deadline, and in fact both are still awaiting completion. More significantly, you also didn't communicate in advance that these tasks would not be completed by the deadline. As a result, inconsistencies in procedures occurred because of undocumented changes in (a) ISO procedures and (b) training and competency assessment.*

- *You are not communicating adequately with your coworkers to provide them with the information that they need to perform their jobs successfully. For example, one coworker shared with me that you do not prepare statistical reports or analysis of your process control questionnaires in a timely manner. These items have been held on your desk for a two- to four-week period rather than being turned around on a regular (meaning at least twice a week) basis. Notification that monthly statistical reports are completed is often not relayed to the proper person until we are in a last-minute push to meet a deadline. Your delays place an undue burden on your coworkers, who must play catchup and stop everything they're doing once you deliver your finished product. For this reason, staff members have had to face unnecessary time crunches in order to get the completed proposals to me on time.*

PERFORMANCE IMPROVEMENT PLAN

1. Measurable/Tangible Improvement Goals: *Jerry, I expect you to meet all departmental standards of performance and conduct. I expect you to openly communicate all information to your coworkers that will help them perform their jobs more efficiently. I expect you to meet all deadlines that you set and not to complain that there simply isn't enough time in the day to complete your work. I also expect you to communicate very clearly with me in advance if, for any reason, you can't complete a project by deadline.*

2. Training or Special Direction to Be Provided: *I plan to work with you closely over the next four weeks to ensure that you are able to manage your time efficiently and meet all the deadlines that are before you. I will work with you to get our ISO procedures and training assessments up to par as quickly as possible. I will also work with HR's training and development department to locate off-site training seminars that will help you manage the work flow in your office and/or more openly communicate your needs to others.*

In addition, I will help you rebuild the lines of communication with your coworkers by setting up brief meetings with your peers to ensure that we all understand (a) the significance of communicating openly and directly with one another and (b) a way of bringing bad news to others' attention that will not seem like an attack.

3. Interim Performance Evaluation Necessary? *No. Your annual performance review is now overdue. Please complete the self-evaluation form that I gave you this week. I will complete your review once I have received your feedback.*

4. Our **Employee Assistance Program** (EAP) provider, Prime Behavioral Health Group, can be confidentially reached to assist you at (800) 555-5555. This is strictly voluntary. A booklet regarding the EAP's services is available from Human Resources.

5. In addition, I recognize that you may have certain ideas to improve your performance. Therefore, I encourage you to provide your own **Personal Improvement Plan Input and Suggestions:**

_____

_____

_____

(Attach additional sheets if needed.)

OUTCOMES AND CONSEQUENCES

Positive: I will remain available to help you and discuss areas where you require additional support. If you meet your performance goals, no further disciplinary action will be taken regarding this issue. *In addition, you'll find your job more rewarding and will have an even greater impact on the department's success if you are able to communicate your needs more openly with me and other members of the staff.*

Negative: *This is a written warning, Jerry, regarding your overall job performance. If at any time within the next ninety days (through February 24, 2018) you fail to meet preset task deadlines, to communicate openly with other members of the staff in order to allow them to maximize their performance, or to meet any other standards of performance and conduct, you may be placed on a final warning. If you fail to meet the terms of this agreement while in the final warning period, you may be dismissed.* A copy of this document will be placed in your personnel file.

Scheduled Review Date: *Thirty days (December 22)*

EMPLOYEE COMMENTS AND/OR REBUTTAL

_____

_____

_____

(Attach additional sheets if needed.)

X _____
Employee Signature

EMPLOYEE ACKNOWLEDGMENT GOES HERE

Bonus Sample: VP-Level Substandard Performance and Conduct

A VP's division consistently scores the lowest among its peer groups, while the VP displays inappropriate workplace behaviors that leave his team constantly scrambling.

PERFORMANCE CORRECTION NOTICE

Employee Name: *Kurt Steiner*   **Department:** *Operations*

Date Presented: *January 14, 2017*   **Supervisor:** *Farid Abdullah*

DISCIPLINARY LEVEL

☐ **Verbal Correction**—(To memorialize the conversation.)

☒ **Written Warning**—(State nature of offense, method of correction, and action to be taken if offense is repeated.)

☐ **Investigatory Leave**—(Include length of time and nature of review.)

☐ **Final Written Warning**

    ☐ Without decision-making leave

    ☐ With decision-making leave (Attach memo of instructions.)

    ☐ With unpaid suspension

SUBJECT: *Notification of substandard job performance and inappropriate workplace behavior*

☐ Policy/Procedure Violation

☒ Performance Transgression

☒ Behavior/Conduct Infraction

☐ Absenteeism/Tardiness

PRIOR NOTIFICATIONS

Level of Discipline	Date	Subject
Verbal	_____	_____
Written	_____	_____
Final Written	_____	_____

Incident Description and Supporting Details: Include the following information: Time, Place, Date of Occurrence, and Persons Present as well as Organizational Impact.

Kurt,

As you and I discussed with Human Resources yesterday, this document will serve as a written warning for overall substandard job performance and inappropriate workplace conduct regarding your position as Vice President, Operations.

I. Substandard Job Performance

Of the eight national divisions, the Midwest division has performed poorly relative to its peers over the past year in the following key performance measurement areas:

Product volume:	*Bottom quartile/7th place ranking (out of 8)*
Product quality:	*Bottom quartile/8th placed ranking (out of 8)*
Division turnover:	*49.8% (highest in the nation)*
Employee Net Promoter Score:	*4 out of 10 ("detractor," lowest eNPS in the nation)*

When asked about the ongoing performance problems of your division, you stated that your regional leaders weren't fully engaged in their work. However, as the divisional general manager, you are responsible for all aspects of leadership and strategy in your group, including productivity, quality, and overall morale and engagement. As such, you are solely responsible for this substandard divisional performance, which has been an ongoing concern for the past year but which has come to a head in this past quarter, as indicated by the statistics above.

II. Inappropriate Workplace Conduct

Members of your team describe your behavior as aggressive, inconsistent, argumentative, abrasive, manipulative, disrespectful, and insensitive. At other times, your conduct has been described as dismissive, apathetic, and disengaged. People state that they don't know how to read you and aren't sure what mood you'll be in at any given time.

In the past, we have intervened when problems occurred between you and your quality management counterparts. Your teams appear to demonstrate a lack of collaboration and teamwork. Senior leaders from your division scramble for a unified response when I ask simple operational questions. I see low morale and an overreactive grapevine among your direct reports, and your team appears to be working in a vacuum without an appropriate amount of communication, structure, or direction stemming from your leadership. The result is that your division continues to perform consistently in the lowest quartile as evidenced above.

In the past, you have admitted to "allowing your tongue to slip" in terms of saying something you realize you shouldn't have said. You likewise admitted to pushing for information that you knew was not your business, like when you insisted on finding out who filed an anonymous EEOC complaint in one of your warehouses. While you stated that you understood that conducting your own investigation was a breach of the company's code of conduct, you admitted at the time that you felt trapped by the incident and compelled to find out who was behind the complaint.

In addition, Kurt, you have admitted that you're not receptive to constructive feedback, and I've told you that you appear to take even marginal feedback as offensive and as a personal attack. As such, it is now appropriate to escalate my concerns and the company's concerns in writing in the form of progressive discipline.

III. Historical Interventions and Attempts to Turn Around Performance

In January 2016, you received a performance improvement plan (PIP) for displaying a "pattern of behaviors unbecoming of an executive." The PIP addressed, among other things, concerns regarding your communication style and decision-making abilities, your need to control and micromanage the people and projects in your area, your failure to delegate appropriately, and your failure to keep promises that you've made. The PIP also addressed your apprehension regarding corporate's involvement in your division and perception of corporate's limiting your control.

Dr. Williams is an organizational psychologist who we assigned to you as part of the PIP development plan to serve as a career coach to help you turn around the performance and interpersonal challenges you were facing as the leader of the Midwest division. After approximately six months of coaching in the first half of 2016, Dr. Williams's assignment ended, and he provided you with tips and tools to excel in your role. However, little has changed since then in terms of your performance or conduct. In fact, at that time, you stated that you were "insulted" by the PIP and by having to work with an executive coach.

PERFORMANCE IMPROVEMENT PLAN

1. Measurable/Tangible Improvement Goals: *Kurt, I expect you to consistently meet all planned performance goals for your division in our key measurement areas of volume, quality, turnover, and Employee Net Promoter Score. Likewise, I expect you to let me know in advance if you suspect that the Midwest division won't meet its performance benchmarks for any given month or any individual project. In our discussion, we can address additional resources that you may need assigned to your division to meet the performance goals outlined for the Midwest.*

I expect you to maintain harmonious relations with your peers, direct reports, boundary partners, and extended team members at all times and on a consistent basis. To do this, you need to deliver constructive, respectful communications to your team members without blame or censure. Furthermore, you must acknowledge your involvement in questionable situations and assume responsibility for things gone wrong within your group, thereby becoming an active agent in resolving complaints.

I expect you to avoid inappropriate information sharing with uninvolved parties, conducting your own unilateral investigations, or engaging in behavior that could be described as bullying, aggressive, or overly controlling.

2. Training or Special Direction Provided: *If there are any additional training and development opportunities that we can provide to help you become a more effective leader or drive more consistent performance in your division, please let us know what you recommend. We will endeavor to provide you with additional training opportunities based on your recommendations, especially anything relating to managing interpersonal conflict in the workplace, effective interpersonal communications, leadership development, and performance management.*

3. Interim Performance Evaluation Necessary? *No*

4. Our **Employee Assistance Program** (EAP) provider, Prime Behavioral Health Group, can be confidentially reached to assist you at (800) 555-5555. This is strictly voluntary. A booklet regarding the EAP's services is available from Human Resources.

5. In addition, I recognize that you may have certain ideas to improve your performance. Therefore, I encourage you to provide your own **Personal Improvement Plan Input and Suggestions:**

_____

_____

_____

(Attach additional sheets if needed.)

OUTCOMES AND CONSEQUENCES

Positive: I will remain available to help you and discuss areas where you require additional support. If you meet your performance goals, no further disciplinary action will be taken regarding this issue. *In addition, you will be able to rebuild relationships, trust, and good-will with a number of leaders and staffers who, like you, have been with our organization for many years.*

Negative: *Overall, however, you are now being placed on formal notice, that your position is in immediate jeopardy of being lost. Failure to demonstrate immediate and sustained improvement may result in further disciplinary action, up to and including dismissal of employment.* A copy of this document will be placed in your personnel file.

Scheduled Review Date: *None*

EMPLOYEE COMMENTS AND/OR REBUTTAL

_____

_____

_____

(Attach additional sheets if needed.)

X _____

Employee Signature

EMPLOYEE ACKNOWLEDGMENT GOES HERE

Bonus Sample: Unacceptable Skip-Level Findings (Director Level)

Newly hired VP meets with her director's staff members to discuss department morale challenges, perceptions of negativity in the group, and overall dissatisfaction and lack of engagement.

PERFORMANCE CORRECTION NOTICE

Employee Name: *Carson Watts*   **Department:** *Communications*

Date Presented: *August 30, 2017*   **Supervisor:** *Dena Taylor*

DISCIPLINARY LEVEL

☐ **Verbal Correction**—(To memorialize the conversation.)

☒ **Written Warning**—(State nature of offense, method of correction, and action to be taken if offense is repeated.)

☐ **Investigatory Leave**—(Include length of time and nature of review.)

☐ **Final Written Warning**

    ☐ Without decision-making leave

    ☐ With decision-making leave (Attach memo of instructions.)

    ☐ With unpaid suspension

SUBJECT: *Ongoing performance and conduct challenges with your team's performance*

☐ Policy/Procedure Violation

☒ Performance Transgression

☒ Behavior/Conduct Infraction

☐ Absenteeism/Tardiness

PRIOR NOTIFICATIONS

Level of Discipline	Date	Subject
Verbal	_____	_____
Written	_____	_____
Final Written	_____	_____

Incident Description and Supporting Details: Include the following information: Time, Place, Date of Occurrence, and Persons Present as well as Organizational Impact.

Carson,

As you are aware, I opted to conduct skip-level meetings in order to hear directly from the staff members of those who report to me. The purpose of those skip-level meetings with your team and the teams of my other direct reports was to gauge the overall culture and level of employee satisfaction and engagement on our team. While my intentions were strictly to listen and not take any specific corrective actions as a result of what I heard, the findings from your team were so concerning that I opted to bring these matters to your direct attention to discuss them with you. Your staff members described your depart-ment's culture and your leadership style as follows:

- *Your department is infected with chronic negativity.*

- *Your communication style is described at times as caustic, confrontational, arrogant, and defensive.*

- *Your team suffers from an overreactive grapevine, meaning that team members gos-sip, "stir the pot," complain about senior leadership, and criticize one another.*

- *You appear to reward employees' negative behavior by pitting certain team members against one another and encouraging others to "stand their ground on principle."*

- *Your team continues to suffer from high turnover, substandard productivity, and overall disengagement, which is consistent with this year's Employee Opinion Survey (EOS) scores.*

When I asked you for your input regarding these findings, rather than demonstrating con-cern for the team based on the feedback that I shared with you, you appeared apathetic and unconcerned. You stated that members of your team suffer from an entitlement men-tality and are spoiled. They stir up trouble because the company doesn't care about them, as evidenced by small merit increases, increasing health-care costs, and the constant need to change things for change's sake. Overall, you assumed little responsibility for the ongoing morale and commitment problems on your team.

As such, it appears that you are not holding yourself sufficiently accountable as a leader and person of authority. Of the eight members of your team whom I interviewed, all but two described your leadership style as lacking, apathetic, or caustic. The majority of those interviewed stated that you not only tolerate caustic behavior but also model and perpetu-ate the negative actions that define your work atmosphere.

Further, the EOS reveals the following scores about you and your leadership of the team. On a scale of 1–9, 9 being the highest, you received aggregate leadership scores in the following areas:

Cares about employee well-being	*1*
Treats others with respect	*2*
Creates an inclusive work environment	*2*
Allows employees to do their best work every day	*1*
Overall supervisor score	**2**

These are the lowest scores of any director in our region. They clearly demonstrate that you are not fully engaged in your role as group lead or otherwise taking your leadership responsibilities seriously. Upon questioning you, I found that you demonstrated little concern for your team's complaints. In fact, you didn't seem to be overly worried or concerned about my findings.

As such, a written warning is warranted for failure to supervise responsibly, lack of commitment to listening to your employees' needs and trying to improve the challenges they bring to your attention, and failure to demonstrate your commitment to this organization in terms of your behaviors toward others.

PERFORMANCE IMPROVEMENT PLAN

1. Measurable/Tangible Improvement Goals: *I expect you take this skip-level feedback in conjunction with your EOS scores very seriously. The level of commitment you demonstrate is clearly within your control. As such, I expect you to complete a full turnaround in terms of your commitment, engagement, and motivation levels. I'm interested to learn what ideas you have for turning around those EOS scores and improving your relationship with your staff, so please schedule time on my calendar next week so we can review your findings.*

2. Training or Special Direction Provided: *None*

3. Interim Performance Evaluation Necessary? *No*

4. Our **Employee Assistance Program** (EAP) provider, Prime Behavioral Health Group, can be confidentially reached to assist you at (800) 555-5555. This is strictly voluntary. A booklet regarding the EAP's services is available from Human Resources.

5. In addition, I recognize that you may have certain ideas to improve your performance. Therefore, I encourage you to provide your own **Personal Improvement Plan Input and Suggestions:**

_____

_____

_____

(Attach additional sheets if needed.)

OUTCOMES AND CONSEQUENCES

Positive: I will remain available to help you and discuss areas where you require additional support. If you meet your performance goals, no further disciplinary action will be taken regarding this issue. *If you commit to reengaging your team and solidifying your relationships with your staff members, you will go a long way in demonstrating your commitment to the organization and to those whom you're privileged to lead. Turning around a flailing team is an important leadership skill set, and I will be open to partnering with you as appropriate. Make note, however, that this is your team, and you are fully responsible for its ultimate success or failure. As such, I expect you to make this a top priority from this point forward.*

Negative: *Feedback on any leader of this magnitude is serious and concerning. If you are either unable or unwilling to demonstrate total commitment and key improvements in this area, your suitability for the leadership role that you currently occupy will be subject to reconsideration and could result in demotion or further disciplinary action up to and including dismissal of employment.* A copy of this document will be placed in your personnel file.

Scheduled Review Date: *Thirty days (September 30, 2017)*

EMPLOYEE COMMENTS AND/OR REBUTTAL

_____

_____

_____

(Attach additional sheets if needed.)

X _____
Employee Signature

EMPLOYEE ACKNOWLEDGMENT GOES HERE

Bonus Sample: Substandard Project Management (Director Level)

Director-level employee fails to manage a large-scale, ongoing project appropriately.

PERFORMANCE CORRECTION NOTICE

Employee Name: *Dmitri Kozlov*   **Department:** *Planning*

Date Presented: *August 25, 2017*   **Supervisor:** *Yona Begay*

DISCIPLINARY LEVEL

☐ **Verbal Correction**—(To memorialize the conversation.)

☒ **Written Warning**—(State nature of offense, method of correction, and action to be taken if offense is repeated.)

☐ **Investigatory Leave**—(Include length of time and nature of review.)

☐ **Final Written Warning**

    ☐ Without decision-making leave

    ☐ With decision-making leave (Attach memo of instructions.)

    ☐ With unpaid suspension

SUBJECT: *Substandard role performance and communication*

☐ Policy/Procedure Violation

☒ Performance Transgression

☐ Behavior/Conduct Infraction

☐ Absenteeism/Tardiness

PRIOR NOTIFICATIONS

Level of Discipline	Date	Subject
Verbal	_____	_____
Written	_____	_____
Final Written	_____	_____

Incident Description and Supporting Details: Include the following information: Time, Place, Date of Occurrence, and Persons Present as well as Organizational Impact.

Dmitri,

As the director of construction planning, you were assigned the lead project management role for the XYZ project in June 2017. You are aware that this included managing the strategy, analysis, communications, project objectives, and risks for the project's overall delivery and completion. The output of your work does not currently represent the level expected of a director. The items in bold parentheses at the end of each paragraph represent the core qualifications violated by your actions.

During the XYZ project, you failed to communicate effectively on numerous occasions with several key stakeholders. On several occasions, members of your team, senior management, and vendors confirmed that they were unclear as to what direction the project was headed in and where they were in regard to established goals. Your failure to provide appropriate overviews, timelines, and progression plans and next steps caused unnecessary confusion and lack of alignment. **(Communication, Strategic Leadership)**

There were several instances when one group thought the other group was doing something, and the work never got completed as a result. For example, your team of construction planners was working on blueprint changes that were never properly communicated to the fiber engineers. This resulted in continued delays of critical milestones necessary to complete the project on time. Since the project's inception, you appeared at weekly meetings unprepared and unable to answer basic status questions about the project (for example, who would take the lead for vendor notification in Walter Nichols's absence). **(Communication, Strategic Leadership, Follow-Up)**

In addition, when you were asked questions requiring your subject matter expertise, you could not consistently answer them and on several occasions provided incorrect and inaccurate responses. For example, a question was asked about the Abel platform and how it was to be integrated into the XYZ project. You responded that Abel wasn't initially compatible with XYZ and required further research, when in fact Abel was selected because of its immediate scalability and systems match capability. This resulted in three weeks of lost time spent researching a solution that wasn't necessary. As a director, you are expected to possess the necessary skills, abilities, and knowledge to answer these types of questions. **(Problem-Solving Skills, Strategic Leadership, Follow-Up)**

Members of your team have informed me that you often appear to be disengaged at work and that they rarely have any type of meetings/communication to go over project updates, goal reassessments, or milestone achievements. This lack of ongoing communication, support, and direction has impacted your group and the XYZ project negatively because your staff members were not able to operate at their highest potential. **(Build Relationship Building, Strategic Leadership)**

PERFORMANCE IMPROVEMENT PLAN

1. Measurable/Tangible Improvement Goals: *From this point forward, Dmitri, you are expected to improve your communication, relationship building, subject matter knowledge, and problem-solving abilities so that overall results are significantly improved. Listed below are the specific expectations that you should hold yourself accountable to:*

Communication

You must demonstrate the ability to communicate effectively with senior management, vendors, direct reports, and to me. Effective communication includes:

1. *The ability to present a compelling business case for opinions and recommendations*

2. *Being prepared for meetings by anticipating questions and being prepared to respond*

3. *Demonstrating business acumen by asking critical questions and providing subject matter expertise*

4. *Providing regular project updates with key project metrics to your team*

Relationship Building

You need to build stronger relationships with extended team members. The following are examples of items that are necessary for improvement:

1. *Holding regular meetings with key stakeholders (field and corporate)*

2. *Clearly communicating to peers, team members, and stakeholders regarding changes in plan, personnel, or due dates*

3. *Looking for synergies and collaboration opportunities to ensure all key stakeholders are in alignment in terms of performance and operational expectations*

Problem-Solving Skills, Knowledge, and Ability

Be able to demonstrate your ability to analyze the business problem or situation at hand and formulate a solution. Areas of concentration are:

1. *Overall project scope, timeline, and cost*

2. *Managing scope change and last-minute changes in plan*

3. *Working through ambiguous or controversial decisions/topics*

4, *Setting, adjusting, and communicating priorities*

5. *Balancing people needs with performance results*

Strategic Leadership

Provide the appropriate strategy and leadership for the direction of this project. Specifically, I expect you to:

1. *Initiate ideas and plans independently*

2. *Meet with your team regularly to go over critical deliverables, changes in plan, and revisions to initial timelines*

3. *Forecast changes in project deadlines and systems support needs, and reassign resources as appropriate*

Overall, Dmitri, you are expected to demonstrate adherence to due dates and action items consistently and complete projects by assigned deadlines.

2. Training or Special Direction Provided: *I will meet you in my office twice a week for the next two weeks and then once a week for the following two weeks to ensure you are on top of this project and informing all boundary partners of changes in plans, resources, or deadlines.*

Please have your to-do list items and execution strategies ready to discuss when we meet, and be prepared to ask me any questions regarding your ability to deliver on this project in a timely manner.

3. Interim Performance Evaluation Necessary? *No*

4. Employee Assistance Program (EAP) provider, Prime Behavioral Health Group, can be confidentially reached to assist you at (800) 555-5555. This is strictly voluntary. A booklet regarding the EAP's services is available from Human Resources.

5. In addition, I recognize that you may have certain ideas to improve your performance. Therefore, I encourage you to provide your own **Personal Improvement Plan Input and Suggestions:**

_____

_____

_____

(Attach additional sheets if needed.)

OUTCOMES AND CONSEQUENCES

Positive: I will remain available to help you and discuss areas where you require additional support. If you meet your performance goals, no further disciplinary action will be taken regarding this issue. *Mastering this matrix project will allow you to meet target deadlines, keep your team members and boundary partners fully informed, and remain flexible and agile as operational changes come your way.*

Negative: *Because the collective output of your work does not currently represent the level expected of a director, please understand that failure to demonstrate immediate and sustained performance may result in further disciplinary action up to and including dismissal.* A copy of this document will be placed in your personnel file.

Scheduled Review Date: *Thirty days (September 25, 2017)*

EMPLOYEE COMMENTS AND/OR REBUTTAL

_____

_____

_____

(Attach additional sheets if needed.)

X _____

Employee Signature

EMPLOYEE ACKNOWLEDGMENT GOES HERE

PART V

Behavior and Conduct Infractions

#51 Profane Language in the Workplace and Insubordination

Graphic artist makes her displeasure known to all around her when she is asked to assist on a project that belongs to another worker. Note that in the meeting following this incident, the employee stated that she was unhappy and wished to look for another job. The employer agreed to allow her limited time off from work over the next thirty days to attend interviews elsewhere during normal working hours.

PERFORMANCE CORRECTION NOTICE

Employee Name: *Denise Kingsley*   **Department:** *Graphics*

Date Presented: *March 7, 2017*   **Supervisor:** *George McMasters*

DISCIPLINARY LEVEL

☐ **Verbal Correction**—(To memorialize the conversation.)

☒ **Written Warning**—(State nature of offense, method of correction, and action to be taken if offense is repeated.)

☐ **Investigatory Leave**—(Include length of time and nature of review.)

☒ **Final Written Warning**

    ☒ Without decision-making leave

    ☐ With decision-making leave (Attach memo of instructions.)

    ☐ With unpaid suspension

SUBJECT: *Written warning: substandard work performance; final written warning: insubordination/abusive language*

☒ Policy/Procedure Violation

☒ Performance Transgression

☒ Behavior/Conduct Infraction

☐ Absenteeism/Tardiness

PRIOR NOTIFICATIONS

Level of Discipline	Date	Subject
Verbal	_____	_____
Written	_____	_____
Final Written	_____	_____

Incident Description and Supporting Details: Include the following information: Time, Place, Date of Occurrence, and Persons Present as well as Organizational Impact.

Denise,

Yesterday, you engaged in insubordinate conduct when you received my email asking you to work with Dorothy Epstein to clean up some imaging work on your graphics project for the sales department. I overheard you from my office, as did other coworkers, stating loudly that you "didn't give a shit what happened to that project" and that you "would be glad" when you "got out of this goddamn place." When I came out of my office, I saw you throw materials into my in-box from several feet away to display your dissatisfaction. Coworkers were concerned about your behavior, which disrupted the entire office. In addition, Denise, on a number of occasions, you have complained about the work that you have been given, whether it has been part of your primary responsibilities or a special project. Attached is your email response to my reasonable request that you provide me with a biweekly inventory account that was to be due on March 1. You stated in your email response that this assignment would "take too much time," that the work you've done on previous inventories was "never right for some strange reason," and then you added, "Isn't it great to work for a company that cares so much about its employees?" Such sarcastic comments are unacceptable because they violate company standards of performance and conduct.

PERFORMANCE IMPROVEMENT PLAN

1. Measurable/Tangible Improvement Goals: *Denise, I expect you to perform all duly assigned tasks at all times. It is your responsibility to ensure that the work in your area is completed by established deadlines. I expect you to talk with me privately and quietly if you have questions about your work or disagree with a work assignment. I also expect you never again to publicly display hostility and anger. You are responsible for creating and maintaining a friendly work environment that is free of harassment and intimidation.*

2. Training or Special Direction to Be Provided: *As we have agreed, we will allow you a reasonable amount of time to conduct a job search and to interview with other companies in the next thirty days.[1] However, understand that your primary responsibility is to complete your work in our department before leaving for any outside interviews. Also, any time that you take off during regularly scheduled hours will come from your accrued vacation and*

---

1 Thirty days was a reasonable amount of time for this individual to find work elsewhere. However, if the employee didn't find a job during that thirty-day window, the company would revisit the issue and determine (a) how the employee was performing, (b) if she needed additional time off work to interview elsewhere, and (c) if it made sense for her to remain employed by the company. Speak with a labor attorney before implementing this third option (i.e., firing the person) lest you be challenged with a wrongful discharge suit for having failed to provide due process.

holiday banks and cannot include sick leave.[2] You must give me twenty-four hours' notice whenever you have an interview scheduled with another company.

In addition, I'm attaching a copy of your job description, which details that you are responsible for work flow backup in our department. Please reread your job description tonight and meet with me tomorrow with any questions. Understand that you remain responsible for all duties listed in your job description while you are employed here.

Note as well that you have already been sent to an off-site training program on handling conflict, anger, and emotion in the workplace. Our company paid for you to attend this workshop, and you were permitted to attend on company time. I expect you to apply the skills that you have learned at that workshop for the remainder of your tenure with our company.

3. Interim Performance Evaluation Necessary? *No*

4. Our **Employee Assistance Program** (EAP) provider, Prime Behavioral Health Group, can be confidentially reached to assist you at (800) 555-5555. This is strictly voluntary. A booklet regarding the EAP's services is available from Human Resources.

5. In addition, I recognize that you may have certain ideas to improve your performance. Therefore, I encourage you to provide your own **Personal Improvement Plan Input and Suggestions:**

_____

_____

_____

(Attach additional sheets if needed.)

OUTCOMES AND CONSEQUENCES

Positive: I will remain available to help you and discuss areas where you require additional support. If you meet your performance goals, no further disciplinary action will be taken regarding this issue. *In addition, we will temporarily continue, at our sole discretion, to support your attempts to locate other employment while you continue working in your current position.*

Negative: *You are now being placed on notice that if you ever again demonstrate hostile behavior toward your supervisors, coworkers, or customers by unreasonably challenging*

---

2 Note that this employee is nonexempt and must therefore clock in and out when leaving company premises to interview. To be paid for time "off the clock" in order to interview, the nonexempt worker will need to access her vacation or holiday accruals; otherwise, the time off would have to be unpaid. However, if the employee were exempt (and not subject to overtime, comp time, or other wage and hour protections), you, the employer, would have to handle this matter differently. Under certain circumstances, exempt workers should not have their pay docked in increments of less than one full day (for example, for two hours). To do so would jeopardize the exempt status of the worker (who could claim that she was indeed treated as a nonexempt employee). And that could land you with a whopping bill for back overtime wages due! Therefore, you wouldn't have the flexibility of allowing the person to use vacation or holiday accruals for interviews. You would, instead, have to pay the exempt worker for the entire day even though the individual leaves your company for several hours to interview elsewhere. Confer with a wage and hour expert before including this line in your disciplinary memo, if you have further questions.

them or willfully refusing to perform properly assigned work, you may be immediately dismissed. In addition, if you ever again purposely demonstrate insubordinate behavior in front of coworkers by using profane language or by loudly stating that you dislike working here or don't care what happens to this institution, disciplinary action up to and including termination will result. A copy of this document will be placed in your personnel file.

Scheduled Review Date: *Thirty days (April 6)*

EMPLOYEE COMMENTS AND/OR REBUTTAL

_____

_____

_____

(Attach additional sheets if needed.)

X _____
Employee Signature

EMPLOYEE ACKNOWLEDGMENT GOES HERE

Note: Since this employee is on final written warning, add this sentence to the Employee Acknowledgment: "I understand that this is my last chance. If I violate any of the terms established in this memo, I will voluntarily resign or be discharged for cause."

#52 Poor Attitude[3]

Cashier fails to make eye contact with customers, doesn't respond when she's greeted, and appears to wish that she were somewhere else other than work.

PERFORMANCE CORRECTION NOTICE

Employee Name: *Eileen Wolfram*   **Department:** *Sales*

Date Presented: *September 30, 2017*   **Supervisor:** *Sid Carpenter*

DISCIPLINARY LEVEL

☒ **Verbal Correction**—(To memorialize the conversation.)

☐ **Written Warning**—(State nature of offense, method of correction, and action to be taken if offense is repeated.)

☐ **Investigatory Leave**—(Include length of time and nature of review.)

☐ **Final Written Warning**

  ☐ Without decision-making leave

  ☐ With decision-making leave (Attach memo of instructions.)

  ☐ With unpaid suspension

SUBJECT: *Unsatisfactory work performance*

☐ Policy/Procedure Violation

☒ Performance Transgression

☒ Behavior/Conduct Infraction

☐ Absenteeism/Tardiness

---

3 It is not good practice to discipline an employee for having a poor attitude. Attitude is a very subjective judgment that courts will dismiss because it is often associated with a mere difference of opinion or personality conflict. It is therefore critical that you avoid that term in the actual disciplinary notice or in the way you describe this to the employee verbally. Instead, use terms like "behavior" or "conduct." Be sure to describe the objective behaviors that create a negative perception of the employee in the eyes of others. Only behaviors and actions that can be observed and documented may be presented as evidence in court.

PRIOR NOTIFICATIONS

Level of Discipline	Date	Subject
Verbal	_____	_____
Written	_____	_____
Final Written	_____	_____

Incident Description and Supporting Details: Include the following information: Time, Place, Date of Occurrence, and Persons Present as well as Organizational Impact.

Eileen,

As a cashier, your primary responsibility is to provide outstanding customer service to patrons who frequent our cafeteria. Over the past two months, I have seen you consistently fail to make eye contact with customers. You rarely look up from the register, and when you do, you look only at the customers' hands as they pass you money. As a result, customers may feel alienated and less inclined to eat at our establishment in the future. In addition, I have heard visitors greet you with a good morning and/or a thank you, and you gave them no response. Yesterday, a long-time customer stated to me that it appears to her that you wish that you were somewhere else other than work. This reflects poorly on our establishment.

It is an essential job requirement to promptly and politely acknowledge the presence of others and to smile when serving a customer. You are consequently not meeting performance and conduct standards.

PERFORMANCE IMPROVEMENT PLAN

1. Measurable/Tangible Improvement Goals: *Eileen, I expect you to greet customers with a friendly hello and a courteous thank you. I expect you to make eye contact and smile so that patrons feel welcome and at home. I also expect you to be more focused on your work and on the people around you so that you create an impression of caring and dedicated attention.*

2. Training or Special Direction to Be Provided: *I will arrange for you to attend an off-site customer service and sales training seminar to increase your skills and awareness in this area.*

3. Interim Performance Evaluation Necessary? *No*

4. Our **Employee Assistance Program** (EAP) provider, Prime Behavioral Health Group, can be confidentially reached to assist you at (800) 555-5555. This is strictly voluntary. A booklet regarding the EAP's services is available from Human Resources.

5. In addition, I recognize that you may have certain ideas to improve your performance. Therefore, I encourage you to provide your own **Personal Improvement Plan Input and Suggestions:**

_____

_____

_____

(Attach additional sheets if needed.)

OUTCOMES AND CONSEQUENCES

Positive: I will remain available to help you and discuss areas where you require additional support. If you meet your performance goals, no further disciplinary action will be taken regarding this issue. _In addition, you will develop a greater sense of your ability to contribute to our restaurant's success._

Negative: _You are now being placed on notice that if you fail to improve in these particular areas or if you violate any other standards of performance and conduct in the next sixty days, further disciplinary action up to and including dismissal may occur._ A copy of this document will be placed in your personnel file.

Scheduled Review Date: _None_

EMPLOYEE COMMENTS AND/OR REBUTTAL

_____

_____

_____

(Attach additional sheets if needed.)

X _____
Employee Signature

EMPLOYEE ACKNOWLEDGMENT GOES HERE

#53 Insubordination

A Human Resources recruiter is disappointed at not receiving a promotion and displays unacceptable conduct toward her supervisor.

PERFORMANCE CORRECTION NOTICE

Employee Name: *Denise Bryant*   **Department:** *Human Resources*

Date Presented: *February 10, 2017*   **Supervisor:** *Janet Farah*

DISCIPLINARY LEVEL

☐ **Verbal Correction**—(To memorialize the conversation.)

☐ **Written Warning**—(State nature of offense, method of correction, and action to be taken if offense is repeated.)

☐ **Investigatory Leave**—(Include length of time and nature of review.)

☒ **Final Written Warning**

   ☒ Without decision-making leave

   ☐ With decision-making leave (Attach memo of instructions.)

   ☐ With unpaid suspension

SUBJECT: *Insubordination, violation of standards of performance and conduct*

☐ Policy/Procedure Violation

☒ Performance Transgression

☒ Behavior/Conduct Infraction

☐ Absenteeism/Tardiness

PRIOR NOTIFICATIONS

Level of Discipline	Date	Subject
Verbal	Jan 6, 2017	Substandard performance
Written	_____	_____
Final Written	_____	_____

Incident Description and Supporting Details: Include the following information: Time, Place, Date of Occurrence, and Persons Present as well as Organizational Impact.

Denise,

Today you displayed unacceptable conduct when I asked you a simple question. You were rude, argumentative, and hostile in front of the entire Human Resources staff and an outside vendor. You used unprofessional language, placed your hands on your hips in a defiant manner, and rolled your eyes when I addressed you. Your outburst disrupted the meeting I was holding and the functioning of the department. Your behavior was clearly insubordinate and in violation of company standards of performance and conduct.

Your conduct has steadily deteriorated over the past two months since you learned you would not be promoted to the position of staffing manager. When I have asked you to update me on projects you are working on, you have responded in a curt and condescending manner. In the past month, three of your coworkers have complained about the abrupt manner in which you treat them.

On January 6, three weeks after you learned that you wouldn't be promoted, I discussed this developing problem with you. I explained that I understood that you were disappointed that you were not promoted, but I informed you that your conduct needed to improve or you would find yourself facing progressive disciplinary actions up to and including dismissal. I told you that I would respect your decision to find work elsewhere, but you assured me that you were fine and that you were happy working here. Unfortunately, your conduct since that meeting has not improved, and this recent blowup is totally unacceptable.

PERFORMANCE IMPROVEMENT PLAN

1. Measurable/Tangible Improvement Goals: *Denise, I expect you to maintain a working environment that is free from any hostility, disruption, or antagonism.*

2. Training or Special Direction to Be Provided: *I am sending you to a one-day off-site training workshop on interpersonal relationships, especially on dealing with conflict in the workplace. While attending this training, I expect you to consider whether further employment with our company is a viable alternative for you.*

3. Interim Performance Evaluation Necessary? *Yes. Although it is not time for your regularly scheduled annual performance evaluation, I will write an appraisal in the next two weeks that reflects your recent conduct infractions and your overall performance year-to-date.*

4. Our **Employee Assistance Program** (EAP) provider, Prime Behavioral Health Group, can be confidentially reached to assist you at (800) 555-5555. This is strictly voluntary. A booklet regarding the EAP's services is available from Human Resources.

5. In addition, I recognize that you may have certain ideas to improve your performance. Therefore, I encourage you to provide your own **Personal Improvement Plan Input and Suggestions:**

_____

_____

(Attach additional sheets if needed.)

OUTCOMES AND CONSEQUENCES

Positive: I will remain available to help you and discuss areas where you require additional support. If you meet your performance goals, no further disciplinary action will be taken regarding this issue.

Negative: *You are now being placed on formal notice that if you ever again display unprofessional conduct with me or any other employees or outside contacts, you may be immediately discharged for cause.* A copy of this document will be placed in your personnel file.

Scheduled Review Date: *Two weeks (February 24)*

EMPLOYEE COMMENTS AND/OR REBUTTAL

_____

_____

_____

(Attach additional sheets if needed.)

X _____

Employee Signature

EMPLOYEE ACKNOWLEDGMENT GOES HERE

Note: Since this is a final written warning, add this sentence to the Employee Acknowledgment: "I also realize that this is my last chance. If I fail to meet the standards established in this memo, I will voluntarily resign or be terminated for cause."

#54 Insubordination and Substandard Work Performance

Lab aide with ten years of seniority engages in insubordinate conduct, makes veiled threats and abusive gestures, and generally refuses to take orders from a newly hired supervisor who is half his age. This is the second in a series of three write-ups leading up to dismissal (see Write-Ups #37 and #55). The letter of termination is located in Part VII, Termination Notices (Write-Up #84).

PERFORMANCE CORRECTION NOTICE

Employee Name: Rick Ricardo   **Department:** Research Lab

Date Presented: October 4, 2017   **Supervisor:** John Josephson

DISCIPLINARY LEVEL

☐ **Verbal Correction**—(To memorialize the conversation.)

☒ **Written Warning**—(State nature of offense, method of correction, and action to be taken if offense is repeated.)

☐ **Investigatory Leave**—(Include length of time and nature of review.)

☐ **Final Written Warning**

    ☐ Without decision-making leave

    ☐ With decision-making leave (Attach memo of instructions.)

    ☐ With unpaid suspension

SUBJECT: Substandard work performance: glass breakage, insubordination

☒ Policy/Procedure Violation

☒ Performance Transgression

☒ Behavior/Conduct Infraction

☐ Absenteeism/Tardiness

PRIOR NOTIFICATIONS

Level of Discipline	Date	Subject
Verbal	Aug 7, 2017	Substandard work performance: unwillingness to perform properly assigned work
Written	_____	_____
Final Written	_____	_____

Incident Description and Supporting Details: Include the following information: Time, Place, Date of Occurrence, and Persons Present as well as Organizational Impact.

Rick,

Yesterday, you placed 100 sixteen-ounce bottles straight out of the autoclave machine/ dishwasher into the cold-water dip tank filled with disinfectant solution. Since the autoclave machine runs at a very hot temperature of about 280 degrees, your placing the bottles directly in the cold water caused them all to crack. It is reasonable for you to know that placing very hot glass bottles into the cold dip tank would result in breakage. These bottles cost our organization $0.68 each. Therefore, the monetary damage done through your careless act amounts to $68.00.

More significantly, you didn't report this breakage to your supervisor, John Josephson. Instead, you simply removed the four racks of bottles from the dip tank and emptied them into the garbage. John later discovered a large amount of broken glass in the waste canister and questioned you about it. You told him that it was none of his concern. When he insisted that it was, you stated in a loud voice, "You're just looking for a reason to fire me, aren't you? Who do you think you are with your two months of experience in this organization? You know, I'm really getting tired of this." You then left the area without allowing him to respond to you.

I met with you to learn about what caused the broken glass, and you told me that you weren't focused on what you were doing because of all the stress you're feeling at work. You told me that you didn't speak to John in a loud voice—you were simply talking over the machines. You stated that he was obviously overly sensitive. Again I am disappointed that you refuse to accept responsibility for your actions or make efforts to open the lines of communication with your supervisor. Your actions constitute insubordination. It is apparent that you didn't take your former warning seriously.

PERFORMANCE IMPROVEMENT PLAN

1. Measurable/Tangible Improvement Goals: *Rick, I hold you accountable for communicating with John whenever you disagree with one of his directives so that you can get an immediate response and not allow your perceptions to fester. I expect you to process all equipment coming into the cage wash area and to ensure adequate clean supplies and to follow all other standard departmental procedures. I expect you to answer any and all questions asked of you by your supervisor or any other members of management. Finally, I want to meet with you tomorrow after you've read this documentation so that you can convince me that we won't ever have to address these issues again.*

2. Training or Special Direction to Be Provided: *I want you to attend a customer service workshop or a training session on dealing with conflict in the workplace. I will arrange for you to attend this workshop within the next month. Expect a call from Human Resources with choices of programs and times. You must attend this training, which will be paid for by the company and which will occur on company time, by the end of November (as long as a program is available).*

3. Interim Performance Evaluation Necessary? *Yes. Although it is not time for your regularly scheduled annual review, I will issue you an out-of-cycle review to more accurately reflect your current level of performance.*

4. Our **Employee Assistance Program** (EAP) provider, Prime Behavioral Health Group, can be confidentially reached to assist you at (800) 555-5555. This is strictly voluntary. A booklet regarding the EAP's services is available from Human Resources.

5. In addition, I recognize that you may have certain ideas to improve your performance. Therefore, I encourage you to provide your own **Personal Improvement Plan Input and Suggestions:**

_____

_____

_____

(Attach additional sheets if needed.)

OUTCOMES AND CONSEQUENCES

Positive: I will remain available to help you and discuss areas where you require additional support. If you meet your performance goals, no further disciplinary action will be taken regarding this issue.

Negative: *You are now being placed into written warning status. If at any time in the next ninety days you fail to process all equipment coming into the cage wash area or to ensure adequate clean supplies, follow your supervisor's reasonable directives, demonstrate respect for your supervisor's authority, or follow any other standard departmental procedures, you may be placed on a formal ninety-day final written warning. If you fail to abide by the terms of this agreement in that final written warning period, you may be discharged for cause.* A copy of this document will be placed in your personnel file.

Scheduled Review Date: *One month (November 4)*

EMPLOYEE COMMENTS AND/OR REBUTTAL

_____

_____

_____

(Attach additional sheets if needed.)

X _____
Employee Signature

EMPLOYEE ACKNOWLEDGMENT GOES HERE

#55 Insubordination and Substandard Work Performance

Lab aide with ten years of seniority engages in insubordinate conduct, makes veiled threats and abusive gestures, and generally refuses to take orders from a newly hired supervisor who is half his age. This is the third in a series of three write-ups (see also Write-Ups #37, 54) leading up to dismissal. The letter of termination is located in Part VII, Termination Notices (Write-Up #84).

PERFORMANCE CORRECTION NOTICE

Employee Name: *Rick Ricardo*   **Department:** *Research Lab*

Date Presented: *November 2, 2017*   **Supervisor:** *John Josephson*

DISCIPLINARY LEVEL

☐ **Verbal Correction**—(To memorialize the conversation.)

☐ **Written Warning**—(State nature of offense, method of correction, and action to be taken if offense is repeated.)

☐ **Investigatory Leave**—(Include length of time and nature of review.)

☒ **Final Written Warning**

    ☒ Without decision-making leave

    ☐ With decision-making leave (Attach memo of instructions.)

    ☐ With unpaid suspension

SUBJECT: *Insubordination and threatening your supervisor*

☒ Policy/Procedure Violation

☒ Performance Transgression

☒ Behavior/Conduct Infraction

☐ Absenteeism/Tardiness

PRIOR NOTIFICATIONS

Level of Discipline	Date	Subject
Verbal	Aug 7, 2017	*Substandard work performance: unwillingness to perform properly assigned work*
Written	Oct 4, 2017	*Substandard work performance: glass breakage; insubordination*

Final Written   _____   _____

Incident Description and Supporting Details: Include the following information: Time, Place, Date of Occurrence, and Persons Present as well as Organizational Impact.

Rick,

On October 25, you were standing on the loading dock with your supervisor, John Josephson, while a cargo truck was backing up to the dock. You called out instructions to the driver in Spanish, and you made sarcastic and disrespectful remarks about your supervisor at that time. Specifically, you called your supervisor a "cabrón, stupido, and bendejo. You called out in Spanish that your supervisor was a little boy with a big ego who was messing with your future by trying to undermine your job.

John interrupted you and instructed you to stop using profane language and not to refer to him as a little boy. You then turned to him and stated, "What are you talking about? You don't even speak Spanish!" John informed you that he does indeed speak Spanish and understood your whole very loud conversation with the vendor. He also shared with you how embarrassed he was to be called vulgar names in front of a vendor.

At that point, you yelled, "Hey! Did anyone ever tell you you're paranoid? Why don't you go off somewhere and do this?" (You gestured to your groin and pretended to masturbate.) You raised your index finger to John's face and told him he'd better back off if he knows what's good for him. Your actions have been confirmed with the vendor, who personally witnessed your physical threats and loud admonitions. Your actions clearly violate company standards of performance and conduct.

PERFORMANCE IMPROVEMENT PLAN

1. Measurable/Tangible Improvement Goals: *Rick, I expect you to reread your previous warnings and discuss any questions you have with me regarding their directives. I expect that you will never again use profane language or make direct or veiled threats to a member of management, a coworker, or anyone doing business on company property. I expect you to strictly follow all policies and procedures without exception from this point forward.*

2. Training or Special Direction to Be Provided: *You have attended an off-site workshop on dealing with conflict in the workplace. You've met one-on-one with your supervisor for individualized training and task clarity. Yet you have refused to cooperate and communicate openly. Consequently, you will now be placed on a one-day paid decision-making leave. A handout is attached that explains the purpose of this leave and the assignment that will be due upon your return—if you choose to return.*[4]

3. Interim Performance Evaluation Necessary? *No*

4. Our **Employee Assistance Program** (EAP) provider, Prime Behavioral Health Group, can be confidentially reached to assist you at (800) 555-5555. This is strictly voluntary. A booklet regarding the EAP's services is available from Human Resources.

---

4 You should attach the decision-making leave document to this warning. (See Figure 2–1.)

5. In addition, I recognize that you may have certain ideas to improve your performance. Therefore, I encourage you to provide your own **Personal Improvement Plan Input and Suggestions:**

_____

_____

_____

(Attach additional sheets if needed.)

OUTCOMES AND CONSEQUENCES

Positive: I will remain available to help you and discuss areas where you require additional support. If you meet your performance goals, no further disciplinary action will be taken regarding this issue.

Negative: *We are not terminating you for insubordination at this time because of your ten-ure with our organization.[5] Understand, however, that if you ever again engage in insubordinate conduct by using foul language or making threatening gestures at your supervisor, you may immediately be discharged for cause. There will be no further chances.* **A copy of this document will be placed in your personnel file.**

Scheduled Review Date: *One month (December 2)*

EMPLOYEE COMMENTS AND/OR REBUTTAL

_____

_____

_____

(Attach additional sheets if needed.)

X _____
Employee Signature

EMPLOYEE ACKNOWLEDGMENT GOES HERE

Note: Since this is a final written warning, add this sentence to the Employee Acknowledgment: "I understand that my job is now in serious jeopardy of being lost. I also acknowledge that this is my last chance. If I fail to abide by the terms of this agreement, I will voluntarily resign or be discharged for cause."

---

5 This is also a logical move, since the ten-year employee is a minority and over forty. This "last chance" that you're providing will strengthen your case should you be sued for wrongful discharge or age or race discrimination.

#56 Misconduct, Fighting, and Horseplay

A company groundskeeper and independent contractor construction worker have words in front of the office building; multiple witnesses observe the confrontation. The employee is disciplined and the construction worker is taken off the job.

PERFORMANCE CORRECTION NOTICE

Employee Name: *Joe Smothers*   **Department:** *Environmental Services*

Date Presented: *October 29, 2017*   **Supervisor:** *Willis Reese*

DISCIPLINARY LEVEL

☐ **Verbal Correction**—(To memorialize the conversation.)

☒ **Written Warning**—(State nature of offense, method of correction, and action to be taken if offense is repeated.)

☐ **Investigatory Leave**—(Include length of time and nature of review.)

☐ **Final Written Warning**

    ☐ Without decision-making leave

    ☐ With decision-making leave (Attach memo of instructions.)

    ☐ With unpaid suspension

SUBJECT: *Misconduct and fighting on company grounds*

☒ Policy/Procedure Violation

☐ Performance Transgression

☒ Behavior/Conduct Infraction

☐ Absenteeism/Tardiness

PRIOR NOTIFICATIONS

Level of Discipline	Date	Subject
Verbal	_____	_____
Written	_____	_____
Final Written	_____	_____

Incident Description and Supporting Details: Include the following information: Time, Place, Date of Occurrence, and Persons Present as well as Organizational Impact.

Joe,

On October 23, at approximately 2:30 P.M., construction workers from BMG Contractors were dismantling their 130-ton crane in front of Lumley Building. The crew's supervisor was directing traffic when you drove by in your company truck. You claim that the supervisor then told you to "Move your damned truck; this crane is costing us over $300 an hour." The supervisor in question claims that you ignored his direction, let your truck idle in the crane's path, stared him down, and gave him the finger.

Although there are witnesses on both sides who agree with these versions of the story, the end result was that the two of you got into a screaming match in front of other company employees and visitors. You were heard saying things like "Up yours, you bastard" and "If you know what's good for you, stay out of my way." The contracting supervisor also made comments along the lines of "Shove it, you piece of shit" and "Go to hell."[6]

Regardless of who started this confrontation or why, your behavior violates company policy 7.04 regarding standards of performance and conduct. Specifically, you engaged this independent contractor in public and used abusive, threatening, and offensive language when you should have immediately reported the incident to your supervisor. The construction worker will be transferred to another project tomorrow; however, your behavior is unacceptable and violates company norms of conduct.

PERFORMANCE IMPROVEMENT PLAN

1. Measurable/Tangible Improvement Goals: *Joe, I expect you to never again engage in conduct that threatens physical harm or uses profane language. If you ever again have such a run-in with another employee, vendor, or independent contractor, I expect you to notify me (or another supervisor if I am unavailable) immediately. I expect that you will never again take matters into your own hands or in any way encourage a confrontation of words or actions.*

2. Training or Special Direction to Be Provided: *Policy 7.04, regarding company standards of performance and conduct, is attached. Note that section 7.04.14 clearly states the following under Prohibited Conduct:*

- *Causing, creating, or participating in a disruption of any kind on Company property*

- *Using abusive language at any time on Company premises*

- *Participating in horseplay or practical jokes on Company time or on Company premises*

These are all subject to disciplinary action up to and including immediate dismissal.

3. Interim Performance Evaluation Necessary? *No*

---

6 I recommend quoting exact language when disciplining an employee for using obscenities, even when the obscenities are much more graphic or crude than the ones we are limited to using in a professional book such as this. This demonstrates the seriousness of the offense as well as your willingness to deal openly with it.

4. Our **Employee Assistance Program** (EAP) provider, Prime Behavioral Health Group, can be confidentially reached to assist you at (800) 555-5555. This is strictly voluntary. A booklet regarding the EAP's services is available from Human Resources.

5. In addition, I recognize that you may have certain ideas to improve your performance. Therefore, I encourage you to provide your own **Personal Improvement Plan Input and Suggestions:**

_____

_____

_____

(Attach additional sheets if needed.)

OUTCOMES AND CONSEQUENCES

Positive: I will remain available to help you and discuss areas where you require additional support. If you meet your performance goals, no further disciplinary action will be taken regarding this issue.

Negative: _If you ever again engage in conduct that constitutes physical threats of harm, open displays of hostility, attempts to engage in a fight, or profane and abusive language aimed at invoking an angry response from another, you will be subject to further disciplinary action including immediate dismissal._ A copy of this document will be placed in your personnel file.

Scheduled Review Date: _None_

EMPLOYEE COMMENTS AND/OR REBUTTAL

_____

_____

_____

(Attach additional sheets if needed.)

X _____
                                         Employee Signature

EMPLOYEE ACKNOWLEDGMENT GOES HERE

#57 Misconduct, Fighting, and Horseplay

Two employees, a secretary and an internal auditor, physically attack each other in the secretary's office. Witnesses rush in a few seconds later, but no witnesses see who made the first strike. The employees are known to dislike each other, and both receive a written warning.

PERFORMANCE CORRECTION NOTICE

Employee Name: *Marion Lemmon*   **Department:** *Marketing*

Date Presented: *April 8, 2017*   **Supervisor:** *Tina Flood*

DISCIPLINARY LEVEL

☐ **Verbal Correction**—(To memorialize the conversation.)

☒ **Written Warning**—(State nature of offense, method of correction, and action to be taken if offense is repeated.)

☐ **Investigatory Leave**—(Include length of time and nature of review.)

☐ **Final Written Warning**

    ☐ Without decision-making leave

    ☐ With decision-making leave (Attach memo of instructions.)

    ☐ With unpaid suspension

SUBJECT: *Misconduct and fighting with a coworker*

☒ Policy/Procedure Violation

☐ Performance Transgression

☒ Behavior/Conduct Infraction

☐ Absenteeism/Tardiness

PRIOR NOTIFICATIONS

Level of Discipline	Date	Subject
Verbal	_____	_____
Written	_____	_____
Final Written	_____	_____

Incident Description and Supporting Details: Include the following information: Time, Place, Date of Occurrence, and Persons Present as well as Organizational Impact.

Marion,

Yesterday, you engaged in inappropriate conduct with a coworker when an argument ensued between the two of you, leading to a physical altercation.[7] You claim that the internal auditor entered your office without permission, threatened you by muttering between her teeth, "I'll get you" or "I'll fix you," and walked toward your desk with an "intent to harm" you. You state that you were physically threatened for no apparent reason, and you immediately attempted to call Security in order to protect yourself.

The internal auditor, however, claims that she entered your office only to use the fax machine that sits right next to your desk. She states that she neither looked at you nor spoke to you and that as soon as she walked through the door, you berated her for walking into your office without permission and then picked up the phone to call Security. She states that you and she have a long history of distrust and dislike for one another and that you were simply looking for an excuse to bring matters to a head.

You state that she took the phone right out of your hand, held it above your head, and "made you jump for it" while she laughed at you. She states that you "used the phone as a weapon" and hit her in the arm with it. She has a welt on her arm to prove it. By that time, witnesses had heard the commotion and rushed into your office only to find the two of you locked in conflict. Both of you were pulled off each other at that point, and both of you seriously violated company standards of performance and conduct.

PERFORMANCE IMPROVEMENT PLAN

1. Measurable/Tangible Improvement Goals: *Marion, I expect you to control your temper and never engage in a physical altercation with a coworker. Furthermore, I expect you to avoid any threatening actions that could invoke a hostile response from another person. If you ever feel threatened in the future, I expect you to call me or another supervisor immediately. You are not to engage in any form of altercation under any circumstances.*

2. Training or Special Direction to Be Provided: *Policy 7.04, regarding company standards of performance and conduct, is attached. Note that section 7.04.14 clearly states the following under Prohibited Conduct:*

- *Causing, creating, or participating in a disruption of any kind on Company property*

- *Using abusive language at any time on Company premises*

- *Participating in horseplay or practical jokes on Company time or on Company premises*

These are all subject to disciplinary action up to and including immediate dismissal.

3. Interim Performance Evaluation Necessary? No

4. Our **Employee Assistance Program** (EAP) provider, Prime Behavioral Health Group, can be confidentially reached to assist you at (800) 555-5555. This is strictly voluntary. A booklet regarding the EAP's services is available from Human Resources.

---

7 Note that the other employee involved received this identical warning.

5. In addition, I recognize that you may have certain ideas to improve your performance. Therefore, I encourage you to provide your own **Personal Improvement Plan Input and Suggestions:**

_____

_____

_____

(Attach additional sheets if needed.)

OUTCOMES AND CONSEQUENCES

Positive: I will remain available to help you and discuss areas where you require additional support. If you meet your performance goals, no further disciplinary action will be taken regarding this issue.

Negative: _If you ever again fight with a coworker or anyone doing business on company premises, or if you engage in conduct that constitutes physical threats of harm, open displays of hostility, or attempts to engage in a fight, you will be subject to further disciplinary action including immediate dismissal._ A copy of this document will be placed in your personnel file.

Scheduled Review Date: _None_

EMPLOYEE COMMENTS AND/OR REBUTTAL

_____

_____

_____

(Attach additional sheets if needed.)

X _____
Employee Signature

EMPLOYEE ACKNOWLEDGMENT GOES HERE

#58 Sexual Harassment

A female supervisor in the company gift shop attempts to date a male cashier despite the cashier's rebuffs.

PERFORMANCE CORRECTION NOTICE

Employee Name: *Cindy Tucker*   **Department:** *Gift Shop*

Date Presented: *March 11, 2017*   **Supervisor:** *Peter Sharpe*

DISCIPLINARY LEVEL

☐ **Verbal Correction**—(To memorialize the conversation.)

☒ **Written Warning**—(State nature of offense, method of correction, and action to be taken if offense is repeated.)

☐ **Investigatory Leave**—(Include length of time and nature of review.)

☐ **Final Written Warning**

    ☐ Without decision-making leave

    ☐ With decision-making leave (Attach memo of instructions.)

    ☐ With unpaid suspension

SUBJECT: *Failure to follow company policies and procedures*

☒ Policy/Procedure Violation

☐ Performance Transgression

☒ Behavior/Conduct Infraction

☐ Absenteeism/Tardiness

PRIOR NOTIFICATIONS

Level of Discipline	Date	Subject
Verbal	_____	_____
Written	_____	_____
Final Written	_____	_____

Incident Description and Supporting Details: Include the following information: Time, Place, Date of Occurrence, and Persons Present as well as Organizational Impact.

Cindy,

This is to document that Richard Caballero, cashier, has today made a formal harassment complaint against you. Richard states that the problem began in November when you, his immediate supervisor, called him at home to ask him out on a date. He declined the invitation. You asked him out again another time in late January or early February, and again he refused the invitation. He states that he had hoped that you would simply lose interest in him.

The situation became acutely more uncomfortable for him yesterday when you began blowing kisses at him while he was working at the cash register and you were taking a meal break at one of the tables.

Although Richard did not confront you yesterday about this incident, he reported it to his union steward, who in turn brought it to me. In our meeting, you confirmed that these events occurred. This written memo confirms that our company strongly disapproves of any conduct that might constitute sexual harassment. We are committed to guaranteeing all of our employees a friendly work environment. Your actions, however, have violated company policy.

PERFORMANCE IMPROVEMENT PLAN

1. Measurable/Tangible Improvement Goals: *Cindy, I expect that you, as a supervisor, will uphold all standards of performance and conduct. I expect that you will create a work environment that treats people with dignity and respect and never again engage in conduct that could diminish a person's self-worth or sense of well-being.*

2. Training or Special Direction Provided: *Our firm's policy on sexual harassment is attached. Please read the policy immediately and see me if you have any questions. In addition, I encourage you to attend a course at a local college or adult school regarding the "politics of sexual harassment."*

3. Interim Performance Evaluation Necessary? *No*

4. Our **Employee Assistance Program** (EAP) provider, Prime Behavioral Health Group, can be confidentially reached to assist you at (800) 555-5555. This is strictly voluntary. A booklet regarding the EAP's services is available from Human Resources.

5. In addition, I recognize that you may have certain ideas to improve your performance. Therefore, I encourage you to provide your own **Personal Improvement Plan Input and Suggestions:**

_____

_____

_____

(Attach additional sheets if needed.)

OUTCOMES AND CONSEQUENCES

Positive: I will remain available to help you and discuss areas where you require additional support. If you meet your performance goals, no further disciplinary action will be taken regarding this issue.

Negative: *You are now being placed on notice that if you ever again fail to respect others' rights regarding their personal lives, or if you ever again violate our organization's policy regarding sexual harassment, disciplinary action up to and including dismissal may result.* A copy of this document will be placed in your personnel file.

Scheduled Review Date: *None*

EMPLOYEE COMMENTS AND/OR REBUTTAL

_____

_____

_____

(Attach additional sheets if needed.)

X _____
Employee Signature

EMPLOYEE ACKNOWLEDGMENT GOES HERE

#59 Sexual Harassment

An employee attempts to rekindle a romance with a former girlfriend, who in turn complains of his advances.

PERFORMANCE CORRECTION NOTICE

Employee Name: *Roger Samson*   **Department:** *Manufacturing*

Date Presented: *April 15, 2017*   **Supervisor:** *Danita Harold*

DISCIPLINARY LEVEL

☐ **Verbal Correction**—(To memorialize the conversation.)

☒ **Written Warning**—(State nature of offense, method of correction, and action to be taken if offense is repeated.)

☐ **Investigatory Leave**—(Include length of time and nature of review.)

☐ **Final Written Warning**

　☐ Without decision-making leave

　☐ With decision-making leave (Attach memo of instructions.)

　☐ With unpaid suspension

SUBJECT: *Failure to follow company policies and procedures*

☒ Policy/Procedure Violation

☐ Performance Transgression

☒ Behavior/Conduct Infraction

☐ Absenteeism/Tardiness

PRIOR NOTIFICATIONS

Level of Discipline	Date	Subject
Verbal	_____	_____
Written	_____	_____
Final Written	_____	_____

Incident Description and Supporting Details: Include the following information: Time, Place, Date of Occurrence, and Persons Present as well as Organizational Impact.

Roger,

It has come to management's attention that while in the elevator you attempted to kiss a fellow worker whom you previously dated after that individual explained to you that she is no longer interested in a personal relationship beyond work. Indeed, since you dated her last year, she has become engaged to another person.

In our meeting, you shared that you "went over the line" because you still have feelings for her, work side by side with her on a daily basis, go to lunch with the same group of friends, and occasionally meet after hours at the gym. You admitted that you "lost focus" in terms of respecting her wishes to be left alone. Finally, you stated that you will respect her in the future and maintain an appropriate distance.

PERFORMANCE IMPROVEMENT PLAN

1. Measurable/Tangible Improvement Goals: *Roger, I expect you to adhere to the commitments you made in terms of respecting your coworker's rights regarding her personal life and her right to feel comfortable working side by side with you.*

2. Training or Special Direction Provided: *Our firm's policy on sexual harassment is attached. Please read the policy immediately and see me if you have any questions.*

3. Interim Performance Evaluation Necessary? *No*

4. Our **Employee Assistance Program** (EAP) provider, Prime Behavioral Health Group, can be confidentially reached to assist you at (800) 555-5555. This is strictly voluntary. A booklet regarding the EAP's services is available from Human Resources.

5. In addition, I recognize that you may have certain ideas to improve your performance. Therefore, I encourage you to provide your own **Personal Improvement Plan Input and Suggestions:**

_____

_____

_____

(Attach additional sheets if needed.)

OUTCOMES AND CONSEQUENCES

Positive: I will remain available to help you and discuss areas where you require additional support. If you meet your performance goals, no further disciplinary action will be taken regarding this issue.

Negative: *Our organization is committed to guaranteeing all of our employees a friendly work environment based on respect of their rights. You are now being placed on notice that if you fail to respect this coworker's or any others' rights regarding their personal lives, you may be dismissed. Furthermore, I remind you that if you retaliate against this employee in any manner, you may likewise be dismissed.* A copy of this document will be placed in your personnel file.

Scheduled Review Date: None

EMPLOYEE COMMENTS AND/OR REBUTTAL

_____

_____

_____

(Attach additional sheets if needed.)

X _____
Employee Signature

EMPLOYEE ACKNOWLEDGMENT GOES HERE

#60 Sexual Harassment

A stockroom clerk charges a coworker with speaking to her in an offensive manner. Although no witnesses were present and the coworker denies having made the statement, his file shows that three years ago he was written up for a similar offense. HR decided that there was merit in the clerk's allegations and placed the coworker on final written warning.

PERFORMANCE CORRECTION NOTICE

Employee Name: *Chris Cicero*   **Department:** *Graphics Services*

Date Presented: *April 7, 2017*   **Supervisor:** *Mark Jones*

DISCIPLINARY LEVEL

☐ **Verbal Correction**—(To memorialize the conversation.)

☐ **Written Warning**—(State nature of offense, method of correction, and action to be taken if offense is repeated.)

☐ **Investigatory Leave**—(Include length of time and nature of review.)

☒ **Final Written Warning**

    ☒ Without decision-making leave

    ☐ With decision-making leave (Attach memo of instructions.)

    ☐ With unpaid suspension

SUBJECT: *Failure to follow company policies and procedures*

☒ Policy/Procedure Violation

☐ Performance Transgression

☒ Behavior/Conduct Infraction

☐ Absenteeism/Tardiness

PRIOR NOTIFICATIONS

Level of Discipline	Date	Subject
Verbal	_____	_____
Written	*Oct 9, 2014*	*Inappropriate workplace conduct*
Final Written	_____	_____

Incident Description and Supporting Details: Include the following information: Time, Place, Date of Occurrence, and Persons Present as well as Organizational Impact.

Chris,

On Wednesday, April 2, a member of the Graphics Department's staff complained that you spoke to her in a rude and offensive manner. The individual reported to Human Resources that you asked her to bend over so that you could "see what she looked like in the doggie position," suggesting that you wanted to look more closely at certain parts of her body. She also complained that you wink at her and make loud kissing sounds on an ongoing basis whenever you see her.

The next day, the employee confronted you to tell you that your behavior was offensive and rude and that she didn't like the way you spoke to her. Your response to her was, "We were only talking. Besides, no one was around, so I'll just deny it if you say anything."

You have denied making these comments. However, you have been previously warned about such behavior on October 9, 2014. The complaint was very similar.

Such actions violate policy 2.54 on sexual harassment. Understand that our institution is committed to maintaining a friendly work environment and has a zero-tolerance policy toward harassment of any kind.

No further transgressions of corporate policy will be tolerated under any circumstances.

PERFORMANCE IMPROVEMENT PLAN

1. Measurable/Tangible Improvement Goals: *I expect you to respect the rights and space of others. I expect that you will never again speak with coworkers in a demeaning way or make gestures or insinuations that could be construed as disrespectful or offensive.*

2. Training or Special Direction Provided: *Our firm's policy on sexual harassment is attached. Please read the policy immediately and see me if you have any questions. In addition, we will schedule you to attend an outside workshop on sexual harassment in the workplace to sensitize you to the needs of others.*

3. Interim Performance Evaluation Necessary? *No*

4. Our **Employee Assistance Program** (EAP) provider, Prime Behavioral Health Group, can be confidentially reached to assist you at (800) 555-5555. This is strictly voluntary. A booklet regarding the EAP's services is available from Human Resources.

5. In addition, I recognize that you may have certain ideas to improve your performance. Therefore, I encourage you to provide your own **Personal Improvement Plan Input and Suggestions:**

_____

_____

_____

(Attach additional sheets if needed.)

OUTCOMES AND CONSEQUENCES

Positive: I will remain available to help you and discuss areas where you require additional support. If you meet your performance goals, no further disciplinary action will be taken regarding this issue.

Negative: *You are now being placed on final written warning. If you ever again make inappropriate gestures or comments or attempt to invade a coworker's space, make a coworker feel like "less of a person," demonstrate offensive behavior, or violate any other standards of performance and conduct, you may be immediately discharged for cause. A copy of this document will be placed in your personnel file.*

Scheduled Review Date: *None*

EMPLOYEE COMMENTS AND/OR REBUTTAL

_____

_____

_____

(Attach additional sheets if needed.)

X _____

Employee Signature

EMPLOYEE ACKNOWLEDGMENT GOES HERE

Note: Since this is a final written warning, add the following sentence to the Employee Acknowledgment: "I also realize that this is my last chance. If I fail to meet the terms and conditions of this directive, I will voluntarily resign or be discharged for cause."

#61 Sexual Harassment

Female supervisor who claimed harassment by a male department head is herself guilty of creating a sexually charged environment.

PERFORMANCE CORRECTION NOTICE

Employee Name: *Anita Ford*   **Department:** *Loan Administration*

Date Presented: *February 28, 2017*   **Supervisor:** *Rudi Logan*

DISCIPLINARY LEVEL

☐ **Verbal Correction**—(To memorialize the conversation.)

☒ **Written Warning**—(State nature of offense, method of correction, and action to be taken if offense is repeated.)

☐ **Investigatory Leave**—(Include length of time and nature of review.)

☐ **Final Written Warning**

    ☐ Without decision-making leave

    ☐ With decision-making leave (Attach memo of instructions.)

    ☐ With unpaid suspension

SUBJECT: *Failure to follow company policy 2.01*

☒ Policy/Procedure Violation

☐ Performance Transgression

☒ Behavior/Conduct Infraction

☐ Absenteeism/Tardiness

PRIOR NOTIFICATIONS

Level of Discipline	Date	Subject
Verbal		
Written		
Final Written		

Incident Description and Supporting Details: Include the following information: Time, Place, Date of Occurrence, and Persons Present as well as Organizational Impact.

Anita,

We have just completed a thorough investigation of the allegations of sexual harassment that you levied against your department manager, Chuck Rourke. We have addressed these allegations with him and are taking appropriate action in light of our findings. During the course of this investigation, however, we obtained information from a number of sources that calls into question your conduct in relation to the company's standards of performance and conduct. These standards are detailed in your employee handbook in section 2.01.

It has been reported to us that you, as a supervisor, initiated, encouraged, and willingly participated in conversations of a sexually explicit nature with your subordinates. In addition, a number of employees reported that it appeared to them you were attempting to initiate a more personal relationship with your department manager and that they witnessed no incidents of misconduct on his part toward you or any other employee. Statements from several employees report that you frequently and openly shared private details of your personal life with Chuck. Such conduct clearly violates our organization's standards of performance and conduct.

We are open to investigating and correcting any and all legitimate claims of harassment that you feel may exist in the workplace. However, we cannot overlook the evidence that you appear to be responsible for unacceptable conduct in this instance.

PERFORMANCE IMPROVEMENT PLAN

1. Measurable/Tangible Improvement Goals: *Anita, I expect that you will follow all company standards of performance and conduct and avoid any and all conversation in the future that can be construed as sexually explicit, provocative, or harassing.*

2. Training or Special Direction to Be Provided: *Please reread section 2.01 in your employee handbook immediately to familiarize yourself with the types of behaviors that are considered inappropriate.*

3. Interim Performance Evaluation Necessary? *No*

4. Our **Employee Assistance Program** (EAP) provider, Prime Behavioral Health Group, can be confidentially reached to assist you at (800) 555-5555. This is strictly voluntary. A booklet regarding the EAP's services is available from Human Resources.

5. In addition, I recognize that you may have certain ideas to improve your performance. Therefore, I encourage you to provide your own **Personal Improvement Plan Input and Suggestions:**

_____

_____

_____

(Attach additional sheets if needed.)

OUTCOMES AND CONSEQUENCES

Positive: I will remain available to help you and discuss areas where you require additional support. If you meet your performance goals, no further disciplinary action will be taken regarding this issue.

Negative: *You are now being placed on notice that if you again engage in conduct that violates any of our organization's standards regarding sexual harassment, disciplinary action may result up to and including termination.* A copy of this document will be placed in your personnel file.

Scheduled Review Date: *None*

EMPLOYEE COMMENTS AND/OR REBUTTAL

_____

_____

_____

(Attach additional sheets if needed.)

X _____
Employee Signature

EMPLOYEE ACKNOWLEDGMENT GOES HERE

Note: Since this is such a serious offense, add the following sentence to the Employee Acknowledgment: "In addition, I understand that if I fail to meet the directives outlined in this memo, I will voluntarily resign or be terminated for cause."

#62 Creating an Intimidating Work Environment

Mechanic creates a "hostile work environment" with coworkers by threatening them with a personal lawsuit.

PERFORMANCE CORRECTION NOTICE

Employee Name: *Dan Marx*   **Department:** *Boiler Room*

Date Presented: *May 6, 2017*   **Supervisor:** *Phyllis Herndon*

DISCIPLINARY LEVEL

☐ **Verbal Correction**—(To memorialize the conversation.)

☒ **Written Warning**—(State nature of offense, method of correction, and action to be taken if offense is repeated.)

☐ **Investigatory Leave**—(Include length of time and nature of review.)

☐ **Final Written Warning**

    ☐ Without decision-making leave

    ☐ With decision-making leave (Attach memo of instructions.)

    ☐ With unpaid suspension

SUBJECT: *Creating an unfriendly work environment*

☒ Policy/Procedure Violation

☐ Performance Transgression

☒ Behavior/Conduct Infraction

☐ Absenteeism/Tardiness

PRIOR NOTIFICATIONS

Level of Discipline	Date	Subject
Verbal	_____	_____
Written	_____	_____
Final Written	_____	_____

Incident Description and Supporting Details: Include the following information: Time, Place, Date of Occurrence, and Persons Present as well as Organizational Impact.

Dan,

Today six of your coworkers came forward to make a formal complaint about your performance and conduct over the past two months. It was discovered that several of these individuals fear retaliation when working with you. Namely, they fear that you will personally sue them for defamation if you conclude that they said something negative about you. One worker stated that you told him, "If I have any health or mental stress problems as a result of working with you, I will hold you personally responsible and sue you." This obviously could create an intimidating and hostile work environment.

In addition, your coworkers stated that you inappropriately share your personal problems and your perceptions of problems at work with others in the boiler room. It has also been confirmed by a number of your peers that you relentlessly reiterate your problems in an effort to find out who said something about you. You have asked multiple coworkers, "Who says things about me? Have you heard anyone mentioning my name? What do others say about me?" This not only wastes valuable time but also diminishes morale.

PERFORMANCE IMPROVEMENT PLAN

1. Measurable/Tangible Improvement Goals: *Dan, I expect you to maintain harmonious relationships with your peers. To do this, you need to deliver constructive, respectful communications to your coworkers without blame or censure. Further, you should acknowledge your involvement in questionable situations and become an active team member in resolving complaints. I expect you to immediately stop threatening your coworkers with lawsuits as well as to stop inappropriately sharing information with uninvolved parties. Finally, I expect you to discuss with me any time you want more information about the goings-on in our workgroup.*

2. Training or Special Direction to Be Provided: *Our company will arrange for you to attend two separate off-site training workshops on (a) interpersonal communications and (b) dealing with conflict in the workplace. The goal of these programs is to sensitize you regarding your method of communicating with others and to expose you to alternative communication means that you may find helpful in your day-to-day dealings.*

3. Interim Performance Evaluation Necessary? *Yes. Although your standard annual review is not due for another three months, I feel it is necessary to issue an interim written evaluation at this point that reflects your current level of performance. We will then review your performance again next quarter at the regularly scheduled time.*

4. Our **Employee Assistance Program** (EAP) provider, Prime Behavioral Health Group, can be confidentially reached to assist you at (800) 555-5555. This is strictly voluntary. A booklet regarding the EAP's services is available from Human Resources.

5. In addition, I recognize that you may have certain ideas to improve your performance. Therefore, I encourage you to provide your own **Personal Improvement Plan Input and Suggestions:**

_____

_____

_____

(Attach additional sheets if needed.)

OUTCOMES AND CONSEQUENCES

Positive: I will remain available to help you and discuss areas where you require additional support. If you meet your performance goals, no further disciplinary action will be taken regarding this issue. _In addition, you will enjoy more positive interpersonal relations with your peers and more satisfaction at work._

Negative: _You are now being placed on notice that you are never again to threaten coworkers with personal lawsuits. Although you have the civil right to sue anyone at any time for any reason, threatening lawsuits in the workplace creates hostility and anxiety. Because our company is committed to providing all employees with a work environment that is free of hostility, if you ever again threaten a coworker, supervisor, or subordinate with a personal lawsuit, you may be immediately discharged._

Furthermore, if you ever again inappropriately share personal information with your coworkers regarding what's being said about you by others or about others' actions toward you, or if you conduct what in essence boils down to an inappropriate "mini-investigation," you may be subject to further disciplinary action up to and including termination. A copy of this document will be placed in your personnel file.

Scheduled Review Date: _Three months (August 5)_

EMPLOYEE COMMENTS AND/OR REBUTTAL

_____

_____

_____

(Attach additional sheets if needed.)

X _____
                Employee Signature

EMPLOYEE ACKNOWLEDGMENT GOES HERE

Bonus Sample: Social Media Cyberbullying

An employee posts offensive and disrespectful material on Facebook and Twitter about a coworker's personal life.[8]

PERFORMANCE CORRECTION NOTICE

Employee Name: *Adriana Cabral*   **Department:** *Customer Care*

Date Presented: *September 25, 2017*   **Supervisor:** *Mohamed Tengku*

DISCIPLINARY LEVEL

☐ **Verbal Correction**—(To memorialize the conversation.)

☐ **Written Warning**—(State nature of offense, method of correction, and action to be taken if offense is repeated.)

☐ **Investigatory Leave**—(Include length of time and nature of review.)

☒ **Final Written Warning**

    ☒ Without decision-making leave

    ☐ With decision-making leave (Attach memo of instructions.)

    ☐ With unpaid suspension

SUBJECT: *Inappropriate workplace conduct/irresponsible behavior*

☒ Policy/Procedure Violation

☐ Performance Transgression

☒ Behavior/Conduct Infraction

☐ Absenteeism/Tardiness

PRIOR NOTIFICATIONS

Level of Discipline	Date	Subject
Verbal	_____	_____

---

8 A word of caution: Disciplining employees for social media misuse is in a state of flux as far as the law is concerned. The National Labor Relations Board prohibits employers from restricting workers' rights to engage in protected, concerted activities, such as online discussions and comments regarding wages, work conditions, and other terms of employment. This example is clearly personal in nature and speaks to abusive behavior; however, companies must likewise take into account workers' rights to privacy and to engage in lawful off-duty conduct without disciplinary or other adverse consequences in the workplace. When in doubt, speak with qualified legal counsel about disciplining employees for social media misuse.

Written   _____   _____

Final Written   _____   _____

Incident Description and Supporting Details: Include the following information: Time, Place, Date of Occurrence, and Persons Present as well as Organizational Impact.

Adriana,

On Friday, September 25, your coworker Sara Mendoza complained to Human Resources that you humiliated and shamed her publicly on Facebook and Twitter. Specifically, she showed HR the postings that you uploaded to those two social media sites with photos of her. The first photo read "Sara's Brain," showing her dancing with a beer in her hand. The second posting read "Sara's Brain on Drugs." In that second posting, Sara had fallen to the ground, and the photo that you posted showed her rolled back with her legs spread open, revealing her undergarments.

In her report to HR, Sara stated that she felt publicly humiliated and embarrassed by the photos that you shared. She also stated that she felt it could adversely affect her ability to do her job because her personal credibility was now placed into question within our workforce and even with our clients. She told HR that you were aware that many of her coworkers and even some of her client contacts are friends with both you and her on social media platforms and that they would surely see her in this compromised state. As such, she needed HR's guidance to determine how to best handle this—by either posting an apology online, calling people directly who might be offended by the photo, or simply remaining silent on the matter.

When asked about this, you stated that you only posted the photos as a joke and a lark because Sara's behavior that night was funny and so "un-Sara." You also informed me that the motivation behind your posting had something to do with ongoing issues you had with Sara about a male companion that you're both pursuing. You likewise stated that you were sorry for your actions, would apologize to Sara, and were willing to make amends with her.

However, anything that could constitute cyberbullying or other acts that could be viewed as humiliating or mean-spirited toward coworkers—for example, embarrassing photos, videos, websites, or fake profiles—is taken very seriously by our company and violates our Social Media policy, which you can find online in our electronic employee handbook. As such, your behavior violates this critical company policy and warrants a final written warning for inappropriate workplace conduct.

PERFORMANCE IMPROVEMENT PLAN

1. Measurable/Tangible Improvement Goals: *Adriana, I expect you to uphold all standards of performance and conduct, especially when it comes to any abusive or humiliating public comments, seen by coworkers and clients, toward your coworkers. I expect you to use much better judgment and discretion when posting anything to your personal social media accounts that have potential connections to the workplace and can be hurtful or abusive toward your coworkers. Likewise, I expect you at all times in the future to foster a work environment with your coworker peers that treats people with dignity and respect at all*

328 BEHAVIOR AND CONDUCT INFRACTIONS

times—and not to engage in any type of activity that could appear to humiliate someone, diminish their sense of self-worth, or potentially strip them of their dignity.

2. Training or Special Direction Provided: *Our company's policy on social media is attached. Please read the policy immediately and see me if you have any questions. I will likewise schedule a meeting for the three of us, including Sara, to discuss expectations in the workplace moving forward and how to ensure that communication remains open and transparent after this event.*

3. Interim Performance Evaluation Necessary? *No*

4. Our **Employee Assistance Program** (EAP) provider, Prime Behavioral Health Group, can be confidentially reached to assist you at (800) 555-5555. This is strictly voluntary. A booklet regarding the EAP's services is available from Human Resources.

5. In addition, I recognize that you may have certain ideas to improve your performance. Therefore, I encourage you to provide your own **Personal Improvement Plan Input and Suggestions:**

_____

_____

_____

(Attach additional sheets if needed.)

OUTCOMES AND CONSEQUENCES

Positive: I will remain available to help you and discuss areas where you require additional support.

Negative: *Note, however, that you are now being placed on formal notice that if you ever again fail to respect others' rights regarding their personal lives or engage in activity that could embarrass or humiliate a coworker or other affiliate at work, disciplinary action up to and including immediate dismissal may result.*

Scheduled Review Date: *None*

EMPLOYEE COMMENTS AND/OR REBUTTAL

_____

_____

_____

(Attach additional sheets if needed.)

X _____
Employee Signature

EMPLOYEE ACKNOWLEDGMENT GOES HERE

I also realize that this is my last chance. If I fail to meet the terms and conditions of this directive, I will voluntarily resign or be discharged for cause.

#63 Veiled or Direct Threats of Violence

A secretary, sick at home, calls a coworker, her former best friend, in the office and leaves a hostile and threatening voice mail message. The secretary claims that the coworker reported her poor performance to management. The voice mail is captured on tape and reported to Human Resources and Security.

PERFORMANCE CORRECTION NOTICE

Employee Name: *Joan Carter*   **Department:** *Marketing*

Date Presented: *April 27, 2017*   **Supervisor:** *Gail Harris*

DISCIPLINARY LEVEL

☐ **Verbal Correction**—(To memorialize the conversation.)

☐ **Written Warning**—(State nature of offense, method of correction, and action to be taken if offense is repeated.)

☐ **Investigatory Leave**—(Include length of time and nature of review.)

☒ **Final Written Warning**

    ☒ Without decision-making leave

    ☐ With decision-making leave (Attach memo of instructions.)

    ☐ With unpaid suspension

SUBJECT: *Making threats to a coworker, indecent conduct*

☒ Policy/Procedure Violation

☒ Performance Transgression

☒ Behavior/Conduct Infraction

☐ Absenteeism/Tardiness

PRIOR NOTIFICATIONS

Level of Discipline	Date	Subject
Verbal	_____	_____
Written	_____	_____
Final Written	_____	_____

Incident Description and Supporting Details: Include the following information: Time, Place, Date of Occurrence, and Persons Present as well as Organizational Impact.

Joan,

Yesterday, you were out sick and called in to the office from your home. Apparently, you were angry with a fellow secretary because you believed that she reported you to management. You left a threatening message on your coworker's voice mail, and you stated: "You'll pay for this . . . I ought to kick your ass, you bitch!" Such direct threats of violence breach company standards of performance and conduct, per policy 8.11.

Specifically, policy 8.11 states under Prohibited Conduct that an employee will face immediate and appropriate disciplinary action, up to and including dismissal, for engaging in any of the following activities:

8.112 Unlawful harassment

8.114 Using abusive language at any time on Company premises

8.116 Causing, creating, or participating in a disruption of any kind

8.118 Provoking a fight during working hours or on Company property

Our company's policy against unlawful harassment further states: "The Company will not retaliate against any employee for filing a complaint and will not tolerate or permit retaliation by management, employees, or coworkers." Your actions constitute a serious breach of conduct as defined by these policies.

PERFORMANCE IMPROVEMENT PLAN

1. Measurable/Tangible Improvement Goals: *Joan, I expect you to never again engage in any conduct or activity that could be construed as harassment, direct threats, or veiled threats. You are responsible for ensuring a friendly work environment at all times. There are absolutely no excuses or exceptions to this performance expectation.*

2. Training or Special Direction to Be Provided: *Attached to this disciplinary document is a copy of policy 8.11. Please review this policy immediately and see me if you believe you will have any difficulty meeting its requirements or if you have any questions about its interpretation.*

3. Interim Performance Evaluation Necessary? *No*

4. Our **Employee Assistance Program** (EAP) provider, Prime Behavioral Health Group, can be confidentially reached to assist you at (800) 555-5555. This is strictly voluntary. A booklet regarding the EAP's services is available from Human Resources.

5. In addition, I recognize that you may have certain ideas to improve your performance. Therefore, I encourage you to provide your own **Personal Improvement Plan Input and Suggestions:**

_____

_____

_____

(Attach additional sheets if needed.)

OUTCOMES AND CONSEQUENCES

Positive: I will remain available to help you and discuss areas where you require additional support. If you meet your performance goals, no further disciplinary action will be taken regarding this issue.

Negative: *If you ever again engage in conduct that could be construed as harassment by inciting a fight, threatening a coworker with physical harm, or creating a work atmosphere charged with hostility, you may be immediately discharged for cause.* A copy of this document will be placed in your personnel file.

Scheduled Review Date: *None*

EMPLOYEE COMMENTS AND/OR REBUTTAL

_____

_____

_____

(Attach additional sheets if needed.)

X _____
Employee Signature

EMPLOYEE ACKNOWLEDGMENT GOES HERE

Note: Since this is a final written warning, add this sentence to the Employee Acknowledgment: "Furthermore, I understand that this is my last chance. If I fail to abide by the directives established in this memo, I will voluntarily resign or be discharged for cause."

#64 Antagonistic Behavior Toward a Coworker

A collector is unwilling to help a coworker and responds to her questions in a belittling and antagonistic tone.

PERFORMANCE CORRECTION NOTICE

Employee Name: *Marge Sorensen*   **Department:** *Accounting*

Date Presented: *June 15, 2017*   **Supervisor:** *Rolf Wagener*

DISCIPLINARY LEVEL

☐ **Verbal Correction**—(To memorialize the conversation.)

☒ **Written Warning**—(State nature of offense, method of correction, and action to be taken if offense is repeated.)

☐ **Investigatory Leave**—(Include length of time and nature of review.)

☐ **Final Written Warning**

    ☐ Without decision-making leave

    ☐ With decision-making leave (Attach memo of instructions.)

    ☐ With unpaid suspension

SUBJECT: *Antagonistic behavior toward a coworker; unwillingness to perform properly assigned work*

☒ Policy/Procedure Violation

☒ Performance Transgression

☒ Behavior/Conduct Infraction

☐ Absenteeism/Tardiness

PRIOR NOTIFICATIONS

Level of Discipline	Date	Subject
Verbal	_____	_____
Written	_____	_____
Final Written	_____	_____

Incident Description and Supporting Details: Include the following information: Time, Place, Date of Occurrence, and Persons Present as well as Organizational Impact.

Marge,

Yesterday, you displayed unprofessional conduct toward a coworker. Namely, when Debbie Carter came to see you to retrieve a folder from your area in order to look at an invoice, she asked you to give her the account file. You did so reluctantly and unwillingly after expressing your dissatisfaction by stating, "God, don't you know how busy I am? I don't have the time to do your work for you. Keep an eye on your own damn files next time, okay?"

The employee complained to me, and I invited Human Resources to investigate the matter. Two witnesses confirmed that your behavior was inappropriate and unacceptable. They stated that you became unduly upset and loudly complained so that others around you would hear you. It was reported that your manner and tone of voice were belittling, antagonistic, and intimidating. This violates our firm's standards of performance and conduct.

PERFORMANCE IMPROVEMENT PLAN

1. Measurable/Tangible Improvement Goals: *Marge, I expect you to foster a sense of community and cooperation in the workplace. You are to assist others in completing their tasks and to treat others with dignity and respect at all times.*

2. Training or Special Direction to Be Provided: *If you would like to attend an outside seminar on dealing with interpersonal conflict in the workplace or on controlling anger, please let me know so that I can arrange it. Otherwise, I want you to meet with me immediately when you feel that you're having difficulty dealing with a particular coworker or situation so that I can help you solve the problem.*

3. Interim Performance Evaluation Necessary? *No*

4. Our **Employee Assistance Program** (EAP) provider, Prime Behavioral Health Group, can be confidentially reached to assist you at (800) 555-5555. This is strictly voluntary. A booklet regarding the EAP's services is available from Human Resources.

5. In addition, I recognize that you may have certain ideas to improve your performance. Therefore, I encourage you to provide your own **Personal Improvement Plan Input and Suggestions:**

_____

_____

_____

(Attach additional sheets if needed.)

OUTCOMES AND CONSEQUENCES

Positive: I will remain available to help you and discuss areas where you require additional support. If you meet your performance goals, no further disciplinary action will be taken regarding this issue.

Negative: You are now being placed on notice that if you ever again act in a manner that can be considered hostile, offensive, or antagonistic toward a coworker, customer, or vendor, disciplinary action up to and including termination may result. A copy of this document will be placed in your personnel file.

Scheduled Review Date: None

EMPLOYEE COMMENTS AND/OR REBUTTAL

_____

_____

_____

(Attach additional sheets if needed.)

X _____
Employee Signature

EMPLOYEE ACKNOWLEDGMENT GOES HERE

#65 Antagonistic Behavior Toward a Coworker

Two supervisors engage in "conduct unbecoming a manager"; each is written up for unacceptable behavior. Note: This is the first of two write-ups for a manager who is arrogant and condescending; the next write-up is for the other manager involved (see Write-Up #66). Since both were equally responsible, notice the similarity in language.

PERFORMANCE CORRECTION NOTICE

Employee Name: *Christopher Rand*

Date Presented: *December 30, 2017*

Department: *Information Systems*

Supervisor: *Mike Forrest*

DISCIPLINARY LEVEL

☒ **Verbal Correction**—(To memorialize the conversation.)

☐ **Written Warning**—(State nature of offense, method of correction, and action to be taken if offense is repeated.)

☐ **Investigatory Leave**—(Include length of time and nature of review.)

☐ **Final Written Warning**

    ☐ Without decision-making leave

    ☐ With decision-making leave (Attach memo of instructions.)

    ☐ With unpaid suspension

SUBJECT: *Antagonistic behavior toward a coworker*

☐ Policy/Procedure Violation

☒ Performance Transgression

☒ Behavior/Conduct Infraction

☐ Absenteeism/Tardiness

PRIOR NOTIFICATIONS

Level of Discipline	Date	Subject
Verbal	_____	_____
Written	_____	_____
Final Written	_____	_____

Incident Description and Supporting Details: Include the following information: Time, Place, Date of Occurrence, and Persons Present as well as Organizational Impact.

Marge,

Over the last six months, but especially in the past two months, you have engaged in conduct unbecoming a manager. Specifically, you have allowed your interpersonal relationship with another manager in your unit to negatively affect the atmosphere in Information Systems. You purposely use arcane language when speaking with this coworker when you know that she is foreign-born. Your assertiveness can easily be construed as aggressiveness, especially when you attempt to intimidate this coworker via your selection of arcane words.

You also need to be sensitive to the fact that others feel that you physically "invade their space" and engage in "intellectual one-upsmanship." For example, you freely mention your wealth, status, and cultural upbringing. You comment freely on how you look down on certain practices (like eating at McDonald's or shopping at Wal-Mart) that most of your coworkers engage in. As such, you alienate yourself from your peers and subordinates, who perceive your comments as arrogant and immature.

PERFORMANCE IMPROVEMENT PLAN

1. Measurable/Tangible Improvement Goals: *Marge, I expect you, as a manager, to solve problems, not create them. I expect you to demonstrate a commitment to open communications and a friendly work environment. I also expect you to manage your personal feelings about others so that they don't spill over into the workplace.*

2. Training or Special Direction to Be Provided: *I will hold a meeting with you and your coworker to air each of your problems and to improve your problem-solving methods when disagreement occurs.*

3. Interim Performance Evaluation Necessary? *No*

4. Our **Employee Assistance Program** (EAP) provider, Prime Behavioral Health Group, can be confidentially reached to assist you at (800) 555-5555. This is strictly voluntary. A booklet regarding the EAP's services is available from Human Resources.

5. In addition, I recognize that you may have certain ideas to improve your performance. Therefore, I encourage you to provide your own **Personal Improvement Plan Input and Suggestions:**

_____

_____

_____

(Attach additional sheets if needed.)

OUTCOMES AND CONSEQUENCES

Positive: I will remain available to help you and discuss areas where you require additional support. If you meet your performance goals, no further disciplinary action will be taken regarding this issue.

Negative: *Our organization is dedicated to guaranteeing all its employees a friendly work environment. Furthermore, your putting your own needs above the needs of your unit constitutes failure to meet organizational standards of performance and conduct. You are now warned that if you ever again engage in activity that can be construed as harassment, verbal abuse, or intellectual one-upsmanship with coworkers, peers, or subordinates, you may be placed on written warning status. If you fail to meet the standards outlined in this notice while in that written warning period, disciplinary action up to and including termination may occur.* A copy of this document will be placed in your personnel file.

Scheduled Review Date: *None*

EMPLOYEE COMMENTS AND/OR REBUTTAL

_____

_____

_____

(Attach additional sheets if needed.)

X _____
Employee Signature

EMPLOYEE ACKNOWLEDGMENT GOES HERE

#66 Antagonistic Behavior Toward a Coworker

Two supervisors engage in "conduct unbecoming a manager"; each is written up for unacceptable behavior. Note: This is the second of two write-ups. This write-up is for a manager who meddles in others' affairs; the previous write-up demonstrates how the other manager was disciplined. Since both were equally responsible, notice the similarity in language.

PERFORMANCE CORRECTION NOTICE

Employee Name: *Marilyn Beckman*   **Department:** *Information Systems*

Date Presented: *December 30, 2017*   **Supervisor:** *Mike Forrest*

DISCIPLINARY LEVEL

☐ **Verbal Correction**—(To memorialize the conversation.)

☐ **Written Warning**—(State nature of offense, method of correction, and action to be taken if offense is repeated.)

☐ **Investigatory Leave**—(Include length of time and nature of review.)

☐ **Final Written Warning**

    ☐ Without decision-making leave

    ☐ With decision-making leave (Attach memo of instructions.)

    ☐ With unpaid suspension

SUBJECT: *Antagonistic behavior toward a coworker*

☐ Policy/Procedure Violation

☒ Performance Transgression

☒ Behavior/Conduct Infraction

☐ Absenteeism/Tardiness

PRIOR NOTIFICATIONS

Level of Discipline	Date	Subject
Verbal	_____	_____
Written	_____	_____
Final Written	_____	_____

Incident Description and Supporting Details: Include the following information: Time, Place, Date of Occurrence, and Persons Present as well as Organizational Impact.

Marilyn,

Over the last six months, but especially in the past two months, you have engaged in conduct unbecoming a manager. Specifically, you have allowed your interpersonal relationship with another manager in your unit to negatively affect the atmosphere in Information Systems. You have purposely intruded in another manager's hiring decisions without having all the facts necessary to claim that your staff members were overlooked for the job available. You have also acted on this incomplete information by inciting negative feelings among staff members in your department. One employee felt that you "baited" him to speak poorly about his supervisor when he had just had a disagreement with that individual. Also, your assertiveness can easily be construed as aggressiveness, especially when you are perceived as pressing issues with problems in other units that are in no way under your scope of authority.

PERFORMANCE IMPROVEMENT PLAN

1. Measurable/Tangible Improvement Goals: *Marilyn, I expect you, as a manager, to solve problems, not create them. I expect you to demonstrate a commitment to open communications and a friendly work environment. I also expect you to manage your personal feelings about others so that they don't spill over into the workplace.*

2. Training or Special Direction to Be Provided: *I will hold a meeting with you and your coworker to air each of your problems and to improve your problem-solving methods when disagreement occurs.*

3. Interim Performance Evaluation Necessary? *No*

4. Our **Employee Assistance Program** (EAP) provider, Prime Behavioral Health Group, can be confidentially reached to assist you at (800) 555-5555. This is strictly voluntary. A booklet regarding the EAP's services is available from Human Resources.

5. In addition, I recognize that you may have certain ideas to improve your performance. Therefore, I encourage you to provide your own **Personal Improvement Plan Input and Suggestions:**

_____

_____

_____

(Attach additional sheets if needed.)

OUTCOMES AND CONSEQUENCES

Positive: I will remain available to help you and discuss areas where you require additional support. If you meet your performance goals, no further disciplinary action will be taken regarding this issue.

Negative: *Our organization is dedicated to guaranteeing all its employees a friendly work environment. Furthermore, your putting your own needs above the needs of your unit constitutes failure to meet organizational standards of performance and conduct. You are now warned that if you ever again engage in activity that can be construed as meddling in another manager's affairs, critiquing his decisions or managerial effectiveness, or baiting others to complain about that person, you may be placed on final written warning status. If you fail to meet the standards outlined in this notice while in that final written warning period, disciplinary action up to and including termination may occur.* **A copy of this document will be placed in your personnel file.**

Scheduled Review Date: *None*

EMPLOYEE COMMENTS AND/OR REBUTTAL

_____

_____

_____

(Attach additional sheets if needed.)

X _____
Employee Signature

EMPLOYEE ACKNOWLEDGMENT GOES HERE

#67 Managerial Retaliation

Wholesale manager retaliates against a subordinate who complained about the manager's sleeping on the job. Newly hired unit director begins disciplinary action against this ten-year manager with a history of acceptable performance evaluations.

PERFORMANCE CORRECTION NOTICE

Employee Name: *John Lambert*   **Department:** *Wholesale*

Date Presented: *December 2, 2017*   **Supervisor:** *Tom Watson*

DISCIPLINARY LEVEL

☐ **Verbal Correction**—(To memorialize the conversation.)

☒ **Written Warning**—(State nature of offense, method of correction, and action to be taken if offense is repeated.)

☐ **Investigatory Leave**—(Include length of time and nature of review.)

☒ **Final Written Warning**

   ☒ Without decision-making leave

   ☐ With decision-making leave (Attach memo of instructions.)

   ☐ With unpaid suspension

SUBJECT: *Written warning: substandard work performance; final written warning: sleeping on the job and managerial retaliation*

☒ Policy/Procedure Violation

☒ Performance Transgression

☒ Behavior/Conduct Infraction

☐ Absenteeism/Tardiness

PRIOR NOTIFICATIONS

Level of Discipline	Date	Subject
Verbal	Oct 7, 2017	*Insubordination, poor communication skills, lack of professional etiquette/courtesy*
Written	Aug 30, 2015	*Sleeping on the job*
	Jan 16, 2013	*Sleeping on the job*
Final Written	_____	_____

Incident Description and Supporting Details: Include the following information: Time, Place, Date of Occurrence, and Persons Present as well as Organizational Impact.

John,

Since the verbal warning meeting that you and I had with Human Resources on October 7, 2017, you have continued to demonstrate unacceptable performance and behavior as manager in Wholesale. Your overall job performance does not currently meet company standards of performance and conduct.

Last Wednesday, you were again found sleeping on the job. Your personnel file demonstrates a previous occurrence of disciplinary action taken against you for this infraction. Specifically, you previously received written warnings about this issue on August 30, 2015, and January 16, 2013. Because you have failed to improve your performance in this particular area, this memo constitutes a final written warning for sleeping on the job.

More significantly, you retaliated against Francis Franco, your subordinate, when you hid an item that she was planning on purchasing. She stepped out of the room, and you placed her item into your desk. When she couldn't find it, you told her to fill out a Loss Report. This would reflect poorly on her work record and could even lead to disciplinary action against her. A coworker saw you place the item into your desk, however, and reported this to me. When I questioned you about it, you admitted that you did this because you were mad at her for reporting your sleeping on the job. Such retaliatory behavior demonstrates a disregard for your responsibilities and obligations to this company, Consequently, this memo also constitutes a final written warning for retaliation.

In addition, this document serves as a written warning because your overall performance is unacceptable. In October, I requested that you compose procedures for all operations for Wholesale services, and as of today's date, those procedures have not been submitted to me (despite my directive and your commitment to complete the task by December 1). You are responsible for communicating with me any time that you cannot keep a commitment as per our agreement in October.

PERFORMANCE IMPROVEMENT PLAN

1. Measurable/Tangible Improvement Goals: *John, I expect that you will never again sleep while on the job. I expect that you will never again act in a retaliatory manner toward any subordinate, peer, or member of management. In addition, as I outlined for you in the October 7 meeting, I expect you to maintain open communications with me regarding the status of your workload, to assume total responsibility for your actions, and to avoid any conduct or behavior that violates company performance and conduct standards.*

2. Training or Special Direction to Be Provided: *You have recently attended our company's customer service training. However, in order to strengthen your skills in this area, we will pay for you to attend an outside seminar on company time regarding interpersonal communications, supervision, or dealing with interpersonal conflict in the workplace. Please let me know which of these workshops would be most beneficial to you. In addition, please instruct me regarding any additional technical training that you believe you need in order to meet the essential functions of your job.*

I am attaching a copy of policy 9.45, regarding standards of performance and conduct. Please read this policy carefully and see me regarding any questions you have or clarification that you require.

Finally, I am attaching a copy of your job description. Please read the entire document and see me if you have any questions that require clarification in any of the areas listed.

3. Interim Performance Evaluation Necessary? *Yes. Although it is not yet time for your regularly scheduled annual review, I will issue you an out-of-cycle review that accurately reflects your overall performance since I assumed responsibility for Wholesale.*

4. Our **Employee Assistance Program** (EAP) provider, Prime Behavioral Health Group, can be confidentially reached to assist you at (800) 555-5555. This is strictly voluntary. A booklet regarding the EAP's services is available from Human Resources.

5. In addition, I recognize that you may have certain ideas to improve your performance. Therefore, I encourage you to provide your own **Personal Improvement Plan Input and Suggestions:**

_____

_____

_____

(Attach additional sheets if needed.)

OUTCOMES AND CONSEQUENCES

Positive: I will remain available to help you and discuss areas where you require additional support. If you meet your performance goals, no further disciplinary action will be taken regarding this issue.

Negative: *John, I expect you to take this warning very seriously. If you ever again engage in conduct that could be construed as retaliation toward a subordinate or coworker, or if you ever again are found sleeping on your job, you may be immediately dismissed.*

Furthermore, if you violate any other standards of performance and conduct, you will be placed on a final written warning. If you fail to abide by the terms of this agreement while in final warning status, you may be dismissed. A copy of this document will be placed in your personnel file.

Scheduled Review Date: *Ninety days (March 2, 2018)*

EMPLOYEE COMMENTS AND/OR REBUTTAL

_____

_____

_____

(Attach additional sheets if needed.)

X _____

Employee Signature

EMPLOYEE ACKNOWLEDGMENT GOES HERE

Note: Since this is a final written warning, add this sentence to the Employee Acknowledgment: "I recognize that my job is now in jeopardy of being lost. If I fail to meet the terms of this agreement, I will voluntarily resign or be discharged for cause."

#68 Intoxication During Work Hours

Employee admits to having an alcohol addiction after damaging his vehicle by backing into a wall.

PERFORMANCE CORRECTION NOTICE

Employee Name: *Walter Meyers*   **Department:** *Engineering*

Date Presented: *November 11, 2017*   **Supervisor:** *Gary Martinson*

DISCIPLINARY LEVEL

☐ **Verbal Correction**—(To memorialize the conversation.)

☐ **Written Warning**—(State nature of offense, method of correction, and action to be taken if offense is repeated.)

☐ **Investigatory Leave**—(Include length of time and nature of review.)

☒ **Final Written Warning**

    ☒ Without decision-making leave

    ☐ With decision-making leave (Attach memo of instructions.)

    ☐ With unpaid suspension

SUBJECT: *Unsafe work practices, improper operation of a company vehicle*

☒ Policy/Procedure Violation

☒ Performance Transgression

☒ Behavior/Conduct Infraction

☐ Absenteeism/Tardiness

PRIOR NOTIFICATIONS

Level of Discipline	Date	Subject
Verbal	_____	_____
Written	_____	_____
Final Written	_____	_____

Incident Description and Supporting Details: Include the following information: Time, Place, Date of Occurrence, and Persons Present as well as Organizational Impact.

Walt,

Issue 1: Yesterday, you backed your company pickup truck into a wall and caused approximately $800 worth of damage to the rear fender and taillights.

Issue 2: When I met with you to find out how that happened, you told me that you had been drinking alone at lunch, and you believe that your judgment was impaired. You further stated that you believe that you are addicted to alcohol, and you requested assistance to enter a rehabilitation program.

Your decision to drive a company vehicle while under the influence of alcohol seriously threatened your safety and the safety of other employees. It violates strict company policy and safety practices that prohibit the use and possession of alcohol and drugs on company property during working hours (see attached policy 2.50).

Under normal circumstances, such behavior is grounds for immediate termination. However, because you have sincerely requested assistance to rehabilitate yourself and because you have committed to remain drug- and alcohol-free, the company will be willing to continue your employment under certain conditions.

PERFORMANCE IMPROVEMENT PLAN

1. Measurable/Tangible Improvement Goals:

• *Walt, I expect you never again to be under the influence of any alcohol or other nonprescribed controlled substance while on company grounds or on company time. Furthermore, you are never again to possess such substances while on company grounds or on company time.*

• *If for whatever reason you use or possess alcohol or any other nonprescribed controlled substance while on company grounds or on company time, you will immediately inform your supervisor of this fact. This will place your position in serious jeopardy and may result in immediate dismissal. You will not operate a company vehicle or any machinery that could injure you or a fellow worker.*

• *You agree to immediately enter an alcohol rehabilitation program. You agree to remain in that program until you receive appropriate written medical certification indicating that you have successfully completed the program.[9]*

---

9 The Americans with Disabilities Act (ADA) provides a measure of protection to workers who confess to having an "irresistible compulsion" or inability to stop themselves from engaging in alcoholic or other addictive behavior. In order to utilize the "irresistible compulsion" defense, workers must complete an alcohol rehabilitation program. The program must be either (a) a program certified by your state's department of health or (b) a reputable nonlicensed program like Alcoholics Anonymous or Narcotics Anonymous. Proof of completion must be in writing by either a physician or a treatment program administrator.

Note, however, that the ADA only protects employees who have completed a drug program and are no longer using drugs or who are "participating in a supervised rehabilitation program and are no longer engaging in such use" [42 USCA Section 12114(b)(2)]. Furthermore, certain states also have statutes protecting employees who have requested and are participating in drug treatment programs.

* *You agree in writing to be randomly tested for the presence of alcohol or drugs in your system for the next two years by a medical testing facility. You agree that we have the right to test you for any reason or for no reason at all at our sole discretion.*[10]

2. Training or Special Direction to Be Provided: *A copy of our company's drug-free workplace policy is attached. Please read this policy immediately and provide me with a memo stating that you (a) have read the policy and (b) agree to abide by it and realize that you will be discharged for failing to abide by it.*

3. Interim Performance Evaluation Necessary? *No*

4. *I am formally referring you to our* **Employee Assistance Program** (EAP) *provider, Prime Behavioral Health Group, today. This call will remain confidential. Prime can be reached to assist you at (800) 555-5555. A booklet regarding the EAP's services is available from Human Resources. Please contact Peter Jaspers, who will be expecting your call.*

5. In addition, I recognize that you may have certain ideas to improve your performance. Therefore, I encourage you to provide your own **Personal Improvement Plan Input and Suggestions:**

_____

_____

_____

(Attach additional sheets if needed.)

OUTCOMES ISSUE 1: CONSEQUENCES

Positive: I will remain available to help you and discuss areas where you require additional support. If you meet the company's and your own performance goals, no further disciplinary action will be taken regarding these issues. *In addition, you will greatly benefit from both a personal and career standpoint by getting help now.*

Negative: *Issue I: If you ever again improperly or unsafely operate company vehicles or machinery, disciplinary action up to and including dismissal may result.*

Issue 2: If you refuse to submit to a random test or if you test positive for controlled substances, you will be immediately discharged for cause. If you fail to abide by the dictates of the rehabilitation program at any time, if you fail to attend the program, or if you in any way '"fall off the wagon," you will immediately be discharged.[11] A copy of this document will be placed in your personnel file.

Scheduled Review Date: *Thirty days (December 11, 2017)*

---

10 Disclaimer: As far as random testing is concerned, nearly every state has drug testing laws. These laws are often extremely complicated and vary widely state by state. In addition, some cities now are starting to regulate drug testing. Therefore, if there is any question about whether any form of random testing would be allowed in your city or state, do not include this language in your disciplinary warning. Again, always check with qualified legal counsel before proceeding.

11 Before actually discharging employees based on a drug- or alcohol-related offense, always consult with your labor attorney. A number of states have some very particular rules in terms of when and under what circumstances an employer may actually discharge for such offenses, so make this a consistent practice at all times.

EMPLOYEE COMMENTS AND/OR REBUTTAL

_____

_____

_____

(Attach additional sheets if needed.)

X _____

Employee Signature

EMPLOYEE ACKNOWLEDGMENT GOES HERE

Note: Since this is a final written warning and the offense involved has legal implications, add the following sentences to the Employee Acknowledgment: "I have also been advised to discuss this document with a labor union representative or any other third party that I deem necessary before agreeing to sign it. I understand that no exceptions will be made under any circumstances and that this is my last chance."

#69 Intoxication During Work Hours

Employee smells of alcohol, demonstrates slurred speech and an unsteady gait, but refuses to admit that he is under the influence of alcohol. The employer agrees not to press the issue by mandating a drug test; however, the employee is given a five-day unpaid suspension plus a mandatory EAP referral, which the employee agrees to.

PERFORMANCE CORRECTION NOTICE

Employee Name: *Greg Bjorn* **Department:** *Ceramics Shop*

Date Presented: *August 7, 2017* **Supervisor:** *Terry Carlisle*

DISCIPLINARY LEVEL

☐ **Verbal Correction**—(To memorialize the conversation.)

☐ **Written Warning**—(State nature of offense, method of correction, and action to be taken if offense is repeated.)

☐ **Investigatory Leave**—(Include length of time and nature of review.)

☒ **Final Written Warning**

   ☐ Without decision-making leave

   ☐ With decision-making leave (Attach memo of instructions.)

   ☒ With unpaid suspension

SUBJECT: *Violation of company policy 2.50, Unsafe Work Practices*

☒ Policy/Procedure Violation

☒ Performance Transgression

☒ Behavior/Conduct Infraction

☐ Absenteeism/Tardiness

PRIOR NOTIFICATIONS

Level of Discipline	Date	Subject
Verbal	_____	_____
Written	_____	_____
Final Written	_____	_____

Incident Description and Supporting Details: Include the following information: Time, Place, Date of Occurrence, and Persons Present as well as Organizational Impact.

Greg,

Two days ago, a coworker reported that he had difficulty holding a conversation with you because you reeked of alcohol. When this was reported to me, I called you into my office to observe your actions. I also smelled a strong odor of alcohol on your breath and saw that your eyes were glassy. You slurred your words, and your gait was impaired because you dragged your right foot as you walked.

I questioned whether you were under the influence of alcohol. You said you were not. I asked you when you had your last drink. You said it had been several days since you had a social drink. I asked you why your eyes were glassy. You stated that you were suffering from allergies. I asked you why you wobbled when you walked, and you explained that you hurt your right knee the night before when playing with your children. I asked you why your speech was slurred, and you stated that you were just tired.

I have cause to believe that you were under the influence of alcohol because of the physical manifestations that I observed. Therefore, I arranged for you to be taken by cab to a chemical laboratory so that you could be tested "for cause." You refused. Although I stated that failure to test could be grounds for immediate dismissal, you insisted that you were not under the influence of alcohol and that you did not want to be fired.

I decided not to force you to undergo drug testing because (a) this is the first time that I have observed such behavior and (b) you agreed to meet with our Employee Assistance Plan (EAP) provider, Prime Behavioral Health Group, within 24 hours. I have instructed the EAP to provide you with a medical clearance/"fit for duty" notice in order for you to return to work. You will not be permitted back to work next week without the EAP's clearance.

PERFORMANCE IMPROVEMENT PLAN

1. Measurable/Tangible Improvement Goals: *Greg, I expect that you will never again appear at work under any condition that could be construed or interpreted as intoxication. I expect you to never again be under the influence of any alcohol or other nonprescribed controlled substance while on company grounds or on company time.*

Furthermore, you are to never again possess such substances while on company grounds or on company time. I expect you to fully explore all alternatives for treatment over the next week. I expect you to reevaluate your role in this company and your commitment to ensuring a safe and productive work environment.

2. Training or Special Direction to Be Provided: *A copy of our company's drug-free workplace policy is attached. Please read this policy immediately and provide me with a memo stating that you (a) have read the policy and (b) agree to abide by it and realize that you will be discharged for failing to abide by it.*

3. Interim Performance Evaluation Necessary? *No*

4. *I am formally referring you to our **Employee Assistance Program** (EAP) provider, Prime Behavioral Health Group, today. This call will remain confidential. Prime can be reached to assist you at (800) 555-5555. A booklet regarding the EAP's services is available from Human Resources. Please contact Peter Jaspers, who will be expecting your call.*

5. In addition, I recognize that you may have certain ideas to improve your performance. Therefore, I encourage you to provide your own **Personal Improvement Plan Input and Suggestions:**

_____

_____

_____

(Attach additional sheets if needed.)

OUTCOMES AND CONSEQUENCES

Positive: I will remain available to help you and discuss areas where you require additional support. If you meet the company's and your own performance goals, no further disciplinary action will be taken regarding this issue. _In addition, you will greatly benefit from both a personal and career standpoint by getting help now._

Negative: _If you ever again appear to be under the influence of any alcohol or controlled substances on company time, or if you demonstrate any manifestations of alcohol or drug abuse, you will be automatically transported to an appropriate medical facility for testing. If you refuse to test, or if you test positive for drugs or alcohol, you will be immediately discharged._[12] A copy of this document will be placed in your personnel file.[13]

Scheduled Review Date: _None_

EMPLOYEE COMMENTS AND/OR REBUTTAL

_____

_____

_____

(Attach additional sheets if needed.)

X _____
  Employee Signature

EMPLOYEE ACKNOWLEDGMENT GOES HERE

Note: Since this is a final written warning, add the following sentence to the Employee Acknowledgment: "I understand that no exceptions will be made under any circumstances and that this is my last chance."

---

12 The Americans with Disabilities Act (ADA) precludes you, as an employer, from discharging a worker who is attending an alcohol or drug abuse rehabilitation program. In this case, however, the employee is apparently refusing to recognize an alcohol problem. Therefore, since rehabilitation is not involved, the ADA will not afford the employee any specific protection. In addition, current alcohol use is not a protected disability.

13 Before actually discharging employees based on a drug- or alcohol-related offense, always consult with your labor attorney. A number of states have some very particular rules in terms of when and under what circumstances an employer may actually discharge for such offenses, so make this a consistent practice at all times.

#70 Intoxication During Work Hours

Employee smells of alcohol and demonstrates slurred speech and an unsteady gait. The employer mandates that the employee be tested "for cause," and the employee tests positive.[14] The employee then asks to be entered into an alcohol detoxification program.

PERFORMANCE CORRECTION NOTICE

Employee Name: Ray Cicero   **Department:** Sales

Date Presented: May 30, 2017   **Supervisor:** Teddy Bachelor

---

DISCIPLINARY LEVEL

☐ **Verbal Correction**—(To memorialize the conversation.)

☐ **Written Warning**—(State nature of offense, method of correction, and action to be taken if offense is repeated.)

☐ **Investigatory Leave**—(Include length of time and nature of review.)

☒ **Final Written Warning**

☐ Without decision-making leave

☒ With decision-making leave (Attach memo of instructions.)

☐ With unpaid suspension

SUBJECT: Unsafe work practices, violation of company policy 2.50

☒ Policy/Procedure Violation

☒ Performance Transgression

☒ Behavior/Conduct Infraction

☐ Absenteeism/Tardiness

---

14 In most states, employers must have a "compelling business interest," "probable cause," or a "reasonable suspicion" in order to administer an invasive drug test. If you have probable cause to suspect that an employee's performance has been impaired by current drug or alcohol abuse, immediately contact your labor attorney to learn of your rights and limitations in ordering the employee to submit to a drug test and/or take corrective action based on drug test results.

PRIOR NOTIFICATIONS

Level of Discipline	Date	Subject
Verbal	_____	_____
Written	_____	_____
Final Written	_____	_____

Incident Description and Supporting Details: Include the following information: Time, Place, Date of Occurrence, and Persons Present as well as Organizational Impact.

Ray,

On May 28, a customer on the sales floor complained that you were exhibiting signs of being intoxicated. The customer stated that your eyes were bloodshot, that you laughed and giggled uncontrollably while conducting your business negotiation, and that you were generally giddy and apathetic about the sale. Apparently, you spoke to the customer about your girlfriend, who had just broken up with you. You made statements along the lines of "Who needs her?" and "Who does she think she is?" You also hiccupped and belched in the customer's presence.

I met with you at that time at the customer's request. I concurred that you exhibited behaviors indicative of being under the influence of alcohol. I also smelled liquor on your breath when I stood about two feet away from you. I stated to you that your behavior constitutes misconduct. In addition, because I had reasonable cause to suspect that you were intoxicated, you volunteered to be tested by a drug lab within the hour.

The test results revealed that your blood alcohol level was above the legal limit. Because you tested positive for alcohol consumption while on company premises and during working hours, you have violated policy 2.50, Drug-Free Workplace, and you are not sufficiently responsible to remain employed by our firm.

However, you then admitted to me that you had a chronic alcohol problem that you truly wished to beat. You stated that you could not help yourself when it came to drinking and that you had taken it upon yourself to make an appointment with a state-certified detoxification program to get help.

You have committed to remain drug-free and to voluntarily enter a detoxification program. The company is therefore willing to continue your employment under certain conditions.

PERFORMANCE IMPROVEMENT PLAN

1. Measurable/Tangible Improvement Goals:

• Ray, I expect you to never again be under the influence of any alcohol or other nonprescribed controlled substance while on company grounds or on company time. Furthermore, you are never again to possess such substances while on company grounds or on company time.

• If, for whatever reason, you use or possess alcohol or any other nonprescribed controlled substance while on company grounds or on company time, you will immediately

inform your supervisor of this fact. This will place your position in serious jeopardy and may result in immediate dismissal. You will not operate a company vehicle or any machinery that could injure you, a customer, or a fellow worker.

- *You agree to remain in the alcohol rehabilitation program until you receive appropriate written medical certification indicating that you have successfully completed the program.*

- *You agree to be randomly tested for the presence of alcohol or drugs in your system for the next two years by a medical testing facility. You agree that we have the right to test you for any reason or for no reason at all at our sole discretion.*[15]

2. Training or Special Direction to Be Provided: *A copy of our company's drug-free workplace policy is attached. Please read this policy immediately and provide me with a memo stating that you (a) have read the policy and (b) agree to abide by it and realize that you will be discharged for failing to abide by it.*

3. Interim Performance Evaluation Necessary? *No*

4. *I am now formally referring you to our* **Employee Assistance Program** *(EAP) provider, Prime Behavioral Health Group. The EAP can be confidentially reached to assist you at (800) 555-5555. A booklet regarding the EAP's services is available from Human Resources. Please ask for Rodd Hope, who is expecting your call no later than tomorrow.*

5. In addition, I recognize that you may have certain ideas to improve your performance. Therefore, I encourage you to provide your own **Personal Improvement Plan Input and Suggestions:**

_____

_____

_____

(Attach additional sheets if needed.)

OUTCOMES AND CONSEQUENCES

Positive: I will remain available to help you and discuss areas where you require additional support. If you meet the company's and your own performance goals, no further disciplinary action will be taken regarding this issue. *In addition, you will greatly benefit from both a personal and a career standpoint by getting help now.*

Negative: *If you refuse to submit to a random test or if you test positive for controlled substances, you will be immediately discharged for cause. If you fail to abide by the dictates of the rehabilitation program at any time, if you fail to attend the program, or if you in any way "fall off the wagon," you will immediately resign or be discharged.*[16]

---

15 Disclaimer: As far as random testing is concerned, nearly every state has drug testing laws. These laws are often extremely complicated and vary widely state by state. In addition, some cities now are starting to regulate drug testing. Therefore, if there is any question about whether any form of random testing would be allowed in your city or state, do not include this language in your disciplinary warning. Again, always check with qualified legal counsel before proceeding.

16 Before actually discharging employees based on a drug- or alcohol-related offense, always consult with your labor attorney. A number of states have some very particular rules in terms of when and under what circumstances an employer may actually discharge for such offenses, so make this a consistent practice at all times.

Furthermore, because you failed to volunteer that you had engaged in alcohol consumption until it was proven via a test, you are being placed on a one-day paid decision-making leave tomorrow. I expect you to reevaluate your role within this organization and your commitment to remain a productive member of our car sales team.

If you choose not to return to work the day after tomorrow, I will respect your decision. However, if you choose to return, understand that you will be held fully accountable for all your actions. If you again appear intoxicated at work, or if you again fail to provide acceptable service to any customer, you will be immediately discharged for cause. A copy of this document will be placed in your personnel file.

Scheduled Review Date: *None*

EMPLOYEE COMMENTS AND/OR REBUTTAL

_____

_____

_____

(Attach additional sheets if needed.)

X _____

Employee Signature

EMPLOYEE ACKNOWLEDGMENT GOES HERE

Note: Since this is a final written warning and the offense involved has legal implications, add the following sentences to the Employee Acknowledgment: "I understand that no exceptions will be made under any circumstances and that this is my last chance."

#71 Drug-Related Impairment During Work Hours

Employee admits to having a cocaine addiction when confronted by her supervisor, who notices erratic and strange behavior.

PERFORMANCE CORRECTION NOTICE

Employee Name: *Rosalyn Murray*   **Department:** *Purchasing*

Date Presented: *November 7, 2017*   **Supervisor:** *John McQueen*

DISCIPLINARY LEVEL

☐ **Verbal Correction**—(To memorialize the conversation.)

☐ **Written Warning**—(State nature of offense, method of correction, and action to be taken if offense is repeated.)

☐ **Investigatory Leave**—(Include length of time and nature of review.)

☒ **Final Written Warning**

    ☒ Without decision-making leave

    ☐ With decision-making leave (Attach memo of instructions.)

    ☐ With unpaid suspension

SUBJECT: *Unsafe work practices, violation of company policy 2.50*

☒ Policy/Procedure Violation

☒ Performance Transgression

☒ Behavior/Conduct Infraction

☐ Absenteeism/Tardiness

PRIOR NOTIFICATIONS

Level of Discipline	Date	Subject
Verbal	_____	_____
Written	_____	_____
Final Written	_____	_____

Incident Description and Supporting Details: Include the following information: Time, Place, Date of Occurrence, and Persons Present as well as Organizational Impact.

Rosalyn,

Last night at 5:00, we met in my office to discuss interpersonal relations problems with your coworkers that you felt were hindering your ability to perform at your maximum. As you spoke, I saw that your eyes were darting back and forth and that you kept rubbing your hands together. I heard you speak at a very high speed that became almost unintelligible, and I noticed that you were not listening to me or properly interpreting what I was telling you. I shared with you that this concerned me because it was very unlike you to act this way. I asked you if you were under the influence of any drug, narcotic, or alcohol, and you assured me that you weren't.

This morning at 8:00, you met with me and voluntarily shared that you were indeed addicted to cocaine. You stated that you had voluntarily contacted our Employee Assistance Program provider, Prime Behavioral Health Group, to get help for your problem, and that Prime's counselor recommended that you take a thirty-day unpaid leave of absence to enter a detoxification program.

Your actions have violated strict company policy and safety practices that prohibit the use and possession of alcohol and drugs on company property during working hours (see attached policy 2.50).

Under normal circumstances, such behavior is grounds for immediate termination. However, because you have sincerely requested assistance to rehabilitate yourself and because you have committed to remain drug-free, the company is willing to continue your employment under certain conditions.

PERFORMANCE IMPROVEMENT PLAN

1. Measurable/Tangible Improvement Goals:

 • *Rosalyn, I expect you to never again be under the influence of any alcohol or other nonprescribed, controlled substance while on company grounds or on company time. Furthermore, you are never again to possess such substances while on company grounds or on company time.*

 • *If, for whatever reason, you use or possess alcohol or any other nonprescribed controlled substance while on company grounds or on company time, you will immediately inform your supervisor of this fact. This will place your position in serious jeopardy and may result in immediate dismissal. You will not operate a company vehicle or any machinery that could injure you or a fellow worker.*

 • *You agree to remain in the drug diversion/detoxification program until you receive appropriate medical certification indicating that you have successfully completed the program.*

> • *You agree in writing to be randomly tested for the presence of alcohol or drugs in your system for the next two years by a medical testing facility. You agree that we have the right to test you for any reason or for no reason at all at our sole discretion.*[17]

2. Training or Special Direction to Be Provided: *A copy of our company's drug-free workplace policy is attached. Please read this policy immediately and provide me with a memo stating that you (a) have read the policy and (b) agree to abide by it and realize that you will be discharged for failing to abide by it.*

3. Interim Performance Evaluation Necessary? *No*

4. ~~Our **Employee Assistance Program** (EAP) provider, Prime Behavioral Health Group, can be confidentially reached to assist you at (800) 555-5555. This is strictly voluntary. A booklet regarding the EAP's services is available from Human Resources.~~[18]

5. In addition, I recognize that you may have certain ideas to improve your performance. Therefore, I encourage you to provide your own **Personal Improvement Plan Input and Suggestions:**

_____

_____

_____

(Attach additional sheets if needed.)

OUTCOMES AND CONSEQUENCES

Positive: I will remain available to help you and discuss areas where you require additional support. If you meet the company's and your own performance goals, no further disciplinary action will be taken regarding this issue. *In addition, you will greatly benefit from both a personal and a career standpoint by getting help now.*

Negative: *If you refuse to submit to a random test or if you test positive for controlled substances, you will be immediately discharged for cause. If you fail to abide by the dictates of the detoxification program at any time, if you fail to attend the program, or if you in any way "fall off the wagon," you will immediately be discharged.*[19] A copy of this document will be placed in your personnel file.

Scheduled Review Date: *Thirty days (December 7, 2017)*

---

17 Disclaimer: As far as random testing is concerned, nearly every state has drug testing laws. These laws are often extremely complicated and vary widely state by state. In addition, some cities now are starting to regulate drug testing. Therefore, if there is any question about whether any form of random testing would be allowed in your city or state, do not include this language in your disciplinary warning. Again, always check with qualified legal counsel before proceeding.

18 Delete this paragraph from the form since the employee has already voluntarily contacted the EAP on her own. This language is struck here only to remind you to remove it from the actual write-up.

19 Before actually discharging employees based on a drug- or alcohol-related offense, always consult with your labor attorney. A number of states have some very particular rules in terms of when and under what circumstances an employer may actually discharge for such offenses, so make this a consistent practice at all times.

EMPLOYEE COMMENTS AND/OR REBUTTAL

_____

_____

_____

(Attach additional sheets if needed.)

X _____

Employee Signature

EMPLOYEE ACKNOWLEDGMENT GOES HERE

Note: Since this is a final written warning, and the offense involved has legal implications, add the following sentences to the Employee Acknowledgment: "I have been advised to discuss this document with a labor union representative or any other third party that I deem necessary before agreeing to sign it. I understand that no exceptions will be made under any circumstances and that this is my last chance. I also agree that if I do not meet the standards outlined in this warning, I will voluntarily resign or be discharged for cause."

Bonus Sample: Failure to Disclose Coworker Inebriation

PERFORMANCE CORRECTION NOTICE

Employee Name: *Scott McMillan*   **Department:** *Sales*

Date Presented: *August 1, 2017*   **Supervisor:** *Joe Rizzo*

DISCIPLINARY LEVEL

☐ **Verbal Correction**—(To memorialize the conversation.)

☐ **Written Warning**—(State nature of offense, method of correction, and action to be taken if offense is repeated.)

☐ **Investigatory Leave**—(Include length of time and nature of review.)

☒ **Final Written Warning**

  ☒ Without decision-making leave

  ☐ With decision-making leave (Attach memo of instructions.)

  ☐ With unpaid suspension

SUBJECT: *Failure to act, failure to disclose, violation of Standards of Business Conduct*

☒ Policy/Procedure Violation

☐ Performance Transgression

☒ Behavior/Conduct Infraction

☐ Absenteeism/Tardiness

PRIOR NOTIFICATIONS

Level of Discipline	Date	Subject
Verbal	_____	_____
Written	_____	_____
Final Written	_____	_____

Incident Description and Supporting Details: Include the following information: Time, Place, Date of Occurrence, and Persons Present as well as Organizational Impact.

Scott,

This document serves to notify you that you are being issued a final written warning for violation of company policy regarding Employee Conduct and Standards of Business Conduct and management's duty to act. Specifically, on July 30, you witnessed another sales manager, Martina Santino, return to the office from lunch intoxicated and smelling of alcohol. Martina was reported to have an unsteady gait, to be slurring her words, and to be "talking gibberish" per several witnesses that had observed her behavior.

It was likewise reported that you had spent approximately fifteen to twenty minutes with her in your office, apparently trying to "sober her up." You knowingly failed to report this serious and high-risk situation to anyone until I contacted you, after hearing about it from another manager. When I questioned you about this, you stated that you knew she was drunk, but you didn't want her to get into trouble. You stated that she didn't have any further client visits or meetings scheduled for that afternoon, and you hoped that she'd be able to work it off at her desk, primarily doing paperwork that afternoon.

Withholding such critical information and failing to report and immediately communicate this behavior to me or to Human Resources is highly unacceptable and unprofessional behavior, especially in light of your role as an organizational leader. As a seasoned representative of our sales team, you are held to the highest standards of conduct and behavior, and your judgment is now questionable. Simply put, you should have known better. Your failure to escalate and disclose this issue undermines our company's efforts at being an ethical employer and an outstanding business partner in our community.

Your unilateral decision to "protect" your peer is a dishonesty-related offense, a knowing misrepresentation of facts, and conduct inconsistent with the role and responsibilities of a leader in our department and in this company.

PERFORMANCE IMPROVEMENT PLAN

1. Measurable/Tangible Improvement Goals: *Scott, you have an affirmative obligation to disclose issues that could require management intervention or support services that could potentially help the person. Going forward, I expect that if you ever again become aware of or witness misconduct of this sort—especially behavior that may jeopardize an employee's job, or otherwise reflect poorly on the company's part in our community—you will immediately report it to Human Resources or to a member of management.*

2. Training or Special Direction Provided: *To emphasize the importance of affirmative disclosure and reporting, you will be required to complete the training: Standards of Business Conduct Overview within thirty days of the issuance of this corrective action. You will likewise be required to review immediately the Employee Conduct and Corrective Action Process policy.*

3. Interim Performance Evaluation Necessary? *No*

4. Our **Employee Assistance Program** (EAP) provider, Prime Behavioral Health Group, can be confidentially reached to assist you at (800) 555-5555. This is strictly voluntary. A booklet regarding the EAP's services is available from Human Resources.

5. In addition, I recognize that you may have certain ideas to improve your performance. Therefore, I encourage you to provide your own **Personal Improvement Plan Input and Suggestions:**

_____

_____

_____

(Attach additional sheets if needed.)

OUTCOMES AND CONSEQUENCES

Positive: I will remain available to help you and discuss areas where you require additional support. If you meet your performance goals, no further disciplinary action will be taken regarding this issue. _This represents an opportunity for you to rethink and reestablish your commitment to the organization and the significance of your role as a leader within the Sales Department._

Negative: _You must clearly understand, however, that failure to demonstrate immediate and sustained improvement may result in further disciplinary action, up to and including dismissal._ A copy of this document will be placed in your personnel file.

Scheduled Review Date: _None_

EMPLOYEE COMMENTS AND/OR REBUTTAL

_____

_____

_____

(Attach additional sheets if needed.)

X _____
                   Employee Signature

EMPLOYEE ACKNOWLEDGMENT GOES HERE

#72 Misuse of Power and Office

Assistant vice president disrupts company courier service and uses the president's name to have a personal package delivered.

PERFORMANCE CORRECTION NOTICE

Employee Name: *Jim Fallon*   **Department:** *Manufacturing*

Date Presented: *March 1, 2017*   **Supervisor:** *Craig Christopher*

DISCIPLINARY LEVEL

☐ **Verbal Correction**—(To memorialize the conversation.)

☒ **Written Warning**—(State nature of offense, method of correction, and action to be taken if offense is repeated.)

☐ **Investigatory Leave**—(Include length of time and nature of review.)

☐ **Final Written Warning**

   ☐ Without decision-making leave

   ☐ With decision-making leave (Attach memo of instructions.)

   ☐ With unpaid suspension

SUBJECT: *Failure to follow company policies and procedures*

☒ Policy/Procedure Violation

☐ Performance Transgression

☒ Behavior/Conduct Infraction

☐ Absenteeism/Tardiness

PRIOR NOTIFICATIONS

Level of Discipline	Date	Subject
Verbal	_____	_____
Written	_____	_____
Final Written	_____	_____

Incident Description and Supporting Details: Include the following information: Time, Place, Date of Occurrence, and Persons Present as well as Organizational Impact.

Jim,

On February 26, 2017, after realizing that you had missed the morning delivery to the corporate office, you requested that our company courier, Steve Martinson, disrupt his daily schedule by returning to your branch office to pick up a package that you needed delivered to corporate. You stated that you had a package for the president/CEO and that it was urgent that it be delivered that morning.

Because Steve knew that returning to your office would make it difficult for him to meet his delivery schedule, he called his supervisor, Janet Smarter. When Janet called you to question you about the delivery, you "ate her head off" (in her words) and shouted that she, a mailroom supervisor, should not question your authority.

It was later discovered that your package was not for the president, as you stated earlier, but for another department for personal reasons. You consequently admitted that you had used the president's name and your authority as assistant vice president to get the courier, in the midst of his deliveries, to return to your branch to retrieve your package. This made it difficult for the courier to meet his delivery deadlines.

Your actions constitute misconduct. As an assistant vice president, you misused your title and authority to disrupt company business for your own personal gain. You verbally humiliated a supervisor over the phone in the process even though she was doing her job and questioning you appropriately. Your conduct violates policy 2.05 and warrants giving you a written warning for these multiple offenses.

PERFORMANCE IMPROVEMENT PLAN

1. Measurable/Tangible Improvement Goals: *Jim, I expect that you will never again misuse your title, improperly invoke the president's office, or verbally humiliate a lower-ranked staff member under any circumstances.*

2. Training or Special Direction to Be Provided: *To assist you in succeeding as an assistant vice president, you will be required to attend an off-site Management Basics seminar conducted by the American Management Association on April 10. This course has been attended and successfully evaluated by other members of our management team, and it will provide you with an overview of management's rights and responsibilities.*

3. Interim Performance Evaluation Necessary? *No*

4. Our **Employee Assistance Program** (EAP) provider, Prime Behavioral Health Group, can be confidentially reached to assist you at (800) 555-5555. This is strictly voluntary. A booklet regarding the EAP's services is available from Human Resources.

5. In addition, I recognize that you may have certain ideas to improve your performance. Therefore, I encourage you to provide your own **Personal Improvement Plan Input and Suggestions:**

_____

_____

_____

(Attach additional sheets if needed.)

OUTCOMES AND CONSEQUENCES

Positive: I will remain available to help you and discuss areas where you require additional support. If you meet your performance goals, no further disciplinary action will be taken regarding this issue. _By realizing that an executive title brings many responsibilities, you will handle future situations appropriately and increase respect and communication in the workplace._

Negative: If you ever again engage in conduct that compromises the integrity of your office, if you misuse your authority by arbitrarily "pulling rank," or if you violate any other standards of performance and conduct, you may be immediately discharged for cause. A copy of this document will be placed in your personnel file.

Scheduled Review Date: None

EMPLOYEE COMMENTS AND/OR REBUTTAL

_____

_____

_____

(Attach additional sheets if needed.)

X _____
Employee Signature

EMPLOYEE ACKNOWLEDGMENT GOES HERE

#73 Union Steward Abuse

Union steward's actions exceeded the range of reasonable conduct when challenging a supervisor's decision in front of the supervisor's subordinate and other employees. Note that neither the union steward nor any unionized workers are employed at will. Therefore, the at-will provision is deleted from the Employee Acknowledgment section.

PERFORMANCE CORRECTION NOTICE

Employee Name: *Frank Valdez*   **Department:** *Environmental Services*

Date Presented: *February 10, 2017*   **Supervisor:** *Norman Elder*

DISCIPLINARY LEVEL

☐ **Verbal Correction**—(To memorialize the conversation.)

☒ **Written Warning**—(State nature of offense, method of correction, and action to be taken if offense is repeated.)

☐ **Investigatory Leave**—(Include length of time and nature of review.)

☐ **Final Written Warning**

    ☐ Without decision-making leave

    ☐ With decision-making leave (Attach memo of instructions.)

    ☐ With unpaid suspension

SUBJECT: *Inappropriate conduct and abuse of union steward privileges*

☒ Policy/Procedure Violation

☐ Performance Transgression

☒ Behavior/Conduct Infraction

☐ Absenteeism/Tardiness

PRIOR NOTIFICATIONS

Level of Discipline	Date	Subject
Verbal	*Apr 17, 2016*	*Improper conduct*
Written	_____	_____
Final Written	_____	_____

Incident Description and Supporting Details: Include the following information: Time, Place, Date of Occurrence, and Persons Present as well as Organizational Impact.

Frank,

Yesterday, you and a member of your union, janitor Barbara Jones, approached Don Smith, supervisor of environmental services, in the hallway to question a scheduling decision he made. Supervisor Smith stated, and janitor Jones confirmed, that you became unnecessarily antagonistic during that meeting.

You made comments to Don Smith in front of his staff member, Barbara Jones, that "you're doing it again—you're playing favorites," "what kind of crap management is this?" and "whoever promoted you into this job was a goddamn fool." You also stated your opinion loudly enough for other employees in the hallway to hear. At face value, your remarks were rude. The tone of your voice, however, made those comments inflammatory and challenging. Consequently, your aggressive representation while acting in your capacity as shop steward has gone beyond the bounds of appropriateness.

Remember as well that when we addressed this issue with you last April, you assured me, the vice president of Human Resources, that you would be more sensitive about how you communicate with managers of this organization. You committed to me that you would not again engage in activity that was seen as too "hot" or "out of control." You also stated that you would conduct controversial meetings in private—not out in the open where everyone could hear. Local 555's business representative, Victor Farmington, agreed at that time to help you abide by your commitment.

PERFORMANCE IMPROVEMENT PLAN

1. Measurable/Tangible Improvement Goals: *Frank, I expect that you will conduct all union-related business in private and in a manner that does not demonstrate contempt for the management of this organization.*

2. Training or Special Direction Provided: *Please work further with Victor Farmington, business representative of Local 555, regarding proper protocol for investigating and filing grievances and intervening between management and union members.*

3. Interim Performance Evaluation Necessary? *No*

4. Our **Employee Assistance Program** (EAP) provider, Prime Behavioral Health Group, can be confidentially reached to assist you at (800) 555-5555. This is strictly voluntary. A booklet regarding the EAP's services is available from Human Resources.

5. In addition, I recognize that you may have certain ideas to improve your performance. Therefore, I encourage you to provide your own **Personal Improvement Plan Input and Suggestions:**

_____

_____

_____

(Attach additional sheets if needed.)

OUTCOMES AND CONSEQUENCES

Positive: I will remain available to help you and discuss areas where you require additional support. If you meet your performance goals, no further disciplinary action will be taken regarding this issue. *In addition, by working more cooperatively with individual managers, you will help our organization work more effectively with Local 555 in resolving employee disputes effectively.*

Negative: *You are now being placed on notice that any further conduct that could be construed as an inappropriate use of your union steward status may lead to disciplinary action up to and including dismissal.* A copy of this document will be placed in your personnel file.

Scheduled Review Date: *None*

EMPLOYEE COMMENTS AND/OR REBUTTAL

_____

_____

_____

(Attach additional sheets if needed.)

X _____

Employee Signature

EMPLOYEE ACKNOWLEDGMENT GOES HERE

Note: Since this employee is governed by a collective bargaining agreement and is not employed at will, it is necessary to delete the at-will clause from the Employee Acknowledgment.

#74 Character Assassination and Defamation

Research scientist maligns her supervisor by sharing inappropriate information with other members of the management team.

PERFORMANCE CORRECTION NOTICE

Employee Name: *Pam Frances*   **Department:** *Research Testing*

Date Presented: *January 11, 2017*   **Supervisor:** *John Sheller*

DISCIPLINARY LEVEL

☐ **Verbal Correction**—(To memorialize the conversation.)

☐ **Written Warning**—(State nature of offense, method of correction, and action to be taken if offense is repeated.)

☐ **Investigatory Leave**—(Include length of time and nature of review.)

☒ **Final Written Warning**

    ☐ Without decision-making leave

    ☐ With decision-making leave (Attach memo of instructions.)

    ☒ With unpaid suspension

SUBJECT: *Insubordination*

☒ Policy/Procedure Violation

☐ Performance Transgression

☒ Behavior/Conduct Infraction

☐ Absenteeism/Tardiness

PRIOR NOTIFICATIONS

Level of Discipline	Date	Subject
Verbal	_____	_____
Written	_____	_____
Final Written	_____	_____

Incident Description and Supporting Details: Include the following information: Time, Place, Date of Occurrence, and Persons Present as well as Organizational Impact.

Pam,

After conducting a detailed investigation involving your annual performance appraisal, I have determined that the following actions needed to be addressed.

First, the way in which you chose to handle your rebuttal was in direct conflict with the chain of command that you are to follow. Any response or rebuttal to your supervisor's evaluation of your performance should have been brought directly to her. Your decision to send your rebuttal to other individuals not directly involved in the appraisal process was inappropriate and against company policy.

Second, you wrote down in your rebuttal that your supervisor ". . . constantly criticizes her supervisor, Dr. Smith, behind her back, as well as Dr. Smith's peers, including Drs. Jones, Winchester, and Chang." By sharing this written rebuttal with the doctors in question, you deliberately attempted to sabotage your direct supervisor's reputation. Such poor judgment and vindictiveness violate our organization's standards of performance and conduct.

PERFORMANCE IMPROVEMENT PLAN

1. Measurable/Tangible Improvement Goals: *I expect you to support this institution's clinical and research efforts by respecting your coworkers and supervisors at all times and by exercising sound judgment in communicating your needs to others. I expect you to communicate with your supervisor, your department head, or the Human Resources Department if you ever feel frustrated with interpersonal relationships or in need of advice. Furthermore, as I have verbally shared with you, I highly recommend that you apologize to your supervisor and to the other members of the management team whom you involved in this.*

2. Training or Special Direction Provided: *Attached is policy 2.30, Company Standards of Behavior and Conduct, along with policy 2.67, Dispute Resolution Procedures. Please read these policies immediately and see me tomorrow if you have any questions about them.*

3. Interim Performance Evaluation Necessary? *No*

4. Our **Employee Assistance Program** (EAP) provider, Prime Behavioral Health Group, can be confidentially reached to assist you at (800) 555-5555. This is strictly voluntary. A booklet regarding the EAP's services is available from Human Resources.

5. In addition, I recognize that you may have certain ideas to improve your performance. Therefore, I encourage you to provide your own **Personal Improvement Plan Input and Suggestions:**

_____

_____

(Attach additional sheets if needed.)

OUTCOMES AND CONSEQUENCES

Positive: I will remain available to help you and discuss areas where you require additional support. If you meet your performance goals, no further disciplinary action will be taken regarding this issue.

Negative: *You are now being placed on formal written notice that if you again fail to follow the appropriate chain of command when communicating with your supervisors, disciplinary action up to and including dismissal may occur.*

In addition, because you demonstrated an intent to damage your supervisor's reputation among her peers, you are being placed on a five-day[20] suspension without pay. You are not to report to work from Monday, January 11, through Friday, January 15. Should you ever again slander, malign, defame, or otherwise speak negatively about your supervisor, senior management, or your subordinates, you may be immediately discharged for cause. A copy of this document will be placed in your personnel file.

Scheduled Review Date: *None*

EMPLOYEE COMMENTS AND/OR REBUTTAL

_____

_____

_____

(Attach additional sheets if needed.)

X _____
Employee Signature

EMPLOYEE ACKNOWLEDGMENT GOES HERE

Note: Since this is a final written warning, insert this sentence in the Employee Acknowledgment: "I also agree that if I do not meet the standards outlined in this warning, I will voluntarily resign or be discharged for cause."

---

20 Exempt workers must be suspended in increments of at least five days in the same workweek without pay; if you suspend exempt employees for less than five days at a time, or if the individual performs any work within the workweek, you may risk the individual's exemption status and may be liable for back overtime pay.

Bonus Sample: "Locker Room" Banter

Male senior manager is overheard making distasteful remarks toward females and homosexuals and discounts his comments as "locker room talk."

PERFORMANCE CORRECTION NOTICE

Employee Name: *Edward Wacker*   **Department:** *Sales*

Date Presented: *November 8, 2017*   **Supervisor:** *Barry O'Sullivan*

DISCIPLINARY LEVEL

☐ **Verbal Correction**—(To memorialize the conversation.)

☐ **Written Warning**—(State nature of offense, method of correction, and action to be taken if offense is repeated.)

☐ **Investigatory Leave**—(Include length of time and nature of review.)

☒ **Final Written Warning**

    ☒ Without decision-making leave

    ☐ With decision-making leave (Attach memo of instructions.)

    ☐ With unpaid suspension

SUBJECT: *Inappropriate workplace behavior, failure to follow company policy, misconduct*

☒ Policy/Procedure Violation

☐ Performance Transgression

☒ Behavior/Conduct Infraction

☐ Absenteeism/Tardiness

PRIOR NOTIFICATIONS

Level of Discipline	Date	Subject
Verbal	_____	_____
Written	_____	_____
Final Written	_____	_____

Incident Description and Supporting Details: Include the following information: Time, Place, Date of Occurrence, and Persons Present as well as Organizational Impact.

Edward,

On Tuesday night, November 7, members of your team and other departments overheard you making distasteful remarks toward female and homosexual coworkers. Specifically, you were overhead commenting about a female team member's "willingness to spread her legs to get ahead." You referenced one particular female manager's "pea brain being more than offset by her big bosom." Likewise, you referred to a male leader within our organization as a "fag, sissy, and total pussy."

When Travis Farrell from Human Resources and I met with you to discuss these allegations, you assumed responsibility for having said them, and you discounted your comments as "nothing more than locker room talk" with some male colleagues.

First, your comments were overheard by female colleagues and were not limited to the male audience that you were intending to address. Second, sharing such inappropriate comments with male workers could easily offend and insult them—even if female or gay coworkers never overhear those comments. Third, your actions not only violate specific company policies regarding respect in the workplace, inclusion, and potentially antidiscrimination, but they are also totally unacceptable and distasteful. I'm disappointed that you would choose to use such language in the workplace so carelessly; I'm likewise surprised that you hold your coworkers is such disregard as to humiliate them publicly behind their backs.

"Locker room talk" is strictly forbidden because it's used as an excuse to use crude language, hate speech, immorality, or coworker denigration. Further, "locker room" banter can never again be used as a "toughening-up exercise," "harmless hazing," or for any type of alleged "team bonding." As a sales leader, I expect you to know how to build your team's morale positively and constructively rather than to use antiquated assumptions, misogynistic beliefs, or some type of over-the-top masculinity.

Such behavior will not be excused in the future. I will leave it to your judgment to apologize not only to the people you were speaking to when you made these remarks but also to those whom you referenced in such a disrespectful way. Further, while various organizations have different standards for what's deemed socially acceptable, understand that in our company, no such banter will be deemed acceptable under any circumstances.

Your "locker room" excuse is not excusable or justifiable under any circumstances within our culture, as it demeans and degrades others while potentially creating an intolerant and intimidating environment. Any future conversations that you "have in private with men" will result in your immediate dismissal from this company.

PERFORMANCE IMPROVEMENT PLAN

1. Measurable/Tangible Improvement Goals: *As stated above, Edward, I expect you never again to engage in conduct or speech that could be interpreted as offensive, disrespectful, condescending, or otherwise crude and distasteful. I expect you to find ways to motive your sales team that go beyond "locker room" banter and focus on positive and constructive feedback that helps all team members feel supported and included in your team's success. Finally, I expect that I'll never have to hold a conversation like this with you again for the remainder of your tenure with this company.*

2. Training or Special Direction Provided: *Reread the employee handbook immediately, especially the sections on Creating a Friendly and Inclusive Work Environment, Leadership Behavioral Standards, and Antidiscrimination. See me if you have any questions about our company policies. I would also recommend that you research and purchase a book on positive team building and motivation strategies to build trust and camaraderie with your team.*

3. Interim Performance Evaluation Necessary? *No*

4. Our **Employee Assistance Program** (EAP) provider, Prime Behavioral Health Group, can be confidentially reached to assist you at (800) 555-5555. This is strictly voluntary. A booklet regarding the EAP's services is available from Human Resources.

5. In addition, I recognize that you may have certain ideas to improve your performance. Therefore, I encourage you to provide your own **Personal Improvement Plan Input and Suggestions:**

_____

_____

_____

(Attach additional sheets if needed.)

OUTCOMES AND CONSEQUENCES

Positive: *I will remain available to help you and discuss areas where you require additional support. If you meet your performance goals, no further disciplinary action will be taken regarding this issue.*

Negative: *If you ever again engage in inappropriate banter or make offensive and demeaning comments about your coworkers' personal characteristics, including but not limited to their gender or sexual preference, you will be discharged immediately for cause. Further, if you talk behind people's backs with the intent of damaging their reputation, inciting favoritism, or creating a toxic environment that pits people against one another, you will likewise be dismissed. Finally, if you violate any other company standards of performance and conduct, you may be immediately terminated.* A copy of this document will be placed in your personnel file.

Scheduled Review Date: *None*

EMPLOYEE COMMENTS AND/OR REBUTTAL

_____

_____

_____

(Attach additional sheets if needed.)

X _____
Employee Signature

EMPLOYEE ACKNOWLEDGMENT GOES HERE

PART VI

Absenteeism and Tardiness

Caution Regarding Restrictions Related to Disciplining or Terminating Employees for Attendance and Tardiness

Following is an important word of caution regarding disciplining employees for excessive absenteeism or tardiness related to an employee's or an employee's family member's health condition: The law is changing constantly in this area, and it is critical that you check with qualified legal counsel to ensure that your attendance policy is up-to-date and that your disciplinary methods and procedures are compliant with state and local laws. These laws protect employees who need time off from work due to their own sickness or health condition, to care for a family member, or for other protected reasons.

The samples that follow in this chapter will be very helpful in terms of setting forth your strategy for dealing with workers who appear to abuse the company's attendance, tardiness, or FMLA policies and practices. However, a "one size fits all" approach to discipline will not work when administering corrective action and potentially terminating for these particular workplace infractions. The landscape has changed drastically in this area, and several states and cities have enacted "paid sick leave" laws that protect workers who are absent or tardy pursuant to these laws. Therefore, it's critical that you proceed with caution before disciplining and especially before terminating workers for excessive absenteeism, tardiness, or FMLA abuse.

Beginning with the passage of the Americans with Disabilities Act (ADA) in 1990 and the Family Medical Leave Act (FMLA) in 1993, substantial limits were placed on employers' abilities to terminate workers under attendance control policies that, for decades, were able to withstand legal scrutiny. The limitations have become even more restrictive with the recent passage of multiple states' and cities' paid sick leave laws, where legislation has made it even more difficult for employers to hold workers accountable for the excessive use or abuse of paid time off or sick leave policies.

As a result, disciplining employees for unscheduled absences now has additional limits. For example, employers may no longer require doctors' notes or specific advance notice under many paid sick leave laws, and "patterns" may not be established just because someone takes off on the Friday before a holiday, provided the employee uses paid sick time pursuant to one of these paid sick leave laws. Therefore, it's critical that you check with qualified legal counsel to redraft your current attendance policy and your proposed disciplinary procedures if your state or city is subject to paid sick leave statutes.

Ensure that your employees who manage leaves of absence know how to distinguish between pure unscheduled absence occurrences and time off from work that may otherwise be protected by the federal ADA and FMLA laws (and similar state laws) and/or your state's or city's paid sick leave laws. Ensure that your leave of absence team understands how to calculate, track, and notify employees about paid sick leave under these statutes. And train your frontline leaders so they understand that when legally mandated paid sick leave is involved, they may not have the discretion to discipline their workers as they have typically done in the past.

Finally, expect a lot more press about paid sick leave and other issues relating to employee rights, minimum wage, gender pay parity, and the like. While these matters may change depending on the administrations in Washington, D.C., and states' and even cities' individualized attempts to govern the workplace, one thing is for sure: These types of laws will continue to evolve and confound employers who are looking for a reasonable and balanced approach to applying attendance rules fairly.

#75 Excessive, Unscheduled Absence: "No Fault" System[1]

This is the first in a series of three write-ups. Note that this company measures incidents rather than days of absence. In other words, three contiguous days off count as one incident without regard for the number of days involved. Note as well that this company measures incidents of absence on a rolling calendar year.[2]

PERFORMANCE CORRECTION NOTICE

Employee Name: *Tom Dalton*   **Department:** *Marketing*

Date Presented: *October 15, 2017*   **Supervisor:** *Jim McDonnell*

DISCIPLINARY LEVEL

☒ **Verbal Correction**—(To memorialize the conversation.)

☐ **Written Warning**—(State nature of offense, method of correction, and action to be taken if offense is repeated.)

☐ **Investigatory Leave**—(Include length of time and nature of review.)

☐ **Final Written Warning**

    ☐ Without decision-making leave

    ☐ With decision-making leave (Attach memo of instructions.)

    ☐ With unpaid suspension

SUBJECT: *Excessive, unscheduled absence*

☒ Policy/Procedure Violation

☒ Performance Transgression

☐ Behavior/Conduct Infraction

☒ Absenteeism/Tardiness

---

1 The law is rapidly changing in this area, and many states and cities are enacting paid sick leave laws protecting employees who need time off from work to care for themselves or a family member or for other protected reasons. Accordingly, it is critical that you check with qualified legal counsel to ensure that your attendance policy is compliant with these laws and certainly before you discipline or terminate any employee for excessive absenteeism or tardiness.

2 A rolling calendar year does not measure events from January 1 through December 31. Instead, it measures the one year preceding the date of a specific event. For example, this write-up is dated October 15, 2017. The rolling calendar year "rolls" backward from that date to October 16, 2016.

PRIOR NOTIFICATIONS

Level of Discipline	Date	Subject
Verbal	_____	_____
Written	_____	_____
Final Written	_____	_____

Incident Description and Supporting Details: Include the following information: Time, Place, Date of Occurrence, and Persons Present as well as Organizational Impact.

Tom,

Maintenance of good attendance is a condition of employment. In order to minimize hardships that may result from illness or injury, our company provides paid sick time benefits to employees for use when their own or a family member's illness or injury prevents them from working. However, periodic sick leave taken on a repeated basis may be viewed as abuse of the system. It is your responsibility to establish legitimate illness or injury in order to receive sick leave pay pursuant to our sick leave policy.

You have incurred five incidents of unscheduled and unauthorized absence (meaning an absence not protected by law or approved by your supervisor) in this rolling calendar year. The dates are:

October 9–October 13, 2017	*16.0 hours*
July 21–July 25, 2017	*38.1 hours*
April 28–April 30, 2017	*24.0 hours*
January 20–January 22, 2017	*24.0 hours*
December 18, 2016	*8.0 hours*

This number of incidents has disrupted the work flow in our unit and could cause our department to incur unscheduled overtime because others have had to carry the extra work load. Five incidents of unscheduled/unauthorized absence in the rolling calendar year constitute failure to meet company standards of performance and conduct (policy 2.14).

PERFORMANCE IMPROVEMENT PLAN

1. Measurable/Tangible Improvement Goals: *Tom, I expect you to immediately improve your attendance to meet company minimum standards.*

2. Training or Special Direction to Be Provided: *A copy of our attendance policy is attached. Please read the policy thoroughly today and meet with me tomorrow morning if you have any questions about the rules.*

3. Interim Performance Evaluation Necessary? *No, your annual evaluation has been completed and is currently in the approval process.*

4. Our **Employee Assistance Program** (EAP) provider, Prime Behavioral Health Group, can be confidentially reached to assist you at (800) 555-5555. This is strictly voluntary. A booklet regarding the EAP's services is available from Human Resources.

5. In addition, I recognize that you may have certain ideas to improve your performance. Therefore, I encourage you to provide your own **Personal Improvement Plan Input and Suggestions:**

_____

_____

_____

(Attach additional sheets if needed.)

OUTCOMES AND CONSEQUENCES

Positive: I will remain available to help you and discuss areas where you require additional support. If you meet your performance goals, no further disciplinary action will be taken regarding this issue. *In addition, you will develop a greater sense of accomplishment in helping our department meet its production goals while minimizing staff rescheduling and last-minute overtime costs.*

Negative: *You are now being placed on notice that, according to company policy if you reach seven incidents of unauthorized absence (meaning an absence not protected by law or approved by your supervisor) in the rolling calendar year, you will be given a written warning. A ninth incident of unauthorized absence in the rolling calendar year will lead to a final written warning.*

As per policy 2.14 on attendance, when an employee is in final written warning status for absenteeism, any unauthorized occurrence of absenteeism or tardiness in the rolling calendar year will result in immediate dismissal. Furthermore, an employee in final written warning status will be ineligible for promotion or transfer. The employee will be ineligible to receive any approved time off except previously scheduled holidays, bereavement, or any time off required by law. A copy of this document will be placed in your personnel file.

Scheduled Review Date: *None*

EMPLOYEE COMMENTS AND/OR REBUTTAL

_____

_____

_____

(Attach additional sheets if needed.)

X _____
Employee Signature

EMPLOYEE ACKNOWLEDGMENT GOES HERE

#76 Excessive, Unscheduled Absence[3]

This is the second in a series of three write-ups. Note the FMLA notice, Consequences language, and Personal Commitment agreement in which the employee acknowledges that his job is in jeopardy of being lost.

PERFORMANCE CORRECTION NOTICE

Employee Name: *Tom Dalton*   **Department:** *Marketing*

Date Presented: *October 21, 2017*   **Supervisor:** *Jim McDonnell*

DISCIPLINARY LEVEL

☐ **Verbal Correction—**(To memorialize the conversation.)

☒ **Written Warning—**(State nature of offense, method of correction, and action to be taken if offense is repeated.)

☐ **Investigatory Leave—**(Include length of time and nature of review.)

☐ **Final Written Warning**

    ☐ Without decision-making leave

    ☐ With decision-making leave (Attach memo of instructions.)

    ☐ With unpaid suspension

SUBJECT: *Excessive, unscheduled absence*

☒ Policy/Procedure Violation

☒ Performance Transgression

☐ Behavior/Conduct Infraction

☒ Absenteeism/Tardiness

PRIOR NOTIFICATIONS

Level of Discipline	Date	Subject
Verbal	*Oct 15, 2017*	*Unscheduled, unauthorized absence*

---

3 The law is rapidly changing in this area, and many states and cities are enacting paid sick leave laws protecting employees who need time off from work to care for themselves or a family member or for other protected reasons. Accordingly, it is critical that you check with qualified legal counsel to ensure that your attendance policy is compliant with these laws and certainly before you discipline or terminate any employee for excessive absenteeism or tardiness.

Written   _____   _____

Final Written   _____   _____

Incident Description and Supporting Details: Include the following information: Time, Place, Date of Occurrence, and Persons Present as well as Organizational Impact.

Tom,

Maintenance of good attendance is a condition of employment. In order to minimize hardships that may result from illness or injury, our company provides paid sick time benefits to employees for use when their own or a family member's illness or injury prevents them from working. However, periodic sick leave taken on a repeated basis may be viewed as abuse of the system. It is your responsibility to establish legitimate illness or injury in order to receive sick leave pay pursuant to our sick leave policy.

You have incurred seven incidents of unscheduled and unauthorized absence (meaning an absence not protected by law or approved by your supervisor) in this rolling calendar year. The dates are:

October 20, 2017	*8.0 hours*
October 16, 2017	*8.0 hours*
October 9–October 13, 2017	*16.0 hours*
July 21–July 25, 2017	*38.1 hours*
April 28–April 30, 2017	*24.0 hours*
January 20–January 22, 2017	*24.0 hours*
December 18, 2016	*8.0 hours*

This number of incidents has disrupted the work flow in our unit and could cause our department to incur unscheduled overtime because others have had to carry the extra work load. Seven incidents of unscheduled/unauthorized absence in the rolling calendar year constitute failure to meet company standards of performance and conduct (policy 2.14).

PERFORMANCE IMPROVEMENT PLAN

1. Measurable/Tangible Improvement Goals: *Tom, I expect you to immediately improve your attendance to meet company minimum standards.*

2. Training or Special Direction to Be Provided: *None at this time. You have already received a copy of company policy regarding absence. I hold you fully responsible for your attendance. If you need to meet with Gail Angel in Human Resources to discuss your rights under the Family and Medical Leave Act, you can reach her at x2279.*

3. Interim Performance Evaluation Necessary? *No*

4. Our **Employee Assistance Program** (EAP) provider, Prime Behavioral Health Group, can be confidentially reached to assist you at (800) 555-5555. This is strictly voluntary. A booklet regarding the EAP's services is available from Human Resources.

5. In addition, I recognize that you may have certain ideas to improve your performance. Therefore, I encourage you to provide your own **Personal Improvement Plan Input and Suggestions:**

_____

_____

_____

(Attach additional sheets if needed.)

OUTCOMES AND CONSEQUENCES

Positive: I will remain available to help you and discuss areas where you require additional support. If you meet your performance goals, no further disciplinary action will be taken regarding this issue. _In addition, you will develop a sense of accomplishment in helping our department meet its production goals while minimizing staff rescheduling and last-minute overtime costs._

Negative: _Failure to meet company absenteeism standards is serious. You are now formally being placed on written warning for unauthorized absence. This indicates that you may not have taken your prior warning as seriously as you should have. You are now formally notified that a ninth incident of unauthorized absence (meaning an absence not to protected by law or approved by your supervisor) in the rolling calendar year will lead to a final written warning._

As per policy 2.14 on attendance, when an employee is in final written warning status for absenteeism, any unauthorized occurrence of absenteeism or tardiness in the rolling calendar year will result in immediate dismissal. Furthermore, an employee in final written warning status will be ineligible for promotion or transfer. The employee will be ineligible to receive any approved time off except previously scheduled holidays, bereavement, or any time off required by law.

Scheduled Review Date: _None_

EMPLOYEE COMMENTS AND/OR REBUTTAL

_____

_____

_____

(Attach additional sheets if needed.)

X _____
Employee Signature

EMPLOYEE ACKNOWLEDGMENT GOES HERE

Note: The following sentence should be added to the Employee Acknowledgment: "By signing this, I commit to improve my attendance to meet company standards and to follow all other standards of performance and conduct. I also now acknowledge that my job is in jeopardy of being lost."

#77 Excessive, Unscheduled Absence[4]

This is the third in a series of three write-ups. Note the specialized last chance agreement language.

PERFORMANCE CORRECTION NOTICE

Employee Name: *Tom Dalton* **Department:** *Marketing*

Date Presented: *December 15, 2017* **Supervisor:** *Jim McDonnell*

DISCIPLINARY LEVEL

☐ **Verbal Correction**—(To memorialize the conversation.)

☐ **Written Warning**—(State nature of offense, method of correction, and action to be taken if offense is repeated.)

☐ **Investigatory Leave**—(Include length of time and nature of review.)

☒ **Final Written Warning**

    ☒ Without decision-making leave[5]

    ☐ With decision-making leave (Attach memo of instructions.)

    ☐ With unpaid suspension

SUBJECT: *Excessive, unscheduled absence*

☒ Policy/Procedure Violation

☒ Performance Transgression

☐ Behavior/Conduct Infraction

☒ Absenteeism/Tardiness

PRIOR NOTIFICATIONS

Level of Discipline	Date	Subject
Verbal	*Oct 15, 2017*	*Unscheduled, unauthorized absence*
Written	*Oct 21, 2017*	*Unscheduled, unauthorized absence*
Final Written	_____	_____

---

4 The law is rapidly changing in this area, and many states and cities are enacting paid sick leave laws protecting employees who need time off from work to care for themselves or a family member or for other protected reasons. Accordingly, it is critical that you check with qualified legal counsel to ensure that your attendance policy is compliant with these laws and certainly before you discipline or terminate any employee for excessive absenteeism or tardiness.

5 There is little need to provide a one-day paid decision-making leave when it comes to excessive absence. The employee doesn't need a day off to contemplate his situation: He's had too much time off already.

Incident Description and Supporting Details: Include the following information: Time, Place, Date of Occurrence, and Persons Present as well as Organizational Impact.

Tom,

Maintenance of good attendance is a condition of employment. In order to minimize hardships that may result from illness or injury, our company provides paid sick time benefits to employees for use when their own or a family member's illness or injury prevents them from working. However, periodic sick leave taken on a repeated basis may be viewed as abuse of the system. It is your responsibility to establish legitimate illness or injury in order to receive sick leave pay pursuant to our sick leave policy.

You have incurred nine incidents of unscheduled and unauthorized absence (meaning an absence not protected by law or approved by your supervisor) in this rolling calendar year. The dates are:

December 14, 2017	*8.0 hours*
November 19, 2017	*8.0 hours*
October 20, 2017	*8.0 hours*
October 16, 2017	*8.0 hours*
October 9–October 13, 2017	*16.0 hours*
July 21–July 25, 2017	*38.1 hours*
April 28–April 30, 2017	*24.0 hours*
January 20–January 22, 2017	*24.0 hours*
December 18, 2016	*8.0 hours*

This number of incidents has disrupted the work flow in our unit and could cause our department to incur unscheduled overtime because others have had to carry the extra work load. Nine incidents of unscheduled/unauthorized absence in the rolling calendar year constitute failure to meet company standards of performance and conduct (policy 2.14).

PERFORMANCE IMPROVEMENT PLAN

1. Measurable/Tangible Improvement Goals: *Tom, I expect you to immediately improve your attendance to meet company minimum standards.*

2. Training or Special Direction to Be Provided: *None at this time. You have already received a copy of company policy regarding absence. You have received verbal and written warnings as dictated by company policy. I hold you fully responsible for your attendance.*

3. Interim Performance Evaluation Necessary? *No[6]*

4. Our **Employee Assistance Program** (EAP) provider, Prime Behavioral Health Group, can be confidentially reached to assist you at (800) 555-5555. This is strictly voluntary. A booklet regarding the EAP's services is available from Human Resources.

---

6 Because attendance is a clear breach of company policy, there is little need to reevaluate this individual's overall performance. Violation of this policy is enough to terminate the employee for just cause.

5. In addition, I recognize that you may have certain ideas to improve your performance. Therefore, I encourage you to provide your own **Personal Improvement Plan Input and Suggestions:**

_____

_____

_____

(Attach additional sheets if needed.)

OUTCOMES AND CONSEQUENCES

Positive: I will remain available to help you and discuss areas where you require additional support. If you meet your performance goals, no further disciplinary action will be taken regarding this issue. *In addition, you will develop a sense of accomplishment in helping our department meet its production goals while minimizing staff rescheduling and last-minute overtime costs.*

Negative: *Failure to meet company absenteeism standards is serious. You are now formally being placed on final written warning for unauthorized absence. It is apparent that you did not take your former warnings seriously. You are now formally notified that any incident of unauthorized absence (meaning an absence not protected by law or approved by your supervisor) in the rolling calendar year will result in immediate dismissal.*

In addition, as per policy 2.14 on attendance, you will be ineligible for promotion or transfer for six months (until June 15, 2018). You will be ineligible to receive any approved time off except previously scheduled holidays, bereavement, or any time off required by law. A copy of this document will be placed in your personnel file.

Scheduled Review Date: *None*

EMPLOYEE COMMENTS AND/OR REBUTTAL

_____

_____

_____

(Attach additional sheets if needed.)

X _____
Employee Signature

EMPLOYEE ACKNOWLEDGMENT GOES HERE

Note: Since this is a final written warning, insert the following sentences into the Employee Acknowledgment: "I understand that I have the right to discuss this with a union official, or anyone else who can advise me of my rights before I sign it. I understand that this is my last chance. No further incidents of unscheduled absence will be allowed. If I fail to meet the terms and conditions of employment as stated in this final warning, I agree that I will voluntarily resign or be discharged for cause."

#78 Pattern of Excessive, Unscheduled Absence[7]

Employee "patterns" her time off around her weekends (i.e., she consistently takes Fridays and Mondays off).

PERFORMANCE CORRECTION NOTICE

Employee Name: *Kathryn Schulteis*   **Department:** *Client Relations*

Date Presented: *August 27, 2017*   **Supervisor:** *Cheryl Yamamoto*

DISCIPLINARY LEVEL

☒ **Verbal Correction**—(To memorialize the conversation.)

☒ **Written Warning**—(State nature of offense, method of correction, and action to be taken if offense is repeated.)

☐ **Investigatory Leave**—(Include length of time and nature of review.)

☐ **Final Written Warning**

   ☐ Without decision-making leave

   ☐ With decision-making leave (Attach memo of instructions.)

   ☐ With unpaid suspension

SUBJECT: *Verbal warning: excessive, unscheduled absence written warning: pattern of unauthorized absence[8]*

☒ Policy/Procedure Violation

☒ Performance Transgression

☐ Behavior/Conduct Infraction

☒ Absenteeism/Tardiness

---

7 The law is rapidly changing in this area, and many states and cities are enacting paid sick leave laws protecting employees who need time off from work to care for themselves or a family member or for other protected reasons. Accordingly, it is critical that you check with qualified legal counsel to ensure that your attendance policy is compliant with these laws and certainly before you discipline or terminate any employee for excessive absenteeism or tardiness.

8 Because establishing a pattern takes time, it is common to start the disciplinary process at the written level rather than the verbal level. Note, however, that "patterns" may not be established just because someone takes off on the Friday before or the Monday after a holiday, provided the employee uses paid sick time pursuant to one of the paid sick leave laws recognized by certain states or cities. In other words, it may not be permissible to discipline an employee for "patterning" if the days in question are considered paid sick leave days (as addressed in the introduction to this section).

PRIOR NOTIFICATIONS

Level of Discipline	Date	Subject
Verbal	_____	_____
Written	_____	_____
Final Written	_____	_____

Incident Description and Supporting Details: Include the following information: Time, Place, Date of Occurrence, and Persons Present as well as Organizational Impact.

Kathryn,

Maintenance of good attendance is a condition of employment. In order to minimize hardships that may result from illness or injury, our company provides paid sick time benefits to employees for use when their own or a family member's illness or injury prevents them from working. However, periodic sick leave taken on a repeated basis may be viewed as abuse of the system. It is your responsibility to establish legitimate illness or injury in order to receive sick leave pay pursuant to our sick leave policy.

1. Unauthorized Absence

You have incurred five incidents of unscheduled and unauthorized absence (meaning time off not protected by law or approved by your supervisor) in this rolling calendar year. The dates are:

> *Friday, August 26, 2016*
>
> *Friday, September 23, 2016*
>
> *Tuesday, October 25, 2016*
>
> *Friday, November 18, 2016*
>
> *Friday, February 17, 2017*

This number of incidents has interfered with the work flow in our unit and could cause our department to incur unscheduled overtime because others have had to carry the extra work load. Five incidents of unscheduled absence in the rolling calendar year constitute failure to meet company standards of performance and conduct (policy 2.14).

2. "Pattern" of Unauthorized Absence

In addition, you have demonstrated a pattern of taking time off around your regularly scheduled weekends:

> *Saturday, August 27, 2016, was your regularly scheduled weekend; you took Friday, August 26, 2016, as an unscheduled, unauthorized day off (meaning time off not protected by law or approved by your supervisor).*
>
> *Saturday, September 24, 2016, was your regularly scheduled weekend; you took Friday, September 23, 2016, as an unscheduled, unauthorized day off.*
>
> *Saturday, November 19, 2016, was your regularly scheduled weekend; you took Friday, November 18, 2016, as an unscheduled, unauthorized day off.*

Our company defines a pattern as a frequent, predictable, and observable employee action that repeats itself over time. Three of your five unauthorized days off were taken around your regularly scheduled weekend, thereby violating our company's absenteeism policy (2.14).

PERFORMANCE IMPROVEMENT PLAN

1. Measurable/Tangible Improvement Goals: *Kathryn, I expect you to immediately improve your attendance to meet company minimum standards.*

2. Training or Special Direction to Be Provided: *A copy of our attendance policy is attached. Please read the policy thoroughly today and meet with me tomorrow morning if you have any questions about the rules.*

In addition, understand that there are three ways to incur a pattern of unscheduled and unauthorized absence:

(a) By taking unauthorized time off around your regularly scheduled weekends or holidays

(b) By taking unauthorized time off once former incidents of unauthorized absence have fallen off the rolling calendar year

(c) By consistently taking unauthorized time off for the maximum number of days per incident without requiring a doctor's note (in our company's case, after three days)

3. Interim Performance Evaluation Necessary? *No*

4. Our **Employee Assistance Program** (EAP) provider, Prime Behavioral Health Group, can be confidentially reached to assist you at (800) 555-5555. This is strictly voluntary. A booklet regarding the EAP's services is available from Human Resources.

5. In addition, I recognize that you may have certain ideas to improve your performance. Therefore, I encourage you to provide your own **Personal Improvement Plan Input and Suggestions:**

_____

_____

_____

(Attach additional sheets if needed.)

OUTCOMES AND CONSEQUENCES

Positive: I will remain available to help you and discuss areas where you require additional support. If you meet your performance goals, no further disciplinary action will be taken regarding this issue. *In addition, you will develop a sense of accomplishment in helping our department meet its production goals while minimizing staff rescheduling and last-minute overtime costs.*

Negative:

Issue 1: You are now being placed on notice that, according to company policy, if you reach seven incidents of unauthorized absence (meaning an absence not protected by law or approved by your supervisor) in the rolling calendar year, you will be given a written warning. A ninth incident of unauthorized absence in the rolling calendar year will lead to a final written warning.

As per policy 2.14 on attendance, when an employee is in final written warning status for absenteeism, any unauthorized occurrence of absenteeism or tardiness in the rolling calendar year will result in immediate dismissal. Furthermore, an employee in final written warning status will be ineligible for promotion or transfer. The employee will be ineligible to receive any approved time off except previously scheduled holidays, bereavement, or any time off required by law.

Issue 2: Furthermore, if any other patterns appear in the next year in terms of how you take your time off—i.e., if you take unauthorized time off either before or after weekends or if you take unauthorized sick time when days have fallen off the rolling calendar year—you may be subject to disciplinary action up to and including dismissal. **A copy of this document will be placed in your personnel file.**

Scheduled Review Date: *None*

EMPLOYEE COMMENTS AND/OR REBUTTAL

_____

_____

_____

(Attach additional sheets if needed.)

X _____

Employee Signature

EMPLOYEE ACKNOWLEDGMENT GOES HERE

#79 Pattern of Excessive, Unscheduled Absence[9]

Employee "patterns" his time off in that he takes additional unscheduled time off once former incidents have fallen off the rolling calendar year.[10] In this case, the company has a policy that states that five incidents of unscheduled and unauthorized absence in the rolling calendar year equals a verbal warning, seven incidents equals a written warning, and nine incidents equal a final written warning. It is therefore possible for employees to incur multiple verbal warnings without progressing to the written warning level, since old incidents of unscheduled and unauthorized absence fall off the rolling calendar as new incidents occur.

PERFORMANCE CORRECTION NOTICE

Employee Name: *Todd Luchow*   **Department:** *Sales*

Date Presented: *February 17, 2017*   **Supervisor:** *Cheryl Marinero*

DISCIPLINARY LEVEL

☒ **Verbal Correction**—(To memorialize the conversation.)

☒ **Written Warning**—(State nature of offense, method of correction, and action to be taken if offense is repeated.)

☐ **Investigatory Leave**—(Include length of time and nature of review.)

☐ **Final Written Warning**

   ☐ Without decision-making leave

   ☐ With decision-making leave (Attach memo of instructions.)

   ☐ With unpaid suspension

---

9 The law is rapidly changing in this area and many states and cities are enacting paid sick leave laws protecting employees who need time off from work to care for themselves or a family member or for other protected reasons. Accordingly, it is critical that you check with qualified legal counsel to ensure that your attendance policy is compliant with these laws and certainly before you discipline or terminate any employee for excessive absenteeism or tardiness. In addition, note that "patterns" may not be established just because someone takes off once former incidents have fallen off the rolling calendar year, provided the employee uses paid sick time pursuant to one of the paid sick leave laws recognized by certain states or cities. In other words, it may not be permissible to discipline an employee for "patterning" if the days in question are considered paid sick leave days (as addressed in the introduction to this section).

10 A rolling calendar year goes from today's date back one year. For example, the date of this write-up is February 17, 2017. The rolling calendar year goes back one year from this date (to February 18, 2016).

SUBJECT: *Verbal warning: excessive, unscheduled absence; written warning: pattern of unauthorized absence*

☒ Policy/Procedure Violation

☒ Performance Transgression

☐ Behavior/Conduct Infraction

☒ Absenteeism/Tardiness

PRIOR NOTIFICATIONS

Level of Discipline	Date	Subject
Verbal	*Feb 16, 2017*	*Five occurrences of unauthorized absence*
	Nov 28, 2016	*Five occurrences of unauthorized absence*
	Oct 25, 2016	*Five occurrences of unauthorized absence*
Written	_____	_____
Final Written	_____	_____

Incident Description and Supporting Details: Include the following information: Time, Place, Date of Occurrence, and Persons Present as well as Organizational Impact.

Todd,

Maintenance of good attendance is a condition of employment. In order to minimize hardships that may result from illness or injury, our company provides paid sick time benefits to employees for use when their own or a family member's illness or injury prevents them from working. However, periodic sick leave taken on a repeated basis may be viewed as abuse of the system. It is your responsibility to establish legitimate illness or injury in order to receive sick leave pay pursuant to our sick leave policy.

Issue 1: Verbal Warning for Unscheduled Absence

You have again incurred five incidents of unscheduled and unauthorized absence (meaning an absence not protected by law or approved by your supervisor) in this rolling calendar year. The dates are:

Monday, July 11, 2016

Monday, September 19, 2016

Tuesday, October 25, 2016 (verbal warning for five incidents)[11]

Monday, November 28, 2016 (verbal warning for five incidents)[12]

February 16, 2017 (yesterday)

---

11 Notice that on November 28, 2016, the first warning listed, November 20, 2015, has fallen off the rolling calendar year.

12 Notice that now, on February 16, 2017, a second warning dated February 17, 2016, has fallen off the rolling calendar year. In other words, the employee keeps accruing new incidents of unscheduled absence, but former incidents are negated because they "fall off" the rolling calendar year. Now's the time to put a stop to this pattern of "playing the system."

This number of incidents has interfered with the work flow in our unit and could cause our department to incur unscheduled overtime because others have had to carry the extra work load. Five incidents of unscheduled and unauthorized absence in the rolling calendar year constitute failure to meet company standards of performance and conduct (policy 2.14).

Issue 2: Written Warning for "Pattern" of Unscheduled and Unauthorized Absence

Our company defines a "pattern" as a frequent, predictable, and observable employee action, which is not authorized and repeats itself over time. You have demonstrated a pattern of taking unauthorized time off once previous warnings have fallen off the rolling calendar year.

On October 25, 2016 and November 28, 2016, you received verbal warnings for incurring five incidents of unscheduled and unauthorized absence. One incident fell off the rolling calendar, and you took another unscheduled and unauthorized day off. On February 16, 2017, you received a verbal warning for incurring five incidents of unscheduled and unauthorized absence. One incident fell off the rolling calendar, and you took another unscheduled and unauthorized day off. You have now received three verbal warnings in a four-month period for taking time off once previous incidents fell off the rolling calendar year, thereby violating our company's absenteeism policy (2.14).[13]

Furthermore, four of the five incidents occurred on a Monday or a Friday. You have therefore also demonstrated a pattern of taking unauthorized time off around your regularly scheduled weekends.

Your repeated abuse of the company's sick leave policy indicates that you may not have taken your formal warnings as seriously as you should have.

PERFORMANCE IMPROVEMENT PLAN

1. Measurable/Tangible Improvement Goals: *Todd, I expect you to immediately improve your attendance to meet company minimum standards.*

2. Training or Special Direction to Be Provided: *A copy of our attendance policy is attached. Please read the policy thoroughly today and meet with me tomorrow morning if you have any questions about the rules.*

In addition, understand that there are three ways to incur a "pattern" of unscheduled absence:

(a) By taking unauthorized time off (meaning time off not protected by law or approved by your supervisor) around your regularly scheduled weekends or holidays

(b) By taking unauthorized time off once former incidents of unauthorized absence have fallen off the rolling calendar year

(c) By consistently taking unauthorized time off for the maximum number of days per incident without requiring a doctor's note (in our company's case, after three days)

---

13 When employees take more than 50 percent of their time off around weekends or holidays, then a pattern may be established. In this case, three of the five occurrences of unauthorized absence occurred on a Monday. Bear in mind, though, that this is a company rule that you establish, not a law or specific definition.

3. Interim Performance Evaluation Necessary? *No*

4. Our **Employee Assistance Program** (EAP) provider, Prime Behavioral Health Group, can be confidentially reached to assist you at (800) 555-5555. This is strictly voluntary. A booklet regarding the EAP's services is available from Human Resources.

5. In addition, I recognize that you may have certain ideas to improve your performance. Therefore, I encourage you to provide your own **Personal Improvement Plan Input and Suggestions:**

_____

_____

_____

(Attach additional sheets if needed.)

<hr>

OUTCOMES AND CONSEQUENCES

Positive: I will remain available to help you and discuss areas where you require additional support. If you meet your performance goals, no further disciplinary action will be taken regarding this issue. *In addition, you will develop a sense of accomplishment in helping our department meet its production goals while minimizing staff rescheduling and last-minute overtime costs.*

Negative:
Issue 1: You are now being placed on notice that, according to company policy, if you reach seven incidents of unauthorized absence in the rolling calendar year, you will be given a written warning. A ninth incident of unauthorized absence in the rolling calendar year will lead to a final written warning.

As per policy 2.14 on attendance, when an employee is in final written warning status for absenteeism, any unauthorized occurrence of absenteeism or tardiness in the rolling calendar year will result in immediate dismissal. Furthermore, an employee in final written warning status will be ineligible for promotion or transfer. The employee will be ineligible to receive any approved time off except previously scheduled holidays, bereavement, or any time off required by law.

Issue 2: Furthermore, if any other patterns appear in the next year in terms of how you take your time off—i.e., if you take unauthorized days off either before or after weekends or if you take unauthorized sick time when days have fallen off the rolling calendar year— you will be subject to further disciplinary action up to and including dismissal.

Human Resources will be notified of every additional occurrence of absenteeism from this point forward in order to provide you with additional counseling and support. It is your responsibility to bring to my or Human Resources' attention any areas or issues that you need assistance with to meet these performance goals.

You are now formally notified that any further occurrences of sick leave must be substantiated by a doctor's note pursuant to our sick leave policy. The doctor's note will be necessary to return to work. A copy of this document will be placed in your personnel file.

Scheduled Review Date: *None*

EMPLOYEE COMMENTS AND/OR REBUTTAL

_____

_____

_____

(Attach additional sheets if needed.)

X _____
Employee Signature

EMPLOYEE ACKNOWLEDGMENT GOES HERE

#80 Excessive, Unscheduled Absence: "Excuse-Based" System[14]

In comparison to a "no fault" absenteeism policy, "excuse-based" systems look for an employee to provide a legitimate reason each time that an unauthorized absence occurs.[15] This company's policy states that three incidents without a proper and legally protected reason will result in a first warning, five incidents will result in a final written warning, and six incidents will result in discharge.

PERFORMANCE CORRECTION NOTICE

Employee Name: *Anna Palmesano*   **Department:** *Engineering*

Date Presented: *May 18, 2017*   **Supervisor:** *Vincent Scungili*

DISCIPLINARY LEVEL

☒ **Verbal Correction**—(To memorialize the conversation.)

☐ **Written Warning**—(State nature of offense, method of correction, and action to be taken if offense is repeated.)

☐ **Investigatory Leave**—(Include length of time and nature of review.)

☐ **Final Written Warning**

    ☐ Without decision-making leave

    ☐ With decision-making leave (Attach memo of instructions.)

    ☐ With unpaid suspension

SUBJECT: *Unauthorized absence*

☒ Policy/Procedure Violation

☒ Performance Transgression

☐ Behavior/Conduct Infraction

☒ Absenteeism/Tardiness

---

14 The law is rapidly changing in this area, and many states and cities are enacting paid sick leave laws protecting employees who need time off from work to care for themselves or a family member or for other protected reasons. Accordingly, it is critical that you check with qualified legal counsel to ensure that your attendance policy is compliant with these laws and certainly before you discipline or terminate any employee for excessive absenteeism or tardiness.

15 Check with qualified legal counsel before implementing this type of policy. State and/or local law may prohibit employers from inquiring into reasons for absences relating to an employee's use of sick leave.

PRIOR NOTIFICATIONS

Level of Discipline	Date	Subject
Verbal	_____	_____
Written	_____	_____
Final Written	_____	_____

Incident Description and Supporting Details: Include the following information: Time, Place, Date of Occurrence, and Persons Present as well as Organizational Impact.

Anna,

Maintenance of good attendance is a condition of employment. In order to minimize hardships that may result from illness or injury, our company provides paid sick time benefits to employees for use when their own or a family member's illness or injury prevents them from working. However, periodic sick leave taken on a repeated basis may be viewed as abuse of the system. It is your responsibility to establish legitimate illness or injury in order to receive sick leave pay pursuant to our sick leave policy.

Yesterday morning at 7:30, you called me to tell me that you would not be able to work. I asked you why that was the case, and you told me that you were obligated to attend a family-related function. If that was indeed the case, you could have advised me in advance of the time you needed away from work.

On April 2, you also failed to report to work without prior notice. When I called you at home at 9:00, you said you were feeling sick and had overslept. I had previously reminded you and other department members that, pursuant to our sick leave policy, if you were ill, you still had the responsibility to contact the company receptionist by 7:00 A.M. (or as soon thereafter as reasonably practicable) so that a temporary worker could be engaged while you were out. Because you had not contacted the company, a half day's productivity was lost as we awaited the temp's arrival.

On February 15, you failed to report to work without notice. I asked you why you were out when you returned to work. You told me that you had no reason but that it wouldn't happen again. I didn't pursue the issue, since this was your first incident of unscheduled absence, and I believed you when you assured me that there would be no further incidents.

Consequently, you have now incurred three incidents of unauthorized absence (meaning an absence not protected by law or not approved by your supervisor) this year. Furthermore, your reasons are not legitimate pursuant to our policy. Your absences are therefore unexcused and unauthorized. Three unexcused absences in a calendar year violate our company's standards of performance and conduct.

PERFORMANCE IMPROVEMENT PLAN

1. Measurable/Tangible Improvement Goals: *Anna, I expect you to immediately improve your attendance to meet company minimum standards.*

2. Training or Special Direction to Be Provided: *A copy of our attendance policy is attached. Please read the policy thoroughly today and meet with me tomorrow morning if you have any questions about the rules. Remember as well that you are obligated to (a) provide a* *legitimate reason whenever you are absent in accordance with our policies and (b) provide the company with advance notice if reasonably possible. Finally, it is company policy that time off for doctors' appointments (absent emergencies) and other personal reasons should be scheduled and approved with one week's advance notice. Same-day notification is not acceptable. Therefore, please provide me with one week's advance notice any time you have a planned medical visit.*

3. Interim Performance Evaluation Necessary? *No*

4. Our **Employee Assistance Program** (EAP) provider, Prime Behavioral Health Group, can be confidentially reached to assist you at (800) 555-5555. This is strictly voluntary. A booklet regarding the EAP's services is available from Human Resources.

5. In addition, I recognize that you may have certain ideas to improve your performance. Therefore, I encourage you to provide your own **Personal Improvement Plan Input and Suggestions:**

_____

_____

_____

(Attach additional sheets if needed.)

OUTCOMES AND CONSEQUENCES

Positive: I will remain available to help you and discuss areas where you require additional support. If you meet your performance goals, no further disciplinary action will be taken regarding this issue. *In addition, you will develop a sense of accomplishment in helping our department meet its production goals while minimizing staff rescheduling and last-minute overtime costs.*

Negative: *According to company policy, a fifth incident of unauthorized absence (meaning an absence not protected by law or not approved by your supervisor) this year will place you on written notice that you are in violation of our company's absenteeism control policy. A sixth incident may result in immediate dismissal.* A copy of this document will be placed in your personnel file.

Scheduled Review Date: *None*

EMPLOYEE COMMENTS AND/OR REBUTTAL

_____

_____

_____

(Attach additional sheets if needed.)

X _____

Employee Signature

EMPLOYEE ACKNOWLEDGMENT GOES HERE

#81 Excessive Tardiness[16]

This is the first in a series of three warnings. Employer has a "no fault" attendance and tardiness policy that allows for five verbal, seven written, and nine final written incidents before a tenth occurrence in the rolling calendar year mandates termination. Note that the supervisor learns of the employee's five incidents of tardiness two months after they occur while conducting a departmental audit.

PERFORMANCE CORRECTION NOTICE

Employee Name: *Tony Epifanio*   **Department:** *Finance*

Date Presented: *April 8, 2017*   **Supervisor:** *Julie Estrada*

DISCIPLINARY LEVEL

☒ **Verbal Correction**—(To memorialize the conversation.)

☐ **Written Warning**—(State nature of offense, method of correction, and action to be taken if offense is repeated.)

☐ **Investigatory Leave**—(Include length of time and nature of review.)

☐ **Final Written Warning**

   ☐ Without decision-making leave

   ☐ With decision-making leave (Attach memo of instructions.)

   ☐ With unpaid suspension

SUBJECT: *Excessive tardiness*

☒ Policy/Procedure Violation

☒ Performance Transgression

☐ Behavior/Conduct Infraction

☒ Absenteeism/Tardiness

---

16 The law is rapidly changing in this area, and many states and cities are enacting paid sick leave laws protecting employees who need time off from work to care for themselves or a family member or for other protected reasons. Accordingly, it is critical that you check with qualified legal counsel to ensure that your attendance policy is compliant with these laws and certainly before you discipline or terminate any employee for excessive absenteeism or tardiness.

PRIOR NOTIFICATIONS

Level of Discipline	Date	Subject
Verbal	_____	_____
Written	_____	_____
Final Written	_____	_____

Incident Description and Supporting Details: Include the following information: Time, Place, Date of Occurrence, and Persons Present as well as Organizational Impact.

Tony,

You have incurred five incidents of tardiness in this rolling calendar year. The dates are:

	Arrival Time
Friday, February 14, 2017	*8:17 A.M.*
Thursday, February 13, 2017	*8:22 A.M.*
Monday, January 12, 2017	*8:06 A.M.*
Wednesday, January 7, 2017	*9:30 A.M.*
Wednesday, December 17, 2016	*8:04 A.M.*

This number of incidents has disrupted the work flow in our unit and has caused our department to incur unscheduled overtime. In addition, your tardiness has impeded the performance of your coworkers, who have had to carry the extra workload. Five incidents of tardiness in the rolling calendar year constitutes failure to meet company standards of performance and conduct.

PERFORMANCE IMPROVEMENT PLAN

1. Measurable/Tangible Improvement Goals: *Tony, I expect that you will assume responsibility for your timely arrival at work and that, from this point on, we won't have to address this issue again.*

2. Training or Special Direction Provided: *A copy of our firm's attendance policy is attached. Please read the policy thoroughly today and meet with me tomorrow with an action plan outlining how you will correct this problem.*

3. Interim Performance Evaluation Necessary? *No*

4. Our **Employee Assistance Program** (EAP) provider, Prime Behavioral Health Group, can be confidentially reached to assist you at (800) 555-5555. This is strictly voluntary. A booklet regarding the EAP's services is available from Human Resources.

5. In addition, I recognize that you may have certain ideas to improve your performance. Therefore, I encourage you to provide your own **Personal Improvement Plan Input and Suggestions:**

_____

_____

_____

(Attach additional sheets if needed.)

OUTCOMES AND CONSEQUENCES

Positive: I will remain available to help you and discuss areas where you require additional support. If you meet your performance goals, no further disciplinary action will be taken regarding this issue. _In addition, you will help our department minimize last-minute overtime costs and staff rescheduling._

Negative: _According to corporate policy, if you reach seven unauthorized tardies in the rolling calendar year, you will be placed in a written warning status. If you reach nine tardies in the rolling calendar year, you will be placed in a final written warning status. If you reach ten tardies in the rolling calendar year, you will be dismissed. A copy of this document will be placed in your personnel file._

Scheduled Review Date: _None_

EMPLOYEE COMMENTS AND/OR REBUTTAL

_____

_____

_____

(Attach additional sheets if needed.)

X _____

Employee Signature

EMPLOYEE ACKNOWLEDGMENT GOES HERE

#82 Excessive Tardiness[17]

This is the second in a series of three write-ups. Note the more aggressive language in the consequences and last chance sections.

PERFORMANCE CORRECTION NOTICE

Employee Name: *Tony Epifanio*   **Department:** *Finance*

Date Presented: *August 19, 2017*   **Supervisor:** *Julie Estrada*

DISCIPLINARY LEVEL

☐ **Verbal Correction**—(To memorialize the conversation.)

☒ **Written Warning**—(State nature of offense, method of correction, and action to be taken if offense is repeated.)

☐ **Investigatory Leave**—(Include length of time and nature of review.)

☐ **Final Written Warning**

    ☐ Without decision-making leave

    ☐ With decision-making leave (Attach memo of instructions.)

    ☐ With unpaid suspension

SUBJECT: *Excessive tardiness*

☒ Policy/Procedure Violation

☒ Performance Transgression

☐ Behavior/Conduct Infraction

☒ Absenteeism/Tardiness

PRIOR NOTIFICATIONS

Level of Discipline	Date	Subject
Verbal	*Apr 8, 2017*	*Excessive tardiness*
Written		
Final Written		

---

17 The law is rapidly changing in this area, and many states and cities are enacting paid sick leave laws protecting employees who need time off from work to care for themselves or a family member or for other protected reasons. Accordingly, it is critical that you check with qualified legal counsel to ensure that your attendance policy is compliant with these laws and certainly before you discipline or terminate any employee for excessive absenteeism or tardiness.

Incident Description and Supporting Details: Include the following information: Time, Place, Date of Occurrence, and Persons Present as well as Organizational Impact.

Tony,

You have incurred seven incidents of tardiness in this rolling calendar year. The dates are:

	Arrival Time
Tuesday, August 18, 2017	*8:25 A.M.*
Thursday, April 30, 2017	*8:06 A.M.*
Friday, February 14, 2017	*8:17 A.M.*
Thursday, February 13, 2017	*8:22 A.M.*
Monday, January 12, 2017	*8:06 A.M.*
Wednesday, January 7, 2017	*9:30 A.M.*
Wednesday, December 17, 2016	*8:04 A.M.*

This number of incidents has disrupted the work flow in our unit and caused our department to incur unscheduled overtime because others have had to carry the extra workload. Seven incidents of tardiness in the rolling calendar year constitutes failure to meet company standards of performance and conduct (policy 2.14).

PERFORMANCE IMPROVEMENT PLAN

1. Measurable/Tangible Improvement Goals: *Tony, I expect that you will assume total responsibility for your timely arrival at work. I am disappointed that we are again addressing this after you committed to fixing this problem back in April.*

2. Training or Special Direction to Be Provided: *A copy of our firm's attendance policy is attached, and it specifically addresses tardiness. I expect you to read this policy again and see me if you have any questions about the organization's rules governing tardiness.*

If you need to meet with Gail Engel in Human Resources to discuss your rights under the Family and Medical Leave Act, you can reach her at x2279.

3. Interim Performance Evaluation Necessary? *No*

4. Our **Employee Assistance Program** (EAP) provider, Prime Behavioral Health Group, can be confidentially reached to assist you at (800) 555-5555. This is strictly voluntary. A booklet regarding the EAP's services is available from Human Resources.

5. In addition, I recognize that you may have certain ideas to improve your performance. Therefore, I encourage you to provide your own **Personal Improvement Plan Input and Suggestions:**

_____

_____

_____

(Attach additional sheets if needed.)

OUTCOMES AND CONSEQUENCES

Positive: I will remain available to help you and discuss areas where you require additional support. If you meet your performance goals, no further disciplinary action will be taken regarding this issue.

Negative: *According to corporate policy, this seventh incident of tardiness dictates that you now be given a written warning. A written warning is a serious transgression, and your position is now in jeopardy of being lost. This indicates you may not have taken your former warning as seriously as you should have.*

If you reach nine tardies in the rolling calendar year, you will be placed on final written warning. As per policy 2.14 on attendance, when an employee is in final written warning status for tardiness, any occurrence of absenteeism or tardiness in the rolling calendar year will result in immediate dismissal. Furthermore, an employee in final written warning status will be ineligible for promotion or transfer. The employee will be ineligible to receive any approved time off except previously scheduled holidays, bereavement, or any time off required by law. A copy of this document will be placed in your personnel file.

Scheduled Review Date: *None*

EMPLOYEE COMMENTS AND/OR REBUTTAL

_____

_____

_____

(Attach additional sheets if needed.)

X _____
　　　　　　　　　　　　　　　Employee Signature

EMPLOYEE ACKNOWLEDGMENT GOES HERE

Note: Add the following sentence to the Employee Acknowledgment: "I also acknowledge that my job is now in jeopardy of being lost."

#83 Excessive Tardiness[18]

This is the third in a series of three write-ups. Note the specialized last chance agreement language.

PERFORMANCE CORRECTION NOTICE

Employee Name: *Tony Epifanio*   **Department:** *Finance*

Date Presented: *December 14, 2017*   **Supervisor:** *Julie Estrada*

DISCIPLINARY LEVEL

☐ **Verbal Correction**—(To memorialize the conversation.)

☐ **Written Warning**—(State nature of offense, method of correction, and action to be taken if offense is repeated.)

☐ **Investigatory Leave**—(Include length of time and nature of review.)

☒ **Final Written Warning**

    ☒ Without decision-making leave[19]

    ☐ With decision-making leave (Attach memo of instructions.)

    ☐ With unpaid suspension

SUBJECT: *Excessive tardiness*

☒ Policy/Procedure Violation

☒ Performance Transgression

☐ Behavior/Conduct Infraction

☒ Absenteeism/Tardiness

---

18 The law is rapidly changing in this area, and many states and cities are enacting paid sick leave laws protecting employees who need time off from work to care for themselves or a family member or for other protected reasons. Accordingly, it is critical that you check with qualified legal counsel to ensure that your attendance policy is compliant with these laws and certainly before you discipline or terminate any employee for excessive absenteeism or tardiness.

19 There is no need to provide a one-day paid decision-making leave when it comes to excessive tardiness. The employee doesn't need a day off to contemplate his situation. Extra time off work will not solve his problem—only a commitment to being responsible about setting the alarm clock will.

PRIOR NOTIFICATIONS

Level of Discipline	Date	Subject
Verbal	Apr 8, 2017	Excessive tardiness
Written	Aug 19, 2017	Excessive tardiness
Final Written	_____	_____

Incident Description and Supporting Details: Include the following information: Time, Place, Date of Occurrence, and Persons Present as well as Organizational Impact.

Tony,

You have incurred nine incidents of tardiness in this rolling calendar year. The dates are:

	Arrival Time
Thursday, December 13, 2017	8:41 A.M.
Thursday, November 13, 2017	8:17 A.M.
Tuesday, August 18, 2017	8:25 A.M.
Thursday, April 30, 2017	8:06 A.M.
Friday, February 14, 2017	8:17 A.M.
Thursday, February 13, 2017	8:22 A.M.
Monday, January 12, 2017	8:06 A.M.
Wednesday, January 7, 2017	9:30 A.M.
Wednesday, December 17, 2016	8:04 A.M.

This number of incidents has disrupted the work flow in our unit and caused our department to incur unscheduled overtime because others have had to carry the extra workload. Nine incidents of tardiness in the rolling calendar year constitutes failure to meet company standards of performance and conduct (policy 2.14).

PERFORMANCE IMPROVEMENT PLAN

1. Measurable/Tangible Improvement Goals: Tony, I expect that you will assume total responsibility for your timely arrival at work and immediately eliminate your tardiness problem.

2. Training or Special Direction to Be Provided: None at this time. You have already received copies of our firm's attendance policy regarding tardiness. You have received verbal and written warnings as dictated by company policy. I hold you fully responsible for your attendance and timely arrival at work.

3. Interim Performance Evaluation Necessary? No[20]

---

20 Because tardiness is a clear breach of company policy, there is little need to reevaluate the individual's overall performance. Violation of this policy is enough to terminate the employee for just cause.

4. Our **Employee Assistance Program** (EAP) provider, Prime Behavioral Health Group, can be confidentially reached to assist you at (800) 555-5555. This is strictly voluntary. A booklet regarding the EAP's services is available from Human Resources.

5. In addition, I recognize that you may have certain ideas to improve your performance. Therefore, I encourage you to provide your own **Personal Improvement Plan Input and Suggestions:**

_____

_____

_____

(Attach additional sheets if needed.)

OUTCOMES AND CONSEQUENCES

Positive: I will remain available to help you and discuss areas where you require additional support. If you meet your performance goals, no further disciplinary action will be taken regarding this issue.

Negative: *According to corporate policy, this ninth incident of tardiness dictates that you now be given a final written warning. You are now formally notified that any unauthorized occurrences of tardiness in the rolling calendar year will result in immediate discharge.*

In addition, as per policy 2.14 on attendance, you will be ineligible for promotion or transfer for six months (until June 14, 2017). You will be ineligible to receive any approved time off except previously scheduled holidays, bereavement, or any time off required by law. A copy of this document will be placed in your personnel file.

Scheduled Review Date: *None*

EMPLOYEE COMMENTS AND/OR REBUTTAL

_____

_____

_____

(Attach additional sheets if needed.)

X _____

Employee Signature

EMPLOYEE ACKNOWLEDGMENT GOES HERE

Note: Since this is a final written warning, insert the following sentences into the Employee Acknowledgment: "I understand that I have the right to discuss this with a union official, or anyone else who can advise me of my rights, before I sign it. I understand that this is my last chance. No further incidents of tardiness will be allowed. If I fail to meet the terms and conditions of employment as stated in this final written warning, I agree that I will voluntarily resign or be discharged for cause."

Bonus Sample—FMLA Abuse: Failure to Provide Appropriate Medical Documentation[21]

PERFORMANCE CORRECTION NOTICE

Employee Name: *Farid Saleem*   **Department:** *Public Affairs*

Date Presented: *December 28, 2017*   **Supervisor:** *Keiko Asaka*

DISCIPLINARY LEVEL

☐ **Verbal Correction**—(To memorialize the conversation.)

☒ **Written Warning**—(State nature of offense, method of correction, and action to be taken if offense is repeated.)

☐ **Investigatory Leave**—(Include length of time and nature of review.)

☐ **Final Written Warning**

    ☐ Without decision-making leave

    ☐ With decision-making leave (Attach memo of instructions.)

    ☐ With unpaid suspension

SUBJECT: *Excessive absenteeism, failure to provide appropriate medical documentation*

☒ Policy/Procedure Violation

☐ Performance Transgression

☐ Behavior/Conduct Infraction

☒ Absenteeism/Tardiness

PRIOR NOTIFICATIONS

Level of Discipline	Date	Subject
Verbal	Oct 3, 2017	*Unscheduled, unauthorized absence*
Written	_____	_____
Final Written	_____	_____

21 The law is rapidly changing in this area, and many states and cities are enacting paid sick leave laws protecting employees who need time off from work to care for themselves or a family member or for other protected reasons. Accordingly, it is critical that you check with qualified legal counsel to ensure that your attendance policy is compliant with these laws and certainly before you discipline or terminate any employee for excessive absenteeism, tardiness, or failure to follow FMLA guidelines.

Incident Description and Supporting Details: Include the following information: Time, Place, Date of Occurrence, and Persons Present as well as Organizational Impact.

Farid,

Maintenance of good attendance is a condition of employment. In order to minimize hardships that may result from illness or injury, our company provides paid sick time benefits to employees for use when their own or a family member's illness or injury prevents them from working. However, periodic sick leave taken on a repeated basis may be viewed as abuse of the system. It is your responsibility to establish legitimate illness or injury in order to receive sick leave pay pursuant to our sick leave policy.

On October 3, you received a verbal warning for five incidents of unscheduled, unauthorized absence (meaning an absence not protected by law or not approved by your supervisor) on the following dates:

> *August 4, 2017*
>
> *August 30, 2017*
>
> *September 15, 2017*
>
> *September 25, 2017*
>
> *October 3, 2017*

On October 8, you reached your one-year anniversary and became eligible for FMLA (Family and Medical Leave). On October 9, you brought in a doctor's note authorizing one to four days off per month as an "intermittent leave," which was granted to you.

In October, you took four days off, which were approved under your leave, and then took off the following two days, even though you had no sick leave left in your bank:

> *October 25, 2017*
>
> *October 30, 2017*

You would normally have received a written warning for this fifth and sixth incident of unauthorized leave, but you then informed me that you would need an FMLA "block leave," stating that your health situation warranted more time off from work. You stated that you would have your doctor amend the current FMLA instructions to move you from an intermittent to a block leave.

In November, you took four days off, which were approved under your original doctor's instructions. However, you then took off the following two days, even though you had no sick leave left in your bank:

> *November 21, 2017*
>
> *November 30, 2017*

This would have normally resulted in a final written warning for nine incidents of unauthorized absence. However, you assured me that you would have a doctor's note authorizing a block FMLA leave within three days.

In December, you took off four days in accordance with your intermittent FMLA leave. You then took off another day on the following date, even though you had no sick leave left in your bank:

December 17, 2017

Normally, this tenth incident would have resulted in your termination.

It has now been almost two months since you stated that you would provide the appropriate medical certification authorizing a block FMLA leave. To date, you have not provided this to us. As a result of your lack of follow-up, this document will serve as a written warning for failure to provide the appropriate medical documentation required under FMLA and to avoid corrective action under our company's disciplinary policy.

In addition, this recent tenth incident warrants an additional written warning for excessive, unauthorized absence.

PERFORMANCE IMPROVEMENT PLAN

1. Measurable/Tangible Improvement Goals: *Farid, I expect you to immediately improve your attendance to meet company minimum standards. I also expect you to remain true to your word and hold yourself accountable for obtaining the appropriate medical documentation necessary to justify your absences, pursuant to the FMLA and our policy.*

2. Training or Special Direction to Be Provided: *A copy of our attendance policy is attached. In addition, we are providing you with another FMLA application to provide to your doctor for the block leave, if you still require it. Please note that you have fifteen calendar days from now to submit the necessary medical certification.*

3. Interim Performance Evaluation Necessary? *No*

4. Our **Employee Assistance Program** (EAP) provider, Prime Behavioral Health Group, can be confidentially reached to assist you at (800) 555-5555. This is strictly voluntary. A booklet regarding the EAP's services is available from Human Resources.

5. In addition, I recognize that you may have certain ideas to improve your performance. Therefore, I encourage you to provide your own **Personal Improvement Plan Input and Suggestions:**

_____

_____

_____

(Attach additional sheets if needed.)

OUTCOMES AND CONSEQUENCES

Positive: I will remain available to help you and discuss areas where you require additional support. If you meet your performance goals, no further disciplinary action will be taken regarding this issue. *Demonstrating proper follow-through and commitment to cooperate with the company by providing the necessary medical documentation will also help our department meet its workforce planning and production scheduling goals.*

Negative: *You are now being placed on notice that according to company policy, if you reach a twelfth incident (the current ten plus two new incidents) of unauthorized absence (meaning an absence not protected by law or approved by your supervisor) in the rolling calendar year, you will be placed on a final written warning. A thirteenth incident of unauthorized absence in the rolling calendar year will result in termination.*

In addition, your current intermittent FMLA leave provides for one to four days off per month to attend to your special needs on an intermittent basis. Unless additional time off is warranted by an updated medical certification, we will honor the current medical instructions. If you take additional, unauthorized time off, you may be subject to further disciplinary action up to and including termination. A copy of this document will be placed in your personnel file.

Scheduled Review Date: *Fifteen days (January 12, 2018)*

EMPLOYEE COMMENTS AND/OR REBUTTAL

_____

_____

_____

(Attach additional sheets if needed.)

X _____
Employee Signature

EMPLOYEE ACKNOWLEDGMENT GOES HERE

Bonus Sample—FMLA Abuse: Failure to Follow the Terms of the Medical Certification[22]

PERFORMANCE CORRECTION NOTICE

Employee Name: *Al Costello* **Department:** *Research & Development*

Date Presented: *April 24, 2017* **Supervisor:** *Mark Gardner*

DISCIPLINARY LEVEL

☐ **Verbal Correction**—(To memorialize the conversation.)

☐ **Written Warning**—(State nature of offense, method of correction, and action to be taken if offense is repeated.)

☐ **Investigatory Leave**—(Include length of time and nature of review.)

☒ **Final Written Warning**

  ☒ Without decision-making leave

  ☐ With decision-making leave (Attach memo of instructions.)

  ☐ With unpaid suspension

SUBJECT: *Excessive absenteeism, failure to follow the terms of the medical certification*

☒ Policy/Procedure Violation

☒ Performance Transgression

☒ Behavior/Conduct Infraction

☒ Absenteeism/Tardiness

PRIOR NOTIFICATIONS

Level of Discipline	Date	Subject
Verbal	_____	*See below for details.*
Written	_____	*See below for details.*
Final Written	_____	*See below for details.*

---

22 The law is rapidly changing in this area, and many states and cities are enacting paid sick leave laws protecting employees who need time off from work to care for themselves or a family member or for other protected reasons. Accordingly, it is critical that you check with qualified legal counsel to ensure that your attendance policy is compliant with these laws and certainly before you discipline or terminate any employee for excessive absenteeism, tardiness, or failure to follow FMLA guidelines.

Incident Description and Supporting Details: Include the following information: Time, Place, Date of Occurrence, and Persons Present as well as Organizational Impact.

Al,

You are being placed on a final written warning and last-chance agreement for excessive and repetitive attendance problems, substandard job performance, inappropriate workplace conduct, and failure to comply with policies and procedures. This is consequently your last chance to continue employment with our company: Failure to meet any of the terms outlined in this final written warning or failure to meet any of our company's standards of performance and conduct will result in your immediate termination.[23]

- *Substandard 2016 annual review*

  Your annual performance review, received in March 2017, shows that you did not meet minimum company expectations in calendar year 2016. Please review the annual appraisal for further details.

- *Multiple, ongoing, and repetitive corrective action notices*

  In your tenure with our company over the past four years, you have been placed on numerous corrective action notices, including:

2017

March 17, 2017	*Written warning for attendance and "patterning"*
February 2, 2017	*Verbal warning for attendance and "patterning"*
January 14, 2017	*Final written warning for substandard job performance*

2016

November 5, 2016	*Written warning for substandard job performance*
September 22, 2016	*Verbal warning for substandard job performance*
May 17, 2016	*Written warning for inappropriate workplace conduct: profane language*
March 28, 2016	*Final written warning for attendance*
February 1, 2016	*Written warning for attendance*
January 20, 2016	*Verbal warning for attendance*

2015

September 12, 2015	*Written warning for substandard job performance*
June 30, 2015	*Verbal warning for substandard job performance*
February 22, 2015	*Verbal warning for attendance*

2014

June 1, 2014	*Written warning for sleeping on the job*
April 17, 2014	*Written warning for attendance*

---

23 I typically don't recommend beginning a written warning with consequential language like this. However, this case is an exception and clearly warrants the consequences in the opening paragraph of the document.

February 28, 2014   Verbal warning for attendance

- *Failure to provide appropriate FMLA medical certification*

The company permitted you to take a block of time between November 17 and December 8 with the understanding that you would remit the appropriate paperwork to convert your intermittent FMLA leave certification to a block FMLA leave. When you finally submitted your FMLA certification paperwork in mid-December, it acknowledged only the need for an intermittent leave of two days per week. You consequently took more time off than approved under FMLA. In addition, the unapproved time off was taken when you did not have any sick leave in your sick bank. You failed to provide the necessary paperwork to substantiate your leave. Had your supervisor reported the discrepancy to Human Resources at that time, you would have been terminated.

- *Excessive, unscheduled, unauthorized tardiness*

Since your most recent written warning for excessive absenteeism on March 17, 2017, you have accrued 3.0 additional occurrences of unauthorized tardiness on the following days:

Friday, April 17, 2017	*7 minutes late (.5 occurrence)*
Tuesday, April 14, 2017	*5 minutes late (.5 occurrence)*
Tuesday, March 30, 2017	*5 minutes late (.5 occurrence)*
Friday, March 27, 2017	*4 minutes late (.5 occurrence)*
Monday, March 23, 2017	*6 minutes late (.5 occurrence)*
Friday, March 20, 2017	*7 minutes late (.5 occurrence)*

We note that you had no sick leave left in your bank justifying any of these tardies. Normally this number of occurrences would have resulted in a final written warning and subsequent termination. However, you told your supervisor that these tardies were covered by your FMLA certification, which he mistakenly believed. You also stated that because Kronos paid you for these occurrences, the occurrences did not violate company policy. In fact, Kronos rounds in seven-minute increments (pre- and post-start time) in the employee's favor; however, according to company policy, these incidents do indeed count as disciplinary infractions under the company's policy, regardless of whether they were under the seven-minute threshold and subsequently paid via Kronos.

Again, it's important to understand that normally you would have been terminated with 3.0 instances of unauthorized tardiness beyond the written warning. It was only because your supervisor was confused as to the nature of your medical certification and the amount of FMLA time that you have available that he failed to discipline you according to company policy.

- *April 23 FMLA violation*

Yesterday, April 23, you called in at 7:30 A.M. to say that you were once again running late. At 8:00 A.M., you then called in and stated that you weren't coming in due to inclement weather.

By 10:00 A.M., the weather warning had lifted, and you then called back and stated that you wished to use intermittent FMLA time instead of an inclement weather day to cover this particular absence. You do not have the discretion to arbitrarily designate time off as FMLA time unless it falls under the terms of your current medical certification.

It was at this point that your supervisor notified Human Resources of the potential abuse of the FMLA system, which, upon further investigation, revealed the numerous infractions outlined above.

It appears you have not taken your previous disciplinary warnings and counseling sessions seriously. Therefore, this final written warning and last-chance agreement will serve to notify you that escalated measures are now warranted and that your position is in serious and immediate jeopardy of being lost.

PERFORMANCE IMPROVEMENT PLAN

1. Measurable/Tangible Improvement Goals: *Al, I expect you to make an immediate 180-degree turnaround in terms of both your performance and conduct from this point forward. Following are the company's expectations if you are to remain employed:*

• Except if authorized (meaning time off protected by law or authorized by your supervisor), if you come in late, it is a tardy regardless of whether you are paid for the time by Kronos. (Again, Kronos rounds in seven-minute increments to the benefit of the employee. This only speaks to pay, not to tardiness.)

• To avoid being tardy in the future, you should be at your desk and ready to begin work at the assigned shift time, absent a legitimate authorized reason.

• We expect you to adhere to the terms of your FMLA medical certification. Excessive use of FMLA outside of the terms of your medical certification is not acceptable and may result in immediate discharge for cause.

• Coming in late to work is not an FMLA-protected activity according to the terms of your current medical certification.

• In addition, any further instances of tardiness or unscheduled absence (meaning an absence not protected by law or approved by your supervisor) will be brought to Human Resources' immediate attention for appropriate interpretation and response.

2. Training or Special Direction to Be Provided: *Please review the attendance guidelines in your employee handbook on pages 16 to 18. An overview of the corrective action policy is provided below.*

Attendance Standards/Corrective Action Guidelines:

Verbal Warning: Employees who reach four (4) occurrences or seven (7) days of unauthorized absence during any twelve-month period may receive a verbal warning.

Written Warning: Employees who reach six (6) occurrences or ten (10) days of unauthorized absence during any twelve-month period may receive a written warning.

Final Written Warning: Employees who reach seven (7) occurrences or eleven (11) days of unauthorized absence during any twelve-month period may receive a final written warning.

Termination: Employees who exceed seven (7) occurrences or eleven (11) days of unauthorized absence during any twelve-month period may be subject to immediate termination.

If you have any additional questions regarding the instructions contained in your FMLA medical certification, how the terms of your current FMLA intermittent leave will be interpreted in the workplace, or the company's sick leave policy, please speak with Karen Franklin in Human Resources immediately.

3. Interim Performance Evaluation Necessary? *No. Your annual review shows that you continue to fail to meet company expectations. This document confirms that no further development has been made in this area in terms of improving your performance.*

4. Our **Employee Assistance Program** (EAP) provider, Prime Behavioral Health Group, can be confidentially reached to assist you at (800) 555-5555. This is strictly voluntary. A booklet regarding the EAP's services is available from Human Resources.

5. In addition, I recognize that you may have certain ideas to improve your performance. Therefore, I encourage you to provide your own **Personal Improvement Plan Input and Suggestions:**

_____

_____

_____

(Attach additional sheets if needed.)

OUTCOMES AND CONSEQUENCES

Positive: I will remain available to help you and discuss areas where you require additional support. If you meet your performance goals, no further disciplinary action will be taken regarding this issue.

Negative: *Failure to provide immediate and sustained improvement in all areas outlined in this final written warning—performance, conduct, attendance, and compliance with company policy—will result in your immediate termination.* A copy of this document will be placed in your personnel file.

Scheduled Review Date: *None*

EMPLOYEE COMMENTS AND/OR REBUTTAL

_____

_____

_____

(Attach additional sheets if needed.)

X _____

Employee Signature

EMPLOYEE ACKNOWLEDGMENT GOES HERE

Bonus Sample—FMLA Abuse: Failure to Consult HR Regarding Leave Request[24]

Supervisor fails to follow company's policies under granting FMLA leave and threatens to discipline a worker for taking time off that would have fallen under FMLA protection.

PERFORMANCE CORRECTION NOTICE

Employee Name: *Kate Vario*   **Department:** *Dispatch*

Date Presented: *October 11, 2017*   **Supervisor:** *Weng Chen*

DISCIPLINARY LEVEL

☐ **Verbal Correction**—(To memorialize the conversation.)

☒ **Written Warning**—(State nature of offense, method of correction, and action to be taken if offense is repeated.)

☐ **Investigatory Leave**—(Include length of time and nature of review.)

☐ **Final Written Warning**

    ☐ Without decision-making leave

    ☐ With decision-making leave (Attach memo of instructions.)

    ☐ With unpaid suspension

SUBJECT: *Failure to consult with HR regarding an employee's FMLA leave request*

☒ Policy/Procedure Violation

☐ Performance Transgression

☐ Behavior/Conduct Infraction

☐ Absenteeism/Tardiness

---

24 The law is rapidly changing in this area, and many states and cities are enacting paid sick leave laws protecting employees who need time off from work to care for themselves or a family member or for other protected reasons. Accordingly, it is critical that you check with qualified legal counsel to ensure that your attendance policy is compliant with these laws and certainly before you discipline or terminate any employee for excessive absenteeism, tardiness, or failure to follow FMLA guidelines.

PRIOR NOTIFICATIONS

Level of Discipline	Date	Subject
Verbal	_____	_____
Written	_____	_____
Final Written	_____	_____

Incident Description and Supporting Details: Include the following information: Time, Place, Date of Occurrence, and Persons Present as well as Organizational Impact.

Kate,

On October 3, Debra Dolgen on your team informed you that she needed to return home to Arkansas to care for her parents. She stated that her father had injured himself and required extensive surgery and then nursing home care while he recovered. Meanwhile, Debra's mother continued to suffer from numerous medical conditions, and she had to be placed in a nursing home because her father was not able to take care of her.

Debra contacted Human Resources from Arkansas and informed HR that you told her that she'd be "written up" for taking this time off, especially since it was in the middle of the telephone system upgrade project. She stated and you confirmed that since Debra had no sick leave in her sick leave bank, and had never requested either FMLA leave or FMLA leave forms prior to leaving, she wasn't covered by our company FMLA policy. Had you checked with HR first, as you are required to do under company policy, you would have learned that an employee does not have to formally use the term "FMLA" to invoke FMLA protections. In fact, HR takes it upon itself to work with employees to educate them on their FMLA rights and provide them with the appropriate forms.

Upon discussing this with you, you stated that you believed that Debra did not have the right to take time off without advanced notice under the FMLA. Further, you mentioned that she did not have any leave time available in her sick leave bank. You also confirmed that you didn't think you were obligated to discuss this leave matter with HR. You likewise confirmed that you now understand that all leave requests must be vetted by HR, and you understand that you have no discretion to discipline, terminate, or take other types of adverse actions against employees for leaves of absence without HR's direction and approval.

Note that the written warning that you told Debra will follow upon her return to work will not be issued. HR will explain to her that she qualifies for FMLA, that this is an FMLA-qualifying event, and that the company wants her to focus on the needs of her family at this difficult time.

PERFORMANCE IMPROVEMENT PLAN

1. Measurable/Tangible Improvement Goals: Kate, I expect you to run all requests for FMLA leave or of other types of leaves of absence by Human Resources before committing to an employee one way or the other. Understand that the FMLA is a complicated law that has many considerations, and no supervisor is expected to understand the intricacies of *the law or the application of its rules; however, all department heads and supervisors are expected to refer FMLA, ADA, workers' comp, and other similar requests relating to illness or injury of the employee or the employee's family members to Human Resources for processing and administration.*

Further, I expect you to demonstrate the appropriate level of care and concern for your team members, especially when family circumstances are at issue. Debra is a tenured employee with little or no history of performance or conduct problems. As such, you had no need to assume that she was taking advantage of the system in any way. Look to balance legal and policy requirements with the personal needs of your staff members to ensure a positive work environment, whenever possible.

Finally, remember that employees are not required to name specific leave laws or worker protections in order to be covered by them. In other words, workers do not have to formally request FMLA or ADA leaves to be protected under those laws. Instead, once employees let their supervisor know there may be a need for time off work, it is up to the company to inform employees when a leave statute or leave policy may protect them, which clearly falls under HR's authority—not yours. HR will determine whether an employee's leave is eligible for worker protections and communicate their findings to you.

2. Training or Special Direction Provided: *Please arrange to meet with Sarah Sweeney, our leave administrator in HR, to discuss not only Debra's specific situational needs but also for an overview of the FMLA and other leave laws. I will notify Debra that you are aware that discipline was not appropriate under the circumstances and that she will not be disciplined when she returns. Otherwise, please refrain from contacting Debra or involving her with any work-related activities until her leave has concluded and her family situation has been taken care of. HR will follow up with her at appropriate intervals.*

3. Interim Performance Evaluation Necessary? *No*

4. Our **Employee Assistance Program** (EAP) provider, Prime Behavioral Health Group, can be confidentially reached to assist you at (800) 555-5555. This is strictly voluntary. A booklet regarding the EAP's services is available from Human Resources.

5. In addition, I recognize that you may have certain ideas to improve your performance. Therefore, I encourage you to provide your own **Personal Improvement Plan Input and Suggestions:**

_____

_____

_____

(Attach additional sheets if needed.)

OUTCOMES AND CONSEQUENCES

Positive: I will remain available to help you and discuss areas where you require additional support. If you meet your performance goals, no further disciplinary action will be taken regarding this issue. *The FMLA and other leave laws are difficult to navigate, which is why our company has a strict policy of referring all requests to one central source in HR for administration. By consistently referring cases to HR, you'll feel more confident in terms* *of what you're communicating to your employees, and you can rest assured that your actions are consistent with company policy and past practices.*

Negative: *Failure to notify HR of leave requests or special circumstances before communicating with an employee is not consistent with our organization's vision for its employees and likewise violates company policy. If you ever again fail to involve HR in a potential leave of absence matter or threaten an employee with discipline or some other type of adverse action for taking time off without further clarification and advanced approval from HR, disciplinary action up to and including dismissal may result.* A copy of this document will be placed in your personnel file.

Scheduled Review Date: None

EMPLOYEE COMMENTS AND/OR REBUTTAL

_____

_____

_____

(Attach additional sheets if needed.)

X _____
Employee Signature

EMPLOYEE ACKNOWLEDGMENT GOES HERE

Bonus Sample: Failure to Engage in the ADA Interactive Process

Long-term office services supervisor with a problematic record of treating people poorly and disrespectfully learns of an employee's diagnosis of a serious health condition and attempts to talk the employee into leaving the company rather than referring the individual to Human Resources for help and support and initiation of the Americans with Disabilities Act interactive process. The supervisor issued the office services supervisor a final written warning with an unpaid suspension as well as a demotion.

PERFORMANCE CORRECTION NOTICE

Employee Name: *Winnie Singh*   **Department:** *Admin Services*

Date Presented: *August 15, 2017*   **Supervisor:** *Walter Ng*

DISCIPLINARY LEVEL

☐ **Verbal Correction**—(To memorialize the conversation.)

☐ **Written Warning**—(State nature of offense, method of correction, and action to be taken if offense is repeated.)

☐ **Investigatory Leave**—(Include length of time and nature of review.)

☒ **Final Written Warning**

    ☐ Without decision-making leave

    ☐ With decision-making leave (Attach memo of instructions.)

    ☒ With unpaid suspension

SUBJECT: *Failure to follow company policy, inappropriate workplace conduct*

☒ Policy/Procedure Violation

☐ Performance Transgression

☒ Behavior/Conduct Infraction

☐ Absenteeism/Tardiness

PRIOR NOTIFICATIONS

Level of Discipline	Date	Subject
Verbal	_____	_____
Written	_____	_____
Final Written	_____	_____

Incident Description and Supporting Details: Include the following information: Time, Place, Date of Occurrence, and Persons Present as well as Organizational Impact.

Winnie,

On August 7, 2017, your employee, office services coordinator Wanda Crawford, called you and notified you that she had just been diagnosed with a serious health condition.[25] She stated that she called you immediately after leaving her doctor's office because she was concerned that any absences that might follow could inconvenience you and the rest of the team. Rather than expressing empathy and concern and referring her to Human Resources for additional help and support, in accordance with company policy, you questioned whether she would be able to perform her basic job duties. At that point, she said she wasn't sure how involved her treatment would be because further tests from additional medical specialists were warranted. As such, she wasn't sure what restrictions her doctors would place on her work in the foreseeable future.

Wanda asked you at that point if you were aware of any easier jobs that might not require so much lifting or physical agility on her part. According to Wanda, you responded that you were not aware of any other openings in the company and that you needed someone who could perform the office services job during the upcoming busy season. Wanda stated that you pressed her to tell you whether she would be able to carry out her duties, and you then told her that there would likely not be any easier jobs in the division.

When Wanda continued to express anxiety about managing her workload, you asked her if she was tendering her two-weeks' notice. Wanda responded that she did not wish to stop working or to leave the company, especially since she was worried about benefits and disability income continuation relative to her newly diagnosed medical condition. Your only response to her at that point was that if she was going to resign, she had to do so in writing. You asked her to prepare a written statement that you would be able to forward to Human Resources for processing and then ended the call.

It was at that point that Wanda reached out to Human Resources and relayed her discussion with you, reaffirming her desire to remain employed with our company, whether in her current capacity or one that would better be able to accommodate any potential medical restrictions. Human Resources assured Wanda that she was not being terminated due to her recent medical diagnosis and that her two-week notice wasn't under consideration and would not be accepted.

---

25 In this case, the employee reported that she was diagnosed with cancer. However, the company opted not to include that specific information in this write-up for employee privacy reasons, instead simply writing "serious health condition."

Further, Human Resources informed her that our company would engage with her in an interactive process to see how we might be able to accommodate her work restrictions. This would include finding out what, if any, reasonable accommodations might be necessary for her to continue working in her current position and would likewise include discussions about other positions in which she could work on an interim basis, if needed.

When we asked you about your understanding of the matter, you confirmed everything Wanda told us. You informed us that you were concerned about her not being able to perform in her current job now that the busy season was upon us, and you assumed she would want to resign if she couldn't meet her current obligations. Therefore, you simply asked her for her resignation letter.

Your conversation with Wanda at the point of her diagnosis was uncaring and unprofessional. Further, it violated specific company policy. This final written warning, in conjunction with an unpaid suspension and demotion, is intended to impress upon you the seriousness of your actions and the significance of your mishandling of the situation with Wanda.

PERFORMANCE IMPROVEMENT PLAN

1. Measurable/Tangible Improvement Goals: *As a twenty-year supervisor with our organization, you are expected to know and apply the basic policies and employment laws covering the workers in your department. You have been trained to refer all requests for medical restrictions and accommodations to Human Resources and failed to do so. Had you reached out to Human Resources, you would have learned immediately that our company has an affirmative obligation to engage in the interactive process, which is a responsibility that each frontline supervisor shares with Human Resources every time this situation arises.*

2. Training or Special Direction Provided: *Please reread the employee handbook and familiarize yourself with leave law matters and policies regarding absenteeism and accommodation. If you have any questions regarding leaves of absence, please see me or a member of the Human Resources team immediately.*

3. Interim Performance Evaluation Necessary? No

4. Our **Employee Assistance Program** (EAP) provider, Prime Behavioral Health Group, can be confidentially reached to assist you at (800) 555-5555. This is strictly voluntary. A booklet regarding the EAP's services is available from Human Resources.

5. In addition, I recognize that you may have certain ideas to improve your performance. Therefore, I encourage you to provide your own **Personal Improvement Plan Input and Suggestions:**

_____

_____

_____

(Attach additional sheets if needed.)

OUTCOMES AND CONSEQUENCES

Positive: I will remain available to help you and discuss areas where you require additional support. If you meet your performance goals, no further disciplinary action will be taken regarding this issue.

Negative: *This correction notice serves as a final written warning that if you ever again fail to engage with an employee who notifies you of a serious medical condition, your employment will be terminated. Likewise, if you fail to notify Human Resources as appropriate or attempt to intimidate your staff members from using available benefits, you will be dismissed.*

Further, your actions in this case demonstrate a lack of care and concern for your team members that would be consistent with the responsibilities of a supervisor and our overall corporate culture and concern for our employees. Therefore, your role within our organization is subsequently being adjusted to that of an office services coordinator with a commensurate adjustment in pay that will remove frontline supervisory duties from your areas of responsibility. Note that your pay will be adjusted to the top of the salary range for that role. Your salary will remain frozen at that maximum until the entire salary range for that position classification is readjusted at some point in the future.

To impress upon you the seriousness of your actions in this case, you will also be placed on an unpaid suspension for one week. Together with the final written warning, demotion, and corresponding adjustment in pay, you are hereby notified that if you ever again engage in conduct that demonstrates such disregard for another employee's well-being or for company policies, you will be immediately dismissed. A copy of this document will be placed in your personnel file.

Scheduled Review Date: *None*

EMPLOYEE COMMENTS AND/OR REBUTTAL

_____

_____

_____

(Attach additional sheets if needed.)

X _____

Employee Signature

EMPLOYEE ACKNOWLEDGMENT GOES HERE

PART VII
Termination Notices

#84 Discharge for Cause: Substandard Performance[1]

December 15, 2017

Rick Ricardo
261 Dorset Street
Brooklyn, New York 11236

Dear Mr. Ricardo:

This is to inform you that you are being terminated immediately for failure to perform your work at an acceptable level. On August 7, 2017, you received a verbal correction for substandard work performance and an unwillingness to perform properly assigned work duties. On October 4, 2017, you received a written correction for substandard work performance, glass breakage, and insubordination. On November 2, 2017, you received a final written warning for substandard work performance, insubordination, and threatening your supervisor.

In this period of time, you were sent to outside training on dealing with conflict in the workplace. You were also placed on a paid one-day decision-making leave to rethink your commitment to this institution.[2]

However, today you committed a serious error in the handling of your cage wash duties. Namely, you failed to place the rabbit rack in the rack washer after spraying it down with acid. Because you did not notify your coworkers about this exception to standard operating procedures, a fellow worker handled the acid-covered rack and was subsequently injured.[3]

Your failure to properly process equipment demonstrates an ongoing inability to perform at an acceptable level and a lack of concern for your job. I consequently have no choice but to immediately sever this employment relationship.

Your final paycheck through the close of business today is attached. Within thirty days, we will issue you a statement of accrued benefits. You may choose to continue your medical insurance coverage at your own expense. Please contact Karen Johannsen in the Benefits Department at your earliest convenience. She will explain the status of your benefits and COBRA options and also arrange for the return of any company property.

Sincerely,

Fred Mertz
Director, Research Lab

---

1 See Write-Up #55.

2 Detailing all your affirmative efforts to rehabilitate the employee in conjunction with the history of formal disciplinary measures taken is a good strategy in a termination letter. Remember that if the ex-employee seeks counsel to sue you for wrongful discharge, this letter will be the first piece of evidence reviewed by plaintiff's counsel. A well-constructed termination letter outlining your actions could function as a repellent to dissuade a lawyer from taking on the case.

3 This was a very minor injury, but it sufficed to make this final incident "clean" in order to warrant a discharge.

#85 Discharge for Cause: Substandard Performance[4]

September 17, 2017

Mary Wellington
25972 Pueblo Court
Canyon Country, CA 91355

Dear Ms. Wellington:

This is to inform you that you are being terminated immediately for failure to perform your work at an acceptable level. On August 31, 2017, you received a final written warning for substandard work performance, an unwillingness to perform properly assigned work duties, excessive telephone usage, refusal to follow proper work instructions, and persistent infractions of properly established work rules.

In this period of time, your supervisor met with you twice a week to assist you in meeting your deadlines and properly administering your accounts. You were also placed on a paid one-day decision-making leave to rethink your commitment to this institution.

However, yesterday you committed a serious error in the handling of your Medicare collections files. Your supervisor, Linda Huntley, discovered that you had missed a sixty-day deadline to submit a claim. When I asked you about this, you stated that you were working denials all day, and that you thought you had six months—not sixty days—to file the Medicare appeal. I asked you whether you felt you used proper judgment and followed standard departmental guidelines. You responded that you didn't think you were "totally in the wrong" because others in the department don't know the guidelines and because if you call the automated phone line at Medicare, you get two or three different answers. Unfortunately, these issues have little to do with the fact that you missed the standard sixty-day deadline. This action is a clear breach of the terms of your August 31 final written warning.

Your failure to properly process Medicare receivables and claims demonstrates an ongoing inability to perform at an acceptable level and a lack of concern for your job. I consequently have no choice but to immediately sever this employment relationship.

Your final paycheck through the close of business today is attached. There will be no severance pay since your termination was for just cause. Within thirty days, we will issue you a statement of accrued benefits. You may choose to continue your medical insurance coverage at your own expense. Please contact Chuck Whitley in the Benefits Department at your earliest convenience. He will explain the status of your benefits and COBRA options and also arrange for the return of any company property.

Sincerely,

David Vigilucci
Director of Accounting

---

4 See Write-Up #28.

#86 Employee Fails to Report to Work on First Day; Company Rescinds Its Employment Offer

November 5, 2017

Lisa Walters
500 Monterrey Avenue
San Francisco, CA 94109

Dear Lisa:

Seeing that you did not appear for work on your first day of employment with us, we have no choice but to rescind our employment offer.

I understand from Jack Larrabee, your intended supervisor, that you called him to tell him that you had to miss orientation yesterday because you had finals. I also checked with Employee Health Services and learned that you had not followed up with the documentation you had agreed to give them in order to begin work. Finally, I left a message for you last night and didn't receive a return call today as of 4:00. My only conclusion is that you've made other plans career-wise and that our firm's opportunity doesn't meet your current needs.

If you have any questions or concerns, you can reach me at (415) 555-5555. Thank you.

Sincerely,

Roger Sommers
Director of Human Resources

#87 Summary Discharge: Falsification of Company Records

Branch manager allows borrower's wife to sign a deed of trust for her husband and is immediately dismissed for violating state notary laws and company policy.

February 22, 2017

Anthony Halverson
122 Oceanside Avenue #3
Las Vegas, NV 89114

Dear Mr. Halverson:

Attached are documents with a borrower's forged signature. Mike Walker, vice president of Branch Operations, visited the Las Vegas branch approximately three weeks ago. While there, Mike reviewed a file with a signed but nonnotarized deed of trust. Mike spoke with you and your staff about the importance of proper notarization procedures at that time.

Now it has been discovered by the Loan Production Department that on February 18, 2017, the signature of borrower Michael Carter was forged by his wife, Corrine. The discrepancies in Mr. Carter's signature were especially notable because he is an amputee and his signature (as documented in the notary log and his Nevada driver's license) is very wobbly and unsteady. In stark contrast, Mr. Carter's signatures on the Short Form Deed of Trust and borrower application are much smoother and flowing.

An untrained eye can immediately notice that Corrine signed for her husband because the husband's and wife's signatures on the document are practically identical. Forgery is grounds for immediate dismissal, and the company could have been legally exposed for failure to follow proper notary procedures as dictated by the Nevada State Notary Commission. We consequently have no choice but to discharge you immediately for violation of company standards of performance and conduct.

Sincerely,

Gary Keller
Senior Vice President, Loan Origination

I have received a copy of this notice.[5]

_____   _____   _____
Anthony Halverson   Date

---

5 The acknowledgement countersignature is an alternative way to construct termination letters. Requiring the employee to sign means that there will be no dispute (as an evidentiary matter) that the employee received the document. Of course, it is not really necessary to have a signature line because there are other signs that the employment relationship has ended. Namely, the employee no longer reports to work and is no longer paid! Still, there's no harm in adding it; it's really more of a stylistic issue. Therefore, add the countersignature requirement if your company is more comfortable with the added closure it may bring to the employment relationship.

#88 Summary Discharge: Employee Time Card Fraud

Clerical support specialist commits time card falsification and is immediately discharged for cause.

April 16, 2017

Dave Regan
666 Calle Arbor Road
Phoenix, AZ 85250

Dear Dave,

This letter is to inform you that you are hereby terminated from our company effective at the close of business today. On April 10, 2017, you clocked out for lunch at 12:08 P.M.[6] You clocked back in at 12:42. This was consistent with your thirty-minute lunch period.

However, you then left the office again and did not return until 1:20 P.M. You also never reported to your supervisor that you were taking additional time. At 1:20, your supervisor, Polly Daniels, witnessed you clocking in again on the Kronos system. However, that swipe with your badge was not valid and did not register because you ran your card backwards through the machine. (There is no entry on the Kronos report for 1:20 P.M.) In addition, your supervisor verified that you were not working at your desk between 12:42 and 1:20.

Consequently, you have violated Timekeeping policy and procedures. Namely, section 2.5.1 states: "Violations that are not subject to the Progressive Discipline policy and will result in immediate discharge include . . . willful falsification of a time record."

Enclosed please find your final check, which represents payment for all days worked through today (including vacation and holiday). You will be notified by the Benefits Office of any benefit continuation for which you may be eligible.

Sincerely,

Don Gardner
Director, Customer Service

---

6 This was reported to management by a coworker who was tired of watching this game go on over an extended period of time.

Bonus Sample: Supervisory Time Card Manipulation

July 30, 2017

Ethan Botha
9245 Regents Road
La Jolla, CA 92037

Dear Ethan,

This letter is to inform you that you are being terminated from our company effective immediately for time card manipulation.

Payroll manager Wei Lui instructed payroll technician Lucas Santos to conduct an audit of employees' time cards from January 13–July 20, 2017. During the course of the audit, Lucas found numerous instances of your manually altering your employees' time cards. You altered time cards of 22 employees on multiple occasions, and an aggregate total of 78 altered punches was identified. Your employees were subsequently underpaid a total of $1,183.36 since the beginning of the year.

When I asked you about this, you confirmed that you altered the time cards in order to minimize overtime payouts. You stated that as a manager, you felt under pressure to attain margin dollars and meet payroll goals. However, meeting budget or capping expenses is never an acceptable reason for engaging in dishonest practices such as this. Further, you stated that you never engaged in similar practices before this year and that this year was the first and only time you've made such manual edits to time cards to reduce hours worked and/or overtime hours.

The employees in question will be immediately repaid for these lost hours. Further spot audits will be conducted for prior years to ensure that your team members were not shorted payroll or overtime dollars. Because your actions constitute such a significant breach of company policy and practices in addition to dishonesty and record falsification, your employment with our organization is hereby terminated today. You will receive your final check separately according to payroll guidelines in addition to information regarding benefits continuation.

Sincerely,

Kai Yazzi
Director, Administration

#89 Summary Discharge: Loss of Current Weapons License

October 9, 2017

Marlene Vassar
13579 Windsor Court
Nashua, NH 19843

Dear Marlene,

On July 31, 2017, your weapons permit expired as issued by the State of New Hampshire. This permit is required to be in full force at all times as a condition of employment as a security officer at our bank. On the expiration date, it was determined that you had completed the required state training and had in your possession all the required documents to obtain the permit. You stated to your supervisor, Dennis Stevens, that "it had been taken care of." Unfortunately, this was not so.

On September 30, 2017, it was discovered that you had failed to send the documents to the State of New Hampshire to obtain renewal of your permit as required. You later told your supervisor that you did not have the necessary funds in late July to complete the filing requirements.

As a result, on October 3, 2017, you were placed on unpaid suspension effective October 6 for three days to obtain your permit. You were advised that failure to comply during the three-day period would result in further discipline up to and including termination.

As of October 8, 2017, you still had not obtained the required permit. You have therefore violated Security Department Manual Section 13-E, Weapons Permits, which provides that:

> 1. It is mandatory that each Security Officer have in his/her possession, while on duty, the following:
>
>> b. Current valid Weapons Permit (.38 Caliber) issued by the State of New Hampshire . . .
>
> 4. Failure to comply with any regulations concerning required permits will result in immediate suspension and can result in termination.

Accordingly, effective today, we must now terminate your employment due to your willful and continuing violation of company policy and state law.

Sincerely,

Larry Collins
Director of Security

#90 Summary Discharge: Possession, Sale, or Being Under the Influence of Alcohol or Illegal Substances

Nurse diverts morphine and tests positive for drugs.

October 8, 2017

Pamela Zuckerberg
123 South Ardmore Street
Fort Smith, AR 75601

Dear Pam:

This letter is to inform you that, effective October 8, 2017, you are discharged from employment as a registered nurse at Victory Memorial Hospital. On September 29, you were placed on investigatory leave because Francis Franco, administrative supervisor, had reason to suspect that you were diverting drugs. Since then, a thorough investigation has been conducted. It was discovered that from September 24 through September 29, using your Personal Identification Number (PIN), you withdrew morphine that you were unable to account for. Specifically, you withdrew morphine for your patients that was not documented in your patients' charts, and you withdrew morphine for other nurses' patients without the other nurses' knowledge. These withdrawals were also not documented in their patients' medical charts.

On October 1, you voluntarily submitted to a drug test at the Ozark Clinic.[7] Your test results were positive for morphine.

As a result, we have no choice but to terminate your employment for violation of the following provisions of hospital policy 2.05, a copy of which is enclosed:

1.2.2 Dishonesty

1.2.5 Using, possessing, . . . or being under the influence of . . . illegal drugs or controlled substances while on duty, while on Corporation property

1.2.10 Falsification or making a material omission on forms, records, or reports, including . . . patient records

1.2.11 Violating safety or health rules or practices or engaging in conduct that creates a safety or health hazard

In addition, we are required to contact the Board of Registered Nursing to inform them of the events leading up to your termination.

Sincerely,

Emma Sbanotto
Vice President, Nursing

---

7 This employee apparently believed that the residual drug would have dissipated to a point where it did not show up in a lab test. She voluntarily submitted to this drug test to strengthen her case that she was innocent.

Bonus Sample: Medical Marijuana Misuse[8]

April 25, 2017

Angelica Reyes
7322 Normandy Blvd
Baker, CA 90000

Dear Angelica,

On April 18, 2017, at 8:45 A.M., you were involved in a vehicle accident while driving the company van. Specifically, you rear-ended the car in front of you when it began moving forward once the light turned green, only to hit its brakes again unexpectedly. The driver of that car was injured, filed a police report, and reported to a medical facility to have his purported neck and back injuries tended to.

As you are aware and as noted in the employee handbook and pursuant to our drug- and alcohol-free workplace policy, post-accident drug testing is permissible in California when an employer has reasonable suspicion that an employee involved in an accident may have been under some influence of drugs and/or alcohol.[9] When you reported the accident to your supervisor, you stated that you weren't currently under the influence but that you had smoked marijuana the night before. You subsequently tested positive for marijuana.

As our drug- and alcohol-free workplace policy highlights, we must terminate your employment "for using, possessing, or being under the influence of drugs or controlled substances while on duty" and while operating a company vehicle. Enclosed, please find your final check, which represents payment for all days worked through today. You will receive additional information from the Benefits Department for benefits continuation under COBRA and other benefits that you may be eligible for.

Sincerely,

Ming Zhang
Director of Operations

---

8 Proceed with caution here! The law is always changing, and nowhere is that more evident than with medical marijuana usage in the workplace. As of this writing, many American jurisdictions allow employers to fire workers for using illegal drugs. Some states have legalized the use of marijuana for medical purposes, and California, Colorado, and Washington have even legalized it for recreational use. This increased decriminalization standard raises the question of whether employers in those states are allowed to fire someone who uses marijuana for medical reasons if such usage can be interpreted as a "reasonable accommodation" under the Americans with Disabilities Act (and similar state law) for ailments such as glaucoma, Crohn's disease, or cancer.

The Supreme Court of California held that employers are not required to accommodate the use of medical marijuana in conflict with employer drug-free workplace policies because marijuana remains illegal under federal law. Employee privacy issues are also involved and remain unsettled in the courts. Always check with qualified legal counsel before implementing a termination or failure to hire for medical marijuana use because state laws are in constant flux about this very matter.

9 This reflects the current law of California and many other states. However, other jurisdictions may not allow random and/or post-accident drug and alcohol testing. Always check with qualified legal counsel before implementing any drug testing policy.

#91 Summary Discharge: Failure to Pass Certification Exam

Two years earlier, it had been mandated that diagnostic technicians pass a CMV examination. This five-year employee was the only one not to pass the test in the first year. The company allowed the technician to retake the test the following year, but he failed to pass that second time. He was discharged as soon as the company learned that he did not pass.

August 15, 2017

Jim DeMattias
9201 Marmora Street
Morton Grove, IL 60053

Dear Jim,

I regret to inform you that our company must exercise its right to terminate you for failure to pass the CMV examination this year. As you know, passing the CMV examination was mandated two years ago as a result of increased demands in the diagnostic laboratory field. Your job description was altered in 2016 to reflect this new requirement. Your annual performance evaluations in 2016 and 2017 also stated that you must pass the CMV exam and obtain your certification in order to retain your position. You acknowledged this requirement by signing your revised job description as well as your performance reviews.

Seeing that this exam is given only once a year, in June, your inability to pass the exam in 2017 could have led to your dismissal at that time. However, as you'll recall, we agreed that you could take the exam in 2017 even though you were the only uncertified lab technician in the department. In June of 2017, you signed a document stating that "if you failed to provide the department with written proof of passing the CMV examination in June of 2017, you would be dismissed."

Yesterday, we received the news that you did not pass the test, and we must consequently sever our employment relationship. I wish you well, Jim, and I thank you for your hard work and commitment to our department and company over the past five years.

Sincerely,

Ron Bauers
Lab Director

#92 Summary Discharge: Terminating an Employee Without Corporate Approval

Manager is discharged for firing a subordinate without receiving corporate approval first.

November 1, 2017

Albert Morehouse
25972 Eisenhower Avenue
Staten Island, NY 10304

Dear Albert,

This letter confirms your termination of employment from Apex Consulting Group at the close of business today for violating company policy and for performance issues relating to the management of employees whom you supervise.

On October 30, 2017, your decision to terminate an employee before discussing this with Human Resources and with me was in direct violation of company policy 2.05, section 2.5.3: "discharge should not be imposed without prior clearance from the Human Resources department in all cases." This is also a violation of a disciplinary memorandum issued to you on February 4, 2017, which stated that "in the event a disciplinary or confidential matter is being discussed, please conference call a representative from Human Resources or Scott Hamilton, associate vice president."

As you know, both before and after the February 4 memorandum, I have had discussions with you regarding continuing problems with the management of the Staten Island office staff. These problems have had an adverse effect on the employees and the organization, recently resulting in three employee resignations directly related to your management behavior.

Enclosed is your final check, which includes your regular pay through today plus accrued vacation and holiday time. You will be notified in a separate letter from the Benefits Department of your COBRA rights and eligibility. If you have any questions, please contact me.

Sincerely,

Albert Napperson
Associate Vice President

#93 Summary Discharge: Misconduct at Company Holiday Party

December 6, 2017

Kathy Yarnell
1234 Lark Lane
Longview, TX 75605

Dear Ms. Yarnell:

This is to inform you that Abacus Insurance has exercised its right to terminate your employment effective today. This decision is based on your violation of our company's standards of performance and conduct at the annual holiday party.[10]

You will receive information regarding conversion of company benefits from the Human Resources department in the near future.

Sincerely,

Sylvia Olshan
Human Resources Manager

---

10 This employee became very drunk, lifted her skirt to male employees whom she found attractive, and attempted to place several men's hands on her breasts. The supervisor chose not to describe these actions in detail in this letter for the sake of propriety.

#94 Summary Discharge: Threatening a Coworker with Bodily Harm

May 18, 2017

Mary Beth Kaline
3000 Peachtree Road
Atlanta, GA 30326

Dear Mary Beth,

As we discussed over the phone, our company will no longer be able to employ you as a security guard. After completing an investigation regarding a coworker's complaints about you and your complaints about the coworker, I have determined that your behavior was inappropriate and that it potentially could have created a hostile work environment.

I base my findings on the fact that you admitted to telecommunications supervisor Denise King that you did indeed make threatening faces at this coworker. You stated to Supervisor King that "if this had occurred anywhere but here, I would have beat the shit out of her."

You also repeated this threat in writing to me in your letter dated May 15, 2017. You wrote in that letter explaining your side of the story that "if we were outside, I would take matters into my own hands." Such direct or veiled threats of violence violate company standards of performance and conduct and preclude us from continuing your employment relationship with this organization.

Thank you for your weekend on-call[11] services over the past two years. If you have any questions or would like to discuss this further, please call me at 555-5555.

Sincerely,

Michael Shanahan
Director of Security

---

11 An "on-call," also known as a "standby," employee does not work a specified schedule but is available to respond to calls to work as needed. Such workers typically do not receive employer-sponsored benefits, and there is generally less of a need to provide formal due process because of the casual nature of the employment relationship. (In other words, you would be less obligated to follow the verbal-written-final written paradigm for on-call workers than for regular full- or part-time workers.) Although it could be argued that a 20-year full-time employee might not be summarily dismissed for this very same incident, most employers retain the flexibility to consider the worker's employment status when administering discipline

#95 Summary Discharge: Terminating the Probationary Employee

February 15, 2017

Patty O'Grady
532 Westminster Court
Portland, OR 97232

Dear Patty,

I'm sorry to inform you that, effective at the close of business today, you will be dismissed from Paragon Real Estate Group for failure to meet the terms of your introductory period. On January 20, you had your initial sixty-day introductory period extended for an additional thirty days because of performance problems, including slow mastery of basic accounting calculations as evidenced by errors, work avoidance, and multiple revisions of your standard paperwork.

Since then, you've made an excessive number of errors in the accounts receivable spreadsheets. As a result, your internal customers have ceased delegating work to you for fear that it would not get done correctly. You have been unable to complete your monthly statement, and your work must now be reviewed and redone by another member of the accounting staff.

Because you have not met the terms of your probation, we must terminate your employment. You will receive information regarding COBRA and any other benefits for which you are eligible from our Human Resources Department in the near future. I wish you well in your career.

Sincerely,

Mark Gathers
Accounting Manager

#96 Letter Confirming Acceptance of an Employee's Verbal Resignation

Employee verbally resigns but does not provide her supervisor with a formal letter of resignation as requested. The supervisor is afraid that this employee may change her mind about leaving, since she's made idle threats before. The supervisor therefore confirms in writing the worker's verbal resignation so that the worker can't rescind her resignation during the two-week notice period.

April 10, 2017

Nina Sam
201 Darcey Street
Brooklyn, NY 11236

Dear Nina,

This letter confirms that you have verbally provided me with two weeks of notice regarding your resignation as financial analyst and that I have accepted your resignation. You stated that your last day of work with our organization will be April 23 because you have found a new position elsewhere.

Thank you for continued support to our company over the past year. I wish you well in your future career endeavors.

Sincerely,

Rae Mauro
Director of Finance

#97 Summary Discharge: Acceptance of Gratuities

January 25, 2017

Molly Stone
135 West Macarthur Blvd
Miami, FL 33323

Dear Molly,

This letter confirms that you are hereby terminated from your employment with our non-profit organization effective at the close of business today for the following reasons:

It was recently learned that you violated policy 2.11, Gratuities, when you personally accepted monetary gifts from the Everglades fund-raising chapter. Our investigation disclosed that you did this on two separate occasions: first, on December 6, 2016, and then again on January 6, 2017.

For this reason, we have no choice but to discharge you immediately for violation of company policy on acceptance of gratuities. Enclosed is your final check, which includes your regular pay, vacation, and holiday accruals through today. You will be notified in a separate letter from the Human Resources Department of your COBRA rights and eligibility.[12] If you have any questions, please contact me.

Sincerely,

Alex Paul
Vice President, Fund-Raising

---

12 You have the right to challenge offering COBRA to an employee who was discharged for gross misconduct. However, although this specific exception exists in the Consolidated Omnibus Budget Reconciliation Act (COBRA), it is very rarely applied. Consult with a labor attorney before attempting to withhold this benefit—no matter how egregious the offense.

#98 Summary Discharge: Insubordination (Inappropriate and Undermining Behavior)

Staff accountant who received prior disciplinary notices, including a recent written warning for refusing to speak with his supervisor or his coworkers, blows up and sends a derogatory email to all members of his department and senior management regarding his perception of his supervisor's ineptness.

March 14, 2017

Ronald Mack
125 South Rockland Court
Newark, NJ 07103

Dear Mr. Mack,

Effective today, your employment as staff accountant with our organization is terminated. Enclosed you will find a check for wages through today and any accrued and unused vacation and holiday pay due you. Your employment is being terminated for the following reasons:

- Insubordination

- Disruption of the business operations of the company and particularly of the Finance Department via your email to the executive staff and every member of the Finance Department regarding your perception of your supervisor's lack of abilities and talents

- Making unfounded and inappropriate allegations against your supervisor[13]

You will be notified in a separate letter from the Human Resources Department of your COBRA rights and eligibility. If you have any questions regarding this notice, please contact me.

Sincerely,

Joanne Rawlinson
Vice President, Human Resources

---

13 A special note regarding interpretations by the National Labor Relations Board (NLRB) in regard to employee conduct: The NLRB as of the time of this writing is exercising extreme discretion in protecting workers' rights to "protected, concerted activity." This may include complaining about supervisors' communication styles and abilities and, absent physical threats, the NLRB has been giving employees substantial leeway at the expense of a company's right to maintain order and respect. When in doubt about terminating a worker for maligning his supervisor, be sure to check with qualified legal counsel.

Bonus Sample: Insubordination
(Violent Employee Reaction to a Disciplinary Notice)

IT director slams door in anger so hard into the office wall that the doorknob breaks through the drywall.

October 11, 2017

Michele Clancy
30 West 16th Street #208
New York, NY 10011

Dear Michele,

This letter is to inform you that, effective immediately, you are discharged from employment as the IT director at Lox Communications. Earlier this afternoon at approximately 2 P.M., I called you into a meeting with Alison DeMarco from Human Resources to discuss team performance issues as well as your willingness and ability to role-model appropriate behaviors for your staff. We informed you at the onset of the meeting that, depending on the outcome of our discussion, formal corrective action might result.

You immediately became defensive and began to raise your voice. Despite our efforts to calm you down and discuss the legitimate business concerns we had about your ongoing behavior and your group's overall performance challenges, your conduct escalated out of control. You made derogatory comments about our company, its leaders, and HR's role in mediating conflicts, and you then began to use profane language to demonstrate your disgust for the entire process.

Before we had a chance to express our concerns and engage in an appropriate dialog about specific challenges that we wanted to discuss with you, you stood up, walked to my door, and slammed it against the back wall with such force that the doorknob broke through the drywall. After seeing the force of your action, you stated in a disrespectful and condescending manner, "Whoops. It looks like you'll either need to make softer doors or stronger walls," and you stormed out of my office and left our facility.

As of 4:30, we have not heard back from you. We are consequently emailing this notice to your personal email address and shipping it via overnight certified mail to your address of record. The hard copy termination letter that you receive tomorrow will contain your final paycheck, paid through the close of business tomorrow, along with accrued but unused vacation as well as your COBRA rights and eligibility, unemployment insurance brochure, and other documents, as required. If you have any questions, please contact me directly.

Sincerely,

Rob Baudette
Vice President, IT

cc: Alison DeMarco, Director of Human Resources

Bonus Sample: Social Media Misuse

October 15, 2017

Roger Ellis
147 N. Broadway
Bangor, ME 04401

Roger,

On October 13, several coworkers of yours complained to Human Resources about a political comment you posted on Facebook that caused them concern about their safety. Specifically, you posted: "The President of the United States should be tried for treason, murder, and crimes against the U.S. Constitution . . . then hung on the Mall in Washington, D.C." You further stated, "White supremacy rules!" Accompanying your comment was a caricature of a blood-spattered hangman with an axe in one hand and a noose in the other.

Such political comments are exceptionally disrespectful and distasteful. They disrupt the workplace, interfere with work, and cause morale issues. Hate speech such as this—whether political or not—is exceptionally offensive and does not reflect the character or the values of our organization. Further, your statements—whether intended as satire or not—have caused concern among your coworkers for their safety in the workplace. The severity and context within which these comments were made clearly violate our company's antidiscrimination, respect in the workplace, and social media policies, especially in light of the fact that we are a government contractor.

As a result, your separation from the company becomes effective immediately. Enclosed please find your final check, which represents payment for all days worked through today. You will receive additional information from the Benefits Department for benefits continuation under COBRA and other benefits that you may be eligible for.

Sincerely,

Adisa Bello
Vice President, Human Resources

#99 Secretarial Layoff: No Severance

Severance was not offered as a result of this office closure. The regional manager flew out to the branch to meet individually with this employee who worked as the only secretary in a two-person office.

May 13, 2017

Marilyn Beckwith
753 Jefferson Court
Washington, DC 20009

Dear Marilyn,

Effective immediately, Randolph Home Loans is closing its Washington, D.C., office. We regret having to take this action. Your last day of employment with the company is today. We are sorry that we were not able to give you more notice. We simply do not have enough business at this location to justify keeping the branch open.

Enclosed is your final paycheck as well as information about converting your health insurance benefits. Please do not hesitate to contact our Human Resources Department in Seattle should you have any questions about the closure of this branch or your benefits. We wish you continued success in your future endeavors and thank you for your excellent service.

Sincerely,

Howard Christie
Regional Manager

#100 Director-Level Layoff, Including Severance Package, Outplacement, and Appropriate Legal Release[14]

October 11, 2017

Gary Putnam
17 S. Vanguard Court
San Diego, CA 92108

Dear Gary,

On October 10, 2017, you were informed that ABC Financial (the "Company") has made the decision to eliminate your position as Controller effective today. This letter sets forth in writing the terms and conditions of an agreement for an amicable separation of your employment (the "Agreement"), which includes payments and benefits to which you would not otherwise be entitled under company policy or applicable law.

Your separation from employment will be effective as of the close of business today. You are being paid your final paycheck today, which will include your pay through October 31, 2017, as well as any accrued but unused vacation and any personal days. We do not pay for unused sick time under our company policy.

As consideration for your release of claims and other promises in this Agreement and your continued compliance with the terms of this Agreement, you will receive twenty-four (24) weeks of severance pay, less applicable withholdings, which will be paid in accordance with our regular biweekly pay cycle beginning as soon as feasible after the Effective Date of this Agreement (defined below).

As part of this separation agreement, you may qualify for unemployment benefits through the California Employment Development Department. ABC Financial will not contest your application for unemployment compensation.

As further consideration for this Agreement, you will receive outplacement assistance under the services of Alexander and Associates. You will participate in their Modified Executive Outplacement Program, which will assist you in finding gainful employment for a six-month period beginning with the Effective Date of this Agreement. Further details about this outplacement arrangement will be provided by Heidi Clair, your outplacement consultant.

---

14 This sample draft is for a California employee who is 40 years of age or older. Further, this Agreement is for a single position elimination, not a group layoff. In cases of group layoffs, the language must change: The company would need to give 45 days instead of a 21-day consideration period under the Older Workers Benefit Protection Act. Further, an Exhibit A would need to be included with the letter, stating something like this: "Attached as Exhibit A, you will find a list of the job titles and ages of employees in the decisional unit affected by the reduction in force of which your layoff is a part, as well as the job titles and ages of employees in the decisional unit that are not included in the reduction in force." Of course, check with qualified legal counsel before issuing a release agreement of any sort to ensure that it is up-to-date and consistent with current law.

Your group coverage for health, dental, and vision insurance will continue through the end of this month. You will be offered the opportunity to elect COBRA continuation coverage at your own expense beginning November 1 for the plans that are subject to this provision and in which you are eligible to participate. If you timely elect COBRA continuation coverage, we will pay, as additional consideration for this Agreement, your premiums for COBRA continuation coverage for you as a single participant for the months of November _____ through April _____ provided that you continue to remain eligible for coverage under COBRA.

You will be entitled to receive your vested retirement benefits in accordance with the terms of the Company's plan.

All other benefits, compensation, and privileges of your employment not specified above will cease as of October 11, 2017. You affirm that you have been paid and/or have received all compensation, salary, wages, bonuses, commissions, expense reimbursements, and/or benefits to which you may be entitled. You further affirm that you have no known workplace injuries or occupational diseases not previously disclosed in writing to the Company.

In consideration for this Agreement, you hereby release ABC Financial and all of its affiliated or related entities as well as past and present officers, directors, employees, representatives, and agents of ABC Financial and any of its affiliated or related entities (collectively, the "Released Parties") from: any and all claims, demands, debts, losses, obligations, liabilities, costs, expenses, attorneys' fees, rights of action, and causes of action of any kind or character whatsoever, whether known or unknown, suspected or unsuspected, arising prior to the date of this Agreement, all of which are also referred to below as the "Released Claims."

You understand and agree that the Released Claims include without limitation any rights or claims you may have that arise out of or are related to your employment with ABC Financial or the termination of that employment and any rights or claims under the Age Discrimination and Employment Act, 29 U.S.C. Section 621 et seq., Title VII of the Civil Rights Act of 1964, the California Fair Employment and Housing Act, as well as any other claims under any federal, state, or local law, or the common law, including without limitation any claims for breach of contract.

To effectuate a full and complete general release as described above, you expressly waive and relinquish all rights and benefits of Section 1542 of the Civil Code of the State of California. Section 1542 of the Civil Code of the State of California states as follows:

> A general release does not extend to claims which the creditor does not know or suspect to exist in his or her favor at the time of executing the release, which if known by him or her must have materially affected his or her settlement with the debtor.

You have had the opportunity to discuss this waive of Section 1542 with counsel of your choosing. You acknowledge that you may hereafter discover facts different from, or in addition to, those which you know or believe to be true with respect to the Released Claims, and agree that this agreement and the releases contained herein shall be and remain effective in all respects notwithstanding such different or additional facts or the discovery of those facts.

Excluded from the Released Claims are any claims that by law cannot be waived in a private agreement between an employer and employee. Moreover, this Agreement does not prohibit you from filing a charge with the Equal Employment Opportunity Commission (the "EEOC") or other federal agency, or the California Department of Fair Employment and Housing or other state agency, nor does this Agreement prohibit you from participating in any EEOC or other federal or state agency investigation. You do, however, agree to waive your right to any monetary recovery should any claim be pursued with the EEOC, state agency, or any other federal, state, or local administrative agency on your behalf arising out of or related to your employment with or separation from the Company.

You represent that you have not filed any charges, complaints, grievances, arbitrations, lawsuits, or claims against the Released Parties, with any local, state, or federal agency. Nothing in this Agreement prevents you from filing a claim for unemployment insurance after the Separation Date.

You acknowledge and agree that in the course of your employment with the Company, you have acquired: (i) confidential information including without limitation information received by the Company from third parties, under confidential conditions; (ii) other technical, product, business, financial, or development information from the Company, the use or disclosure of which reasonably might be construed to be contrary to the interests of the Company; or (iii) any other proprietary information or data, including but not limited to customer lists, which you may have acquired during your employment (collectively referred to as "Confidential Information"). You understand and agree that such Confidential Information was disclosed to you in confidence and for use only on behalf of the Company. You understand and agree that you: (i) will keep the Confidential Information confidential at all times; (ii) will not disclose or communicate Confidential Information to any third party; and (iii) will not make use of Confidential Information on your own behalf, or on behalf of any third party, without the express authorization of the Company. In view of the nature of your employment and the nature of the Confidential Information you received during the course of your employment, you agree that any unauthorized disclosure to third parties of Confidential Information or other violation, or threatened violation, of this Agreement would cause irreparable damage to the Company, and that, therefore, the Company and/or its affiliated companies, shall be entitled to an injunction prohibiting you from any such disclosure, attempted disclosure, violation, or threatened violation.

You affirm that you have returned all of the Company's property, documents, and/or any Confidential Information in your possession or control. This includes without limitation any and all work product, notes, reports, files, memoranda, records, cardkey passes, door and file keys, safe combinations, laptop computers, computer access codes, disks and instructional or personnel manuals, and other physical or personal property that you received or prepared or helped to prepare in connection with your employment with the Company.

You and the Company acknowledge and agree that the terms and conditions set forth in any Confidential Information and Priority Rights Agreement (the "Confidential Information Agreement") that you signed shall continue in full force and effect after the Separation Date, and its terms shall be incorporated by reference into this Agreement.

Except as otherwise provided by law, you agree that you shall not make any disparaging statements or comments to the media or third parties about the Company's business, technologies, market position, employment policies and practices, employees (past and present), operations, products or services, either as a statement of fact or opinion, which impugns or potentially injures the reputations, goodwill and business relationships of the Company or other individuals involved. Nothing in this Agreement shall prohibit you from providing accurate information to any court or governmental entity or to any person or organization in response to legal process or as otherwise required by law.

This Agreement represents a compromise of claims and shall not be construed as an admission by any party of any liability or any contention or allegation made by any other party, or a suggestion that any claims or liabilities exist or would have any basis.

You agree that you will not disclose the terms of this Agreement to any third party, including without limitation other current, past, or future employees of the Company, except that you may disclose the terms to your spouse or significant other or to your attorney, accountant, or tax preparer (provided that each of the persons to whom you make disclosure agrees to maintain the strict confidentiality of the terms of this Agreement), or otherwise as may be required by law.

You will have a period of twenty-one (21) days from the date of this letter to review and consider this Agreement, with the assistance of counsel should you so choose, before signing it. You may take as much of this twenty-one-day period of time to consider this agreement as you wish prior to signing it.

You may revoke this agreement within seven (7) days after you sign it. Revocation may be made by delivering a written notice of revocation to me within the seven-day period. If you revoke this agreement in a timely fashion, it shall not become effective or enforceable, and all payments provided in this agreement other than your final paycheck, including without limitation severance payments, will not be made. The Effective Date of this Agreement will be the day after the seven-day revocation period expires following your signature of this Agreement.

If any provision of this Agreement is determined to be invalid or unenforceable, in whole or in part, this determination will not affect any other provision of this Agreement, and the remaining provisions of this Agreement shall remain in full force and effect.

You represent and warrant that you have not previously assigned or transferred, or purported to assign or transfer, to any person, corporation, partnership, or any other type of entity, any of the Released Claims. You agree to indemnify and hold harmless against any claim, demand, obligation, liability, cost, expense, right of action, or cause of action arising out of or in connection with any such transfer or assignment. This Agreement will bind the heirs, personal representatives, successors, and assigns of both you and the Company, and inure to the benefit of both you and the Company, and their heirs, successors, and assigns.

This Agreement shall be governed by California law. It represents the entire agreement between the parties and supersedes all prior negotiations, representations, or agreements between the parties, either written or oral, on its subject matter (except for the Confidential Information Agreement referred to above, which remains in effect). You acknowledge that you have not relied on any representations, promises, or agreements of any kind made to you in connection with your decision to accept this Agreement, except for those set forth in this Agreement. This Agreement may be amended only by a document designated as an amendment to agreement and executed by the parties to it.

In the event of a breach of any provision of this Agreement, either party may institute an action specifically to enforce any term or terms of this Agreement and/or to seek any damages for its breach. The prevailing party in any such action shall be entitled to recover reasonable attorneys' fees and costs.

It is unfortunate that this reduction in force is necessary. The Company and I thank you for your dedication to our Company over the past eight years. Please review this offer carefully, with the assistance of counsel if you choose. If you accept the offer, please sign below and return the original of this letter so that I receive it within twenty-one (21) days. Please contact me with any questions you may have.

Sincerely,

Addie Droz
Chief Financial Officer

I have read and understood the content of this letter, and I accept the offer by ABC Financial and agree to the terms of agreement contained in the letter.

_____   _____
Gary Putnam   Date

#101 Job Abandonment

This letter is sent to an employee who has missed work for two days without calling in to report his absence. If the employee does not report to work the next day, he will be discharged for violation of company policy.

September 28, 2017

Gerhardt Hauptmann
62 Music Row
Nashville, TN 37214

Dear Gerhardt:

You were scheduled to work this Saturday, September 27, at 3:30 P.M. When you did not appear at work, your supervisor, Ralph Jones, called you at 4:00 to find out if you were planning on reporting to work that day. You told your supervisor that you wouldn't be able to get to work until 5:00, one hour later, because you had personal business that needed your immediate attention.

However, at 5:00, you neither called nor showed up to the office. Today, Sunday, September 28, you neither called in nor showed up to work for your regularly scheduled shift. You are scheduled to report to work tomorrow, Monday, September 29, at 3:30 P.M. If you do not call or report to the office for work at the time of your regular shift starting time (3:30), you will have violated company policy regarding job abandonment.

Policy 2.21 on seniority states:

1.4.2 Seniority will be lost *and all employment rights cease* for any of the following reasons . . .

1.4.2.3 *Failure to report to work without notice for any period of time longer than three consecutive work days.*

Since it has now been two consecutive workdays since you have reported to work or contacted your supervisor, *if you fail to report to work tomorrow, you will be dismissed effective tomorrow.* I have left a message on your home telephone answering machine with this information at (615) 555-5555. In addition, this letter is being sent to you via express overnight delivery to your last known address.

If there are any extenuating circumstances that we should consider, please contact your supervisor immediately. Otherwise, we will process your termination effective tomorrow, September 29, 2017.

Sincerely,

Dick Kaufmann
Vice President, Human Resources

Index

Selected Additional Titles from the Society for Human Resources Management (SHRM®)

*View from the Top: Leveraging Human
and Organization Capital to Create Value*
Edited by Patrick M. Wright, Dave Ulrich,
Richard L. Antoine, Elizabeth "Libby" Sartain

*California Employment Law: An Employer's Guide,
Revised & Updated for 2017*
By James J. McDonald. Jr.

*Developing Business Acumen SHRM Competency Series:
Making an Impact in Small Business HR*
By Jennifer Currence

*Applying Critical Evaluation SHRM Competency Series:
Making an Impact in Small Business HR*
By Jennifer Currence

Touching People's Lives: Leaders' Sorrow or Joy
By Michael R. Losey

*From Hello to Goodbye: Proactive Tips for Maintaining
Positive Employee Relations, Second Edition*
By Christine V. Walters

Defining HR Success: 9 Critical Competencies for HR Professionals
By Kari R. Strobel, James N. Kurtessis, Debra J. Cohen, and Alexander Alonso

HR on Purpose: Developing Deliberate People Passion
By Steve Browne

*A Manager's Guide to Developing Competencies in HR Staff:
Tips and Tools for Improving Proficiency in Your Reports*
By Phyllis G. Hartman

Developing Proficiency in HR: 7 Self-Directed Activities for HR Professionals
By Debra J. Cohen

Manager Onboarding: 5 Steps for Setting New Leaders Up for Success
By Sharlyn Lauby